Putin's Virtual War

Acknowledgements

I want to express my deep gratitude and pleasure at having had the opportunity to work with the outstanding Pen and Sword editorial team of Lisa Hooson, John Grehan, Martin Mace, and Lori Jones, who were always as kind as they were professional, to Jon Wilkinson for his cover design and to Mat Blurton for the layout and design of the book. I am especially grateful to John and Martin for pointing out a dozen or so passages where perhaps my wording was too blunt. Although I didn't pull any punches, I did glove them and the book is much better for that. Finally, the team may merit a Guinness Book record for the speed with which they carried *Putin's Virtual War* from proposal to print.

Putin's Virtual War

Russia's Subversion and Conversion of America, Europe and the World Beyond

William Nester

FRONTLINE
BOOKS

First published in Great Britain in 2019 by
Frontline Books
An imprint of
Pen & Sword Books Ltd
Yorkshire – Philadelphia

ISBN 978 1 52677 118 6

A CIP catalogue record for this book is
available from the British Library.

Printed and bound in the UK by TJ International Ltd,
Padstow, Cornwall.

Pen & Sword Books Limited incorporates the imprints of Atlas,
Archaeology, Aviation, Discovery, Family History, Fiction, History,
Maritime, Military, Military Classics, Politics, Select, Transport,
True Crime, Air World, Frontline Publishing, Leo Cooper, Remember
When, Seaforth Publishing, The Praetorian Press, Wharncliffe
Local History, Wharncliffe Transport, Wharncliffe True Crime
and White Owl.

For a complete list of Pen & Sword titles please contact

PEN & SWORD BOOKS LIMITED
47 Church Street, Barnsley, South Yorkshire, S70 2AS, England
E-mail: enquiries@pen-and-sword.co.uk
Website: www.pen-and-sword.co.uk

Or

PEN AND SWORD BOOKS
1950 Lawrence Rd, Havertown, PA 19083, USA
E-mail: Uspen-and-sword@casematepublishers.com
Website: www.penandswordbooks.com

Contents

Tables

Introduction

The collapse of the Soviet Union was the biggest geopolitical catastrophe of the century.

(Vladimir Putin)

The emphasis in methods of struggle is shifting toward widespread use of political, economic, informational, humanitarian, and other nonmilitary measures, implemented through the involvement of the protest potential of the population...supplemented by covert military measures, including... information struggle and...special operations forces. Overt use of force, often under the guise of peacekeeping and crisis management, occurs only at a certain stage, primarily to achieve definitive success in the conflict.

(General Valery Gerasimov)

With his elfin poker face, receding short golden hair, diminutive but muscular body, and stiff clipped gait, Vladimir Putin is among the world's most recognizable leaders.[1] He has tightly ruled Russia since December 31, 1999, and will firmly assert power from the Kremlin for the foreseeable future. Many fear and loath him for his brutality, for ordering opponents imprisoned on trumped up charges and even murdered. Yet most Russians adore him for rebuilding the economy, state authority, and national pride.[2] His rise to power was extraordinary. He was not a charismatic politician but a stolid apparatchik or bureaucrat who climbed steadily up the power pyramid through a mix of professionalism, connections, and luck along with one more vital ingredient. Not surprisingly, as a former KGB officer, he excels "at manipulating information, suppressing information, and creating pseudo-information."[3]

What lurks beyond Putin's bland personality and ruthless character? Like any politician, he tries to enhance his popular image. Wanting to be celebrated as a fearless action man, he has staged himself "discovering" Roman vases while diving in the Black Sea and stalking and tranquilizing a "wild" Siberian tiger. The vases were planted and the tiger was actually a zoo inmate that died because the tranquilizer was too powerful. In August 2018, Russian television channel *Rossiya 1* began broadcasting each Sunday an hour-long special celebrating Vladimir Putin as a great adventurer, humanist, and man of the people. During one episode depicting Putin in the wilderness, his press secretary Dmitri Peskov reassured viewers that they need not fear for their president's safety because: "Imagine, bears aren't idiots. If they see Putin, they will behave properly."[4] Left unsaid was the fine model those docile bears displayed for all Russian citizens. Propaganda rarely gets that hamfisted in every sense of the word. Alas, Putin does not confine his fake news industry to self-aggrandizement.

What drives Putin? His personal aim is simple: to become as rich and powerful as possible. At that, he has been stunningly successful. He is Russia's supreme leader and among the world's richest men with his wealth estimated from $20 billion to $100 billion.[5] He loves vacationing at a vast palace near Sochi overlooking the Black Sea, the most grandiose of twenty official residences along with 58 planes and 4 yachts.[6]

To get that rich and powerful, Putin collaborated with a coterie of trusted oligarchs, most from his KGB career. Russian politics is essentially a spoils system whereby one buys one's way to a powerful position then milks it for all it is worth in bribes, kickbacks, and protection money. Analyst Karen Dawisha described Putin's system as grounded on the old Russia adage: "For my friends, anything. For my enemies, the law."[7] As that system's core, Putin is the number one recipient of the tribute.[8] Oligarch Boris Berezovsky explained: "The Russian regime has no ideology, no party, no politics – it is nothing but the power of a single man."[9]

That regime is perhaps best called a kleptocracy, or government of the thieves, by the thieves, and for the thieves. Yergeniy Gontmakher, who directs Moscow's Institute of World Economy and International Relations, observed that: "there is no state in Russia," only "a certain structure in which millions of people who call themselves bureaucrats work … Instead of the state as an institution implementing the course of a developing country, we have a huge and uncontrolled private structure which is successfully diverting profits for its own use."[10] *The Economist* depicted the authoritarian system through which Putin and his cabal rule Russia: "The job of Russian law enforcers is to protect the interests of the state, personified by their particular boss, against the people. This psychology is particularly developed among former KGB members who have gained huge political and economic power in the country since Mr. Putin came to office. Indeed, the top ranks in the Federal Security Service (FSB) describe themselves as the country's new nobility – a class of people personally loyal to the monarch, and entitled to an estate with people to serve them."[11]

Yet much more than greed for money and power animates Vladimir Putin. He is a zealous nationalist deadset to make Russia great again.[12] He mourns the Soviet Union's breakup as "the greatest political catastrophe of the twentieth century." Putin's nostalgia is understandable. The Russian empire peaked in territory, population, military power, and prestige when it was the Soviet Union.

Putin was indoctrinated to view America as Russia's nemesis and to do everything possible to defeat that threat. The communist system imposed the indoctrination that the KGB deepened. The subsequent collapse of communism and the Soviet empire did little to alter that view. America remains the world's greatest military, economic, and cultural power that leads western civilization and the global system. Putin genuinely believes that: "America does not want to humiliate us: It wants to subjugate us. It wants to solve its problems at our expense."[13] Since becoming president on New Year's Eve 1999, he has devoted his power to reversing history, to rebuilding the Russian empire and corroding American influence around the world.

In Putin's mind, Russia can only rise as far as its rivals fall. To that end, he seeks to diminish and, ideally, break up America, western civilization, and the global political economic system, ultimately making the rest of the world as authoritarian and corrupt as Russia. Of course, most countries are already like that, but for those that are not, the Kremlin aims at transforming liberal democracies into illiberal democracies, and illiberal democracies into dictatorships.[14] Specifically, the Kremlin is doing whatever it can to crumble the North Atlantic Treaty Organization

(NATO) and the European Union (EU), the respective military and economic alliances undergirding western civilization. Russian foreign policy also seeks to destroy the liberal global trading system that Washington created after World War II, including such international organizations as the World Trade Organization (WTO), International Monetary Fund (IMF), and International Bank for Reconstruction and Development (World Bank), along with regional organizations like the existing North American Free Trade Association (NAFTA) and Trans-Pacific Partnership (TPP), and the proposed Trans-Atlantic Trade and Investment Partnership (TTIP).

Ideally, Putin would have Moscow replace Washington as Europe's leader: "If Europe wants to be independent and a full-fledged global power center, the shortest route to this goal is good relations with Russia."[15] Putin has embraced the concept of Eurasianism to counter America's Atlanticism. If Washington's Atlanticism represents a policy of upholding western civilization through NATO, the EU, and other institutions, then Eurasianism is Putin's policy of uniting Europe and Asia in a web of bilateral and multilateral strands centered on Moscow that strangle Atlanticism.[16]

Putin has mastered the art of power. Depending on what is at stake that involves the deft wielding of appropriate or "smart" ingredients of "hard" physical power like armored divisions, multinational corporations, and assassins, and "soft" psychological power like diplomats, honey-traps, cyber-trolls, and fake news factories to defeat threats and seize opportunities. Putin learned the art of power through his black belt in judo, a martial art whereby one defeats one's opponents by manipulating their own strengths against them. He revealed how vital judo is to his life: "Judo is not just a sport. It is a philosophy."[17]

For Russia, a war against the United States, NATO, and other allies is inconceivable, suicidal. America, Europe, and Japan collectively enjoy an overwhelming advantage in hard military, economic, financial, and technological power. To finesse that, the Kremlin has conceived a new type of warfare. General Valery Gerasimov, the army's chief of staff, explained just what that involves: "The emphasis in methods of struggle is shifting toward widespread use of political, economic, informational, humanitarian, and other nonmilitary measures, implemented through the involvement of the protest potential of the population … supplemented by covert military measures, including … information struggle and … special operations forces. Overt use of force, often under the guise of peacekeeping and crisis management, occurs only at a certain stage, primarily to achieve definitive success in the conflict."[18] The Russians also have a strategy to deter any attack: "To avert military conflict, our plan calls for a comprehensive set of…measures embracing the entire state apparatus. These will be based on political, diplomatic, and foreign economic measures…closely interconnected with military, information, and other measures. Their general aim is to convince potential aggressors of the futility of any forms of pressure on the Russian Federation and its allies."[19]

Putin's assertions of military power have rendered mixed results. In August 2008, the Russian Army trounced Georgia's army in less than a week followed by the Kremlin recognizing the "independence" of Georgia's rebel provinces of Ossetia and Abkhazia under Russian domination. With the American army bogged down in Iraq and Afghanistan, President George Bush acquiesced to that blatant Russian imperialism. Not only did Washington and Brussels impose no significant sanctions, NATO suspended indefinitely its previous offer to Georgia and Ukraine to become members. But, in 2014, President Barack Obama worked with NATO and the EU to assert tough sanctions against Russia for conquering and annexing Crimea and detaching Ukraine's two eastern mostly Russian speaking provinces as the "independent" People's Republics of Donetsk and Luhansk.

Putin has largely succeeded in wielding hard economic power. Entangling other countries in a web of Transneft oil and Gazprom gas pipelines is a key Kremlin foreign policy goal.[20] Russia's giant oil and gas corporations buy controlling or exclusive shares of each link in a country's energy industry including production, refining, transport, storage, and marketing. That strategy is called *agentura*, the same term for networks of intelligence officers and informants. Moscow has not hesitated to exploit Europe's worsening dependence on Russian oil and gas by cutting the flow and raising prices to punish defiance, and increasing the flow and lowering prices to reward compliance. Russia's political influence over Europe deepens with Europe's energy dependence. Russian businessmen and intelligence officers annually distribute tens of millions of petrodollars to bribe European politicians and bureaucrats.

Putin's greatest victories have come from asserting soft psychological power through information warfare.[21] Disinformation, or fake news as it is now called, is designed to bolster one's alliances and disintegrate one's enemies by exacerbating class, racial, ethnic, political, ideological, and religious divisions. For instance, during America's 2016 presidential election, Russia's cyber-trolls created thousands of fake websites seen by more than 120 million people that promoted vicious lies about candidates and groups. Information warfare also seeks to reveal scandalous hidden truths. Russian hackers penetrated the Democratic National Committee (DNC) and Hillary Clinton's campaign organization, extracted tens of thousands of potentially embarrassing emails, and posted them on WikiLeaks, which is accused of being a Russian front organization.[22] Moscow wielded the same disinformation warfare to warp Britain's 2016 referendum on the European Union. It cannot be precisely determined how many millions of voters the Kremlin's cyber-offensives swayed to elect Donald Trump to the White House or Britain to leave the European Union.

Tragically, since January 20, 2017, Putin's greatest ally in realizing his ambitions has been America's president. Donald Trump is the Kremlin's dream come true, an extraordinary gift that just keeps on giving. In spy-speak, whether Trump is merely a naïve "useful idiot" or a conscious "agent of influence" is murky. What is clear is that Trump has been a one man wrecking ball to American democracy, national security, western civilization, and the global economy. Just for violations of American law, by autumn 2019, there were a score or so legal and congressional investigations of Trump for conspiracy, obstructing justice, campaign finance violations, money laundering, witness tampering, emoluments, and tax, insurance, and charitable foundation fraud.

Trump does not conceal his desperate need to cosy-up to Putin and win his approval. His attraction to the dictator has persisted for some time. During the 2013 Miss Universe contest that he held in Moscow, Trump was dying for a meeting with Putin, tweeting: "Will he become my new friend?"[23] All along, Putin knew the best way to manipulate Trump was to play hard to get while doling out occasional praise and requests that the president cannot refuse.[24]

What explains Trump's obsession with Putin? Does the Kremlin have *kompromat* on Trump, a rumored video of him performing kinky sex with prostitutes during one or more of his three Moscow visits? Is it his dependence on more than two billion Russian mob-laundered dollars borrowed to underwrite his business empire over the decades that began in the 1980s? Is it his obsession with erecting a massive Trump Tower in Moscow, for which he tried to cut a deal with Putin via intermediaries throughout most of the 2016 election campaign? Regardless, what is obvious is Trump's fawning subservience.

Trump is not Putin's only collaborator, only the most glaring. Numerous political parties and groups share key interests with Russia. Of course, during the Soviet era, communist parties around the world more or less toed Moscow's line. These days the ties are more subtle but still profound. A 2018 European Council on Foreign Relations study of 252 political parties across the European Union found that 30 were "hard-core anti-Western parties" that "support closer ties between their country and Russia, oppose sanctions on Russia, or have contacts with the Russian regime." The most prominent of those anti-Western parties included France's National Front, Italy's Five Star Movement and Lega, Britain's United Kingdom Independent Party, Germany's Alternative für Deutschland, and Hungary's Fidesz. In America that includes Trump's wing of the Republican Party.[25]

Interest groups are also among Putin's kingpins. During the Cold War, the Kremlin either secretly sponsored or infiltrated an array of movements like the Russian American Chamber of Commerce, Campaign for Nuclear Disarmament, World Federation of Trade Unions, and Christian Peace Federation. Today's Kremlin enjoys an even more diverse list. For instance, Britain's Stop the War movement was tied to two Russian organizations, the Institute of Globalization and Social Movements (IGSU) and the Anti-Globalization Movement of Russia (AGMR). Moscow targeted America's National Rifle Association (NRA) and Conservative Political Action Conference (CPAC), and events like the National Prayer Breakfast and evangelical Freedom Fest for co-option with invitations for its leaders to collaborate via agents like

Maria Butina. The most influential organisation that shares Moscow's interests is WikiLeaks, a website run by Julian Assange and dedicated to revealing stolen secrets that embarrass the United States and other western countries. Of course, most members of these groups are unaware or dismissive of any Moscow links.[26]

Like anyone, Vladimir Putin is understandable only in history. Putin did not create Russia's kleptocratic political system or its imperialistic foreign policy. He much more reflects than shapes the Russian empire's legacy, especially its extreme Soviet version. As the Kremlin's latest ruler, like most of his predecessors, he is as realistic as he is ruthless. He knows the limits of Russian hard and soft power while constantly trying to expand them. He is doing whatever he can to advance Russian national interests as he interprets them. In Putin's mind, Russia can rise only as far as the West can fall. And, on multiple fronts he is methodically advancing those ends. *Putin's Virtual War* reveals just how and why he does so, and the dire consequences for America, Europe, and the world beyond.

Part I

Russian Power and Culture

Chapter 1

The Russian Empire's Rise and Fall

Historical analysis brings out a certain cyclical pattern in the evolution of Russia: major periods of modernization were always brought about by a brutal collision with the outside world, which only tended to underscore the inadequacy of a backward and xenophobic Russia.

(Sergei Kozyrev)

We do not belong to any of the great families of humanity, to either the West or the East, and have no traditions of either. We exist outside of time.

(Peter Chaadayev)

Each individual is some dynamic mix of mostly nature shaped by nurture. Character is each person's unique bundle of fundamental values, beliefs, interests, skills, and behaviors that largely determines that person's choices, opportunities, and constraints over a lifetime. Most psychologists find that our characters are shaped by around age seven and thereafter change little. A culture is a group's character. Cultures, like characters, limit if not determine behavior. Political culture involves the dynamic between beliefs and behaviors, or how a nation's values shape, and are shaped by, politics. Cultural values include how people collectively perceive, express, and assert what is important about their nation's past, present, and future; how they promote their traditions and aspirations; how they see themselves and believe others see them; how they determine appropriate and inappropriate behavior according to circumstances. Some cultures like some characters are pathological and so promote pathological behavior.

Vladimir Putin is a product of a twelve-hundred-year-old political culture characterized by autocracy, xenophobia, and imperialism.[1] Historically, these traits made perfect sense as defense mechanisms against a succession of invaders who sought, and sometimes succeeded, to conquer Russia. An autocrat was vital for mobilizing the producers and fighters vital to repelling invaders and expanding Russia's territory in all directions toward defensible frontiers like seas, rivers, and mountain ranges. Russians could feel less insecure the more distant those frontiers became. The strategy against an invader was to trade space for time, for the army slowly to withdraw fighting rearguard actions back toward the heartland with its concentration of military recruits, manufacturers, and farmers as the enemy's supply lines stretched to the snapping point. Ideally, Russia's great ally, winter, would bog down the invader, which the Russian army could then advance against and destroy. That happened most decisively against the Swedes in 1709, the French in 1812, and the Germans from 1942 to 1944. National security demands that virtually all but exceptional individuals and groups are expendable, pawns to be sacrificed to preserve the Russian people, and, most importantly, the state that protects them.

Looking back through Russian time, autocrats have prevailed. At the heart of Russian political culture is the belief that it is better to be feared than loved, that the more ruthless one is against one's enemies, the greater the chance that one will die peacefully in bed rather than by their hands. Communism capitalized on the very worst of Russia's political culture as Vladimir Lenin and Joseph Stalin had tens of millions of people murdered to amass more power. Historically, sweeping changes in Russia rarely happened, and when did they almost always came from those already in power. The exceptions were the takeovers by liberals in April and by Bolsheviks in November 1917. Peter the Great, Stalin, Nikita Khrushchev, Vladimir Putin and Mikhail Gorbachev were firmly ensconced in the Kremlin when they initiated policies that radically transformed Russia, whether for better or worse. Even "enlightened" rulers like Peter I, Catherine I, Alexander I, Alexander II, Gorbachev and Boris Yeltsin who all imposed genuine reforms on Russia could only do so as autocrats. Perhaps only Alexander Kerensky, who led the flawed democracy that briefly emerged in 1917, Gorbachev and Yeltsin can cautiously be called "liberals".

Russians tend to see themselves as victims and martyrs of forces largely beyond their control. Political scientist Robert Nalbandov explained how, in their political culture, most Russians tolerate repression, exploitation, imprisonment, torture, and even murder, because they have no other choice and fear becoming victims if they protest let alone resist:

> In these relationships born out of state-level fear, the horrors are amplified when, by mutual acceptance of state and citizens, fear of the state is institutionalized as the basis for the social contract in Russia. Essentially, the population resembles a wife who is being abused by her husband but still refuses to divorce. She consciously accepts the hardships and ill treatment just for the sake of having a husband instead of having none .... As a hugely politically incorrect Russia saying goes, *Be't znachit lubit* – he is beating his wife because he loves her. The effectiveness of such a love-hate relationship depends on the durability and duration of fear, and on the sense of legitimacy – on the willful acceptance of coercion.[2]

In his *Writer's Diary*, Fyodor Dostoyevsky explored Russian political culture's masochistic dimension:

> I think the principal and most basic spiritual need of the Russian People is the need for suffering, incessant and unshakeable suffering .... A current of martyrdom runs through their entire history .... There is always an element of suffering even in the happiness of the Russian People, and without it their happiness is incomplete. Never, not even in the most triumphant moments of their history, do they assume a proud and triumphant air.[3]

Collectivism and conformity are to Russians what individualism and humanism are to Americans. Different historical developments explain those different cultural values. Political Scientist David Satter contrasted those values and their consequences:

> Russia differs from the West in its attitude toward the individual. In the West, an individual is treated as an end in himself. His life cannot be disposed of recklessly in the pursuance of the political schemes, and recognition of its values imposes limits on the behavior of the authorities. In Russia, the individual is seen by the state as the

means to an end, and a genuine moral framework for political life does not exist.[4]

Until their emancipation in 1861, most Russians were serfs or essentially slaves forced to farm someone else's land and forbidden to leave. People inhabited villages surrounded by the lands they collectively harvested. *Mir*, the word for village, is the same as that for world. Although the landlord had the ultimate say on what they produced and how much they gave him, villagers had autonomy to decide issues that solely affected themselves. Elders debated and slowly forged a consensus on how to deal with problems, with the communal outlook and lifestyle called *obshchina* and communal farming called *kolknov*. The Orthodox Church bolstered communalism as powerful priests dominated tight-knit congregations or *sobor*. Communism transformed the peasants back into serfs and exploited them systematically and rapaciously.

Political culture is not just about shared values, beliefs, and aspirations. Those set the acceptable choices for what to do to protect or enhance national interests. Peter the Great initiated a great debate that has ebbed and flowed in intensity over four centuries and will persist for the indefinite future. He asserted that opening Russia's empire to European trade and ideas would strengthen it, overcoming those who argued that Russian security depended on autarky within a vast Slavic, Orthodox empire. The power balance in that tug-of-war between so-called Westernizers and Slavophiles has varied over time. Slavophiles first peaked with Nicolas I, who had dozens of liberal Decembrists executed and hundreds imprisoned in Siberian labor camps. Then came Stalin who, to perfect "socialism in one country," had millions of "enemies of the people" executed or starved to death and millions more imprisoned as slave laborers. Recently, Putin has promoted a third possibility, Eurasianism, whereby Russia would lead both sides of that vast continent. For now, that outlook dominates Russian foreign policy.

So, how did Russia become Russia?[5] Russia emerged from Dark Age shadows more than twelve hundred years ago. Ironically, a foreigner named and organized the Russian people. The key year was 862 when Viking chief Rurik and his band settled at Novgorod and convinced the region's Slavic tribes to swear allegiance to him. That loose-knit slowly expanding people became known as the Russ. Rurik and his heirs built a network of trading towns and fealty that extended across a vast swath of territory between the Baltic and Black Seas. Rurik's dynasty died with his last male heir in 1012. By then the center of Russ political, economic, and cultural gravity had shifted a thousand miles southward to Kiev, which exceeded Novgorod economically with its milder climate, richer soil, and easier access to opulent markets in the distant Byzantine, Persian, Arab, and Seljuk empires beyond the Black Sea.

Another key year in Russia's development was 988 when Kievan Russ converted to Christianity. Had Prince Vladimir chosen a Muslim rather than Christian bride and converted to her faith, he would have sharply altered the subsequent history of Russia, Europe, and the world beyond. He actually carefully examined the beliefs and practises of other religions before choosing Christianity. He rejected Judaism because the Jews had lost their empire and were scattered. He rejected Islam because that religion forbade imbibing alcohol, a pleasure he and his people could never forego. Vladimir adapted Orthodox Christianity to Russia. The liturgy was in the region's dialect rather than Byzantine Greek, and the local bishop enjoyed autonomy from the Patriarch in faraway Constantinople. Within decades nearly all the Russ people northward had converted.

The Mongols conquered most of Russia in the 1230s, destroyed Kiev, and extracted tribute for the next two and a half centuries. During that time, Russia had little contact with Europe westward as its princes literally and figuratively bowed eastward. In 1147 Moscow first appears in written records as a trade town with a fortress known as the Kremlin. The drain of tribute combined with short growing seasons, poor soil, and long winters to crimp the ability of Muscovy's princes, merchants, and landowners called *boyars* to amass and invest wealth in enterprises that diversified the economy. In 1382 the Mongols sacked Moscow along with other Russian towns after they rebelled.

But, like all empires, the Mongol peaked, declined, and eventually collapsed. By the 1480s the Mongol shadow disappeared completely from Russia. Meanwhile, another rising power would eventually become a Russian enemy. In 1453 the Ottoman Turks captured the Byzantine

Empire's last stronghold, Constantinople, and made that city their own capital. The Ottomans then expanded north-west into Europe, eventually conquering as far as Hungary. The Ottomans also established vassal states on the north shores of the Black and Caspian Seas.

Three centuries after its emergence, Moscow finally amassed enough economic, political, cultural, and military power to assert its own empire. Grand Prince Ivan III annexed Yaroslavl in 1471, Novgorod in 1478, and within a generation engulfed most Russians. For now, the Polish-Lithuanian empire blocked any further expansion westward and dominated the Baltic Sea basin. Nonetheless, Russia's power grew with Moscow's swelling tribute and trade profits. Moscow's patriarch asserted independence from and superiority to Kiev's patriarch as head of Russia's Orthodox Church.

Russia's next important ruler was Ivan IV, appropriately known as "the Terrible" for his murderous autocracy from 1547 to 1584. He was the first Grand Prince to be crowned with the added title of Tsar, derived from Caesar, in hopes of achieving equal status in the minds of distant European rulers. Ivan's troops conquered Astrakhan, the region where the Volga river flows into the Caspian Sea. He began receiving tribute from some of the Muslim khans along the Black Sea's north coast. Russia expanded to the Arctic Ocean, planted ports at Archangel and Murmansk, and traded with western Europe. Learning about England's virgin queen, Ivan the Terrible sent Elizabeth a marriage proposal, which she politely declined. He set up the *Oprichina*, or death squads, that he wielded to arrest, torture, and murder anyone he suspected of opposing him, with eventually thousands of victims. In 1581 he murdered his own son as a potential rival.

The three decades following Ivan's death was known as the "Time of Troubles" because of the blood-soaked civil wars, coups, and series of short-lived tsars. Then, in 1612, the Zemsky Sobor, an assembly of boyars, priests, and merchants, elected Mikhail Federovich Romanov the tsar. Thus began the Romanov dynasty that would rule and often misrule Russia for three centuries until it was overthrown in 1917.[6]

Russia expanded eastward, conquering tribes and small states along the way, and reached the Pacific Ocean in 1639. In 1689 Russian and Chinese diplomats signed the Treaty of Nerchinsk that designated the

Amur river the boundary between their empires. Then, in 1696, a new tsar took power who was determined to transform Russia from an Asiatic into a European power.

Peter I, appropriately known as "the Great", was Russia's most important autocrat before Lenin.[7] He expanded Russia's empire through wars with the Turks from 1695 to 1696, 1701 to 1717, and 1722 to 1723, and the Swedes from 1709 to 1717. The most crucial new territory was the Baltic Sea's eastern shore where Peter founded St Petersburg in 1702 as "a window to the west". He and a coterie had already visited Europe in 1697 and 1698, mostly England and Holland, studying advanced techniques of shipbuilding, astronomy, metal-forging, finance, engineering, architecture, public administration, and law-making. After returning, he implemented as many reforms as possible including, symbolically, forcing the boyars and nobles to shave their beards and, with their wives, exchange their oriental robes for European-style clothing. However, it was a victory in war that heralded Russia's emergence as one of Europe's great powers, the destruction of Swedish King Charles XII's invading army at Poltava in 1709. Peter added a title to his job description. In 1721 he declared Russia an empire and himself emperor, titles his successors would proudly assert. Fittingly, he established Russia's Academy of Sciences in 1725, the year of his death, as a lasting intellectual legacy. Nonetheless, his reforms were controversial during his lifetime and ever since, with Russians bitterly split between Westernizers and Slavophiles, and their relative power often seesawing convulsively over time.[8]

Three tsarinas, Anna from 1730 to 1740, Elizabeth from 1741 to 1761, and Catherine from 1762 to 1796, carried on Peter's vision and completed the Russian nobility's transformation into a European-style court. Catherine, who was born in the German duchy of Anhalt-Zerbst and later also known as "the Great," was especially devoted to bringing the Enlightenment to Russia, well aware that her adopted country was lost in the dark ages when Western Europe experienced the revolutionary changes that embraced humanism and individualism during the Renaissance and Reformation. She was a great patron of painting, music, poetry, and architecture. Her greatest contribution to Russia's enlightenment was the hundreds of schools she established, with equal opportunities for girls and boys. Ironically, she took power by a very unenlightened Russian method – a cabal murdered her autocratic, erratic, and estranged husband Peter. It was under Catherine that the Russian empire conquered most of the Black Sea's north coast, including Crimea in 1783, and established a Russian naval base at Sevastopol. After the French Revolution erupted in 1789, her despotism became much less enlightened as the secret police arrested any potential Russian revolutionaries.

Like his grandmother Catherine, Alexander I had supreme power thrust upon him through murder; a cabal strangled his tyrannical father Paul and placed him on the throne. Nonetheless, Alexander shared Catherine's enlightened despotism that faded steadily through his rule from 1801 to 1825. The series of wars with Napoleon hardened Alexander, especially when the French emperor invaded Russia with half a million troops and devastated the country all the way to Moscow in 1812. It was under Alexander that a Russian army fought its way the farthest west. The tsar led his troops into Paris in April 1814, as part of the allied coalition that defeated Napoleon. Fortunately, Alexander eventually withdrew his soldiers and thereafter no Russian army has appeared in Western Europe. After Napoleon's final defeat at Waterloo in 1815, Alexander formed with the leaders of Prussia and Austria the Holy Alliance dedicated to crushing any liberal or nationalist revolution in their lands or other European states.

Nicholas I, who followed his brother Alexander onto the throne, asserted that policy when he had the secret police round up hundreds of liberal army officers, known as Decembrists, on charges of plotting to overthrow the tsarist regime in 1825. He had five ringleaders executed, 121 sent to Siberian labor camps, and another four hundred demoted or cashiered. Count Sergei Uvarov, the tsar's education minister, justified the crackdown for preserving Russia's essence of Orthodoxy, autocracy, and imperialism. But no matter how determined the tsar and other conservative European rulers were to crush any revolutionaries, the forces of liberalism and nationalism were too widespread and deeply embedded in countless hearts and minds to eradicate completely.

Then a new revolutionary creed emerged in the mid-nineteenth century. Karl Marx developed what became known as Marxism in reaction to the industrial revolution in which factory owners reaped vast profits by exploiting workers with abysmal hours, conditions, and wages. He called for a revolution by the workers, whom he called the proletariat, against the bourgeoisie who owned the factories, mines, banks and other industries. The industrial revolution began in England during the late-eighteenth century, spread to America, France, and the Low Countries in the early-nineteenth century, central Europe by mid-century, and Russia in the late-nineteenth century.

Marxism had an ideological rival that Russian radicals found especially appealing. Anarchism is the belief that all governments are repressive and exploitative, and thus should be destroyed and replaced by local people ruling themselves through consensus. Mikhail Bakunin and Nikolai Chernyshevsky were Russia's leading theorists who inspired extremists to form terrorist groups like Land and Freedom and People's Will, dead set to assassinating the tsar and other members of the ruling elite. Most adherents were college students with St Petersburg University a radical hotbed.

Ironically, in 1881, anarchists succeeded in murdering Tsar Alexander II who was committed to reforming Russia. By decree, he emancipated the serfs from their landlords in 1861; authorized villages, towns, and city districts to establish *zemstvos* or committees of local leaders to run their own affairs in 1864; permitted jury trials in 1864; eased censorship laws in 1865; and reduced army enlistments from twenty-five to six years in 1874. When he was murdered, he was planning to make zemstvos the foundation for a national assembly. His ultra-conservative brother replaced him on the throne as Alexander III. The new tsar's crackdown not just on terrorist groups, but also the zemstvos and even Jewish communities as scapegoats, had the typically perverse effect of radicalizing more alienated Russians.

Meanwhile, Slavophiles, or ultra-Russian nationalists, became increasingly powerful. That outlook was partly in reaction against "alien" creeds like liberalism, Marxism, and anarchism, but was especially enraged at Russia's defeat by the United Kingdom, France, Turkey, and Austria in the Crimean War from 1853 to 1856. Adherents demanded that Russians establish an empire that championed all Slavic peoples and Orthodox Christians. Ironically, Slavophiles found inspiration in another western creed, this one developed by Englishman Herbert Spencer and called Social Darwinism, that justified imperialism as the natural conquest by the fittest nation of lesser nations in a constant struggle for survival and power.

Amidst all this political ferment, Russian high culture flourished during the nineteenth century into the early twentieth century. There were brilliant poets like Alexander Pushkin and Mikhail Lermontov; novelists like Ivan Turgenev, Nikolai Gogol, Fyodor Dostoyevsky, and Leo Tolstoy; playwright and short-story writer Anton Chekov; painters like Alexander Ivanov, Ilya Repin, Vasilii Vereshchagin, Vasilii Surikov, Ivan Shishkin, and Isaak Levitan; composers and musicians like Mikhail Glinka, Anton Rubinstein, Alexander Borodin, Peter Tchaikovsky, Nicolai Rimsky-Korsakov, Modest Mussorgsky, and Igor Stravinsky; ballet choreographers like George Balanchine and Sergei Diaghilev; and ballet dancers like Vaslav Nijinsky and Anna Pavlova. These artists excelled in each genre by reinterpreting western models through Russian culture. The Communists would destroy the chance for Russia's creative geniuses to express themselves, usually by imprisoning or murdering those who did not escape into foreign exile.

Industrialization came a century later to Russia than Britain, and several generations after western European countries and America.[9] However, Russia rapidly narrowed that gap with annual economic growth rates averaging 5.7 per cent from 1885 to 1913 that peaked at 8 per cent from 1909 to 1913. Russian wheat and rye exports accounted for one-quarter and two-thirds respectively of the global market. The ranks of industrial workers tripled from one million to three million.[10] The economy diversified with classes and occupations. The middle class of small business owners, middle managers, lawyers, engineers, doctors, and teachers was growing, but still represented only about one in five Russians. Two in three Russians were impoverished factory, mine, railroad, dock, or farm laborers while only one in twenty-five were members of either the ancient nobility or the new industrial class. Most people still lived in the country but, by 1914, one in three inhabited cities. Poverty afflicted two in every three Russians. University students were an increasingly important class as their numbers soared from 5,000 to 69,000 between 1860 and 1914. During those same years, the number of newspapers skyrocketed from thirteen to 856 and the literacy rate from 10 per cent to 40 per cent. The result was ever more people aware and enraged at how backward, impoverished, and repressive Russia was, and determined to change that through collective action. Political parties, labor unions, demonstrations, and strikes were illegal, but mushroomed from the 1890s through 1914 with 3,543 strikes involving 1,337,458 workers or nearly half of all workers. Russia became Europe's most strike-ravaged country as workers protested their abysmal pay, hours, and conditions.[11]

Every revolution has its own unique set of causes, of which many may appear similar to those of other revolutions. For instance, the royal families of France in 1789 and Russia in 1917 both had weak kings and unpopular foreign queens. Atop Russia's power pyramid from 1894 was Nicholas II, known for his conservatism, love of his family, mild manners, and indecisiveness. When his father died, then twenty-six year old Nicholas wailed: "What is going to happen to me and to all of Russia? I am not prepared to be a Tsar. I never wanted to become one. I know nothing of the business of ruling. I have no idea of even how to talk to the ministers."[12] Those may be the most insightful words the tsar ever uttered. Every revolution has a unique array of causes, but one key perennial component is a weak-willed, ignorant, inept, vacillating leader who seesaws between brutal repression and bumbling appeasement toward reformers and revolutionaries alike.

As the twentieth century dawned, two groups posed the worst Marxist threats to Russia's tsarist regime: the Social Democratic Workers' Party or Social Democrats founded in 1898, and the Socialist Revolutionary Party or Social Revolutionaries founded in 1901. Those parties differed in two critical ways. One was orientation as Social Revolutionaries championed peasants and Social Democrats championed industrial workers. The other was that among the Social Democrats was a profound theorist and ruthless rising leader named Vladimir Ilych Ulyanov who called himself Lenin.[13]

Lenin revolutionized Marxist theory through his 1902 book *What Is To Be Done?* and 1916 book *Imperialism: The Highest Stage of Capitalism.* He argued that Marx had failed to anticipate that each industrial country's ruling elite would finesse revolutionary conditions with reforms that ameliorated workers and peasants, paid for by profits reaped from recently conquered colonies in Africa and Asia. Revolution was possible only if a secret zealous elite group called the Dictatorship of the Proletariat led it. Lenin scored a decisive propaganda victory during the international congress of Marxist parties in London in 1903. The Social Democrats split between his followers dedicated to violent communist revolution, led by a Dictatorship of the Proletariat, and Julius Martov's followers who advocated overthrowing the tsarist regime and replacing it with a Marxist dominated democratic system. Although Lenin had fewer adherents, he called his faction the Bolsheviks or Majoritarians and denigrated Martov's majority as Mensheviks or Minoritarians. The labels stuck as a classic example of fake news trumping reality.

A communist revolution would never have engulfed Russia had Nicholas II and his advisors avoided two devastating wars. The first was between the Russian and Japanese empires for supremacy in northeast Asia. The Russians were completing the Trans-Siberian Railroad to its eastern terminus at Port Arthur on the Pacific Ocean. That railroad and port were actually in China's north-eastern region called Manchuria. Beijing had succumbed to St Petersburg's pressure to lease Russian access to that region for the railroad, port, chain of towns, and even troops to protect those assets. Meanwhile, the Russians pressured Korea's government for similar concessions. Japan had defeated China in a war from 1894 to 1895, and won a huge indemnity and the island of Taiwan. Now the Japanese were dead-set to drive the Russians from Manchuria and Korea, and conquer those lands for themselves. On February 9, 1904, they destroyed Russia's Pacific Fleet in a sneak attack, invaded Manchuria, besieged Port Arthur, eventually captured it, and then advanced on Mukden. The Kremlin dispatched its Baltic fleet all the way around the world, but the Japanese navy destroyed that fleet on May 27, 1905. Eventually, President Theodore Roosevelt ended the war by pressuring Russian and Japanese envoys to make concessions and sign the Treaty of Portsmouth on September 2, 1905. Although the Russians had to surrender their Manchurian sphere of influence to Japan, the tsar and his government were eager to cut their losses because a revolution had erupted in their midst.

That revolution began with a mass demonstration before the tsar's Winter Palace in St Petersburg on January 22, 1905. The protesters, led by radical priest Georgii Gapon, had gathered to beseech the tsar to alleviate worsening economic conditions caused by industrialization exacerbated by war. Nicholas could have dispersed a mostly grateful and adoring crowd by appearing on a balcony and making vague promises. Instead, the Imperial Guard opened fire then charged the protesters, killing over a hundred and wounding hundreds more. Radicals called for a general strike to force the tsar to enact reforms. Although there were no legal unions, most workers walked out and formed "soviets" or councils to decide and implement what to do. The result was more violence. During this time the Bolsheviks played a minor rabble-rousing role, but no radical group led the revolution. On October 30, the tsar promised to establish a constitution with a *duma* or general assembly. That was good enough for most workers who returned to their jobs. However, Lenin and his Bolsheviks tried carrying on the struggle but were crushed by the police and army in December. Lenin fled with his coterie into foreign exile, moving restlessly among cities until he finally made Zurich his headquarters. The Bolsheviks would later call the aborted 1905 revolution a dress rehearsal for the 1917 version.

The tsar did inaugurate a constitution known as the Fundamental Laws and a Duma on April 27, 1906. Unfortunately, neither the document nor institution proved to be anything more than symbolic gestures void of genuine democratic substance. The Duma had no lawmaking or investigative powers. The tsar issued decrees and his appointed State Council determined all laws and whitewashed serious problems. The Duma's largest party was the Constitutional Democrats, or Kadets, with 153 of 445 seats, followed by Labourites, or Trudoviks, with 107 seats; there were no Social Revolutionaries or Social Democrats because they had boycotted the election.

The only important reform to emerge from the Duma was to privatize communal village lands so that peasants could buy and farm them freely. Believing that land reform threatened rather than bolstered his reign, the tsar dissolved the Duma on June 3, 1907. Yet no mass protests erupted. The revolutionary zeal among most previous adherents was exhausted. That left the radicals in the underground with nothing to do but plot and impatiently await the next disaster inflicted on Russia by the tsarist regime. That opportunity soon arose.

No great power wanted a European-wide war in August 1914 even though over preceding decades each had prepared for just such a possibility.[14] Europe was split between the Central Alliance of the German, Austro-Hungarian, and, in September, Ottoman Empires, and the Triple Entente of France, Russia, and the United Kingdom. The result was a self-fulfilling prophecy. The First World War would result in at least 14 million dead, including 9 million soldiers and 5 million civilians; the shattering of the Russian, Austro-Hungarian, German, and Ottoman Empires; and Russia's communist revolution.[15]

Terrorism is the threat or use of violence against innocent people for political purposes. As such, terrorism is probably as old as humanity. One man, Gavrilo Princeps, committed the terrorist act with history's most catastrophic consequences on June 28, 1914. He was a member of the Black Hand, a Serbian terrorist group committed to driving Austria from Bosnia-Herzegovina. He shot to death Archduke Franz Ferdinand, Austria's crown prince, and his wife Sophie in Sarajevo, Bosnia's capital. Austria's secret police captured him and several other Black Hand conspirators and, during the interrogation, learned that Serbia's Military Intelligence supported them. Vienna issued a list of demands to Belgrade that would trigger war if the Serbs did not immediately accept them all. After Belgrade refused, Austria mobilized its army to invade Serbia. That provoked Russia to mobilize its army to defend its ally Serbia. Germany in turn mobilized its army against Russia, which provoked the mobilization of first the French and then the British to do the same. On August 4, 1914, the Germans struck first with a massive assault through Belgium toward France.

Tsar Nicholas II's decision to take Russia to war led to a series of catastrophes.[16] Although the tsar's announcement that Russia was at war inspired patriotism in most of his subjects, that enthusiasm diminished rapidly. The Germans inflicted devastating defeats on the Russian army at Tannenberg and the Masurian Lakes in autumn 1914, and then pushed eastward into Russia until their offensive finally ground to a halt. The result was a stalemate on that front along with the Western Front for the next four years. The technologies of machine guns and barbed wire made defense the superior strategy, although that did not inhibit generals from ordering human-wave assaults that resulted in mass slaughter.

The unwinnable war steadily corroded the legitimacy of the tsar and his regime. Nicholas had destroyed his lofty father-figure image with most Russians, especially peasants and workers, when his troops slaughtered protesters outside his Winter Palace in January 1905. He then compounded the mass loathing and dismay for him as word spread of the bizarre advisor that he and his wife had adopted. Grigori Rasputin was a wandering libertine and mystic who mesmerized most people, especially women, with his seeming prophetic and healing powers atop his tireless sexual prowess in all-night orgies. In December 1905 Nicholas and Alexandria invited him to the palace to cure their son Alexia's hemophilia. Amazingly, Rasputin appeared to staunch the boy's bleeding. For the next eleven years the tsar and tsarina relied on Rasputin for spiritual, emotional and even political advice. Nicholas may have later rued not heeding this plea from Rasputin: "Let Papa not plan war because war will mean the end of Russia and yourselves and you will lose to the last man."[17] And he may have also rued taking Rasputin's advice that he go to the front and head the army in September 1915. Fearful and jealous of his influence, a cabal of army officers murdered Rasputin on December 16, 1916. Although apparently Rasputin did not predict his demise, he exuded superhuman strength in resisting death. Lured to an orgy, he was poisoned with cyanide-laced food and drink, shot several times, strangled, then dumped in the freezing Neva river, but somehow crawled back on shore where an officer shot him in the head.

Russia's government appeared to have disappeared. After the war erupted the Duma's delegates voted to dissolve their body for the duration to avoid divisiveness. St Petersburg's name was changed to Petrograd, which sounded Russian rather than German. Nicholas recalled the Duma on July 19, 1915, but dissolved it on September 2 after its delegates issued too many criticisms and demands. Then the tsar himself left for the front.

By early 1917 Russians had endured two and a half years of worsening defeats, casualties, shortages, prices, taxes, confiscations, debt, and despair. By the war's end the Russian army had suffered 1,811,000 dead, 1,450,000 wounded, and 3,500,000 captured or 6,761,000 casualties along with several million dead civilians; a hundred thousand or more troops had deserted.[18] In St Petersburg and other cities, workers enjoyed growing bargaining power with their managers. Strikes began in 1915 and grew in length and violence. Social Revolutionaries, Mensheviks, and Bolsheviks vied to rally workers and army deserters into their respective radical movements. Factory workers formed Red Guard militia units and Soviets, or councils. The Soviets in turn formed the All-Russian Congress of Soviets that the communists were determined to make an alternative government.

Meanwhile, the tsar's decision to go to the front and command the army worsened Russia's war effort. Nicholas knew nothing of substance about military affairs and his meddling compounded the indecision, chaos, and abysmal morale plaguing the army. The Germans inflicted more devastating defeats on the Russians. Those soldiers who survived along with civilians across the country blamed the tsar for those disasters. Nicholas abdicated on March 15, 1917.

Prince Georgii Lvov, who headed the Union of Zemstrovs, worked with other opposition groups to form a coalition government that included Kadets, Social Revolutionaries, and Mensheviks in the cabinet and the Duma, renamed the Constituent Assembly. Lvov's right-hand man was Alexander Kerensky, a prominent lawyer and socialist, who he chose to be first his justice minister and then his war minister. Lvov and his unwieldly coalition made a critical decision that discredited them. They chose to honor Russia's treaty commitment to the alliance and continue to wage war, thus alienating countless people across the political spectrum who hoped the new government would negotiate peace.

Upon learning about the tsar's overthrow, Lenin sought to return to Russia to instigate a communist revolution. Berlin was well aware that Vladimir Lenin was a radical Russian leader. When Lenin and a dozen of his followers applied for transit visas to return to Russia, German officials not only promptly granted those visas but assigned them a special train carriage. After reaching St Petersburg on April 2, Lenin wrote, had printed, and distributed what became known as the April Thesis. With the tsar's overthrow, Russia had experienced a bourgeois revolution. With that done, the time had come for a communist revolution that established a dictatorship of the proletariat whose key leaders were now Lenin, Leon Trotsky, Grigory Zinoviev, Lev Kamenev, and Joseph Stalin.

Kerensky became prime minister on July 8. He sought to bolster his power by naming conservative General Lavr Kornilov the commander-in-chief. However, Kornilov was more interested in defeating the government than the Germans. Kornilov attempted to overthrow Kerensky's government, but loyal troops defeated him on September 14. Kerensky followed up this victory by having the *Okhrana*, or secret police, round up communist radicals. To evade arrest, Lenin escaped to Finland. His latest exile would be brief.

Chapter 2

The Soviet Empire's Rise and Fall

Without lies, the Soviet Union had no legitimacy.

(Arkady Ostrovsky)

I came to hate Lenin and Stalin – those monsters who had cruelly deceived me.

(Alexander Yakovlev)

I'm not sure we've absorbed the full impact of what happened ... But communism died this year ... By the grace of God, America won the Cold War.

(George H.W. Bush)

Vladimir Lenin slipped back to St Petersburg from Helsinki on October 23. Assessing the situation, he realized that the Bolsheviks were as strong in the cities as they were largely absent in the countryside. A revolution could only succeed if the workers and peasants united. To bolster Bolshevik power, he forged a coalition with the Social Revolutionaries as a junior partner. His next step was to convince his inner circle of Bolsheviks that the time for a coup had come. Joseph Stalin and Leon Trotsky agreed immediately and they pressured reluctant Lev Kamenev and Grigory Zinoviev to go along. Collectively they got the Central Committee to approve.

Red Guards stormed the Winter Palace and captured most of the provisional government on November 7; Kerensky somehow escaped. Backed by his cabal, Lenin announced the coup and got the All-Russian Congress of Soviets to declare the creation of the Soviet Socialist Republic of Russia. The Congress then approved a coalition government of People's Commissars with Bolsheviks packing the key posts but minor ones going to Mensheviks and Social Revolutionaries. Lenin was the chief commissar, Trotsky the foreign affairs commissar, and Stalin the nationalities commissar. The Bolsheviks sought popularity by promising "bread, land, and peace," what nearly all Russians wanted above all else. But that government soon faced a rival.

Although the Constituent Assembly's elections took place before the Bolshevik coup, officials were still counting the votes. On January 18, 1918, when the Constituent Assembly first met, the Bolsheviks were a minority having won only 24 per cent of the vote compared to the Social Revolutionaries with 38 per cent. That did not intimidate Lenin who declared the Constituent Assembly a counter-revolutionary institution and had Red Guards eject the delegates. He then designated the All-Russian Congress of Soviets the revolution's legislature and transferred the capital from St Petersburg to Moscow. Within the Central Committee, he formed the Political Bureau or Politburo with a chairman, general secretary, and secretaries of what amounted to ministries. Initially, the Politburo included Lenin at its head along with, most prominently, Stalin, the general secretary, Kamenev, the head of Moscow's party, Zinoviev, the head of St Petersburg's party, Trotsky, the war commissar, and Nikolai Bukharin, the editor of the newspaper *Pravda*. In July he had a constitution written to legitimize and systematize all these new government institutions. That communist system of repression and exploitation would endure until 1991.[1]

The Communists had seized power in St Petersburg, Moscow, and a handful of other cities. The next step was to assert total control over the entire Russian empire. That posed a dilemma. The Communists would have to inflict harsh measures that alienated people in order to commandeer the resources to subject them. On December 7, 1917, Lenin set up the secret police called the "All Russian Extraordinary Commission for the Struggle against Counter-Revolution, Sabotage, and Speculation," better known by its acronym *Cheka*. The Cheka's first chief was Felix Dzerzhinsky, who was utterly ruthless in having his police round up any opponents on trumped-up charges, find them guilty in kangaroo courts, then either sentence them to one of 132 labor camps by 1922 or execution. Lenin's Red Terror committed at least a million murders.[2] Among the victims were Tsar Nicholas, his wife, three of his four daughters, and son, executed by the communists at Ekaterinburg on

July 16, 1918. Trotsky spoke for all communists when he explained: "Red Terror is a weapon utilized against a class, doomed to destruction … Without the Red Terror, the Russian bourgeoisie, together with the world bourgeoisie, would throttle us long before the coming of the revolution in Europe … The very fact of the existence of the Soviet system must also sanction the Red Terror."[3]

The Communists achieved peace with the treaty of Brest-Litovsk which Trotsky signed with German and Austrian diplomats on March 3, 1918. Under the treaty, Russia transferred the Baltic States and Belarus to Germany and Ukraine to Austria in return for diplomatic recognition. In all "the Soviet Republic lost 34 per cent of its population (55 million people), 32 per cent of its agricultural land, 54 per cent of its industrial enterprises and 89 per cent of its coalmines."[4]

The Communist grip on power could only be secure after eliminating all their enemies. They faced Russian generals Lavr Kornilov, Anton Denikin, Peter Krasnov, Alexander Kolchak, and Peter Wrangel who all gathered armies in remote regions. The trouble with those "White" armies was that they were widely separated on the sparsely populated periphery, failed to coordinate their strategies, and were often starved of supplies despite support from contingents of British, French, American, Polish, and Japanese troops. The worst foreign threat came in 1920 from the newly liberated Poles who advanced into Belarus, Ukraine, and Lithuania before being repelled. The Japanese tried and failed to conquer Russia's far eastern provinces. The Americans, British, and French mostly deployed troops to guard and extract military supplies that they had shipped to their former ally Russia and now sought to prevent the Bolsheviks from transferring to their enemy Germany. By 1922 all foreign troops had withdrawn. Soviet "history" books claimed that the Cold War actually began during the civil war with that foreign intervention. What the Soviet books neglected to explain was that after withdrawing the troops, President Woodrow Wilson despatched Herbert Hoover, the American Relief Administration's director, to Moscow to help alleviate the mass violence, starvation, and disease plaguing the Russians.

Lenin charged Trotsky with winning the civil war by any means possible. Trotsky's strategy, which he called War Communism, involved mobilizing all the human and natural resources needed to destroy the enemy. On February 23, 1918, he ordered the Red Army to confiscate grain, livestock, and other foods from the peasants to feed the soldiers and workers. In the cities Red Guards stormed into the homes of the wealthy and well-to-do to confiscate their money, jewels, and anything else of value, provoking a stampede of, eventually, two million Russians into foreign exile. Across Russia the communists seized the property of the Orthodox Church and other religions. On June 28, 1918, they nationalized all mines, factories, and railroads. With conscription, the Red Army's ranks soared from a million men in 1919 to five million in December 1920, while the Communist Party and government officials expanded to 1.4 million and 5.4 million, respectively.[5] Strategically, the communists capitalized on the advantage of controlling Russia's heartland and its rail network, along which Trotsky transferred troops and supplies where they were most needed. Psychologically, the communists wielded terror against not just the enemy but their own soldiers and civilians for a very simple reason – ruthlessness worked at every level. Lenin boasted that "we're applying the model of the French Revolution and putting on trial and even executing the senior commanders if they hold back and fail in their actions" as well as shooting "conspirators and waverers without asking anyone or any idiotic red tape".[6] By 1922 the communists had eliminated each White army and won the civil war, but at the horrific cost of around eight million people who died from violence, disease, and starvation, twice the four million who perished in the First World War.[7]

Lenin believed that communism in Russia would only succeed if communist revolutions succeeded elsewhere. To realize that, he established the Communist International or Comintern in March 1919. Comintern was a coalition of the world's communist and other revolutionary parties controlled by Moscow that provided money, training, experts, and arms. Comintern racked up a series of failed attempts to provoke revolutions in Hungary, Germany, Serbia, Greece, Austria, Romania, and Mexico. The only genuine success was by Comintern agent Mikhail Borodin who, during the 1920s, nurtured China's Communist Party that Mao Zedong eventually led to victory in a civil war against the Nationalist Party and various warlords from 1927 to 1949.

Lenin recognized that if the Communist Party exploited the peasants and workers too harshly they would likely rebel. With the White armies defeated, War Communism was no longer needed. During the Communist Party Congress in March 1920, he convinced the delegates to approve a New Economic Policy (NEP) whereby the state retained control of the largest industries but tolerated privately-owned small businesses, farms, and homes that paid 20 per cent of their wealth in money or kind to the state. He justified this by arguing that communism could not be implemented until Russia completed the bourgeois development phase. To manage the economy he established the State Planning Commission or Gosplan within the Supreme Economic Council. Then, on December 30, 1922, he and his cabal established the Soviet Union among Russia, Ukraine, Belarus, and the Transcaucasian Federation, later split among Georgia, Armenia, and Azerbaijan. Moscow would conquer and transform other lands into Soviet republics until there were fifteen, with four – Lithuania, Latvia, Estonia, and Moldova – Second World War spoils.

Lenin suffered the first of three strokes on May 25, 1922 with the final killing him on January 21, 1924. The first two strokes partly paralyzed his body and slurred his thought and speech. He had moments of lucidity when he may have written his "Testament," in which he warned his fellow communist leaders to beware of Stalin: "I suggest that the comrades think about a way to remove Stalin."[8] That warning was unheeded whether Lenin actually wrote it, which is disputed.[9]

What followed was a four-year power struggle in which Stalin eventually eliminated his rivals and became the Soviet Union's supreme leader. His Politburo colleagues had unwittingly given him the rope with which to hang themselves in April 1922 when they granted his request to be the Communist Party's general secretary. He wielded that position to pack the party with 10,000 communists who owed their positions to him. Presented with Lenin's criticism, Stalin pretended to accept it humbly and assured his comrades that he would be a better communist worthy of their trust. He displayed his devotion to the deceased leader by creating a cult of worship of Lenin with his body embalmed and displayed in a glass coffin in a massive mausoleum in Red Square beneath the Kremlin's medieval walls. That done, he turned against Trotsky, his most ruthless rival, whom he accused of "factionalism". Zinoviev and Kamenev backed Stalin; although they feared both men's ambitions, they believed that Trotsky posed the worse threat because he was brilliant and ruthless, unlike Stalin who was merely ruthless. The Central Committee stripped Trotsky of his power in January 1925 and party membership in November 1927. Stalin then targeted Zinoviev and Kamenev who belatedly tried to rehabilitate Trotsky; he got the Central Committee to strip them of their posts and membership in December 1927. The party reinstated Kamenev and Zinoviev after they recanted their errors and begged forgiveness. Trotsky refused and instead went into foreign exile. Finally, Stalin attacked Bukharin, the last of Lenin's inner circle.

Stalin's first significant policy was downgrading Comintern's efforts to foment revolution abroad; he terminated Comintern in 1940. Instead, the Kremlin would concentrate on achieving "socialism in one country" and thus make the Soviet Union a model for communist revolutionaries around the world. Stalin issued the first five-year economic plan in 1929. That plan involved communizing the economy by abolishing all private property and having the government impose five-year production goals for every now state-owned factory, mine, farm, and construction project. With these policies, the communists did not eliminate the class system; they simplified it. Essentially, they created a modern version of feudalism with themselves as the lords. Less than 5 per cent of Soviets could join the exclusive Communist Party, which was organized in a pyramid of power. The communists destroyed the rich and middle classes, and took their place to monopolize what little wealth the system produced. From their feast, they distributed the leftovers among the 95 per cent remaining people whom they repressed, exploited, and, when they resisted, imprisoned or outright murdered. Most families were crammed into a room and shared a kitchen, toilet, and bath with other families on the same floor or complex. Virtually all non-party member Soviets existed in chronic poverty, malnutrition, and bleak despair.

Communism was an economic catastrophe. Production figures revealed the starkly different results between working for the state and working for one's own profit. About 40 per cent of vegetables and 66 per cent of meat was produced on the tiny gardens that the collectivized peasants were allowed to nurture in their time off. Pre-revolutionary Russia exported grain; the Soviet Union had to import grain because collective farms were so inefficient and wasteful.[10] Industrial products were shoddily made. Everything was in short supply. Shop shelves were usually bare except for times when a rare shipment of some product would appear. People spent hours daily standing in lines hoping to purchase goods that often sold out before they got to the counter.

The Communists believed that achieving a communist economy was inseparable from achieving a communist society. To that end, they sought to transform everyone into a model Soviet man or woman who exemplified communist ideals of collectivism, conformity and sacrifice. That, of course, proved to be difficult since those ideals conflict with such natural human drives as individualism, materialism, enterprise and spirituality. Incessant propaganda through the mass media and schools was one way to socialize or brainwash people into communism. Stalin had himself promoted alongside Lenin as perfect communist cult leaders. Then there were the model communist followers like a fifteen-year-old boy named Pavlik Morozov whom the Kremlin celebrated for betraying his parents to the police for their counter-revolutionary attitudes. However, the Communists swiftly recognized that, ultimately, obedience could only be coerced with the most brutal methods of repression for all and prison or outright murder for dissidents. As Stalin enjoyed putting it, "you can't make an omelette without breaking eggs."

Stalin's policies caused 15 million or so deaths from execution, overwork, disease and starvation. Around 8.5 million died after Stalin ordered agriculture collectivized. Those convicted of crimes were either shot or imprisoned in the Gulag, the acronym for the Main Administration of Corrective Labor Camps and Colonies, a network of sixty concentration camps located mostly east of the Ural Mountains in Siberia; of the 14 million people sentenced to the Gulag, half died.[11] Then came Stalin's "Great Terror" from 1936 to 1938 that officially included 1.5 million arrests, of whom 681,692 were executed, and 1.3 million were condemned to the Gulag.[12] Among those murdered were 80,000 army officers, many veterans of the First World War and the civil war, leaving mostly inexperienced generals and lower-ranking officers in command to face Germany's onslaught in June 1941. The communists executed 42,000 Orthodox priests, or 95 per cent, from 1918 to 1930.[13]

Thousands of creative people like painters, playwrights, sculptors, poets, novelists and dancers were also murdered or enslaved. Of course, to Stalin's victims must be added Lenin's 7 million or so victims, bringing the total communist genocide to around 22 million.[14]

And atop that holocaust inflicted by Lenin and Stalin were the 27 million Soviets who died in the Second World War. Among the dead were 158,000 Red Army troops shot for various reasons atop another 436,000 imprisoned and 422,000 who served in penal units.[15] After the Second World War Stalin had imprisoned most of the 3 million Soviet soldiers who had been German prisoners, fearing that they might infect his communist utopia with dangerous ideas; hundreds of thousands died as slave laborers. That carnage might have been avoided or reduced had Lenin and Stalin not mass murdered or enslaved tens of millions of people and thus devastated Soviet military and economic power, including most of the army's officers, thus inviting Hitler's assault. So Soviet communism's total death toll may well exceed 50 million.[16]

Stalin believed that his non-aggression pact with Hitler, signed on August 23, 1939, would avoid war with Germany and let the Soviet Union retake lands ceded to Germany in 1918. After Germany invaded western Poland on September 1, the Red Army invaded eastern Poland as well as Estonia, Latvia, and Lithuania. France and Britain declared war against Germany, but not the Soviet Union. To complete the conquest of those countries, the Soviets imprisoned 420,000 Poles and murdered half, including 15,000 Polish officers and 7,000 civilians at Katyn, in Belarus.[17] The communists also imprisoned hundreds of thousands and murdered tens of thousands of Baltic peoples. In November 1939 Stalin launched a war against Finland that inflicted half a million Soviet and Finn casualties. In March 1940 the Finns agreed to a peace treaty in which they ceded part of their territory to the Soviet Union.

Stalin was stunned when the German army invaded the Soviet Union on June 22, 1941. Over the next five months the Germans and their allies killed, wounded or captured millions of Soviet troops until the invasion bogged down in the mud of autumn downpours, then winter blizzards and sub-zero temperatures. The war would not end until the Nazi government surrendered on May 8, 1945, after Soviet armies from the east and American and British armies from the west overran Germany.

Perversely, the Second World War legitimized communist rule more than any other Kremlin policy. Historian Orlando Figes explained:

> The Second World War did not interrupt the Revolution. It intensified and broadened it. Bolshevism came into its own during the war – with its military discipline and cult of sacrifice, its willingness to expend human life to meet its goals, and its capacity to militarize the masses through its planned economy.[18]

To mobilize the population against the invaders, Stalin set aside communist ideology and appealed to Russian patriotism in what the Kremlin dubbed the "Great Patriotic War". During that war, Hitler unwittingly provided indispensable aid to Stalin. People in the western Soviet Union initially greeted the Germans as liberators from communist mass exploitation and murder until the Nazis began mass round-ups for their own slave labor camps and slaughtered those who resisted.

It was not just Stalin's ruthlessness and Hitler's blunders that ultimately led to the Soviet victory and German defeat in May 1945. The Soviet Union, the United States, and the United Kingdom were allies in a classic example of that maxim, the enemy of my enemy is my friend. Washington supplied Moscow with $11 billion in military and economic aid including, most prominently, 13,303 armored vehicles, 427,284 trucks, 35,170 motorcycles, 1,911 steam locomotives and 2,670,371 tons of petroleum products. America's aid to the Soviet Union was crucial first for its survival and then for its steamroller offensive all the way to Berlin.[19]

The three major allied leaders, Stalin, President Franklin Roosevelt, and Prime Minister Winston Churchill met twice, at Tehran from November 28 to December 1, 1944 and Yalta from February 4 to 11, 1945. They debated and reached broad agreements on, first, how to win the war, and, then, how to win the peace. That was not easy given the mutual suspicions. Stalin's paranoia was understandable. After all, it was Churchill who in 1919 declared: "Bolshevism is not a ... creed; it is a disease", and in 1954 would bitterly reflect that "we might have strangled Bolshevism in its cradle, but everyone turned their hands and said, 'How shocking.'"[20] And Harry Truman, who became vice president in 1944, earlier argued that "If we see that Germany is winning the war we ought to help Russia, and if Russia is winning, we ought to help Germany, and in that way let them kill as many as possible."[21]

Stalin's priority was for the Americans and British to invade France as soon as possible to divert resources from Germany's war against the Soviet Union. In that Roosevelt was in complete accord but Churchill feared a cross-Channel attack and instead advocated a series of offensives against what he claimed was the enemy's "soft underbelly" in southern Europe. That split between Roosevelt and Churchill delayed what became the Normandy landing until June 6, 1944. Roosevelt's priority was for Stalin to join the war against Japan. Although Roosevelt was aware that America's nuclear program was making progress, there was no guarantee that it would ultimately succeed. If not, then Japan would have to be invaded by at least a million troops who would suffer hundreds of thousands of dead and wounded before finally crushing the enemy. So Roosevelt wanted Moscow to share that horrific burden. Actually, to advance Soviet interests in north-east Asia, Stalin intended to attack Japan as soon as possible after Germany's defeat but played hard to get to get to garner more concessions. Both Roosevelt and Churchill pressured Stalin to agree to democratic elections in the eastern European countries after the war. The three agreed to split Berlin and the rest of Germany into three occupation zones which each army would de-nazify and demilitarize; later Charles de Gaulle pressured Roosevelt and Churchill into giving part of their zones to France. A major concession that Roosevelt and Churchill gave Stalin was to redraw Poland's territory westward so that the Soviet Union took eastern Poland and Poland took northwestern Germany to the Oder river. They also agreed to establish a United Nations Organization to be, hopefully, an improved version of the League of Nations that had failed to prevent the Second World War. Power would reside in a Security Council in which each of the five major allies, the Soviet Union, United States, United Kingdom, France and China, would have veto power. Churchill and Stalin welcomed a Roosevelt notion known as "the Four Policemen," whereby each great power would assert hegemony over its own sphere of influence and not meddle in other spheres. That would let the Soviets dominate eastern Europe and central Asia, the Americans the Western Hemisphere, the British their empire and the Chinese East Asia.

Thereafter Roosevelt, Churchill and their successors fumed as Stalin systematically violated all his promises. As the Red Army fought its way westward, political commissars established communist regimes in each conquered country's capital and other cities. To eliminate opponents and assert total control, the communists wielded strategies appropriate to each country. By 1948 Moscow had embedded communism in East Germany, Estonia, Latvia, Lithuania, Poland, Czechoslovak, Hungary, Bulgaria and Romania. Yugoslavia was also communist, but its dictator, Josip Broz Tito, had led his own guerrilla movement against the German army and refused to let the Soviet army remain after they joined forces in 1945.

Harry Truman became president on April 12, 1945, when a brain hemorrhage killed Roosevelt. Truman was ill prepared for the job as Roosevelt had failed to brief his vice president about such vital matters as diplomacy with the Soviet Union and the nuclear weapons program's existence. With swelling dismay and rage, Truman and his advisors watched communists take over one country after another, debated how that threatened American national security and what, if anything, to do about that.

George Kennan, the acting ambassador in Moscow, provided powerful answers to those questions that became the foundation for America's Cold War containment policy. On February 22, 1946, he sent an eight-thousand-word "Long Telegram" that explained the historical, cultural, and ideological sources of Soviet imperialism and how to counter that. The Soviet Union had inherited the traditional Russian policy of expanding the empire as far as possible in all directions, but justified that as liberating people with communism. Having advanced to the heart of Europe, Stalin would concentrate on asserting totalitarian control over his conquests. He did not want a war with the West and was eager to reduce defense spending to rebuild the Soviet economy, especially the devastated western regions. A Soviet threat existed but was political, not military. Communism appeals to victims of mass poverty, violence, corruption and chaos that prevailed in the war-shattered countries of Europe and Asia. Unlike its economy, Moscow's foreign policy was opportunistic rather than minutely planned. The Kremlin had broad goals and flexible means for achieving them. The Soviets would take advantage of any chance for local communists abetted by Soviet agents to bolster their power in any country.

Kennan then explained how to contain that threat. Washington could reduce communism's appeal only by transforming mass poverty into mass prosperity with massive economic aid. That aid would focus on rebuilding the industrial powerhouses of Western Europe and Japan, and re-integrating them into a global free trade system regulated by international organizations. This strategy should be immediately implemented to reinforce existing democratic European and Japanese forces in those countries. All along, statesmanship, patience, firmness and adaptation were the proper responses to the inevitable challenges and outright crises that the Kremlin would provoke to test Washington's resolve.

Elsewhere around the world, communists would undoubtedly take over some countries like China that were so deeply mired in poverty, corruption, incompetence and brutality that they were beyond reform. That, however, did not threaten American security for nationalistic, practical, and ideological reasons. Nationalism lurked beneath the international communist fraternity and would eventually break that up as the traditional conflicting interests of Russia and China re-asserted themselves. Then there was the pragmatic need for communist regimes to trade for products that they could not produce themselves; the greater a communist country's dependence on the outside world, the more likely it would moderate its policies. Finally, communism would eventually self-destruct everywhere it was imposed. Communism may be the perfect system for repressing, mobilizing and exploiting people, and imprisoning or murdering anyone who resists. However, communist regimes would economically fall further behind the West because they stifle rather than encourage the creativity, experimentation and entrepreneurship that drive development. The containment policy would accelerate communism's destruction. Kennan's analysis was brilliantly prescient both in how to contain communism and the reasons for its ultimate fate.

President Truman essentially declared Cold War on March 12, 1947. Although he and his advisors had mulled over Kennan's analysis since receiving it, the immediate catalysts were Soviet pressure on Turkey to make territorial concessions in the Caucasus region and the threat that a communist revolution would overwhelm Greece. Traditionally, the eastern Mediterranean region was a British sphere of influence, but London informed Washington that it could no longer afford to assert power there. So, Truman asked Congress to approve an aid program to bolster the pro-western Greek and Turkish governments. He did not mention communism or the Soviet Union, but instead spoke of totalitarian forces again threatening freedom around the world. Congress granted that aid program. That was just the down payment. In June Secretary of State George Marshall would recommend what became known as the Marshall Plan that distributed $12.731 billion in aid to Western European countries and another $2.2 billion to Japan.[22]

Thus began America's Cold War containment strategy.[23] The policy actually had two versions and four phases. The "selective" version was Kennan's original concept that how and where to contain communism should be limited – industrial Europe and Japan should be rebuilt and integrated with America in the global economy through aid in return for political reforms. Paul Nitze, a high-ranking State Department official, asserted what became known as "global" containment in a report entitled NSC-68 and circulated in April 1950. Nitze argued that Moscow directed a monolithic global communist movement with a grand strategy to systematically conquer the world. That threat must be contained militarily as well as economically everywhere a revolution threatened to engulf a country, no matter how remote or poor. A communist revolution in any country would soon spread to neighboring countries, a catastrophe later called the "domino effect". Diplomacy was virtually impossible with communists who would see it as a sign of weakness and opportunity to exploit. Nitze's vision could not have differed more starkly from Kennan's whereby policymakers must first understand the complex histories, cultures, parties, personalities and interests of other countries before deciding how best to advance American interests with or against them.

When events appeared to discredit one version of containment, the White House embraced the other version. Selective containment lasted from Truman's Cold War declaration on March 12, 1949, until communist North Korea's invasion of non-communist South Korea on June 25, 1950. That invasion was the culmination of a series of ominous events that appeared to discredit selective containment, including the Berlin crisis from June 1948 to May 1948 during which the Soviets cut off the land routes from West Germany to West Berlin; the Soviet testing of an atomic bomb in August 1949; and the Communist Party's conquest of China in a civil war that had raged since 1927. America, Britain and its Commonwealth and France, responded to the Berlin crisis by airlifting supplies to the western sectors, and along with other countries formed the North Atlantic Treaty Organization (NAT0), a military alliance that eventually included twenty-eight countries. Washington could only react to a Soviet bomb by producing many more of its own. Kennan had predicted communist victory in China's civil war and recommended playing on Beijing's nationalist sentiments eventually to entice it from Moscow. The Truman administration responded to North Korea's invasion by initiating a United Nations Security Council resolution that empowered the United States and any willing allies to repel that invasion.

That inaugurated a global containment phase that lasted until January 20, 1969, when Richard Nixon became president and shifted the strategy back to selective. What happened during those nineteen years discredited the global version. The Korean War lasted three years and ended in a stalemate during which 36,516 American troops, 900,000 Chinese troops, and a couple of million Korean troops and civilians on both sides died. Elsewhere Washington established military alliances and supplied massive military aid to governments facing communist revolutionaries. Global containment culminated with the war in Vietnam, in which more than 58,220 American troops and two million Vietnamese troops, and civilians on either, side perished. Moscow helped underwrite America's Korean War stalemate, Vietnam War defeat, hundreds of thousands of casualties, and hundreds of billions of mostly squandered dollars with massive military and economic support to its communist allies.[24]

Nixon sought to realign America's strategic commitments with its genuine interests. He got the Europeans and Japanese to spend more on their own defense, a policy known as "burden sharing". He devalued the dollar and took America off the gold standard to revive the economy. He declared that henceforth Washington would only aid those countries that demonstrated will and ability to fight a communist insurgency. He played off Moscow and Beijing against each other by pursuing *détente* with each.

He negotiated the Strategic Arms Limitation Treaty (SALT) and Anti-Ballistic Missile Treaty (ABM) with the Soviet regime. Tragically, a series of catastrophes in the late 1970s appeared to discredit Nixon's version of selective containment. In 1975 communist North Vietnam conquered South Vietnam, while communist movements also engulfed Cambodia and Laos. The decisive blows to the strategy came in 1979. In February an Islamist anti-American and anti-Western revolution in Iran led by Ayatollah Ruhollah Khomeini overthrew the government of pro-American Shah Mohamad Reza Pahlavi. In August the communist Sandinista movement took over Nicaragua. Finally, on December 25, 1979, the Soviets invaded Afghanistan to solidify a communist regime that took power there.

That last event provoked President Jimmy Carter to shift containment back to its global version as his administration began sending military aid to the Afghan *mujahideen*, or holy warriors, fighting the Soviets. After becoming president in 1981, Ronald Reagan expanded global containment by aiding anti-communist movements in Angola, Mozambique and Nicaragua and doubling the military budget over eight years. During a speech on March 8, 1983, Reagan called the Soviet Union an "evil empire" and unveiled his Strategic Defense Initiative (SDI), soon dubbed "Star Wars," as an anti-ballistic missile system. The Kremlin was terrified that Reagan was constructing Star Wars as a shield behind which to launch a first-nuclear strike that would devastate the Soviet Union. The Soviet leaders debated whether to attack first before the Americans constructed what Reagan promised would be an impregnable defense.

Mercifully, this second version of global containment did not include any disastrous unwinnable wars. Nonetheless, it was exorbitantly expensive. Reagan's policies quadrupled America's national debt during his eight years as president followed by George H.W. Bush's four years. This last containment policy phase ended on December 25, 1991, with Premier Mikhail Gorbachev's announcement that the Soviet Union would cease to exist.

During forty-seven years of Cold War when Washington see-sawed between selective and global containment Moscow asserted the same grand strategy of manipulating opportunities to expand influence and outright control around the world. In September 1947 Moscow set up the Communist Information Bureau (Cominform) as a global propaganda network of publications, radio broadcasts, and, eventually, television broadcasts. The Kremlin's "rope a dope" strategy was its most effective. Moscow drained American power by provoking Washington into unwinnable wars in Korea and Vietnam, then massively aiding its communist partners. Throughout the Cold War Washington diverted into the military literally trillions of dollars from potential investments in infrastructure, high technology and education that could have enriched Americans.

The Stalin regime's greatest success was developing nuclear weapons. Stalin initiated research in 1943 during the Second World War, but accelerated it after the Americans detonated an atomic bomb in July 1945 and demonstrated its decisive impact on warfare as Tokyo agreed to surrender on August 14 after atomic bombs destroyed Hiroshima on August 6 and Nagasaki on August 9. The Kremlin launched a multi-billion ruble equivalent of America's Manhattan Project. Just four years later, on August 29, 1949, the Soviets detonated their own atomic bomb. Soviet spies embedded in the American and British nuclear projects accelerated that achievement by at least a year or so.[25]

Stalin's death on March 5, 1953 initiated a deadly scramble for power. Initially, Nikita Khrushchev, Georgy Malenkov, and Viacheslav Molotov took his place and consolidated power, first by having KGB chief Lavrentii Beria, their rival, arrested and executed. Over the next three years Khrushchev achieved supreme power by forcing Malenkov and Molotov into premature retirement. Then Khrushchev detonated an ideological and political bombshell during the Communist Party Congress on February 25, 1956 when, during a four-hour speech, he detailed Stalin's horrendous crimes against humanity.

The greatest Soviet accomplishments under Khrushchev were beating the Americans into space, first by launching the Sputnik satellite in 1957 and then the first human in 1961. That accelerated the nuclear arms race as each side sought to produce and deploy more powerful intercontinental ballistic missiles (ICBMs), intermediate range ballistic missiles (IRBMs) and submarine launched ballistic missiles (SLBMs). That swelling nuclear power emboldened Khrushchev. The closest the world came to nuclear Armageddon was during the October 1962 missile crisis. Mercifully Kennedy, Khrushchev and their advisors managed to defuse that crisis through sensible diplomacy. Had they miscalculated, they might have initiated a nuclear war that immediately killed a hundred million or so people and destroyed the global economy leading to hundreds of millions of more deaths from mass starvation and radiation poisoning. Khrushchev's enemies combined to oust him on October 14, 1964, by accusing him of grossly bumbling the Cuban missile crisis.

The Central Committee replaced Khrushchev with Leonid Brezhnev, a stolid apparatchik. Brezhnev remained the Soviet premier until a stroke killed him on November 12, 1982. During his eighteen years in power, he dealt with a series of presidents, Lyndon Johnson, Richard Nixon, Gerald Ford, Jimmy Carter and Ronald Reagan. All along, he grounded Soviet foreign policy on the principle of "peaceful co-existence," which he explained as:

> The Communist Party of the Soviet Union has always held … that the class struggle between the two systems – the capitalist and the socialist – in the economic and political, and … ideological domains will continue. That is to be expected because the world outlook and the class aims of socialism and capitalism are opposite and irreconcilable. But we shall strive to shift this historically inevitable struggle onto a path free from the perils of war, of dangerous conflicts, and an uncontrolled arms race.[26]

Relations between Moscow and Washington see-sawed through the Brezhnev years. *Détente* was Nixon's attempt to transform Moscow's peaceful co-existence into genuine co-operation on managing common interests. Nixon established a working relationship with Brezhnev, meeting with him in Moscow and even inviting him to spend the night in the White House. Washington and Moscow cut deals that expanded bilateral trade and travel, and, most importantly, attempted to slow the nuclear arms race through the SALT I and ABM Treaty of 1972. However, the Soviets killed *détente* in December 1979 with the Kremlin's decision to invade Afghanistan. Carter imposed economic sanctions on the Soviet Union, forced American athletes to boycott the 1980 Moscow Olympics, withdrew the 1979 SALT II from Senate ratification and began aiding the rebels fighting the Soviets and their puppet regime in Afghanistan. Carter justified these retaliatory policies with calm rational explanations that promised to end them if the Soviets withdrew from Afghanistan. If Carter appealed to the reason of Soviet rulers, the rhetoric and behavior of the man who replaced him in the White House provoked their paranoia with nearly apocalyptic results.

After the Cuban missile crisis, the second closest crisis that might have led to nuclear Armageddon came in November 1983. Yuri Andropov, Brezhnev's successor and former KGB chief, was well positioned to understand America but Ronald Reagan and his conservative movement baffled him. During the two years since Reagan became president, his rhetoric about winning a nuclear war, expansion of America's nuclear forces to achieve superiority and launching of the Stars War anti-ballistic missile system terrified Andropov and his Politburo colleagues that a devastating nuclear attack on the Soviet Union was imminent. They concluded that they could only save themselves by launching a pre-emptive strike against the United States. They nearly did so during NATO's Able Archer training exercises that they assumed was the cover for a nuclear attack. Mercifully, Andropov and his colleagues stood down at the last moment. They recognized that while a first strike might destroy most of America's land-based missiles, the United States would still have enough invulnerable submarine-launched missiles to destroy the Soviet Union. The logic of Mutually Assured Destruction (MAD) preserved the peace.[27]

To his credit, after Reagan learnt how close the Soviets came to launching a pre-emptive strike in response to his own reckless rhetoric and policies, he changed his tune. Thereafter he repeatedly tried to reassure the Kremlin and convince his conservative supporters that "a nuclear war should never be fought and can never be won". Yet he persisted in expanding America's nuclear and conventional forces. Hair-trigger tensions persisted through the rest of Andropov's short tenure as premier and then that of Konstantin Chernenko, who replaced Andropov when he died on February 9, 1983, then himself died of a heart attack on March 10, 1985.

The rapid succession and demises of elderly, diseased Soviet leaders symbolized communism's pathologies. The Soviet Union and other communist regimes were falling further behind the West by every economic measure. For instance, although the Soviets mined eight times more iron ore than Americans, they produced only three times more pig iron and only twice as much steel. A Soviet construction project took five times longer than a similar American project and consumed

> 1.8 times more steel ... 2.3 times more cement, 7.6 times more fertilizer, and 1.5 times more timber. The USSR produced 16 times the number of grain harvesters, but harvested less grain and became dependent on grain imports .... In the 1980s, the Soviet Union bought more than 15 per cent of the world's imported grain.[28]

The Soviet military industrial complex was at least 15 per cent of the economy, a burden three times worse than Americans shouldered for their own military-industrial complex. Consumer spending accounted for two-thirds of America's economy but only a quarter of the Soviet command economy, and what was available was shoddy. Even food supplies were sporadic. People daily endured long lines to purchase necessities like bread or toilet paper. Cynically, the communists encouraged the production of cheap vodka as an opiate for the masses; the result was tens of millions of alcoholics and the accompanying crime, broken homes and addled brains on the job and elsewhere. The unregulated spewing of industrial, agricultural, and mining toxins into the air and water poisoned and stunted the lives of tens of millions of victims.

People grumbled louder at the worsening conditions but mostly still behind closed doors. Although, after Stalin died, the state stopped murdering dissidents it still imprisoned them on trumped-up charges or committed them to insane asylums on trumped-up psychoses. The true number of persecuted dissidents is unknowable, but one authoritative count found:

> Between 1958 and 1966, 3,448 people were found guilty of anti-Soviet agitation and propaganda. In the period 1967–75, there were 1,538. In 1971–74 ... 63,100 had been given 'prophylactic work,'

meaning that Soviet citizens suspected of thinking differently had been handled by the secret police.[29]

The most famous dissident was Alexander Solzhenitsyn, whose novels *One Day in the Life of Ivan Denisovich* (1962) and *History of the Gulag* (1974) revealed the horrors of Soviet concentration camps, while his *First Circle* (1968) more broadly condemned Stalinism. The Kremlin stripped Solzhenitsyn of his citizenship and exiled him in 1974. The Soviet Union's second most prominent dissident was Andrei Sakharov, the brilliant physicist and father of the atomic bomb, who was exiled to Gorky for his outspoken demands for reform in 1980. Thousands of other dissidents surreptitiously photocopied and circulated essays and books known as *samizdat* or received smuggled copies from exiled dissidents in the West and known as *tamizdat*. And then there was the influence of American-sponsored Radio Free Europe that broadcast western views and rock music to avid listeners across the Soviet Union and communist eastern Europe; at least 80 per cent of college students listened regularly.[30] American pop culture's soft power was insidiously changing countless young minds across the communist empire.

Mikhail Gorbachev became the Soviet Union's premier on March 10, 1985. In stark contrast to his decrepit predecessors, Gorbachev was then a mentally and physically vigorous fifty-four years old, a relative child in the Politburo's gerontocracy.[31] He was also the best educated, having graduated with a law degree from Moscow University. His drive and optimism came from this observation, "There are no unreformable social systems; otherwise there would not be any progress in history."[32] He abhorred violence and repression, wanting "no blood on his hands".[33] What was critical about Gorbachev was his open-minded pragmatism. British Prime Minister Margaret Thatcher first met Gorbachev when he visited London in December 1984. He impressed her so much with his intelligence, knowledge, flexibility, and dedication to peacefully resolving difference that she declared: "I like Mr Gorbachev. We can do business together".[34]

Of Chernenko's possible successors, only Gorbachev was committed to systematically reforming rather than propping up the communist system. Nonetheless, his colleagues unanimously supported him to become premier. They understood that decisive action was vital even if they had no idea what to do. Gorbachev's mission was aptly described as being at once "Pope and Luther" or communism's high priest and scourge.[35] However, when he took power, he had no blueprint for reconstructing communism, only the drive somehow to devise one.

For that, Gorbachev's appointment of Alexander Yakovlev as the ideology and propaganda minister was critical. Yakovlev was a worldly foreign ministry diplomat who had spent a year at New York's Columbia University in 1958 and served as ambassador to Canada from 1973 to 1983, a high-ranking communist whose faith faded the higher he climbed and the more he compared the Soviet Union with the West. In December 1985 he wrote a report that attacked the "dogmatic interpretation of Marxism and Leninism" as "so unhygienic … Marxism is nothing but a neo-religion subjected to the interests and whims of the absolute power …. Political conclusions of Marxism are unacceptable for civilization." The only way to save communism was to destroy it: "Socialism without a market is a utopia and a bloody one at that." He abhorred communism for its repression and exploitation of the people, and for the pathological mendacity that permeated the system and every human within it: "Civil society is poisoned by lies."[36]

It took Gorbachev and Yakovlev more than two years to devise a plan and then forge a Politburo consensus behind it. The reforms were a bundle of three related policies, *glasnost*, or openness, *perestroika*, or restructuring and *demokratizatsiya*, or democracy that they sincerely believed would realize rather than destroy communism. Reform's most implacable foe was Yegor Ligachev, the Central Committee secretary. Gorbachev continually implored Ligachev and other hardliners, "Don't be afraid of your own people. Glasnost is the true socialism."[37]

As Gorbachev built a consensus for reform, he issued a series of pardons that symbolized the new society that he sought. In December 1986 he let Andrei Sakharov, a Nobel-prize winning author and dissident, return to Moscow from his exile in Gorky. In February 1987 he amnestied and released 140 imprisoned dissidents. In June 1988, the Soviet Supreme Court reversed the guilty convictions of fifty high-ranking people, most of whom had been executed during Stalin's reign of terror.

Two catastrophes, one continuing and the other unexpected, enabled Gorbachev and Yakovlev to forge Politburo approval. After invading Afghanistan in December 1979 the Soviet army sank deeper into a military quagmire. That war eventually cost 14,453 Soviet lives, 53,753 wounded and 415,932 illnesses among the 620,000 who served, along with the destruction of 147 tanks, 118 aircraft, 333 helicopters and 11,369 trucks for a total cost of $48.192 billion.[38] Then came the Chernobyl nuclear power plant's meltdown on April 26, 1986. Over the next decade, radiation poisoning killed at least 148,000 people, including 100,000 workers mobilized to clean up the catastrophe.[39] Annual budget deficits skyrocketed from 18 billion rubles in 1985 to 400 billion rubles in 1989, while the price of oil which, along with natural gas, accounted for two-thirds of exports and most revenues plummeted from $35.52 in 1980 to $13.52 in 1986.[40] The Kremlin filled that widening gap by borrowing from international banks and issuing monetary credits. In desperation the Communist Party's Central Committee approved Gorbachev's reform plan in June 1987.

Boris Yeltsin was critical to implementing those reforms.[41] He had won acclaim for the reforms he imposed as Sverdlovsk province's communist chief. He was hard-drinking, outspoken, charismatic and tough. Gorbachev saw Yeltsin as a perfect reform ally as they played complementary "good cop" and "bad cop" roles. Gorbachev gave Yeltsin a politburo seat and appointed him as Moscow's party leader. Yeltsin relished his role, especially blistering conservative Ligachev during a Central Committee meeting on October 21, 1987.

Gorbachev fervently wanted to save communism but his reforms ultimately destroyed it.[42] Two experts explained why:

> Gorbachev was a firm believer in the sovietization myth. The underlying assumption of *perestroika* itself was that a loyal Soviet people existed. Once freed from bureaucratic constraints by *glasnost* and *demokratizatsiya*, this Soviet people would use its newly found freedoms to pull the USSR from its stagnation, reinvigorate the Soviet economy, and accelerate the USSR's historical progress toward communism.[43]

The biggest, and ultimately, fatal flaw in Gorbachev's reforms was their emphasis on political rather than economic freedom. They let people openly criticize the system without having the ability to raise their living standards and quality of life, which continued to deteriorate. The only step toward economic reform was Gorbachev's approval of KGB chief Vladimir Kryuchkov's plan to set up joint ventures with foreign business corporations to acquire expertise, capital and markets. But that only benefited the well-placed insiders, soon called oligarchs, who could capitalize on those ties. During several meetings with Gorbachev, Secretary of State George Schultz gave him carefully prepared seminars on how a market economy works and why it is vastly superior to a communist command economy. Gorbachev listened intently, asked pertinent questions, and accepted the truths that Schultz presented. He just could not figure out how to transform a command into a market economy without inflicting vast disruptions and pain on most people.

During its Congress in July 1988 the Communist Party approved Gorbachev's plan to establish a Congress of People's Delegates with 2,250 members, including 1,500 freely elected, 750 allocated to various groups, and only 100 reserved for the Communist Party. In the election held on March 26, 1989, the Communists won about 85 per cent of the seats, an extraordinary event since they were used to winning nearly 100 per cent of previous rigged votes. The Congress convened in May 1989. Gorbachev presided but asked Sakharov to sit beside him and address the assembly. He was enraged when Sakharov announced that the Soviet empire would soon collapse, then called for the Communist Party's abolition and the enactment of genuine democracy. The Congress's main duty was to elect a working legislature, a 542-member Supreme Soviet with seats split equally between a Union Council and a Nationalities Council. Although communists won 475 seats and non-communists the remaining 67 seats, most representatives were committed to sweeping reforms.

Gorbachev's greatest success was nuclear arms control. Through a series of summits, he and Reagan forged a consensus that eventually led to the 1987 Intermediate Nuclear Forces (INF) Treaty, whereby they openly demolished all land-based missiles with a range between 311 and 3,420 miles for a total of 2,692 weapons, including 846 American and

1,846 Soviet.[44] Astonishingly, during their 1986 meeting at Reykjavik, Iceland, they actually agreed to abolish all nuclear weapons, but Reagan's insistence on retaining his Star Wars anti-missile system scuttled any possibility of doing so. From a realistic perspective, that failure was an enormous relief. Realists supported mutually reducing nuclear forces to a "minimal deterrent" whereby MAD still kept the peace but at a fraction of the financial cost. Realists also understood the Kremlin's fear that if the White House had a nuclear "shield," an ideologically belligerent president and his advisors might be tempted to thrust their ICBM "spear" against the mostly land-based Soviet missiles as American attack submarines torpedoed Soviet nuclear submarines at sea, and thus "win" a nuclear war.

Gorbachev explained to his colleagues the significance of his summits and agreements, and the lessons they provided not just for Soviet foreign policy but for the democratic reforms he was trying to implement:

> For the first time we realized how much the human factors means in international politics. Before … we treated such personal contacts as simply meetings between representatives of opposed and irreconcilable systems. Reagan for us was merely the spokesman of the most conservative part of American capitalism and its military-industrial complex. But it turns out that politicians, including leaders of government if they are really responsible people, represent purely human concerns, interests, and the hopes of ordinary people – people who vote for them in elections and who associate their leaders' names and personal abilities with the country's image and patriotism.[45]

Yet another Gorbachev policy critical for imploding the Soviet empire was announcing that Moscow would not militarily intervene to aid any communist government in Eastern Europe facing a democratic revolution. In doing so, he reversed Soviet policy whereby the Red Army brutally crushed attempts by Eastern European countries to liberate themselves, including East Germany and Poland in 1953, Hungary in 1956, Czechoslovakia in 1968 and Poland in 1981. Now each government stood alone in deciding how to deal with its swelling democracy movement. Wags dubbed this policy the "Sinatra", or "I did it my way", doctrine.

Yet another Gorbachev policy bolstered the democratic movements swelling across Eastern Europe. The Kremlin faced a dilemma. It desperately needed international finance but could only service its worsening debt by selling the West more oil and gas. With its decrepit technology, fuel production was actually plummeting. "The number of wells required to produce 1 million tons grew from 16 in 1975 to 165 in 1990" while production fell from 568 million tons in 1988 to 461 million tons in 1991.[46] So, to sell more oil and gas to Western Europe, the Soviets had to divert subsidized sales from its empire in Eastern Europe. Rising prices and shortages of oil and gas in Eastern Europe helped fuel anti-communist and pro-democracy movements.

Faced with hundreds of thousands of protesters, one communist dictator after another agreed to dismantle the regime and allow free elections. Symbolically and substantively, the most critical event of Eastern Europe's democratic revolutions occurred on November 9, 1989, when demonstrators swarmed atop the Berlin Wall and began demolishing it.

Eastern Europe's democratic revolutions were non-violent with two exceptions. Romania's dictator Nicolae Ceausescu tried to crush the revolt on Christmas Day. Revolutionaries overran the palace, placed Ceausescu and his wife Elena against a wall, and shot them. The Soviets tried to suppress Lithuania's assertion of freedom. On January 8, 1991, Soviet paratroopers killed fourteen people and wounded more than 700 in a battle to take over the national television station but eventually withdrew, leaving embittered Lithuanians ever more determined to rid themselves of communism and the Russian empire.

The most critical geopolitical question was Germany's future. West German Chancellor Helmut Kohl insisted on Germany's re-unification. President George Bush supported German re-unification, but Gorbachev, Thatcher and French President François Mitterrand were reluctant. From July 14, 1990, Kohl met with Gorbachev in Moscow and, in a series of meetings, convinced him not just to accept re-unification, but Germany's NATO membership. West and East Germany unified on

October 3, 1990. Then envoys of NATO and the Warsaw Pact signed the Conventional Forces in Europe Agreement (CFEA) in Paris on November 19, 1990. The terms included the reduction of the Soviet military from 2.8 million personnel to 2.1 million by 1996, while Germany could retain its 375,000 troops, with restrictions where each alliance could move or base troops and weapons. The Warsaw Pact dissolved itself on July 1, 1991.

Meanwhile the democratic revolutions spread to the Soviet Union itself. The Soviets conquered the three Baltic states of Lithuania, Latvia, and Estonia as part of the non-aggression pact that Stalin made with Hitler on August 23, 1939. As chaos and democracy movements spread across the Soviet empire, the people of those countries asserted their freedom. The first step came in February 1990 with referenda in which 90 per cent of Lithuanians and Estonians, and 77 per cent of Latvians voted for independence. The next step came when the governments of those peoples declared independence from the Soviet Union in April 1990.

The other Soviet republics held elections for the Congress of People's Delegates on March 4, 1990. In Russia, liberals won 20 per cent of the seats, including 63 of 64 Moscow seats and 25 of 34 Leningrad seats. Liberals Gavril Popov and Anatoly Sobchak became the respective mayors of Moscow and Leningrad. Russia's legislature had the same ponderous structure as the Soviet Union's. Russia's Congress consisted of 1,068 constituencies that would meet twice yearly to debate and vote on any proposed constitutional changes and once every four years to select a chairman and a Supreme Soviet of 248 voting members and 138 non-voting members. Congress elected Boris Yeltsin its chairman after three ballots on May 29, 1990. The vast majority of Russia's parliamentary members voted for a Declaration of Sovereignty on June 12, 1990. Majorities subsequently approved the establishment of Russia's own Academy of Sciences, Komsomol, trade unions and KGB. Communists declared themselves the Russian Communist Party, initially headed by Ivan Polozkov but soon succeeded by Gennady Zyuganov. On October 23, 1990 the parliament asserted that Russian law would supersede Soviet law.

Gorbachev agreed to a referendum on whether the Soviet Union should continue or be dissolved. Nine of the Soviet Union's fifteen states held what became a revolutionary election on March 17, 1991. Voters answered whether the Soviet Union should persist as "a federation of equal sovereign republics, in which the rights and freedoms of the individual of any nationality will be guaranteed?" This, of course, was an unintended trick question. In reality, the Kremlin had always dominated the Soviet Union, which was simply another name for the Russian empire, and individuals had no rights but were suppressed and exploited by the Communist Party and were imprisoned and even murdered if they resisted. Nonetheless, apparently most voters shrugged as they voted, with 76.2 per cent supporting the Soviet Union's persistence. In Russia, 71.3 per cent voted for and 26.3 per cent against. The Russian vote also included a question of whether to introduce the post of an elected president. More than two-thirds or 69.85 per cent were in favor.[47] On April 23, 1991 those nine republics" renamed their association the Union of Soviet Sovereign Republics, with a common president charged with foreign policy and defense and a common parliament, but all other sovereign powers retained by each member's government. The governments of Lithuania, Latvia, Estonia, Moldavia, Georgia and Armenia refused to join.

Russia held its first presidential election on June 12, 1991. Boris Yeltsin won with 57.3 per cent of the vote against five other candidates. Elections in Moscow and Leningrad resulted in liberals Gavril Popov and Anatoly Sobchak becoming mayors with 69 per cent and 54 per cent respectively of the votes. The Communist Party suffered two powerful blows. Yeltsin issued a "depoliticization" and "departification" decree on July 20 that banned the Communist Party and its members from Russian government bureaucracies and enterprises. Gorbachev announced on July 26 that in December a special congress would convene to transform the Communist Party into a social democratic type party.

During the Group of 7 summit among the leaders of the United States, Japan, Britain, Germany, France, Italy and Canada in London in July 1991, Gorbachev pleaded for as much as $50 billion in foreign aid for at least five years to transform Russia from a communist into a market economy. The seven leaders gently explained that that was far too much for such a vague idea, and asked him to devise a detailed plan. Meanwhile, they would provide Russia with a $24 billion aid package consisting of low-interest loans and guarantees.

Bush met Gorbachev in Moscow on July 29, 1991. Bush wanted the Soviet Union to remain intact, fearing chaos and violence if it broke up. In Kiev on August 1, he gave what infamously became known variously as his "Chicken George" or "Chicken Kiev" speech in which he urged the Ukrainians to remain good Soviets:

> Freedom is not the same as independence. Americans will not support those who seek independence in order to replace a far-off tyranny with a local despotism. They will not aid those who promote a suicidal nationalism based on ethnic hatred.[48]

Communist hardliners were just as committed to holding the Soviet empire together. They became increasingly frantic as Gorbachev's reforms undermined rather than revitalized the Soviet Union. The treaty that would transform the Soviet Union into the Union of Soviet Sovereign Republics was to be signed by nine of the Soviet republics on August 20, 1991. The hardliners resolved to stop that from happening. In mid-August they concocted a coup plan to gain total power and destroy all the liberal reforms. The key leaders included Prime Minister Valentin Pavlov, KGB chief Vladimir Kryuchkov, Defense Minister Dmitry Yazov and Vice President Gennady Yanayev. Gorbachev was vacationing at his dacha at Foros in Crimea on August 18 when the coup leaders demanded that he issue a decree granting the government emergency powers and then revoke all the reforms. Gorbachev angrily refused, warning "You will destroy yourselves, but that is your business and to hell with you. But you will also destroy the country and everything we have already done."[49] Gorbachev's resistance provoked a debate among the cabal over what to do. They decided to carry through the coup. On August 19 they detained Gorbachev and issued television and radio announcements that they were imposing a six-months state of emergency to repeal the reforms that had provoked chaos and economic collapse.

Fortunately, the coup leaders failed to have Russian President Yeltsin arrested. After hearing the broadcast, Yeltsin hurried to the White House,

Russia's parliament building, scrambled atop a tank parked outside and announced: "We call on the people of Russia to respond appropriately to the putschists and to demand that the country be allowed to return to its normal course of constitutional development." Thousands of people packed into the square and rallied around Yeltsin while similar mass protests erupted across the Soviet Union. Violence was limited. Security forces killed three protesters in Moscow but the soldiers refused to fire on the people. On August 22 the coup leaders released Gorbachev and surrendered to the authorities. Gorbachev flew back to Moscow.

Yeltsin summoned Gorbachev to the White House. With Gorbachev beside him and parliament assembled before him, Yeltsin decreed the Communist Party's suspension and transformed Russia's flag from the red hammer-and-sickle flag into the traditional tricolor of descending horizontal white, blue, and red strips. Elsewhere in Moscow angry protectors committed their own symbolic act. They massed before KGB headquarters and tore down the statue of Felix Dzerzhinsky who had created the communist secret police.

The tottering Soviet Union imploded over the next four months. Gorbachev resigned as the Communist Party's General Secretary, although he remained the Soviet premier. On August 29 the Supreme Soviet suspended the Communist Party. Two "republics" had already declared independence, Lithuania on March 11, 1990 and Georgia on April 9, 1991. Then came Estonia's declaration on August 20, Latvia's on August 21, Ukraine's on August 24, Belarus's on August 25, Moldova's on August 27, Azerbaijan's on August 30, Kyrgyzstan's and Uzbekistan's on August 31, Tajikistan's on September 9, Armenia's on September 23 and Turkmenistan's on October 27. Russia and Kazakhstan were the last holdouts. In November negotiations intensified among diplomats from all the republics except the Baltic states for what became the Commonwealth of Independent States.

The presidents of Russia, Ukraine and Belarus signed at Belovezh, Belarus, a treaty that abolished the Soviet Union and created the Commonwealth of Slavic States (CSS) among Russia, Belarus and Ukraine on December 8, 1991, then changed the name to the Commonwealth of Independent States (CIS) and invited the other Soviet states to join. Most did sign the treaty in Almaty, Kazakhstan, on December 21. Georgia,

Moldova and Azerbaijan would join later; Lithuania, Latvia and Estonia never would. On December 25 Gorbachev gave humanity a priceless Christmas present when he announced his resignation as the Soviet premier and the Soviet Union's abolition effective from December 31.

Communism's death was inevitable; it was just a question of when and how. At once evil and inept, communism essentially self-destructed. Communism was an evil system that eventually enslaved and exploited over a billion humans and murdered directly or indirectly tens of millions of other humans. It was also an inept system, often failing to feed the masses of exploited people or satisfy their other basic needs. Most years, Russia exported grain while most years the Soviet Union imported grain. The tiny gardens that the communists let Soviet peasants cultivate represented 3 per cent of farmland but produced 40 per cent of farm production.[50]

Arkady Ostrovsky explains why the communist regime collapsed so swiftly. He first asserts that: "The Soviet system rested on violence and ideology." He then quotes Alexander Bovin, Leonid Brezhnev's speechwriter, who points out another key ingredient: "Only the lies – the end product of the ideologists – provided the effectiveness of the violence (real or potential) which the system rested upon." Ostrovsky then argues that:

> Once the ideology and propaganda started crumbling, the system came down, crushing those who had aimed to reform it. The Soviet collapse happened not so much by the economic meltdown, by a revolutionary uprising in the capital, or by a struggle for independence on the periphery of the empire ... as it was by the dismantling of lies. Without lies, the Soviet Union had no legitimacy.[51]

Perceptive Soviets were well aware of the unbridgeable and widening gap between the communist regime's lies and realities. To avoid prison or execution, one had to ignore those realities. Alexander Yakovlev, Gorbachev's right-hand man, explained:

> All of us, and particularly the nomenklatura ... lived a double, or even a triple, life. Step by step, such amorality became a way of life and was deemed "moral," while hypocrisy became a way of thinking.

Yet, secretly "I came to hate Lenin and Stalin – those monsters who had cruelly deceived me."[52] In other words, like Toto pulling aside the curtain to reveal that the Wizard of Oz was not supernatural but merely a frail manipulative man, once the matrix of lies was exposed, their system swiftly crumbled.

Communism died in both the Soviet Union and China, but the Communist Party retained power in China and lost power in Russia and the other states that emerged from the Soviet empire's collapse. The completely different policies pursued by Mikhail Gorbachev and Deng Xiaoping explain those completely different results. By emphasizing political reforms and neglecting economic reforms, Gorbachev unleashed seven decades of pent-up mass rage against the communist system that had repressed, exploited and often imprisoned or outright murdered them. The subsequent worsening political and economic chaos discredited and drove the Communist Party from power. By emphasizing economic reforms and crushing any political dissent, Deng guaranteed the Communist Party's persistence in power even as it abandoned communism for an increasingly privatized economy and widening gaps in wealth among the rich, middle and poor classes.

During his 1992 State of the Union address President George H.W. Bush triumphantly declared:

> In the past twelve months the world has known changes of almost Biblical proportions .... I'm not sure we've absorbed the full impact of what happened .... But communism died this year .... By the grace of God, America won the Cold War.[53]

Part II

Putin and Power

Chapter 3

Putin's Rise to Power

Anyone who does not regret the collapse of the Soviet Union has no heart. And anyone who wants to see it recreated in its former shape has no head.

(Vladimir Putin)

Enough of living according to [Vladimir] Ilyich [Lenin]... Enough of utopia, the future is business! A man who can turn a dollar into a billion is a genius.

(Mikhail Khodorkovsky)

Vladimir Putin was only vaguely aware of the Soviet Union's insidious decay from the 1970s into the 1980s. Although, as a KGB officer, he had access to information and experiences far more revealing than most Soviets, even that left him unprepared for the fast-paced revolution from 1989 to 1991 that destroyed the Kremlin's empire in Eastern Europe and then the Soviet Union itself. As astonishing was his own steady rise from obscurity to the pinnacle of power. During the 1990s he played increasingly substantive roles in Russia's rebirth and development until he became president on New Year's Eve 1999. Putin's life has been an astonishing rags to riches triumph.

He was born in Leningrad on October 7, 1952. His father, Vladimir, was a disabled commando veteran of the German siege of Leningrad and worked in an automobile factory. His mother, Maria, held a series of menial jobs. Diseases had killed two earlier sons and they were in their forties when they had their third. Like most Soviets the Putins lived in poverty in a twenty-square-metre room that shared a kitchen and toilet with other families crammed into other rooms on the floor of a large, shabbily constructed building; there was no bath or hot water, only the chronic smells of boiled cabbage, tobacco and human waste. His father was stern and aloof; he punished with belt-whippings. His mother was affectionate and had her son secretly baptized.

As a small and skinny boy, Putin attracted bullies. He soon learnt that to deter attacks, he needed allies and had to fight back and never cry or tattle. He was a mediocre student who got into trouble by skipping school, brawling and petty thefts. As punishment he was not allowed to be a Young Pioneer until he was twelve, two years after most of his classmates. That reprieve encouraged him to study harder and behave better. He began practicing sambo, a Soviet martial art that mixed judo and karate, which developed his body and mind. His classmates rewarded his transformation by electing him their Pioneer chief. In eighth grade, he joined Komsomol, the communist youth organization.

The spy novel *The Shield and the Sword* inspired him to join the KGB. He later explained: "What amazed me most of all was how one man's efforts could achieve what whole armies could not. One spy could decide the fate of thousands of people."[1] He visited KGB headquarters in Leningrad and asked to apply. He was told that he first needed a university degree and that if the KGB thought he was worthy it would recruit him. He studied law and made the judo team at Leningrad University. He abstained from cigarettes and alcohol, had just one girlfriend, and tore around Leningrad in his mother's car that she won in a lottery. After graduating in 1975 a stranger asked to meet privately with him.

Over the years the KGB had kept its eyes on him and concluded that he had potential. Essentially, the KGB had two classes of personnel. Of 300,000 employees, only 5,000 formed the tiny elite of highly intelligent, sophisticated, gregarious, tough people trained to be spies and despatched abroad to recruit foreigners and conduct other covert operations; the best ended up in Paris, Tokyo, Washington, and other glamorous cities. And then there were the masses of functionaries (apparatchiks) organized in a vast bureaucracy designed to repress any dissent or rebellion within the Soviet Union or its adjoining empire in Eastern Europe. The qualifications for being a functionary were simple – unthinking obedience to one's superiors and utter ruthlessness to those one was ordered to observe, bully or recruit. Putin turned out to be an ideal functionary.

The KGB tested his capabilities by posting him to Bonn as a TASS reporter but recalled him to Leningrad after he burgled an operation.

He lived at home with his parents who had moved to a two-bedroom apartment. At one point his arm was broken in a fight with hooligans. In 1983 he married Lyudmila Putina, an Aeroflot flight attendant. Then, in 1985, after training at the Academy of Foreign Intelligence outside Moscow, he was posted to Dresden, East Germany, where he stayed until 1990. The Putins' first daughter, Maria, was born in 1985, followed by Ekaterina in 1986. They enjoyed living in Dresden because they got their own apartment and had access to more goods and food than in the Soviet Union. His diligence as a functionary got him steady promotion until he reached the rank of lieutenant colonel.

Putin worked in a building jointly occupied by the KGB and East Germany's secret police, the Stasi. His most important activities were recruiting western businessmen and stealing technological secrets, known as Operation Luch (Beam). His most nefarious known acts were conspiring with Red Army Faction terrorists who murdered people in a series of attacks in West Germany and elsewhere. He may have traveled to West Germany several times. Putin later admitted how fruitless those operations were:

> The results of our own research ... that were obtained by 'special means,' were not actually introduced into the Soviet Union's economy. We did not even have the equipment to introduce them. And so there we were, working away, gathering away, essentially for nothing.[2]

Putin described East Germany:

> as an eye-opener for me .... It was a harsh totalitarian country, similar to our model, but thirty years earlier. And the tragedy is that many people sincerely believed in all those communist ideals. I thought at the time: if we begin some changes at home, how will it affect the fates of these people.[3]

He was aware of the reforms that premier Mikhail Gorbachev had launched back in the Soviet Union. He supported Gorbachev's reforms, hoping that they would save communism and the Soviet Union. Like

Gorbachev, Putin did not anticipate that by promoting political reforms without economic reforms, the throttled rage by most people against communism would eventually destroy it. Putin was astonished how quickly the system imploded: "all the ideals, all the goals that I had when I went to work for the KGB collapsed."[4]

Putin's years in Dresden coincided with the collapse of Moscow's communist empire in Eastern Europe. On January 15, 1989 protesters surrounded the Stasi-KGB building and appeared ready to storm it. Putin went outside to try to divert them as his colleagues burned their secret documents. He recalled that only then did "I realize that the Soviet Union was ill. It was a fatal illness called paralysis. A paralysis of power".[5] The next month the KGB recalled Putin to the Soviet Union.

After returning to Leningrad, the Putins moved back into his parents' two-bedroom apartment. He received an assignment to be assistant to the rector of the international relations program at Leningrad University. That job let him gain information on foreign students or Soviet students who studied aboard. In May he met Anatoly Sobchak, a charismatic and eloquent law professor whose classes he had taken when he was a student. Sobchak had recently won two elections, one to Leningrad's city council and then as mayor. Sobchak asked Putin to be his advisor. Aware that Putin worked for the KGB, Sobchak welcomed him as a liaison and protector. Putin swiftly earned Sobchak's trust by his diligence and honesty. Sobchak repaid Putin with duties that enabled him to develop a network of loyal and increasingly wealthy men who capitalized on the privatization of Soviet enterprises and property.

Meanwhile, Boris Yeltsin swiftly amassed more power and solidified Russia's new political system.[6] In 1991, he was elected Russia's president on June 12, was granted emergency powers for a year by Russia's Congress on November 2, and named himself prime minster on November 6. Yeltsin decisively made the most of those powers.

Yeltsin's key military reform was to banish the Communist Party from its ranks just as he had banished it from politics. Commissars no longer shadowed officers to record any ideologically incorrect career-destroying utterance or act. The small army of commissars was broken up and deployed for more practical pursuits. That helped downsize the military from 2 million personnel in 1990 to 1.2 million in 2000.

Yeltsin announced a sweeping economic liberalization and privatization policy on October 28, 1991, that would begin on January 1, 1992.[7] Finance Minister Yegor Gaidar and Chief of Staff Anatoly Chubais would implement that plan. For his key advisor, Gaidar enlisted Jeffrey Sachs, a Harvard professor. Sachs advocated "shock therapy" or ending all economic restrictions and privatizing all property as swiftly as possible. Shock therapy's core policy was to grant each Russian a voucher with which to buy shares of privatized companies or sell to someone else. People who worked for companies with fewer than 200 people or collective farms received discounts on the prices they paid for shares of their own enterprises.

A vast insurmountable problem with shock therapy soon became glaring. Seven decades of communism had destroyed any entrepreneurial spirit and skills in most Russians. The only people familiar with markets were either black-marketeers or KGB officers posted overseas who dealt with businessmen and managed various front companies and financial accounts. As a result, most of Russia's entrepreneurs were former or current KGB officers, including two-thirds of those who set up the stock market.[8] Nearly all Russians ended up selling their vouchers, with prices averaging twenty dollars, to enterprising brokers who, after they bought most of the economy, were called "oligarchs". The vouchers' face value was a mere $10 billion for the entire Russian economy that was probably worth at least twenty times that, or more.

Thus did the Kremlin sell hundreds of billions of dollars' worth of 15,000 state industries, companies, and other property for pennies on the dollar. Within two years 70 per cent of the economy was privatized, and the oligarchs snatched most of that. For instance, Gazprom then controlled about one-third of the world's known natural gas reserves. A group of investors pooled their vouchers, outbid rivals and paid $250 million for Gazprom. Three years later, Gazprom was worth $40 billion on Moscow's stock exchange. The oligarchs usually "won" non-competitive bids that accounted for only 3 per cent to 10 per cent of an asset's market value, and then received low or no interest loans from the government to pay for the property, an insider deal known as "shares for loans". In return Yeltsin and his "family" which included relatives, friends, and allies, pocketed billions of dollars in kickbacks. Seven oligarchs received the lion's share of the privatization: Boris Berezovsky of Logovaz Holding Corporation and Russian One Television (ORT); Vladimir Potanin of Uneximbank; Mikhail Khodorkovsky of Menatep-Rosprom and Yukos oil company; Vladimir Gusinsky of Most Bank; Pyotr Aven a financier; Mikhail Fridman of Alfa Bank; and Alexander Smolensky of Stolichny Savings Bank. By one estimate, "85 per cent of Russia's sixty-four largest privately-owned companies, with sales of $109 billion in 2000, was controlled by just eight shareholder groups."[9]

Khodorkovsky captured the mindset of that oligarch feeding frenzy in a memoir he somehow found time to write, called *Man with a Ruble*:

> We aspire to be billionaires .... Membership in the Communist Party was a good school for us .... The Party took away a lot, but it also gave us a lot: experience, connections, life status .... Enough of living according to [Vladimir] Ilyich [Lenin] .... Enough of utopia, the future is business! A man who can turn a dollar into a billion is a genius.[10]

In response to criticism of shock therapy, Chubais later admitted the dilemma he and others in Yeltsin's administration faced: "Our market approach was completely unsuitable for building a democracy. But we believed that a market economy and the creation of a middle class would result in a democracy."[11] Tragically, what Russians got instead was a political and economic oligopoly that has only strengthened with time.

"Shock therapy" revolutionized the economy, but from an austere command into a gaudy crony capitalism, not a free market. The result was skyrocketing price, joblessness, homelessness, corruption, poverty, malnutrition and crime rates, because nearly everyone else lacked the connections, skills and money to survive, let alone thrive in a cut-throat Darwinian market dominated by moguls and mobsters. The hyperinflation was the most devastating as it wiped out people's savings and rendered worthless people's fixed incomes. In 1992 prices soared 2,333.30 per cent! One controversial sign of the continuing economic revolution was the mushrooming of McDonald's fast food outlets, with the first opening in Moscow's Pushkin Square on January 31, 1990, and over 500 outlets by 2015. McDonald's at once represented a business model of efficiency, uniformity and profit while providing a bland, soulless international product.

Table 3.1 Russia's Economy Under Yeltsin from 1990 to 1999.[12]

	Gross Domestic Product Change from Previous Year	Purchasing Power Parity	Inflation Rate
1990	−3.0	$3,485	78
1991	−5.0	$3,485	138
1992	−14.5	$3,095	2,323
1993	−8.7	$2,929	844
1994	−12.7	$2,663	202
1995	−4.1	$2,665	131
1996	−3.6	$2,643	21.8
1997	1.4	$2,737	11
1998	−5.3	$1,834	84.4
1999	6.4	$1,330	36.5

Compounding the vicious economic cycle was the Russian government's bankruptcy as receipts dwindled and bills soared. Yeltsin and his coterie learned about a huge potential source of revenue if it was recoverable. In the months before the coup, the KGB transferred the Communist Party's wealth to its foreign bank and business front organizations through which it was laundered and either invested or underwrote other clandestine operations. Astonishingly, that may have included as much as 544 tons of gold that disappeared as Russia's reserves plummeted from 784 tons to 240 tons from 1990 to 1991.[13] Putin helped facilitate some of these financial transfers. The Yeltsin government was determined to retrieve as much of all that money and gold as possible. On February 18, 1992 Gaidar contracted Kroll Associates, an American financial investigation firm, to track down all the wealth that the KGB had hidden overseas. They never recovered more than a fraction.[14]

Yeltsin was determined to tame an increasingly chaotic nascent democracy.[15] He announced on March 20, 1993 that a referendum would be held on April 25 with four questions concerning his own policies and future elections. The results boosted his authority, with 58.7 per cent supporting the president, 53.0 per cent approving his administration's policies, and 49.5 per cent and 67.2 per cent backing early elections for the presidency and parliament. He impatiently waited five months before trying to capitalize on that referendum. On September 21 he decreed the abolition of Congress and the Supreme Soviet, and the transfer of those powers to a bi-cameral Federal Assembly, with an upper house Federation Council of members appointed by the regions and a lower house Duma whose members would be elected on December 12. He justified doing so as critical to overcoming an existential national political crisis:

> Parliament has been seized by a group of persons who are pushing Russia toward the abyss. The security of Russia and its people is more important than formal obedience to contradictory norms created by the legislature. I must break this disastrous vicious circle … to defend Russia and the world from the catastrophic collapse of Russian statehood and of anarchy with the vast potential of nuclear-arms.[16]

The obstructionists and anarchists that Yeltsin warned about were a coalition of communists and ultra-nationalists led by Vice President Alexander Rutskoi. They refused to leave the White House where those institutions were located. Yeltsin had police and troops ring the building and sever its electricity and water. The protestors remained defiant, then, on October 2, surged out to attack the police. On October 4 Yeltsin declared a state of emergency and ordered the army to open fire, then clear the building. During the fighting 146 people died and more than 800 were wounded. Moscow had not suffered such horrendous domestic violence since the 1917 communist coup.[17]

Meanwhile, a committee was busy drafting a constitution that was presented for approval in a referendum along with the Duma election on December 12, 1993. The constitution was approved by 58.43 per cent of the voters.[18] The 1993 Constitution established the formal political system that, with some significant alterations, still governs Russia. France was the model with its hybrid of presidential and parliamentary systems. A president and prime minister lead the executive branch as a duopoly. The people elect the president; if no candidate receives more than half the votes, a run-off between the top two vote-getters is held two weeks later. The president nominates a prime minister for the Duma to approve. The president is the head of state, commander-in-chief and diplomat-in-chief. He has the power to issue legally binding decrees, veto laws, appoint ministers and judges, grant amnesties and declare a state of emergency that imposes martial law. The prime minister heads the government of ministers who administer Russia. The offices of Russia's president and prime minister are in separate buildings in different parts of Moscow, with the former located in the medieval fortress called the Kremlin and the latter in the modernist parliamentary building called the White House.

The Federal Assembly is Russia's bi-cameral legislature with elections every four years. The lower house Duma was originally designed to be an authentic democratic legislature empowered to raise revenue, make laws and investigate wrongdoing. Of the Duma's 450 members, half are elected as candidates from single-member districts and half are awarded to parties in proportion to their share of the votes if they get more than 5 per cent of the total. A voter carries two ballots into the poll, one with a list of candidates from his district and the other with a list of parties eligible to run across the country. The upper house Federation Council has 178 members with two from each of the eighty-nine regional districts; a district's executive and legislature each selects a member. The Central Electoral Commission officially oversees elections. The Federal Assembly can override vetoes and impeach the president and other officials with two-thirds of the votes from each chamber.

The Constitution can be amended with the approval of two-thirds of the Duma and three-quarters of the Federation Council. A Constitutional Court of fifteen judges determines whether proposed bills are constitutional. The president appoints the judges who serve until they must retire at age seventy – originally sixty-five before 2001. Citizens have the rights of speech, assembly, press, religion, residence, travel, property and work. The government is forbidden to establish a state ideology, censor media, or monitor citizens unless they are engaged in criminal activities. Without a formal charge, a criminal suspect must be released after forty-eight hours of detention. Judges determine most trials with juries only for the most serious indictments like murder.

During the December 12, 1993 Duma elections, of thirteen vying parties, two alliances among them with diametrically-opposed visions dominated. Boris Yeltsin's Russia's Choice and Grigory Yavlinsky's *Yabloko* or Apple championed democracy and markets. Gennady Zyuganov's Communist Party of the Russian Federation (CPRF) and Vladimir Zhirinovsky's ultra-nationalist misnamed Liberal Democratic Party of Russia (LDPR) promoted authoritarianism.

Table 3.2 Top Six Political Parties in the December 1993 Duma Election.[19]

	Party List		Single-Member	Total Seats	
	Percentage	Seats	Seats	Number	Percentage
Russia's Choice	15.51	40	30	70	15.6
Liberal Democrat	22.92	59	5	64	14.2
Communist	12.40	32	16	48	10.7
Agrarian	7.99	21	12	33	7.3
Yabloko	7.86	20	3	23	5.1
Women of Russia	8.13	21	2	23	5.1
		213	88	311	

Amidst the political and economic uncertainties, a revolt erupted in Chechnya, a mostly Muslim Caucasus province.[20] On September 6, 1991 Dzhokhar Dudayev, a former Soviet air force general, led a cabal that took over Chechnya's parliament and had himself declared president. Then, on November 1, 1991, Dudayev declared Chechnya's independence. Yeltsin's government refused to recognize that act but for now was too weak and beleaguered to contest it. By February 1994 Yeltsin felt that he had consolidated enough power to authorize a coup that retook Chechnya for Russia. That coup failed, and the Chechens paraded captured Russian agents through the streets. Yeltsin ordered the Russian army to invade Chechnya on December 11, 1994. During the next nineteen months, Grozny, the capital was destroyed, more than 100,000 Chechens along with as many as 14,000 Russian troops died in the fighting, and hundreds of thousands of people became refugees, but the Chechen rebels refused to surrender. On August 31, 1996 Yeltsin agreed to a ceasefire and Chechnyan autonomy. Chechnyan President Aslan Maskhadov re-affirmed his country's independence.

If Chechnya was a disastrous failure, Yeltsin's greatest success was working with American President George Bush to reduce nuclear weapons. After the Soviet Union imploded in December 1991 there remained 27,000 nuclear weapons maintained by 900,000 personnel, of whom 5,000 were experts in plutonium and 2,000 in nuclear weapons design, scattered in bases and factories across Russia, Belarus, Ukraine and Kazakhstan. On July 31, 1991 Presidents Yeltsin and Bush signed the Strategic Arms Reduction Treaty (START) whereby each side would cut its nuclear weapons to 6,000 warheads atop 1,600 intercontinental ballistic missiles (ICBMs) within a decade. The next step was getting Belarus, Ukraine and Kazakhstan to agree to render those weapons and facilities to Russia. The toughest holdout was President Leonid Kuchma who wanted to retain his nuclear weapons. Months of negotiations led to a treaty signed on December 30, 1991 that obliged Ukraine, Belarus and Kazakhstan to transfer all their nuclear weapons by July 1, 1991. Under the follow-up Lisbon Protocol of May 23, 1992, Ukraine, Belarus and Kazakhstan agreed to join the Non-Proliferation Treaty (NPT) as non-nuclear members.

Table 3.3 Soviet Nuclear Weapons, 1991.[21]

Republic	Type	Carriers	Warheads
Russia	ICBM	1,064	4,278
	SSBN/SLBM	62/940	2,804
	HB	101	367
Ukraine	ICBM	176	1,240
	HB	21	168
Kazakhstan	ICBM	104	1,040
	HB	40	320
Belarus	ICBM	54	54

ICBM: Intercontinental Ballistic Missile; SSBN: Nuclear Powered Ballistic Submarine; SLBM: Sea Launched Ballistic Missile; HB: Heavy Bomber.

If the mutual interests of America and Russia in nuclear arms reduction united them, a different geopolitical problem bitterly split them. Like a miniature Soviet Union, communist Yugoslavia began breaking up into its six constituent states in 1991. Tragically, two horrific wars marred that break-up.[22] The first erupted in April 1992 over Bosnia-Herzegovina among its Catholic Croat, Orthodox Serbs and Muslim populations which resulted in more than 200,000 dead, hundreds of thousands of wounded, and more than a million refugees. Serb militants in Bosnia were supplied with arms and troops by Serbian President Slobodan Milosevic, backed by Russian President Yeltsin, a fellow Slav and Orthodox Christian. Around 3,000 Russian mercenaries fought alongside the Serbs while the Kremlin supplied Belgrade with an array of weapons. The United Nations Security Council authorized humanitarian aid and peacekeepers but Milosevic blocked their efforts. German Chancellor Helmet Kohl talked a reluctant President Bill Clinton into wielding NATO to pressure Milosevic into accepting a ceasefire and settlement. Clinton tried to get a Security Council resolution to authorize NATO's potential use of force if diplomacy failed, but the Russians vetoed it. NATO issued Milosevic an ultimatum to begin peace talks then, after he remained defiant, bombed Serbian military positions in August and September 1995. Milosevic finally agreed to talks. Clinton had Ambassador Richard Holbrooke broker negotiations among the three warring factions at Dayton, Ohio. Under the Dayton Accord, signed on December 14, 1995, Bosnia was transformed into a federation in which each faction had its own autonomous region. The Russians protested in NATO's war against Serbia, arguing that it was unjust and illegal without Security Council approval. As a goodwill gesture, Clinton told Yeltsin that NATO would let Russian troops join the post-war peacekeeping force.

Yet another divisive issue between Moscow and the West was NATO's planned expansion eastward to embrace former countries newly liberated from the Soviet empire. That provoked anger across Russia's political spectrum. Russia's reform leaders explained to Clinton administration officials that their "resistance to NATO enlargement stemmed not from … worries about a NATO attack on Russia but from the problems created by the enlargement debate for liberal reformers in Russia."[23] In other words, the communists and nationalists seized on NATO enlargement to trump up fears about a non-existent threat to swell their popularity. Prime Minister Yevgeny Primakov admitted that "the expansion of NATO is not a military problem, it is a psychological one."[24] For that very reason, many American experts also opposed NATO's expansion.

Among them was George Kennan, the architect of America's Cold War containment strategy, who argued that it would backfire:

> Such a decision may be expected to inflame the nationalist, anti-Western and militaristic tendencies in Russian opinion; to have an adverse effect on the development of Russian democracy; to restore the atmosphere of the Cold War to East-West relations, and to impel Russian foreign policy in directions decidedly not to our liking.

He blasted expansion as "a tragic mistake" that "shows so little understanding of Russian history and Soviet history …. The Russians will react quite adversely."[25]

To allay those fears, NATO agreed on January 10, 1994 to invite the Kremlin into a Partnership for Peace that gave Russia observer status in NATO. Then, the Group of 7 leaders of the United States, Japan, Britain, Germany, France, Italy, and Canada, asked Yeltsin to join them at the Denver summit in June 1997 and promised to facilitate Russia's membership in the World Trade Organization (WTO). Clinton talked Yeltsin into signing the NATO-Russian Founding Act on Mutual Relations on May 27, 1997, whereby Russian accepted the alliance's enlargement in return for assurances and assistance: "NATO and Russia do not consider each other as adversaries. They share the goal of overcoming the vestiges of earlier confrontations and competition and of strengthening mutual trust and co-operation." During the Madrid summit in July 1997, NATO issued invitations to Poland, Hungary, and the Czech Republic. Those three nations formally joined NATO on March 12, 1999.

Meanwhile, the imploding economy and worsening conditions for most Russians discredited the free market philosophy that instigated it. That, along with the Yeltsin government's failure to alleviate the prevailing misery, led to huge communist and nationalist gains in the Duma election on December 17, 1995; Yeltsin's Our Home – Russia Party emerged with only 55 seats to the Communist Party's 157 seats and the ultranationalist Liberal Democratic Party's 51 seats. The liberal centrist *Yabloko* Party, led by Grigory Yavlinsky, won only 45 seats.

Table 3.4 Top Four Political parties in the December 1995 Duma Election.[26]

	Party List		Single Member	Total Seats	1993 Seats
	Percentage	Seats	Seats		
Communist	22.30	99	58	157	45
Liberal Democrats	11.18	50	1	51	64
Our Home – Russia	10.13	45	10	55	n.a.
Yabloko	6.89	31	14	45	23
		225	225		

Yeltsin's worst rival for the presidential election, scheduled for June 16, 1996, was Communist Party chief Gennady Zyuganov. Polls revealed that Zyuganov would crush Yeltsin. Many of Yeltsin's inner circle urged him to assert emergency powers, cancel the election and suspend the constitution. Yeltsin was about to do so when his daughter and closest confidante, Tatyana, along with liberal advisors Anatoly Chubais and Alexander Olson, talked him out of it. Instead, they got Yeltsin to curb his excessive eating and drinking, while exuding his nature's better side. Olson explained: "I proposed creating a new Yeltsin, a Yeltsin that people wanted to see, who was cheerful, humane, kind, who knew what the problems were and tried to solve them, who looked after the weak and... gave opportunities to the strong."[27]

Yeltsin's political makeover was one critical reason for his upset victory. Three others were also vital: massive infusions of oligarch money to buy votes; control over most of the mass media; and shameless vote stuffing. Of the oligarchs, Boris Berezovsky and Vladimir Gusinsky contributed the most cash, media and connections. Finally, the Kremlin convinced General Alexander Lebed, a charismatic communist, to run and so split the red vote.

The 1996 election had two rounds on June 16 and July 3. During the first round, Yeltsin edged out Zyuganov by 35.28 per cent to 32.03 per cent, while Lebed received 14.52 per cent. Yeltsin nearly failed to show up for the second round when he was rushed to the hospital after suffering a heart attack, his fifth; he was released just before the run-off. Despite his array of physical and political handicaps, Yeltsin trounced Zyuganov in the second round by winning 53.82 per cent to 40.31 per cent of the votes.[28]

Although Yeltsin retained the presidency, he was powerless to turn around the deteriorating economy. Indeed, the prevailing incompetence and corruption largely caused the financial collapse on August 17, 1998, when the Kremlin declared itself bankrupt, defaulted on its soaring debt, and devalued the ruble. That was the culmination of a decade of bad policies. Throughout the 1990s Russia annually hemorrhaged as much as $30 billion in capital flight to safe foreign havens. The economy contracted 54 per cent and industrial production 60 per cent from 1990 to 1999. Meanwhile, government employees rose from 1.15 million to 2.8 million while revenues fell from 44 per cent to 28 per cent of the budget. With oil exports critical to Russia's economy, the price of a barrel fell from around $50 to $12 during that decade.[29] A majority in the Duma reacted to the collapse on August 21, 1998 by demanding that Yeltsin resign. Instead, Yeltsin fired Prime Minister Sergei Kiriyenko and submitted Yevgeny Primakov as his replacement to the Duma. On September 11 the Duma approved Primakov. The economy continued to freefall. On July 18, 1998 the International Monetary Fund (IMF) and the World Bank issued Moscow a $22.6 billion financial package in return for the Kremlin's commitment to raise revenues and cut spending. The economy bottomed out and slowly began to revive.

Then came NATO's 1999 war against Serbia. Kosovo was a Serbian province whose population was 90 per cent Muslim. For years a group called the Kosovo Liberation Army (KLA) had fought against Serbia for Kosovo's independence. As in Bosnia, several thousand Russian mercenaries fought with the Serbs in Kosovo while Moscow supplied Belgrade with weapons. The fighting intensified in 1998. Serb militia massacred several groups of Muslims, both in retaliation for KLA attacks but also in hopes of stampeding the Muslims to neighboring Albania. Eventually more than 200,000 Muslims fled Kosovo. Washington and Brussels issued repeated protests and warnings to President Slobodan Milosevic, but the massacres persisted. Moscow vetoed a U.N. Security Council resolution by the Americans, British, and French that would empower NATO to pressure the Serbs to stop the atrocities. NATO forged a consensus to act on its own and, on October 13, gave Serbia four days to halt the massacres. Clinton despatched Richard Holbrooke to ensure that Milosevic heeded that warning. Milosevic agreed to grant Kosovo autonomy within Serbia. Tragically, the fighting between Serb militia and the KLA continued, with more Muslims fleeing to Albania. Negotiations opened at Rambouillet, France, on February 6, 1999 but for weeks the Serbs, backed by Moscow, rejected NATO's insistence on deploying 28,000 peacekeeping troops in Kosovo. On March 23 Holbrooke flew to Belgrade and gave Milosevic a last chance to accept the peacekeepers or face war. Milosevic defiantly replied, "Go ahead and bomb us but you will never get Kosovo."[30] Russian Prime Minister Yevgeny Primakov hoped to avert NATO's assault by flying to Washington for direct talks with Clinton but, when he heard that war was imminent, he ordered his plane to turn around and head back to Moscow.

NATO's war against Serbia came just a week after Hungary, Poland and the Czech Republic joined the alliance. The war began on March 24, 1999 with a NATO bombing campaign that lasted seventy-eight days and systematically destroyed Serbia's military and economic infrastructure. Milosevic finally agreed to an armistice, the withdrawal of Serbian troops from Kosovo, and a NATO peacekeeping force in Kosovo. The Russians felt humiliated by NATO's decisive victory over the Serbs who were fellow Slavs and Orthodox Christians, and whose military Russia had armed and trained. Clinton tried to assuage Yeltsin by inviting Russian troops to join a peacekeeping force. That presented a dilemma to Yeltsin who wanted a Russian military presence in Kosovo but not under NATO command.

Then on June 12, General Leonid Ivashov, who commanded the Russian peacekeeping force in Bosnia, airlifted 200 troops to the airport outside Pristina, Kosovo's capital, and began mobilizing another 4,000 troops to follow. That unauthorized deployment nearly resulted in fighting that might have led to war between NATO and Russia. General Wesley Clark, NATO's commander, ordered ground commander Lieutenant General Sir Michael Jackson to force the Russians to stand down. Jackson disobeyed, declaring, "Sir, I'm not starting World War Three for you."[31] Instead, NATO sealed off the airport and forbade any Russian supply flights from landing. Eventually, diplomats cut a face-saving deal that designated a small zone for those 200 troops while forbidding any reinforcements.

Meanwhile, Vladimir Putin acquired a series of increasingly powerful positions throughout the 1990s, culminating with Russia's presidency. St Petersburg Mayor Anatoly Sobchak named Putin to chair the Committee for Foreign Liaisons (KVS) in June 1991 and oversee Leningrad's gambling industry in December 1991. For the next five years Putin wielded his power to privatize Soviet industries, sell excess production, license joint ventures between Russian and foreign businesses and skim money from the government's per cent share of casinos. He formed the St Petersburg Association of Joint Ventures (SPAG) for all the businesses he was authorizing. Dresdner Bank, based in Germany, was the key conduit for international financial deals. The result was an oligarchy among his friends and allies with himself their chief. Eventually they called themselves the Force (*Siloviki*). The oligarchs grew fabulously richer through their expanding web of corporations that monopolized trade and investments flowing through Leningrad and beyond, either to foreign countries or elsewhere in Russia.

Putin headed a vast tribute system. Just to meet him could cost the supplicant anywhere from $5 million to $10 million. He took a standard 25 per cent fee for real estate deals.[32] He owned shares in many of the businesses that he licensed. He frequently traveled abroad to conduct business, most often to Finland, Germany and Spain. He worked closely with Russian criminal gangs. For instance, in return for huge sums of money, he licensed the Tambov crime syndicate to take over St Petersburg's port and the St Petersburg Fuel Company.

Indeed, the distinction between the government and organized crime disappeared in the prevailing kleptocracy of bribery, corruption, kickbacks, money-laundering, no bid contracts, insider information and the occasional beating or even murder of anyone who resisted. CIA Moscow station chief Richard Palmer revealed that Putin's system flourished by spending:

> about 50 per cent of its billions in profits to bribe officials that remained in government and be the primary supporters of all the political candidates. Then, most of the stolen funds, excess profits, and bribes would have to be sent off to offshore banks, for safekeeping. Finally, while claiming that the country was literally bankrupt and

needed vast infusions of foreign aid to survive, this conspiratorial group would invest billions in spreading illegal activities to develop foreign countries.[33]

Marina Sal'ye, a Russian democratic leader and investigator, explained one common way that Putin and his cronies got so rich:

Cook up a legal defective contract with a person, take a license to the Custom Office, on the basis of this license open the border and send the goods abroad, sell the goods and put the money in your pocket … .They needed their 'partners' … of the shadow economy, criminal and mafia structures, front companies that could ensure this ambitious scam. These were Putin's 'partners'.[34]

Yet Putin and his family still lived humbly with an apartment in the city and a dacha on the shore of Lake Komsolmoskyoe northeast of St Petersburg. A fire destroyed his dacha in August 1996. From the ruins, he found the aluminum cross his mother had given him to bless when he visited Jerusalem. On November 10, 1996 Putin and seven St Petersburg oligarchs founded the Ozero (Lake) Dacha Consumer Co-operative as an exclusive gated community on Lake Komsolmoskyoe.

Elections determined the latest twist in Putin's career as he lost his job with Sobchak and got one from Yeltsin in Moscow. Sobchak faced thirteen rivals for his reelection bid as St Petersburg's mayor in May 1996. He won a relative majority in the first round but lost in the second round. The procurator general promptly charged Sobchak with corruption. Putin was instrumental in helping Sobchak escape Russia to a hospital in Paris. During the June 1996 presidential election, Yeltsin's chief rivals were Communist Party leader Gennady Zyuganov and Afghan war hero Alexander Lebed. Yeltsin won a relative majority with 35 per cent of the vote in the first round and 54 per cent to Zyuganov's 40 per cent in the run-off.

Yeltsin appointed Putin to head the Presidential Property Management Department (PPMD) in Moscow in July 1996. The PPMD controlled all foreign Soviet and Communist Party property that included at least 715 sites in seventy-eight countries potentially worth $600 billion.[35] During his eight months as PPMD's chief, Putin privatized much of that property to his cronies. In March 1997 Yeltsin appointed Putin to head the Main Control Directorate (GKU), which oversees the implementation of decrees, laws and regulations. Putin wielded his latest power to terminate investigations of himself and his cronies and prevent new ones from arising by eliminating the Directorate for Economic Counterintelligence and the Directorate for Counterintelligence Protection of Strategic Sites. The most tragic potential new case was a high-speed crash by Putin's driver that killed a boy on December 12, 1997; the driver received amnesty before being convicted of reckless driving and manslaughter. Putin served as first deputy chief of Russia's eighty-nine regions for three months from May 1998; during that time his investigations of officials found 460 guilty of malfeasance in office.[36]

Amidst all that, in June 1997, Putin received an advanced degree from Leningrad University's Mining Institute even though he never attended a class, took a test or wrote a paper, let alone the thesis. Ghostwriters took care of all that for him, mostly by plagiarism. It was all a Potemkin to give him the status of a diploma to hang on his wall.[37] And that provides an insight into Putin's character. He shamelessly paid a lot of money to get his hands on a prized symbol that he never merited. That would render his diploma worthless in most people's minds but does not stop him from showing it off to those he is confident are ignorant of the backstory.

A dream came true for Putin on July 25, 1998 when Yeltsin named him chief of the Federal Security Service (FSB), the renamed and re-organized KGB. During his year there he filled the FSB's upper ranks with allies while purging thousands from the lower ranks to streamline the organization and abolishing the organized crime unit that might have incriminating evidence against him and his cronies. On March 29, 1999 he received an additional duty as secretary of the Kremlin's Security Council.

As Putin rose, Russia's problems worsened as war erupted again with Chechnya.[38] Rebels captured Gennady Shpigan, the Interior Minister's special envoy to Chechnya, on March 5, 1999 and later murdered him when Yeltsin refused to ransom him. Then, on March 20, a bomb exploded at a market in Vladikakaz, Chechnya, killing fifty-three people. No one claimed the bombing. The Kremlin blamed Chechnyan terrorists, severed talks with Chechnyan separatists and launched an offensive into Chechnya. Simultaneously, Yeltsin issued decrees that suppressed Russia's media and dissidents and strengthened presidential powers.

The Communist Party, which controlled a third of the Duma seats, opened impeachment proceedings on May 11 against Yeltsin on political rather than legal charges, including causing the Soviet Union's collapse, suspending parliament in 1993, warring in Chechnya, demoralizing the army and diminishing the Russian people. The following day, looking for a scapegoat, Yeltsin sacked Primakov and replaced him as prime minister with Sergei Stepashin, a feckless sycophant. Before the impeachment vote on May 15 Yeltsin bought off enough Duma deputies so that the 283 in favor fell short of the 300 required for conviction.

Primakov headed the opposition All Russia Party (Vsya Rossiya) in the Duma and prepared to enter the 2000 presidential campaign. Yuri Luzhkov was Moscow's mayor and head of the Fatherland Party (Orechestvo) that he formed in December 1998. On August 17 Primakov and Luzhkov formed a centrist coalition, the Fatherland-All Russia Party (OVR), to campaign for the Duma and presidential elections. They solicited support from the centrist Union of Right Forces (URF), a coalition of nine small parties. Primakov faced two other prominent challengers, Vladimir Zhirinovsky who led the grossly misnamed far right Liberal Democrat Party of Russia (LDPR), and Gennady Zyuganov, the Communist Party chief. Yet Primakov was the frontrunner with his center-right views, financial backing by energy giants Gazprom, Lukoil and Yukos, and mass media mogul Vladimir Gusinsky. Then Yeltsin nominated someone unknown to the public as a potential candidate who, over the next seven months, would astonish everyone by skyrocketing in popularity and winning the election.

A crisis provoked Yeltsin's choice. On August 7 Chechen rebel leader Shamil Basayev and his men invaded Dagestan and seized three villages. To head the fight against the invaders, Yeltsin needed a prime minister who was tough rather than compliant. He also wanted someone who might become a viable presidential candidate and, after winning, could ensure that Yeltsin and his political "family" enjoyed a lucrative rather than litigated retirement. Vladimir Putin appeared to be a good choice. Yeltsin later recalled that

I had a pretty good understanding of his performance in St Petersburg under Sobchak. And when he moved to Moscow, I started watching him especially closely. I could see that he was not just an intelligent and well-educated person but also decent and self-controlled.[39]

On August 9 Yeltsin forced Stepashin to resign and replaced him with Putin. On August 16 the Duma approved Putin by 233 votes, seven beyond the minimum 226 votes. Putin asked and received from Yeltsin "absolute power" to crush the rebellion.

Putin flew to Grozny to consult with Russian army leaders. Several weeks of fighting between the rebels and Russian troops resulted in 307 deaths and 1,700 wounded. Then Basayev announced that he and his men had withdrawn from Dagestan on August 23, the day that Putin had promised the rebellion would be crushed. That may have been coincidental but later a recorded phone call emerged of oligarch Boris Berezovsky offering to pay Chechen rebel leaders to raid Dagestan. Had Yeltsin and his cronies staged the whole war to rally the public behind him and his successor?[40] Regardless, Basayev's invasion was only the first phase of a war in which major fighting persisted until May 2000, followed by Russian attempts to wipe out the last pockets of resistance that stretched until 2009.

Then six bombs exploded in Russian cities between August 31 and September 16, three in Moscow and one each in Buynaksk, Dagestan and Volgodonsk, killing 301 people and wounding 2,000. Three other bombs were discovered and defused in Moscow. The Kremlin accused Chechen terrorists. Investigative journalists uncovered mounting evidence that the Kremlin may have staged the terrorist attacks to justify warring against Chechnya and cracking down on dissidents at home. The tipping point came on September 22 after residents at a building in Ryazan reported two men and a woman carrying containers into the basement. Police discovered the explosive hexogen in three fifty-kilogram bags; hexogen was the same explosive used in the previous bombings. A police dragnet of 1,200 officers caught the two men but released them after they produced FSB identity cards. FSB chief Nikolai Patrushev claimed that the operation was a training mission and the bags were filled with sugar, but virtually no one believed that. The aborted Ryazan bombing was similar to those in Moscow. Later incriminating evidence surfaced that implicated the FSB with all the bombings. Among the more blatant signs of conspiracy was Duma Speaker Gennady Seleznyov's announcement on September 13 that a bomb had exploded the previous night in Volgodonsk instead of three days later when the actual bombing occurred.[41]

Putin got the Duma to suppress any motions to investigate and to seal any evidence for seventy-five years. He then went on television to reassure the Russian people that: "No one in the Russian special services would be capable of such a crime against his own people. The very supposition is amoral. It's nothing but part of the information war against Russia."[42] Is that true? Had Yeltsin, Putin or other key officials ordered Russian citizens mass-murdered to justify their autocracy and war against Chechnya? If so, they ineptly covered their tracks yet got away with it. Historian Sergey Kovalev explained the significance of the bombings for Russia's political development and Putin's role:

These explosions were a crucial moment in the unfolding of our current history …. How … can you negotiate with people who murder children at night in their beds? War was the only solution! … What little is known about the people suspected of having some responsibility for the explosions indicates is that this is likely a false trail: the individuals … are not even ethnic Chechens. But the absence of evidence doesn't prevent the population from continuing to enthusiastically support the government's actions … The explosions were needed only as an initial excuse … While I do not believe Putin himself created this excuse, I have no doubt that he cynically and shamelessly used it; just as I have no doubt that the war was planned in advance … Putin will either resurrect Soviet power or resuscitate the archaic myth of Russian statehood. More likely he will build … an authoritarian police regime that will preserve the formal characteristics of democracy.[43]

Kovalev was prescient.

Regardless, Putin proved to be an extraordinary candidate who not only won the 2000 presidential election, but decisively shaped the preceding 1999 Duma election's results.[44] He exuded the tough, decisive, but calm leadership that Russians craved after a decade of flamboyant leaders like Yeltsin and Zhirinovsky. His poll numbers soared from 31 per cent when he served as prime minister in August 1999 to 84 per cent in January 2000.[45] Yeltsin tasked Sergei Shoigu and Vladislav Surkov, two of his key advisors, to run Putin's campaign and form a political party that could work with him in parliament. They founded the Unity Party (Yedinstvo), also called the Bear Party (Medved), and pressured the oligarchs for massive contributions to pay for mobilizing voters and television advertisements. Boris Berezovsky became Unity's key patron. Meanwhile, Putin built a coalition behind the scenes among as many of eighty-nine governors as possible, of whom many already supported the Fatherland-All Russia Party led by Primakov and Luzhkov. On August 13 he met in Tomsk with nineteen Siberian governors and eventually got thirteen to endorse him. That started a bandwagon effect. On September 24 Yeltsin received a petition from twenty-four governors asking him to resign and appoint Putin in his place as president. Yeltsin would eventually do just that. Putin made his pitch to all the governors who he convened at the Kremlin on September 27; another thirty-two governors endorsed Unity. Putin himself did not publicly embrace Unity until November 24 when he deemed it viable enough to be an asset rather than a distraction.

Table 3.5 Top Four Political parties in the December 1999 Duma Election.[46]

	Party List		Single Member	Total Seats	
	Percentage	Seats	Seats	Number	Percentage
Communist	24.29	67	47	114	25.9
Unity	23.32	64	9	73	16.6
Fatherland-All Russia	13.33	37	29	66	15.0
Union of Right	8.52	24	5	29	6.6
Zhirinovsky Bloc	5.98	17	0	17	3.9
Yabloko	5.93	16	4	22	4.5%
		225	94		

The December 19 Duma election officially resulted in the Communists winning nearly one of four votes, trailed slightly by Unity, and then a ten-per-centage point drop to the third largest recipient, Fatherland-All Russia. Disturbingly, the two largest authoritarian parties, Communist and Zhirinovsky Bloc, won 29.8 per cent of the Duma seats. Even worse, the actual support for extremists may have been far higher. As usual in Russia appearances were deceiving. Observers from the Organization for Security and Cooperation in Europe (OSCE), the European Election Observation Mission and the Parliamentary Assembly of the Council of Europe (PACE) found evidence of widespread fraud with votes given to some parties and taken from others. One investigation found shocking differences between the official and actual results, with the Communist's 24 per cent and 33 per cent, Unity's 23 per cent and 14 per cent, Fatherland-All Russia's 12 per cent and 21 per cent, Union of Right Forces' 9 per cent and 3.4 per cent, Yabloko's 6 per cent and 12 per cent, and Zhirinovsky Bloc's 6 per cent and 4.5 per cent.[47] Most upsetting was that one of three Russians embraced the communists.

During his New Year's Eve address to the nation, Yeltsin made two stunning announcements. One was to apologize:

> that many of our dreams failed to come true .... I am sorry that I did not live up to the hopes of people who believed that we could, with a single effort ... jump out of our gray, stagnant, totalitarian past and into a bright, wealthy civilized future.

The other was that:

> I am going to resign .... Russia should enter the new millennium with new politicians, new faces, new, smart strong energetic people .... Why should I hold on to my seat for six more months when the country has a strong person who deserves to become president and to whom virtually every Russian has linked his hopes for the future?[48]

Yeltsin's resignation required a time change for the presidential election from its scheduled June date to March, since the constitution permits only three months between a president's resignation and the next election to choose his successor.

Vladimir Putin became Russia's acting president just before midnight on December 31, 1999. His first presidential decree was to grant Yeltsin all the perks of a former president including pay, staff and dacha. That was atop his private assurance of immunity from prosecution for any crimes that Yeltsin and his "Family" committed in office. He then terminated every government investigation of alleged crimes by himself and his cronies while bullying the mass media into halting their own investigations.

Amidst the presidential campaign Putin suffered the death of his former mentor, boss and friend, Anatoly Sobchak. In July 1999 Sobchak flew back to St Petersburg after three years of foreign exile to announce that he would run for the Duma in the December 1999 election. He lost. With mixed feelings at one point he described Putin as "a new Stalin, not as bloodthirsty but no less brutal and firm because that is the only way to get Russians to do any work."[49] Sobchak died on February 18, 2000; the official cause was a heart attack, but since his two bodyguards also sickened, a deadly toxin spread on his bedside lightbulb was the likelier culprit. Putin gave the eulogy and wept at Sobchak's funeral.

The parallel strategy to building Unity was to destroy the reputations of the two centrists, former Prime Minister Yevgeny Primakov and Moscow Mayor Yuri Luzhkov, leaving voters with a choice between Putin and Communist candidate Gennady Zyuganov. To undermine Luzhkov, Moscow's government was fined $140 million for violating currency-trading laws. Then, with the elections three days away, the government announced an investigation over allegations that Primakov's organization had broken election rules. The television station ORT, spearheaded by Sergey Dorenko's "news" show *Vremya*, mercilessly attacked Primakov and Luzhkov. Not all national government institutions followed the Kremlin. The Central Electoral Commission (CEC) criticized the Kremlin for trying to tilt the election.

Putin refused to join any debates with other candidates. Instead, the Kremlin or his crony-controlled mass media televised images of Putin performing his duties as prime minister. Support for Putin rose after he announced that the army had captured Grozny on February 6. He flew to Grozny, reviewed the troops and handed out medals on March 20, just six days before the election. He reassured the public that the army was mopping up rebels there and elsewhere in Chechnya. He asserted that "This [war] is not just about restoring the honor and dignity of the country. It is about putting an end to the disintegration of Russia."[50]

According to the 1993 constitution, if no presidential candidate wins more than half the votes, a run-off between the top two candidates occurs two weeks later. Eleven candidates qualified to be on the ballot for the presidential election held on March 26, 2000. The Kremlin manipulated the votes to ensure that no run-off occurred. The Central Electoral Commission announced that Putin had won 52.94 per cent of the vote, while his nearest rival, Communist Party chief Zyuganov got only 29.21 per cent and liberal candidate Grigory Yavlinsky came in a dismal third with only 5.80 per cent.[51]

As with the Duma election, international observers found widespread voter fraud including ballot stuffing and ballot destruction. One method of ballot stuffing is the "caterpillar vote," whereby an operative outside the polling place gives a voter a filled-out ballot who then receives a blank ballot after he registers inside the polling place; he deposits the filled-out ballot then returns to the operative and receives 100 rubles for the blank ballot which the operative fills out and gives to someone else, and so on. One blatant manipulation was the number of registered voters rising from December 1999 to March 2000 from 108,073,956, of whom 61.99 per cent voted in the Duma election, to 109,372,046, of whom 68.64 per cent voted in the presidential race despite the fact that Russia's population experienced a net loss of 182,000 people.[52]

Despite the machinations, most Russians enthusiastically supported Putin. One expert explained Putin's appeal by comparing him with Yeltsin:

He provided both 'continuity' and 'contrast.' Yeltsin was old, ailing and increasingly divorced from reality. Putin was young, sharp and energetic. Yeltsin had a large frame, a swollen face, and gray hair. Putin was short, had chiseled features and thin hair. Putin could fly a military jet, pose on a warship and fight on a judo mat. He spoke clearly, calmly and decisively. After Yeltsin, who was quintessentially

Russian – emotional, a drinker, impulsive – Putin seemed almost un-Russian. He was secretive, restrained, sober, unemotional, and almost pedantic ... The fact that Putin seemed to have come from nowhere, had no political 'baggage' and was not associated with Perestroika or the Communist worked in his favor.[53]

Vladimir Putin gave a very mixed message in his inaugural address on May 7, 2000. On one hand, he declared:

I promise you that any attempts to act contrary to the Russian law and constitution will be cut short .... We will be able to see the true importance of what Boris Yeltsin has done for Russia only after some time has passed. However, it is clear already now that it was thanks to the president that Russia has opted for democracy and reform and is moving toward those goals, and has become a strong and independent state.

Yet he celebrated not the Russian people but the place that had repressed and exploited them for half a millennium:

For today's solemn event we are gathered here in the Kremlin, a place which is sacred for our people. The Kremlin is the heart of our national memory. Our country's history has been shaped here, inside the Kremlin walls, over centuries. And we do not have the right to be heedless of our past. We must not forget anything. We must know our history, know it as it is, draw lessons from it and always remember those who created the Russian state, championed its dignity and made it a great, powerful, and mighty state.

Finally, he expressed a goal for all Russians to share: "We want our Russia to be a free, prosperous, rich, strong and civilized country, a country of which its citizens are proud, and which is respected in the world."[54] He would be false to his first promise, true to his second, and is struggling to realize the third.

Chapter 4

Putin's System of Power

The Kremlin is the heart of our national memory ... We must know our history ... and always remember those who created the Russian state, championed its dignity and made it a great, powerful, and mighty state.

(Vladimir Putin)

You have shown yourself to be as barbaric and ruthless as your most hostile critics have claimed. You have shown you have no respect for life, liberty, or any civilized value ... You may succeed in silencing one man, but a howl of protest from around the world will reverberate, Mr Putin, in your ears for the rest of your life.

(Aleksander Litvinenko)

Vladimir Putin has a unified vision for Russia, its vital interests, and how to realize them. He first publicly articulated his worldview in his 5,000-word essay "Russia on the Threshold of the New Millennium", which appeared on the Kremlin's website on December 29, 1999. He called for making Russia great again by rebuilding its economy, military, society and, above all, state (*gosudarstvo*) and bolstering the symbiotic relationship among mother Russia (*mat Rossiya* or *Rodina*), the government and the people. In return for protection, the people devote themselves to serving Russia, personified by its state. Being a good Russian concerns obedience not freedom. In a January 2012 newspaper article, he wrote: "The Russian people have confirmed their choice time and again during their thousand-year history – with their blood, not through plebiscites or referendums." On November 27, 2011, he declared: "We will do anything to uphold civil peace and harmony. At stake is the future of our statehood, the well-being of our citizens…we are a single Russian nation, a united and indivisible Russia." Putin wants not just to retain what is left of the Russian empire but ideally expand it to its former heights. He mourns the Soviet Union's break-up as "the greatest political catastrophe of the twentieth century". His nostalgia is understandable. The Russian empire peaked in territory, population, military power and prestige when it was the Soviet Union.[1]

In the hyphenated notion of nation-state, Putin champions the state above the nation:

> For Russians, a strong state is not an anomaly to fight against. Quite the contrary, it is the source and guarantor of order, the initiator and the main driving force of any change. Society desires the restoration of the guiding and regulating role of the state. In Russia, a collective form of life has always dominated over individualism. It is also the fact that paternalism is deeply grounded in Russian society. The majority of Russians associate the improvement in their lives not so much with their own endeavors, initiative, and entrepreneurship as with the help and support of the state.[2]

Putin sees a dynamic among a strong state, unified people, economic development, and international power:

> In the end, economic growth, prosperity, and geopolitical influence all derive from societal conditions; from to what extent citizens of a given country consider themselves a unified nation, to what extent they are anchored in their own history, values and traditions; whether they are united by common goals and responsibilities. In this sense, the question of finding and strengthening national identity is fundamentally Russian.[3]

As for what kind of economy was best for Russia, Putin admitted that communism is:

> less efficient than a market economy. History has staged two experiments that are very well known in the world: East Germany and West Germany, North Korea and South Korea … But this does not mean that everything is alright in a market economy. If we would introduce so-called wild capitalism, would it lead to anything good,

would it ever produce anything beneficial? So, what are we aiming for? A market economy, but a socially oriented market economy.[4]

During an April 2011 meeting with the oligarchs, Putin explained why they should be grateful to the Kremlin:

We supported the private entrepreneurs, we backed you, gave you loans, helped your refinance from Western banks, put up collateral …. But we did not proceed to nationalization of our economy … we don't want to create a system of state capitalism – we want to create a system of socially oriented market economy.[5]

Putin's concept of power is known as *derzhavnost* or:

a strong, paternalist, and to some extent expansionist state. Rather than nationalism, this ideology is a return to a traditional Russian form of legitimacy characteristic of the tsarist and Soviet periods, in which the idea of a strong state replaces that of a nation and the state is situated above society.[6]

Putin's world view has five elements, including

emotive nationalism; intrusive social conservativism; the retrieval of the Soviet legitimizing mythology (most of all about the Second World War and Stalin); the Russian Orthodox Church as arbiter and enforcer of national mores; and Russian ethnicity as the backbone of the Russian state.[7]

Related Putin concepts are "state-centeredness" (*gosudarstvennichestvo*), "traditional Russian values" (*rossiiskie*), ethnic Russian people (*Russkii narod*), Russian world of ethnicity, Orthodox Christianity, and language (*Russkii mir*), multi-ethnic Russian people (*rossiiskii narod*), "universal human and primordial Russian values" (*iskonnye rossiiskii*) and "state-forming nation" (*gosudarstvo obrazuiushchii narod*), "Russian civic nation" (*rossiiskaia grazhdanskaia natsiia*) and united Russian nation (*rossiiskaia natsiia*).[8]

Putin's world view reflects traditional Russian autocracy, imperialism and nationalism. His favorite philosopher is Ivan Ilyin, a Bolshevik and Russian Revolutionary but who, in 1922, the Communist Party expelled for his heterodox views. Ilyin was essentially a Russian nationalist who advocated a strong state and condemned both liberalism and communism. In 2005 Putin actually had Ilyin's body disinterred from its obscure grave and re-interred in Moscow's Donskoi Monastery. In 2014 he had Ilyin's book *Our Tasks* distributed as required reading for Russia's governors and United Russia Party leaders. He frequently cites two other thinkers and their books as expressing his world view, Nikolai Berdayev's *Philosophy of Inequality* and Vladimir Solovyov's *Justification of the Good*.

Putin sought to bolster national unity, patriotism, and thus his own legitimacy by officially embracing popular symbols of both Tsarist and Soviet Russia. He designated the old imperial blue, white and red flag as the Russian flag on December 8, 2000 and the two-headed eagle as the national emblem and the old Soviet anthem with updated words as the national anthem on December 25, 2000. Atop that he designated three patriotic holidays, "Victory over Germany Day" on May 9, "Russia Day" on June 12, and "National Unity Day" on November 4, while eliminating the Soviet Union's "Russian Revolution Day" on November 7 and Yeltsin's "Constitution Day" on December 12. On May 9, 2008 he resumed military parades through Red Square that Gorbachev cancelled in 1990. He resisted liberal pressure to remove Lenin from his tomb in Red Square with a nuanced explanation:

> If we accept the fact that in no way could we use the symbols of the previous epochs including the Soviet one, thus we must admit that our mothers and fathers lived useless and senseless lives, that they lived their lives in vain. I can't accept it with either my mind or my heart.[9]

The state that Putin rules is a hybrid of superficially democratic institutions established by the 1993 Constitution rooted in an authoritarian political culture twelve hundred-years old. Theoretically, there are constitutional checks to Putin's power. The Constitutional Court is empowered to determine the constitutionality of any law or decree. Elections for the

Duma or lower legislative house appear to be democratic with competing political parties. Electoral results vary among elections. Voters freely cast their ballots to the candidates and parties they find most appealing or, for some, the least offensive. The upper house Federal Assembly can override a presidential veto of a law with two-thirds votes in favor. Yet beneath the surface Russia's electoral system has deep flaws.

After taking power on New Year's Eve 1999 Putin steadily transformed Russia's illiberal democracy into an outright authoritarian regime, what he called the "vertical of power" based on a "dictatorship of the law". Putin's "dictatorship of the law" is surely better than a "dictatorship of the proletariat," but still involves egregious abuses of power. He makes the most of his presidential power to issue legally binding decrees. Around seven out of every ten laws come from the executive rather than the legislature. Putin invariably signs any laws passed by the Federal Assembly because they reflect his will.

Putin sent two bills to the Duma on May 13, 2000. One bill changed the Federation Council's 178 members from an elected into an appointed body. Henceforth, a district's executive and assembly would each pick one of their two Federation Council members for Russia's president to approve or reject. The other bill empowered the president to remove and replace any governor suspected of wrongdoing. The eighty-nine districts would be split among seven regions that corresponded to the military regions, each with a presidential envoy who would oversee politics within his region. On May 17 he introduced a law that stripped the Federation Council of its power to veto laws passed by the Duma. On September 1 he decreed that he could appoint as many governors as he wished to join the eighty-nine governors already in the Federation Council.

Putin just as systematically reduced the Duma's powers. In July 2001 he had the Duma pass a law that diminished the array of parties by requiring each to have at least 10,000 registered members with at least 100 each in more than half of the federal districts before they could compete, and forbidding any regional parties. That was designed to force a series of mergers until two or three large parties survived. The number of registered parties plummeted from 197 to 56. In January 2006 the minimum number of party members was raised to 50,000 with at least 500 in more than half the federal districts, while raising the minimum vote share for Duma seats from 5 per cent to 7 per cent. That new standard cut the number of registered parties in half. Putin, the United Russia Party, and its allies have dominated the Duma since the 2003 election. Putin dismisses any suggestions that he is an authoritarian ruler with a rubber stamp legislature: "My influence on the Duma is naturally substantial but is overly exaggerated because parliamentarians have their own opinion on some issues." He cited capital punishment that he opposed but did not try to impose because "I do not raise issues that would arouse a negative reaction or rejection".[10]

Nearly all of Russia's political parties represent authoritarian rather than liberal values. The oldest surviving political party is the ultra-nationalist Liberal Democratic Party (LDPR) founded by Vladimir Zhirinovsky in March 1990. The next oldest is the Communist Party of the Russian Federation (CPRF) founded by Gennady Zyuganov in February 1993. Viktor Chernomyrdin and Vladimir Ryzhkov founded the conservative Our Home is Russia (NDR) in May 1995. The centrist Fatherland-All Russia Party (Orechestvo-Vsya Rossiya, OVR) was a short-lived coalition forged among smaller parties led by former Prime Minister Yevgeny Primakov, Moscow mayor Yuri Luzhkov and St Petersburg Mayor Vladimir Yakovlev in August 1999. Liberal parties only garner from 5 to 10 per cent of the vote, with Yabloko the most prominent from its founding in 1993 until it died in the 2007 election and A Just Russia from 2007 through today. The party that spearheads Putin's agenda was first called Unity (Yedinstvo) when Sergei Shoigu formed it in September 2001. Putin endorsed the party then, on December 1, 2001, cut a deal with Primakov and Luzhkov that merged their parties into the new United Russia Party.

Not just nearly all the political parties but the law itself backs Putin's autocracy. Russia's political and legal system reflects "rule by law, but not rule of law," contrary to the liberal principle that "everything is permitted unless it is forbidden".[11] Regardless, Putin strengthened the overloaded judicial system by appointing hundreds more judges who decide nearly all criminal and civil cases. For instance, in 2005, juries decided only 1,389 cases or 1 per cent of 1,263,000 people charged with crimes. Russia's legal system has a 99 per cent conviction rate, with judges and juries respectively finding those charged guilty 99.3 per cent and 85 per cent of the time. That compares to respective European Union and American conviction rates of 85 per cent and 75 per cent. Russia's prison system is notorious for its rampant disease, filth, rape, murder and torture for convicts and those who often wait years before their trials. Execution still punishes the most heinous crimes even though Putin opposes the death penalty.[12]

And then there are Russia's political criminals.[13] Amnesty International summarized Russia's human rights situation for 2018 as:

> There were further restrictions to the rights to freedom of expression, association and peaceful assembly. Harassment and intimidation of human rights defenders and independent NGOs continued. Cultural rights were reduced, including through reprisals and self-censorship. Religious minorities continued to face harassment and persecution. The right to a fair trial was frequently violated. Torture and other ill-treatment persisted; the word of independent monitoring bodies for places of detention was further eroded. Serious human rights violations continued in the North Caucasus .... Migrants and refugees were denied protection of their rights. Some forms of domestic violence were decriminalized. LGBT people continued to face discrimination and violence.[14]

Putin actually revived the post-Stalin Soviet punishment of condemning outspoken dissidents to insane asylums in 2007. Yuri Savenko, who heads the Independent Psychiatric Association of Russia, explained: "We're returning to this Soviet scenario when psychiatric institutions were used as punitive instruments. I call this not even punitive but police psychiatry, when the main aim is the protection of the state." Horrendous as indefinite imprisonment in a psychiatric ward is, dissidents could suffer even worse fates.[15]

Boris Nemtsov was an outspoken liberal leader and Putin critic. He governed Nizhni Novgorod from 1991 to 1997, then came to Moscow as Yeltsin's first deputy prime minister. Relations soon decayed between the progressive, honest Nemtsov and the cynical, erratic, increasingly authoritarian Yeltsin. In February 2008 Nemtsov and Vladimir Milov published a book that exposed the financial machinations of Putin and his cabal, including that of Dmitri Medvedev who was running for president. He denounced Russia's takeover of Crimea in 2014. An assassin shot Nemtsov six times as he crossed a bridge leading to the Kremlin on the night of February 27, 2015, one year after Russia annexed Crimea. Yet outright murdering a political opponent is rare even in Putin's Russia.

Marina Sal'ye was a prominent geologist who became a leader of the democratic movement during the late 1980s and was elected to Leningrad's assembly and Russia's Congress of People's Deputies. She and her followers backed Yeltsin. She was on the committee that drafted the 1993 constitution. She helped found and lead the Free Democratic Party and the Democratic Party of Russia. She headed what was called the Sal'ye Commission that investigated allegations of corruption by Putin and his coterie in Leningrad. When Putin became president in 2000 Sal'ye went into hiding. In 2011 she emerged and prominently joined the Party of National Freedom dedicated to opposing Putin's autocracy. An apparent heart attack killed her at age seventy-eight on March 21, 2012.

Ksenia Sobchak is the daughter of Anatoly Sobchak, St Petersburg's mayor and Putin's mentor during the early 1990s. During the 2000s she became a prominent style-leader for young women, then, from 2011, an outspoken critic of Putin's autocracy. After his 2012 inauguration Putin had Interior Ministry police arrest her for tax evasion after a raid discovered and confiscated over a million dollars at her home. Her mother, Lyudmila Narusova Sobchak, lost her seat on the Federation Council. Ksenia had a weekly political talk show on an independent station. In 2018 she ran against Putin for president but won only 1.68 per cent of the vote. For good reasons she still lives to criticize Putin's regime. The Kremlin views her as essentially a harmless political gadfly, useful to point at and claim that Russian democracy and a spectrum of opinions is vigorous. Atop that, Putin is not a monster. He would not want any physical harm inflicted against the daughter of the man who propelled him up the power pyramid, however annoying her barbs against him.

Russia's most prominent activist is Aleksei Navalny who has been arrested dozens of times for protesting Putin's autocracy and corruption. He made a fortune in real estate before becoming an activist in 2011. In 2017 alone he spent 110 days in prison on six separate convictions. In September 2018 the authorities tried to break him by re-arresting him on trumped-up charges just as he stepped out of prison. Instead, that appears to have strengthened his resolve. On November 15, 2018 the European Court of Human Rights ruled that Russia's government had violated Navalny's human rights and ordered it to pay him €63,678 or around $72,000 in compensation. Although Navalny will probably never see a ruble of that money, the ruling was encouraging for him and other dissidents. Russia then had 10,950 complaints filed against it in the European Court of Human Rights, about 19 per cent of the total.[16]

As for governing Russia, Putin is a skilled administrator who knows how to pick and oversee the right people for key positions. When he was later asked his KGB years' best lessons, number one was "the experience of working with people …. If you want to achieve results, you have to respect your partner. You need to make that person an ally … that you have common goals." After that was "the ability to work with a large amount of information" and "selecting what is most important".[17]

When Yeltsin handed Putin the presidency it came with Yeltsin "Family" members like Prime Minister Mikhail Kasyanov, chief of staff Alexander Voloshin and deputy Anatoly Chubais. With time Putin eased them out and replaced them with people whose foremost loyalty was to himself. He has a tight circle of longstanding friends from his KGB career that he has placed in key posts and calls his *siloviki* or security cabal including Igor Sechin, Sergei Ivanov, Viktor Ivanov, Vladimir Ustinov, Viktor Zubkov and Sergei Stepashin. Putin described his governing coterie as "I have a lot of friends but only a few that are really close to me. They have never gone away. They have never betrayed me, and I have never betrayed them."[18] The share of *siloviki* in Putin's third presidential term was 47 per cent, sharply up from 25 per cent under Yeltsin and a mere 8 per cent under Gorbachev.[19] Then there are the *Civiliki* or civilians, mostly liberal lawyers and businessmen from St Petersburg who Putin helped amass wealth and power like Dmitri Medvedev, Aleksey Kudrin and German Gref. Tension and debate persist between the *Siloviki* and *Civiliki* as the former tend to be Slavophiles or Eurasianists and the latter Westernizers. Finally, there is Vladislav Surkov, a former bohemian and Putin's visionary political advisor, propagandist and mass media expert.[20]

Beyond Putin's inner circle of Kremlin advisors and ministers is his outer circle of allied billionaire oligarchs. Upon taking power Putin's priority was to consolidate it. He sought to eliminate any rivals either by forcing them to swear loyalty to him or confiscating their power bases. On July 28, 2000 he summoned twenty-one key oligarchs to a barbecue at his palace in Novo-Orgaryovo and told them that they could continue freely to enrich themselves as long as they avoided politics and unquestionably supported his presidency and policies. Otherwise the Kremlin would destroy them with thick files of compromising material (*kompromat*) on each of them. The choice was theirs. Nearly all chose to conform. These became known as Putin's deep "pocket oligarchs" who can be relied upon to implement Kremlin polices as directed, including buying targeted companies, businessmen and politicians, foreign as well as domestic. And to ensure that everyone gives and takes their fair shares, Putin established the Financial Monitoring Agency in November 2001 to monitor how much Russia's largest corporations earn and how they earn it.

Putin has crushed any oligarch who dared to resist him. Mikhail Khodorkovsky was once Russia's richest man who became a multi-billionaire through his holding company Menatep-Rosprom, with oil corporations Yukos and Sibneft the most lucrative. He was among privatization's greatest exploiters. For instance, he and five partners paid $309 million for Yukos and $100 million for Sibneft whose respective shares soared to $6 billion and $3 billion in value within a few months. He fiercely opposed the Kremlin's tax reforms. Yet he was a philanthropist who gave Moscow University $100 million and formed the Open Russia Foundation (*Otkrytaya Rossiya*) dedicated to promoting democracy. He helped bankroll the liberal political parties Yabloko and Union of Right Forces. He openly condemned Putin's autocracy and the corruption pervading Russia. He questioned why the government-owned Rosneft Oil Company, then deeply in debt, was attempting to buy Northern Oil, a small company, for the bloated price of $600 million. He was also negotiating for a merger of Yukos with Russia's Sibneft Oil Company and America's ExxonMobil.[21]

And for all that Putin was determined to bring down Khodorkovsky. His first step was to have two of Khodorkovsky's associates arrested, Aleksei Pichugin, his security chief, on murder charges, and Platon Lebedev, who headed Menatep Bank which owned 61 per cent of Yukos, on fraud charges. That caused the price of Yukos shares to plummet, wiping out $7 billion or 15 per cent of the company's value over two weeks. That did not stop Khodorkovsky from merging Yukos with Sibneft Oil Company whose chairman was Roman Abramovich, Chukotka province's governor and Boris Berezovsky's business partner. Putin then had Khodorkovsky arrested on trumped-up charges of fraud and $3.4 billion of tax evasion on October 25, 2003. Share prices for Yukos-Sibneft plunged until Rosneft bought the company at fire-sale prices. Khodorkovsky was convicted on various charges and imprisoned until December 2013 when he went into exile. Expert Richard Sakwa explained that Putin relentlessly persecuted him because Khodorkovsky "was advancing an alternative vision of a pluralist democracy with an active civil society within the framework of a national liberalism, thus challenging the administrative regime's basis of power."[22]

Putin and his cronies dominate a vast kleptocracy, or government of the thieves, by the thieves, and for the thieves. Andrei Illarionov was a Putin advisor for five years until 2005 when he was fired for protesting the worsening autocracy. He defected to the United States and, in testimony before Congress explained the "ethics" of Putin's oligarchy or Corporation as he called it:

> The members … share strong allegiance to their respective organizations, strict codes of conduct and of honor, basic principles of behavior, including among others the principle of mutual support to each other in circumstances and the principle of omertà [southern Italian code of silence]. Since the Corporation preserves traditions, hierarchies, codes and habits of secret police and intelligence services, its members show a high degree of obedience to the current leadership, strong loyalty to each other, rather strict discipline. There are both formal and informal means of enforcing these norms. Violators of the code of conduct are subject to the highest forms of punishment, including the highest form.[23]

Corruption is the illicit exploitation of public resources for private gain. Corruption pervades Russia's entwined economic and political systems. Cronyism, connections (*blat*) and cash rather than merit largely determine who gets what in jobs and contracts. Government bureaucracy has become a bribe-for-service organization with prices for supplicants rising with the pecking order. Lower-ranking officials explain that the extra "fees" supplement wages that are too low to sustain oneself.

Organized crime compounds corruption.[24] Putin inherited then exacerbated a system that merges government institutions and mobsters. Russia's mafia engages in the full array of typical crimes including prostitution, narcotics, gambling and protection rackets, then invests some of the profits in legitimate businesses. Just as the line between legal and illegal activity is hazy, so, too, is that between organized crime and government. In 1997 President Yeltsin acknowledged that "the criminal world has openly challenged the state and launched into open competition with it".[25] Criminals get away with their crimes including murder by paying off police and judges. The Kremlin's intelligence agencies and most Russian corporations have close ties with Russia's organized crime gangs. For stiff prices, the gangs will launder money, smuggle goods, arms, drugs, and people, and blackmail, bully, or outright kill pesky opponents, and gather intelligence. When Putin came to power, criminals controlled around 40,000 businesses and one of three banks while there were 32,000 or so murders. Legitimate businesses either pay protection money to gangsters or pay for expensive private security. Corruption and protection money soared from $33 billion in 2001 to $316 billion in 2005. The tentacles of Russia's mafia extend worldwide but are especially powerful in New York and Tel Aviv.[26]

Then, there are the street thugs whom the Kremlin wield to bully those who dare to demonstrate publicly against the regime. The Night Wolves and Cossacks are motorcycle gangs and paramilitary groups that the Kremlin unleashes against its opponents. The Nashi or Ours are an ultra-nationalist youth organization set up by Vladislav Surkov, Putin's closest advisor, on February 17, 2005. The Nashi swiftly established branches across Russia and then abroad to former Soviet states. They hold frequent rallies and congresses to vent their rage against liberals, Jews, Muslims, gays and other persecuted minorities. Two other nationalist groups, Russia March and Slavic Union, also engage in mass protests and commit violence against any groups that oppose them.

Yet another auxiliary of Putin's power are so-called "think tanks," although they only merit being called that if they sponsor genuine scholarship. An organization that peddles views regardless of the facts is nothing more than a "propaganda tank". The Kremlin still has plenty of those, most influentially the Paris-based Institute of Democracy and Co-operation and the Berlin-based Dialogue of Civilizations Research Institute. Alexander Dugin is a charismatic Moscow State University professor and Slavophile who founded and leads the International Eurasian Movement with 30,000 members in Russia and a score of other countries. The movement receives funding from the Kremlin, Moscow's Patriarch, and the Central Spiritual Administration for Russian Muslims. Eurasianism is a concept that justifies Russia hegemony over that vast continent.

The most vital essence of pre-Revolution Russia that Putin has fully restored is the Orthodox Church. Under communism the Kremlin persecuted religions, limited the number of houses of worship and tolerated only religious leaders who collaborated with the state to spy on and apprehend any "enemies of the people" in their congregations. Among Mikhail Gorbachev's reforms was to loosen the controls on Orthodox Christianity, allowing more churches to open and more priests to be ordained as long as the patriarch and his hierarchy collaborated with the state. That alliance between state and church persists now by promoting Putin and Russian nationalism. Putin has forged very close ties with Patriarch Kirill, whose original name is Vladimir Gundyaev. In 2011 Kirill received an elaborate complex of offices within the Kremlin. Kirill in turn endorsed Putin's 2012 presidential campaign by celebrating him as "a miracle from God" who had "rectified the crooked path of history".[27]

Putin has also tried to co-opt Russia's Jews who are a wealthy, powerful minority with deep channels in America, Israel, international business and organized crime. In 2014, Jews numbered forty-eight of Russia's two hundred richest people. To his credit Putin spurns the anti-Semitism common among Russians and genuinely respects Jewish people. He assigned two Jewish oligarchs, Roman Abramovich and Lev Leviev, to form the Federation of Jewish Communities in Russia led by Rabbi Berel Lazar of the Hasidic sect Chabad-Lubavitch. He did so to counter the power of the Russian Jewish Congress founded by oligarch Vladimir Gusinsky, who turned against him. Chabad-Lubavitch is a messianic sect established in Brooklyn in the nineteenth century and very influential among American Jews. Among the members is Charles Kushner, the "diamond king" of New York and father of Jared Kushner who married Donald Trump's daughter Ivanka.[28]

Then there is the mass media. A free press is vital as a liberal democratic government's informal fourth branch with the watchdog duty of exposing crimes and blunders, corruption and incompetence within that country's related political, economic military and social systems, and beyond. Systematically, Putin has taken over or cowed the mass media and justified it as the Doctrine of Informational Security. Increasingly, the Kremlin has the final word on what journalists can write or say. Putin explained why during a stop at Columbia University during a week-long visit to America in September 2003. When a student asked him if he was impeding freedom of speech in Russia, Putin replied:

> We have never had freedom of speech in Russia, so I can't understand what I am impeding. At the beginning of the Nineties, we had the onset of a renaissance of freedom. This was also understood in different ways in society, and by the press as well … freedom and freedom of the press in particular was … a free-for-all, as anarchy and as a destruction at any price and at any cost.[29]

Putin's imperative to control the mass media accelerated after its blistering criticism of how he mishandled his first crisis as president. On August 12, 2000 a torpedo accidently exploded inside the *Kursk*, a nuclear-powered submarine cruising in the Barents Sea. The blast immediately killed all but twenty-three of the 118 crew members and disabled the *Kursk*, which settled on the sea bottom 108 metres deep. At the time Putin was vacationing at his palace near Sochi on the Black Sea. Although he quickly learned of the disaster he did not hold a press conference to convey sympathy on behalf of the crew, their families and the Russian people until after five days passed, and did not fly back to Moscow until the eighth day. Meanwhile, he and other officials rejected the Norwegian government's offer to rescue the crew with vessels in the immediate area, instead insisting that Russia's navy would save its own crew. But by the time a Russian vessel reached the site the survivors had perished. As that vessel lacked the means of breaching the submarine, Moscow finally gave a NATO vessel permission to do so on August 21. The NATO divers opened the escape hatch within six hours. To obscure its criminal incompetence, the Kremlin propagated such lies as NATO warships had somehow sabotaged or rammed the *Kursk* while rough weather and deep water delayed any rescue attempt. In the minds of Putin's more discerning supporters, the transparent lies atop his indifference and callousness damaged the image of the decisive, virile leader that he and his regime tried so hard to cultivate. Putin would find ways to rebuild that image.[30]

Putin scapegoated the independent mass media companies that exposed his negligence:

There are people on TV today who shout and scream, yet over the past decade they're the ones who've destroyed the army and navy in which people are now dying. Today they're lined up to defend the armed forces, but tomorrow they'll try to ruin them even more! They've stolen everything and have everyone in their pockets! ... They stole money, bought up the media, and now manipulate public opinion .... We need to implement our own information policy. But that requires effort, money and right-minded people.[31]

Putin did whatever he could to eliminate any mass media moguls or muckraking journalists who opposed him, and bully the free mass media to join his regime's propaganda machine. The Kremlin trumped up charges to arrest editors and journalists, fine, buy or bankrupt the companies, cyber-attack websites and plant fake news in puppet media.

The first victim was Vladimir Gusinsky, who owned Media Most, Russia's largest media corporation with the NTV television network and newspaper *Sevodnya* its most politically powerful assets. Two days before the March 2000 election, NTV's program *Independent Investigation* reported that the FSB was behind the 1999 terrorist bombing in Ryazan. The next day a cyber-attack damaged the network that needed days to be repaired. That did not intimidate Gusinsky into restraining NTV's weekly satirical puppet show *Kukly* which caricatured Putin as a jug-eared, bug-eyed elf who could be obsequious or petulant. Putin was not amused but what enraged him even more was Sergei Dorenko, who hosted the news show *Vremya* and accused him of lying about various issues. On May 11, 2000 FSB police raided Media Most's headquarters and confiscated "evidence" of alleged crimes. Procurator General Vladimir Ustinov summoned Gusinsky for questioning, then ordered his arrest. After being released on bail, Gusinsky fled to his villa in Spain. In April 2001 Gazprom took over NTV when Gusinsky was unable to repay a $281 million loan.

Putin then targeted Boris Berezovsky, whose business empire included Channel One (ORT). During the 1990s Berezovsky capitalized on his doctorate in mathematics by making a fortune in financial speculations and developing the Logovaz holding company that owned ORT. He threw his financial and media power behind Yeltsin's 1996 presidential campaign. Putin summoned Berezovsky and demanded that either he sell ORT or be arrested on trumped-up charges. Berezovsky fled to the West, eventually finding sanctuary in Britain. In September 2000 Berezovsky published a letter to Putin in his newspaper *Kommersant* with this warning:

> Mr. President, please stop before it is too late! Don't let the genie out of the bottle. The genie of unlimited power. He ravaged our country for more than seventy years. You are not equal to the task. Both you and Russia will be destroyed.[32]

Nonetheless, in October 2000, he sold his shares in ORT to his partner Roman Abramovich who sold them to the Kremlin. Berezovsky was found hanging by a cord in his London apartment on March 23, 2013; suicide was his death's likely cause.

The Kremlin now controls nearly the entire television industry. The state owns 51 per cent of Channel 1 Russian Public Television (ORT), 100 per cent of Channel 2 Russian Television and Radio (RTR), 100 per cent of Channel 4 (NTV), and 100 per cent of Channel 5 Culture, although it does not carry political advertisements or an overt message.

The city of Moscow controls Channel 3 TV-Center. Only TV-6 is private. According to law, any political party can buy advertising time on any public or private television station that must charge the same rate. Of course, only the best-funded parties can afford to buy time, especially when demand is highest during political campaigns. Beyond elections, the Kremlin is the gatekeeper for what television news programs report, how they report it and who they interview. Vladimir Posner, president of the Russian Academy of Television, admitted that "he submits a list of guests he would like to have on his show to Channel One Management, who let him know whom he can and cannot invite".[33]

Journalism in Russia is a highly risky business. Anyone who looks too deeply and reveals too much about Russian kleptocracy, becomes a bullseye for assassins paid and despatched by the investigation's target. Fifty-eight journalists have been murdered in Russia since 1991; none of their murderers have been brought to trial.[34]

A Duma investigation of the 1999 terrorist bombings led to the identification of nine suspects. Five were killed, two fled overseas and two were tried in 2003. But most of the key journalists and witnesses who revealed the 1999 FSB terrorist bombings also suffered imprisonment or murder. The key witness against them was Mikhail Trepashkin, a former FSB officer then journalist who exposed the Kremlin's complicity in the bombings. To prevent his testimony, Putin had him arrested, whereupon a court convicted him of illegal weapons possession for which he served five years in prison. The two suspects were convicted. Artyom Borovik, an independent journalist working on the case, died in a plane crash on March 9, 2000. Two key witnesses against the FSB 1999 bombers were murdered in 2003, Sergey Yushenkov by gunshot on April 17 and Yuri Shchekochikhin by poison on July 3.

Other journalists were persecuted or murdered for criticizing Putin. Yuri Shutov once worked for Mayor Sobchak, then wrote a tell-all book that included accusations that Putin was guilty of blackmail and corruption. He was merely imprisoned. Anatoly Levin-Utkin was a journalist whose stories revealed Putin's machinations under Sobchak; Levin-Utkin was beaten to death on August 24, 1998. Yelena Tregubova wrote a bestselling account of Putin's Russia called *Farewell to the Kremlin Digger*. Although she escaped injury, she fled to foreign exile after a bomb exploded on her doorstep on February 12, 2004. Paul Klebnikov was not so lucky. He was an American journalist who worked for Forbes, published articles and a book, *Godfather of the Kremlin*, on the Russian mafia and was murdered in Moscow on July 6, 2004.[35] Anna Politkovskaya, an investigative reporter who wrote the book *Putin's Russia* about his autocracy, was shot to death in her apartment building's elevator on October 7, 2006, the president's fifty-fourth birthday.[36]

Three journalists, Orkhan Dzhemal, Aleksandr Rastorguev and Kiril Radchenko, were shot to death alongside a remote stretch of rural road in the Central African Republic on the night of July 30, 2018. They were murdered for investigating the Wagner Group, a secret paramilitary unit linked to the GU and Yevgeny Prigozhin, part of Putin's *siloviki* and among those indicted by Special Counsel Robert Mueller for attacking America's electoral system through his Internet Research Agency in 2016. Around 175 Wagner Group operatives were assisting the Central Africa Republic's government. The evidence that the Kremlin had authorized the murders was at once circumstantial and obvious. Russia's Foreign Ministry did not condemn the murders but instead rather absurdly implied that the journalists somehow caused their own deaths for visiting on tourist rather than journalist visas. State-controlled media focused on the journalists' investigation being funded by Investigation Control Center that was set up by Mikhail Khodorkovsky, the former billionaire and philanthropist who was imprisoned for a decade for violating tax and money laundering laws before being released and going into exile in Britain. This was Putin's latest brutal warning to journalists not to go too far, literally and figuratively.[37]

Russia has a vast intelligence and counter-intelligence system with many overlapping and competing organizations and functions.[38] Vladimir Lenin issued a decree establishing the secret police or "All Russian Extraordinary Commission for the Struggle against Counter-Revolution, Sabotage and Speculation," whose acronym was Cheka, on December 20, 1917. Since then the secret police have performed the same functions of spying at home and abroad even as they occasionally experienced name changes. The Cheka was renamed the Soviet Political Police or OGPU in 1922, the People's Commissariat of Internal Affairs or NKVD in 1934 and the KGB in 1954. Like any intelligence agency, the KGB set up numerous foreign front businesses and organizations through which it spied, recruited agents, laundered money and funded operations, political parties, revolutionary movements, criminal gangs and terrorist groups. Blackmail with kompromat or compromising recordings of illegal or immoral acts is a standard Russian intelligence community method. The KGB's most successful recruitments of Americans included CIA officer Aldrich Ames, who betrayed nine Russian agents, and FBI agent Robert Hanssen, who betrayed three Russian agents spying for the United States.

For its complicity in the aborted August 1990 coup, Yeltsin broke up the KGB into separate organizations including the Foreign Intelligence Service (SVR), the Federal Agency of Government Communications and Information (FAPSI) for electronic surveillance, the Ministry of Security for domestic surveillance, renamed the Federal Counter-intelligence Service (FSK) in 1995, and the Main Administration for the Protection of the Russian Federation (GUO), renamed the Federal Protective Service (FSO) in 1996. Gradually, by 2003, most of those organizations were re-united in the Federal Security Service (FSB) with the departments of Counter-intelligence, Military Counter-intelligence, Analysis and Strategic Planning, Protection of the Constitutional Order and Border Guard Protection.

FSB duties include not just counter-intelligence against foreigners but fighting organized crime, terrorism and drug smuggling. The FSB is criticized for being heavily involved in corruption, bribery, extortion and other organized crime activities, including murder. Then there is the Ministry of Security and Internal Affairs (MBVD), with 135,000 employees, that controls the police, militias and prisons, and spies on dissidents and terrorists.

Russia's largest foreign intelligence service is the armed services' Main Directorate (GU), renamed from the Main Intelligence Directorate (GRU) in 2010. The GU is the latest name for the army's military intelligence unit that was established in 1810. The GU may have six times more personnel than the SRV that is both its rival and partner. The GU is far more powerful in employees, missions and budget than the Pentagon's Defense Intelligence Agency (DIA) or the National Security Agency (NSA) since it includes the equivalent of both those American organizations. The GU conducted most of the hacking and trolling of America's 2016 election, with SVR a secondary player. Deputy Justice Secretary Robert Rosenstein issued indictments against a dozen GU officers in July 2018 although those were most readily identifiable leaders of hundreds involved in the operation. Wagner Group is a quasi-private paramilitary organization that works closely with the Kremlin and GU to promote Russian foreign policies. Among Wagner Group's directors is Yevgeny Prigozhin, among Putin's *Siloviki* and head of the Internet Research Agency troll factory that spearheaded the massive assault on America's electoral system during the 2016 election.[39]

The Foreign Intelligence Service (SVR) reports directly to the president, and has about 15,000 employees, of which around 500 are paramilitary forces. SVR is the CIA's closest Russian equivalent since both are civilian, use diplomatic cover or "official cover" (OCs) for most officers, use an array of non-official covers (NOCs) for many officers, and conduct espionage, counter-espionage and covert actions. SVR is at once GU's partner and rival.

Putin despises traitors and defectors and authorizes Russian assassins to hunt down and kill them.[40] In 2010 he publicly vented his rage when he was prime minister and learned that President Medvedev had agreed to swap a dozen Russian spies caught in America, for four Russians imprisoned for spying for Britain or America:

A person gives his whole life for his homeland and then some bastard comes along and betrays such people .... Whatever they got for those thirty pieces of silver they were given, they will choke on them .... They will have to hide their whole lives .... They live by their own rules, and these rules are well known by everyone in the intelligence services.[41]

Putin's assassins caught up to at least two turncoats with horrific results.

Alexander Litvinenko was a career KGB officer who defected to Britain in 2000 after serving nine months in prison for criticizing Yeltsin's regime for an array of crimes including assassinating opponents. In exile, he wrote two books critical of Putin's regime, *The Gang from Lubyanka* and *The Secret Plot to Bring Back KGB Terror*. He died on November 23,

2006, three agonizing weeks after a Russian assassin coated his bedside lamp's lightbulb with Plutonium-210 that activated with the heat.[42] Putin may have authorized the assassination after Litvinenko publicly insinuated that the Russian president was bisexual or gay. Before his death Litvinenko declared this to the man who ordered his murder:

> You may succeed in silencing men, but that silence comes at a price. You have shown yourself to be as barbaric and ruthless as your most hostile critics have claimed. You have shown you have no respect for life, liberty, or any civilized value .... You may succeed in silencing one man, but a howl of protest from around the world will reverberate, Mr Putin, in your ears for the rest of your life.[43]

Sergei Skripal worked for the GRU for fifteen years before becoming a double agent for MI6 in 1996.[44] In 2004 he was arrested, convicted of espionage and began a thirteen year sentence. In 2010 he was one of four imprisoned Russians who had spied for the West exchanged for ten Russian spies caught in America. The GRU is committed to murdering any defector, a policy it makes clear to its agents during their training when they are forced to watch a film in which a double agent is burned alive. The GRU was especially determined to murder Skripal who may have revealed the names of more than 300 GRU agents to MI6. On March 4, 2018 two GRU agents caught up to Skripal in Salisbury, England, and smeared the chemical Novichok on his home's doorknob. Skripal and his daughter Yulia nearly died and spent weeks under twenty-four-hour protection in the hospital before being released to a safe house elsewhere. Two Britons who handled the discarded Novichok container, a vial of Nina Ricci's Premier Jour perfume, also became contaminated and one of them died. Prime Minister Theresa May retaliated by expelling twenty-three Russian spies under diplomatic cover from Russia's London embassy.[45]

No country's armed forces are organized under a more diverse array of types and commands than those of Russia. The president is the commander-in-chief of all Russian troops and chairs the Security Council that directly commands the Internal Affairs Ministry, the Federal

Security Service (FSB) with its Border Troops, the National Guard, the Foreign Intelligence Service (SVR), the Federal Protective Service and the Civil Defense Forces. The Defense Ministry commands the army or Ground Forces, Aerospace Forces, Navy, Strategic Missile Force and Airborne Force. The Interior Ministry has authority over Logistical Support, Railway, Signal, and Construction troops. The military is organized into five regional Strategic Commands – Western, Northern, Southern, Central and Eastern; the Navy is split among five fleets with the Baltic under the Western Command, the Black and Caspian under the Southern, the Pacific under the Eastern, but the Northern Fleet its own Joint Command. The Russians conduct annual military exercises known as *Zapad* (Western front) and *Vostok* (Eastern front).

Russia's defense spending annually averages about 4 per cent of the economy. Although that burden is four times less than that borne by the Soviet Union, Moscow still struggles to pay for it. The economic sanctions imposed by Washington and Brussels after Russia's imperialism against Ukraine forced the Kremlin to cut its military budget. By one estimate the budget peaked in 2015 then declined through 2019.[46] Russia's military will never be better than the military-industrial complex that supplies its weapons and equipment. Russia's military-industrial complex has fallen further behind America's as it has failed to overcome problems of corruption, inefficiency, outdated design and manufacturing techniques, poorly trained workers, bloated bureaucracy and red tape.

Putin understands that a nation's military might can only be as great as its underlying economic might. That should be obvious, but hubris often blinds national leaders to that reality. Indeed, in 2006, Putin felt completed to remind his own National Security Council that "the level of military security depends directly on the pace of economic growth and technological development." He insisted that:

We must not repeat the mistakes of the Soviet Union, the mistakes of the Cold War era …. We must not solve the problem of military construction at the expense of the development of the economic and social spheres. This is a dead end that will only lead the country to waste its resources.[47]

Table 4.1 American and Russian Military Spending in Constant 2016 Billions of Dollars.[48]

	1992	1993	1994	1995	1996	1997	1998	1999	2000
America	521	494	466	439	415	413	403	404	420
Russia	40	35	33	22	20	22	13	15	20
	2001	2002	2003	2004	2005	2006	2007	2008	2009
America	423	475	541	590	618	628	644	692	747
Russia	22	24	25	26	30	33	36	40	42
	2010	2011	2012	2013	2014	2015	2016	2017	2018
America	768	758	715	659	618	603	600	597	609
Russia	43	46	53	55	59	64	69	55	66

Table 4.2 Comparison of American and Russian Military Spending as Economic Shares.[49]

	1992	1993	1994	1995	1996	1997	1998	1999	2000
America	4.7%	4.3%	3.9%	3.6%	3.4%	3.2%	3.0%	2.9%	2.9%
Russia	4.9%	4.6%	4.9%	4.1%	4.1%	4.3%	3.0%	3.3%	3.6%
	2001	2002	2003	2004	2005	2006	2007	2008	2009
America	2.9%	3.2%	3.6%	3.8%	3.8%	3.8%	3.8%	4.2%	4.6%
Russia	3.8%	4.1%	3.9%	3.5%	3.6%	3.5%	3.4%	3.3%	4.1%
	2010	2011	2012	2013	2014	2015	2016	2017	2018
America	4.7%	4.6%	4.2%	3.8%	3.5%	3.3%	3.2%	3.1%	
Russia	3.9%	3.5%	3.8%	3.9%	4.1%	4.9%	5.5%	4.3%	

Despite these disadvantages, Putin can still boast that Russia is powerful enough "to destroy America in half an hour or less".[50] He is deadly correct about that. And, of course, the reverse is also true. America's ability to destroy Russian since 1945 most likely has prevented a third world war. Around 93 per cent of all nuclear weapons are either in Russian or American hands. Russia has nine types of intercontinental ballistic missiles (ICBMs) and three types of submarine launched ballistic missiles (SLBMs) capable of destroying American cities within thirty minutes of launch. The most advanced Russian missile is the RT-2PM2 Topol-M (SS-27) which can be launched from land, air and sea sites and can evade counter-measures by changing its flight path. Thanks to a series of treaties, the number of nuclear weapons has dropped from the peak of 70,300 in 1986 to 14,485 in 2018. Yet, if Washington and Moscow emptied their arsenals at each other, they would not just mutually destroy themselves but most of the rest of humanity with the global economy's subsequent collapse and nuclear winter that would destroy crops and livestock worldwide.[51]

Table 4.3 World Nuclear Forces, 2018.[52]

	First Nuclear Test	Deployed Warheads	Stored Warheads	Other Warheads	Total
United States	1945	1,750	2,050	2,650	6,450
Russia	1949	1,600	2,750	2,500	6,850
Britain	1952	120	95		215
France	1960	280	10	10	300
China	1964		280		280
India	1974		130–140		130–140
Pakistan	1998		140–150		140–150
Israel			80		80
North Korea	2006			10–20	10–20
Total		3,750	5,555	5,160	14,465

Table 4.4 Comparison of Russian and American Nuclear Forces, 2018.[53]

	ICBMs	SLBMs	Bombers	Non-Strategic	Total
Russia	1,136	768	616	1,830	4,350
United States	800	1,920	880	200	3,800

As for conventional warfare, while Russia's military may have impressive numbers of personnel, weapons, and equipment, its land, air and sea forces suffer from poor training, morale, tactics and leadership. Despite Putin's military reform efforts, not much has changed in the decades since the Soviet Union collapsed. The Soviet Union's military forces were rigid command and control organizations. Anyone at any level who departed from an order and seized a tactical opportunity or thwarted a threat would more likely be shot than awarded. Unthinking obedience was constantly drilled into conscripts and officers alike. As for tactics, brute mass firepower and mass attacks prevailed. Under communist doctrine, soldiers were as expendable and interchangeable as workers, mere pawns to be sacrificed by the millions if need be on the altar of victory at any price. The doctrine of mass warfare demanded numbers of troops, tanks, trucks, aircraft and other machinery of war to be at least twice and ideally three times greater than that of the enemy. The Kremlin achieved those numbers with the Warsaw Pact's combined forces of the Soviet Union and the Eastern European satellite armies.

Table 4.5 Comparison of Key Russian and American Military Forces, 2018.[54]

	Russia	*America*
Total Population	142,257,519	326,625,791
Total Military Personnel	3,586,128	2,083,100
Active Personnel	1,013,628	1,281,900
Reserve Personnel	2,572,500	801,200
Total Aircraft	3,914	13,362
Fighter Aircraft	818	1,962
Attack Aircraft	1,416	2,830
Transports	1,524	5,248
Total Helicopters	1,451	5,758
Attack Helicopters	511	973
Tanks	20,300	5,884
Armored Fighting Vehicles	27,400	38,822
Total Navy Vessels	352	415
Aircraft Carriers	1	20
Submarines	62	66

The Soviet doctrine of mass numbers and firepower worked in the Russian Civil War and the Second World War, but failed in Afghanistan. Mercifully, that doctrine was not tested against NATO. Had the Third World War erupted, whether the Warsaw Pact would have overrun NATO is unknowable. The Soviet empire's collapse rendered that doctrine obsolete. The Russian army that emerged was numerically far inferior to NATO. Obviously, the need now was to emphasize the quality of troops and encourage tactical initiative at all levels. Yet most of Russia's high command clung to the doctrine that had been drummed into them through their careers.

That began to change with NATO's 1999 air campaign against Serbia. After seventy-eight days of systemic precision bombing that destroyed Serbia's military and economic infrastructure, President Slobodan Milosevic yielded to all of NATO's demands. During that offensive the Serbs, armed with Russian air defense weapons, shot down only two NATO planes and the pilots were rescued. NATO won decisively without any ground combat.

Debates arose within Russia's military command over how to adopt that strategy and tactics. That debate accelerated after the American campaigns in Afghanistan in 2001 and Iraq in 2003 that swiftly destroyed the Taliban and Saddam regimes and overran those countries. Then came the increasingly prominent role of drones and satellites in tracking and killing enemy Jihadist leaders. The debate expanded to how to master drone technology and tactics. On March 1, 2011 American special forces with real-time satellite-born information flew in stealth Black Hawk helicopters from their Afghanistan base to Abbottabad, Pakistan, landed in a walled compound, entered the building, killed Osama bin Laden and four others and flew away with his body without suffering any casualties. Now Russian commanders mulled how their own Special Forces (Spetsnatz) could adopt innovative technologies and tactics.[55]

An obsolete doctrine is one of many problems plaguing Russia's military. Each branch, especially the army, suffers from poor quality recruits, inadequate training and equipment, abysmal and often delayed pay, wretched housing, and so dismal morale. Indeed, each year the bullying of recruits and harsh conditions for nearly all soldiers provokes several hundred to kill themselves. During the two wars in Chechyna many Russian soldiers sold arms through the black market to their enemies. From a lack of fuel and spare parts, air force pilots annually fly only dozens rather than hundreds of hours. The navy's ships mostly rust at anchor in various ports. The *Kursk's* sinking was emblematic of the submarine fleet whose sailors deride them as underwater steel coffins.[56]

An analogy personified these challenges facing the Kremlin. Somehow, Russia's military had to be transformed from an obese Sumo wrestler who, through sheer bulk shoved his opponent out of the ring, into a lean judo master who rolled with his opponent's attacks and ended up on top. With his black belt in judo, Putin understood that analogy and was committed to realizing it. He took the first step toward reform in March 2001 when he appointed his friend Sergei Ivanov, an SVR general, as defense minister. But Ivanov made little progress against the entrenched traditionalists.

Putin initiated a major overhaul of the armed forces in 2009 that, by 2012, cut the number of personnel from around 1,200,000 to 800,000; cut the number of officer training schools from sixty-five to ten; made brigades rather than divisions the key army formations; made air bases rather than regiments the key air force unit; had volunteers surpass conscripts in number; had conscripts serve one rather than two years; abolished all draft exemptions except for college students; and raised pay and granted citizenship to foreign recruits after three years of service.

Putin's decisive reform was to replace "mass" with "hybrid" warfare, also known as "new type," "new generation," "asymmetrical," "sixth generation," "network-centric," and, in America, the "Revolution in Military Affairs" (RMA).[57] Ideally, Russia conducts hybrid wars without declaring or even acknowledging them and wins them without firing any shots or killing anyone. The end remains the same, destroying the enemy's will to resist. The means are virtual rather than physical attacks in which cyber-trolls rather than armored divisions spearhead offensives designed to exacerbate existing ethnic, racial, class, ideological and religious divisions in the enemy country and thus provoke groups to fight each other and the government. The worse the disunity and violence, the more likely that government will yield to Moscow's demands. The side wins that asserts misinformation superiority over the other. Then men in suits armed with lots of petrodollars rather than uniformed men with Kalashnikovs occupy the defeated country and forge joint ventures with business corporations in which Russian investors have commanding shares.

Of course, disinformation alone will not defeat every adversary. Some wars will still require killing people and systematically destroying the enemy's military-industrial complex weakened by cyber-attacks. And that will best be achieved by unleashing cutting-edge weapons like drones, precision-guided munitions and robotics guided by quantum computers and satellites. In the air stealth unmanned aircraft will replace manned aircraft. At sea stealth submarines will replace surface ships. Boots on the ground initially are Special Forces that seize key elements of the enemy's infrastructure; only after the enemy is devastated might large numbers of troops and tanks race in to inflict the *coup de grâce*. And, of course, Russia's hybrid defensive forces must be as formidable as its offensive forces. Russia's National Defense Management Center is in charge of the military dimension of hybrid warfare. Hybrid warfare is promoted through think-tanks like the Military Academy and Center for Military Strategic Studies, and journals like *Military Thought*. Leading thinkers include Generals Valery Gerasimov, Alexander Burutin, Vladimir Slipchenko and Vladimir Kruglov and academic Andrei Kokoshin.

Hybrid warfare is not new, but is a cyber version of the political warfare that prevailed during the Cold War. George Kennan's 1946 "Long Telegram" was arguably the most consequential foreign policy analysis in American history. Kennan explained the ends and means of Soviet foreign policy, then proposed what became known as the "containment strategy" to counter it. His insights are as valid today as they were then. For instance, the Kremlin's propaganda warfare was designed:

> to undermine [the] political and strategic potential of major Western powers ... to disrupt national self-confidence ... to increase social and industrial unrest, to stimulate all forms of disunity. All persons with grievances, whether economic or racial, will be urged to seek redress, not in mediation and compromise, but in defiant, violent struggle. Everything possible will be done to set major countries against each other. Anti-British talk will be plugged among Americans, anti-American talk among British ... Germans will be taught to abhor both Anglo-Saxon powers. Where suspicions exist, they will be fanned; where not, ignited.[58]

To those ends and means, the Kremlin sought to master all mass communication channels. Radio Moscow was founded in 1929 and at its peak broadcast propaganda in seventy languages around the world. The *Sovinform* Agency, renamed *Novsti*, published sixty newspapers, magazines and journals. Today, the Kremlin's Federal News Agency and Sputnik News Agency spew streams of propaganda-laden articles that find their way into newspapers around the world. Moscow still has plenty of foreign media fronts, most notoriously Britain's *Morning Star*, France's *L'Humanité* and Italy's *Il Manifesto*. The Kremlin's most blatant propaganda cable television corporation with global reach is RT, once called Russia Today, founded in 2005. RT has a $300 million budget, more than 500 employees, and bureaux in New York, London, Brussels and Jerusalem dedicated to propagating fake news and conspiracy theories twenty-four hours a day, seven days a week. Like Fox News that its producers emulate, RT does so under the guise of "balanced, professional reporting". RT has a "Top Ten List of Russophobes" with Senator John McCain number one and the recipient of a "lifetime achievement award for services to Russophobia". Although McCain did not pick up his award, he proudly bore it until his death.[59] Given its focus on exposing western secrets while avoiding doing the same for Moscow's secrets, WikiLeaks appears to be another Russian propaganda organization; Julian Assange launched it in October 2006. In 2012, RT began broadcasting a show hosted by Assange that revealed WikiLeaks secrets. These days the Kremlin's most powerful propaganda flows through hundreds of thousands of social media sites like YouTube, Facebook, Twitter and Instagram. Subverting liberal democracies through social media is extremely cost-effective. For instance, the Russian cyber-trolls paid only $6,000 for posting on Facebook the inflammatory "Independence or Patriotism" that was seen 529,205 times.[60] Propaganda works to the degree it is believed. For that propaganda must be believable. The Kremlin has not just mastered propaganda's conduits but its contents.

Chapter 5

Putin's Assertion of Power

In 2008 I was Russia's number one politician. I could have gotten re-elected, but the Constitution didn't allow it. I played by the rules and handed power to you. But we agreed that when the day came, we'd sit down and decide what to do next. And now that day has come.

(Vladimir Putin)

We, Russia and Ukraine, have always been united and our future lies in this unity.

(Vladimir Putin)

Vladimir Putin is highly popular among Russians for many reasons, but perhaps the most vital is that his policies transformed most people's lives from a vicious cycle of worsening poverty into a virtuous cycle of increasing prosperity.[1] He was lucky to take power as Russia emerged from its economic collapse during the transition from a command to a crony economy. If 1992 is 100 per cent, the economy bottomed out in 1994 at 87.3 per cent then rose to 109 per cent in 2000. The 1992 budget deficit was minus 25.6 per cent of the economy but was 1.9 per cent in surplus in 2000. Oil prices reached a nadir of $12 a barrel in 2000 then rose steadily in two stages, one after the terrorist attacks on September 11, 2001 and the other after the American invasion of Iraq on March 19, 2003. By the summer of 2008 an oil barrel was worth nearly $150. Putin ensured that Russia made the most of that windfall. When he became president Russia owed $133 billion to foreigners and had only $8.5 billion of financial reserves. By 2007 Putin's policies and rising oil prices had combined to reduce Russia's foreign debt to $37 billion while its foreign reserves skyrocketed to $600 billion. From 1999 to 2008 Russia expanded from the twenty-third to the ninth largest economy with annual growth rates averaging 6 per cent.[2]

Table 5.1 Russia's Economy under Putin, 1999 to 2018.[3]

	Gross Domestic Product Change from Previous Year	Purchasing Power Parity	Inflation Rate
1999	6.4	$1,330	36.5
2000	10.0	$1,771	20.2
2001	5.1	$2,100	18.6
2002	4.7	$2,375	14.0
2003	7.3	$2,975	12.0
2004	7.1	$4,102	11.7
2005	6.4	$5,323	10.9
2006	6.9	$6,920	9.0
2007	7.6	$9,101	11.9
2008	5.2	$11,635	17.9
2009	-7.8	$8,562	1.9
2010	4.5	$10,674	14.1
2011	5.2	$14,351	23.6
2012	3.6	$15,434	9.0
2013	1.7	$16,007	5.4
2014	0.7	$14,125	7.5
2015	-2.8	$9,329	8.3
2016	-0.2	$8,748	3.5
2017	1.5	$10,743	5.2
2018	1.7	n.a.	n.a.

Putin's key economic reform transformed the tax system. When he took power:

> the tax code consisted of nearly two hundred different taxes, augmented by twelve hundred presidential decrees and government orders; three thousand legislative acts; and four thousand regulatory acts and instructions from ministries and agencies. In addition, regional governments added more than a hundred of their own additional taxes to the system.[4]

Tax evasion by households and businesses was chronic. Designed by Finance Minister Aleksei Kudrin, the new tax code eliminated that

Gordian knot in January 2002 by setting income taxes at a flat 13 per cent, Europe's lowest, social welfare at 5 per cent for households and 2 per cent on wages, and lowering corporate taxes from 35 per cent to 24 per cent. Audits of suspicious accounts became routine rather than sporadic. In 2001 authorities audited 440,000 companies and 311,000 individuals and gleaned another 52 billion rubles in revenues. Although the tax burden fell from 35 per cent to 31 per cent of the economy, the state began running budget surpluses.[5] The Kremlin reinvested that surplus by refurbishing infrastructure or paying down the debt and stabilizing financial markets that in turn stimulated more growth and thus revenues, and so on. The economy received a further boost when the government removed most remaining restrictions on buying and selling private property freely.

Another critical reform targeted the pension system. A vast and growing state burden is the retired population. Men can retire when they are sixty, women when they are fifty-five; workers in hazardous occupations can retire even earlier. The hyperinflation of the 1990s devastated retiree savings while the pension system faced bankruptcy. The ratio of payers to retirees plummeted from 2.1 to 1 in 1992 to 1.4 to 1 in 1997. Only one of four businesses paid their share. German Gref, the Strategic Research Center's director, spearheaded the pension reform policy that forced contributors to pay what they owed which the government promptly transferred to retirees.[6]

Gref also pushed through laws that reformed the banking system by strengthening the Central Bank's power to adjust reserve requirements and interest rates, and to revoke the licenses of banks with shady practices. During the 2000s the number of banks fell by half while twice as many offered mortgages. Tighter monetary policy also caused inflation and capital flight to drop and enticed more foreign investment in Russia. Gold and foreign exchange reserves soared.

Putin's reforms may have improved the lives of most people but Russia's economy has changed little. Russia remains a petro-state with oil and gas accounting for more than half of exports, while natural resources of all kinds are around 80 per cent of exports. In exchange, Russia imports consumer goods and machinery for exploiting natural resources. Being a petro-state is both a curse and blessing as Russia's economic and thus political power varies with the roller-coaster of oil and natural gas prices. Like most other petro-states, Russia has not just failed to invest its profits in other industries to diversify its economy but has neglected its oil and gas industry that has fallen ever more behind most of its rivals technologically. Many oil and gas fields are remote, deep, diminishing and thus increasingly expensive to tap and transport. Other minerals like gold, chrome and coal suffer similar challenges of extraction and transport. The reason for the failure to reinvest profits is simple – the oligarchs divert profits to their own hidden bank accounts.

Table 5.2 Comparison of Russian and American Petroleum Industries, 2018.[7]

	Russia	*America*
Oil Production	10,550,000 barrels daily	8,853,000 barrels daily
Oil Consumption	3,320,000 barrels daily	19,000,000 barrels daily
Proven Reserves	80,000,000,000 barrels	36,520,000,000 barrels

Nonetheless, oil and gas exports are the Kremlin's greatest source of hard power and Putin plays that for all its worth. Russia's expanding web of oil producers and natural gas pipelines empower the Kremlin to the degree of a foreign country's dependence on it. The Kremlin has not hesitated at times to raise or lower prices or cut off supplies to force countries like Ukraine or Georgia to yield to its demands. As Russia's largest corporation, Gazprom spearheads the Kremlin's assertion of petro-state power. Gazprom accounts for about 11 per cent of global gas exports and 17 per cent of global reserves. The government owns 51 per cent of Gazprom. After Putin took power, he fired Gazprom's chairman, Viktor Chernomyrdin, and replaced him with Dmitri Medvedev, his right-hand man, and planted cronies in most of the eighteen other board seats. Medvedev chaired Gazprom from 2000 until he became Russia's president in 2008; Aleksei Miller has chaired Gazprom since then. All along Gazprom expanded by buying other energy companies, including Yukos, financed by loans from Dresdner Bank. Putin and his coterie have milked Gazprom for billions of dollars. The financial magazine *Barron's* named Gazprom "the worst managed company on the planet" in 2014.[8] Nonetheless, Putin wields Gazprom like a geopolitical club to bully energy dependent customers into following Kremlin policies. He boasted that Gazprom "is a powerful political and economic lever of influence over the rest of the world".[9]

Those Russians whose lives Putin's economic policies and patriotic sentiments improved expressed their gratitude in the December 2003 Duma election when Putin's United Russia Party won 223 of 450 seats. Independents captured 76 seats, down from 106 in the 1999 election. By buying the votes of independents or getting support from the centrist Motherland Party, United Russia could enact into law its entire agenda. No party had ever garnered that much power in the decade after the 1993 constitution was implemented. United Russia's gains were mostly at the expense of the radical Communists and Liberal Democrats. Yabloko, the liberal party, picked up only four seats.

Table 5.3 Top Five Parties in the December 2003 Duma Election.[10]

	Party List		*Single Member*	*Total*
	Percentage	*Seats*		
United Russia	37.57	120	103	223
Communist	12.61	40	12	52
Liberal Democrats	11.45	36	0	36
Motherland	9.02	29	8	37
Yabloko	4.30	0	4	4

Putin was so confident of being re-elected for the 2004 presidential election that he "ran no campaign ads, held no rallies, and offered no clear proposals for a second term except to continue to be the living embodiment of Russia's stability."[11] As in 2000 he refused to debate his rivals. He had the debate scheduled for 8 o'clock in the morning to ensure a small audience. With his command of television, he simply had his twenty-nine-minute speech announcing that he would run for re-election repeatedly broadcasted.

Putin's popularity was so great that no one important dared run against him for fear of being humiliated. Grigory Yavlinsky, Gennady Zyuganov and Vladimir Zhirinovsky, the respective heads of the Yabloko, Communist and Liberal Democratic parties, got underlings to run as sacrificial lambs. By now Putin's repressive measures had intimidated most prominent dissidents within Russia. However, five exiled Russians – Boris Berezovsky, Elena Bonner, Vladimir Bukovsky, Ruslan Khasbulatov and Ivan Rybkin – dared to take out a full-page article in the *New York Times* entitled "Seven Questions to President George Bush about his Friend Vladimir Putin".[12] Berezovsky underwrote a campaign by Ivan Rybkin, a Yeltsin advisor and Duma speaker. Then, bizarrely, when Rybkin was in Kiev, he was drugged, kidnapped, filmed having sex with men, then released four days later.

Not surprisingly, Putin won a decisive victory on March 14, 2004 with 71.31 per cent of the vote, while the nearest rival, Communist Nikolai Kharitonov attracted only 13.69 per cent. Indeed, in some regions the support for Putin achieved Soviet style unanimity especially among Muslims with 92 per cent in Chechnya, 94 per cent in Dagestan, 96 per cent in Kabardino-Balkaria and 98 per cent in Ingushetia.[13]

Terrorism was an issue in the 2004 presidential campaign.[14] A year and a half before on October 23, 2002, forty-one Chechen terrorists led by Movsar Barayev invaded a theater packed with 912 people in Moscow. The terrorists demanded that Russia withdraw from Chechnya or else they would kill all the hostages. Putin allowed three days of negotiations as he ringed the theater with counter-terrorist units. Before dawn on the fourth, the commandos pumped an odorless knock-out gas into the theater and then stormed inside. Although the gas subdued the terrorists, it also killed many of the hostages who choked to death on their vomit. More hostages died as nervous commandos opened fire. In all 129 hostages either died from the terrorists or the rescuers. The commandos did kill all the terrorists. Memories of those horrors were fading when, on February 16, 2004, a suicide bomber murdered forty-one people and wounded more than 200 outside a Moscow subway station. That latest horror may have boosted votes for Putin as his tough but calm reaction reassured most Russians. Tragically, the attacks continued.

The year's most consequential terrorist attack took place on May 9, 2004 during a Victory Day celebration in Grozny, Chechnya's capital. The bomb killed Chechen President Akhmad Kadyrov and twelve others. Kadyrov had been a rebel leader during the 1990s before 1999, when he accepted Putin's offer to become Chechnya's president if he swore allegiance to Russia. Putin selected his eldest son, Ramzan Kadyrov, to take his father's place. There was a catch. Kadyrov would have to wait three years until he turned thirty and became eligible to be president. In the interim Putin made him deputy prime minister, then prime minister. Putin would later extoll Ramzan for fulfilling all his hopes:

> Ramzan gets things done. I honestly didn't expect him to be so hands on. I was in Grozny ... I was walking among the ruins and thinking: 'When can it be rebuilt? Can it be rebuilt at all?' Ramzan took charge and got it done.

Later Putin described Ramzan as "like a son to me".[15]

"Black Widows" are Chechen women who become terrorists to avenge their husbands who were killed in the civil war. On August 24, 2004 two Black Widows with bombs strapped to their bodies somehow got through Moscow's Domodedovo Airport security and boarded separate planes. Shortly after take off, each detonated her bomb which destroyed the aircraft, murdering all ninety people abroad one flight and all forty-six aboard the other. Then, on August 31, another Black Widow killed nine people and wounded fifty others when she blew himself up at a Moscow metro station.

Thirty-one Chechen terrorists overran a school in Beslan, North Ossetia, on September 1, 2004 and declared that they would murder all 1,020 hostages unless the Kremlin withdrew its troops from Chechyna and recognized its independence. To prove their point, the terrorists began executing men and dumping them from windows. Then they released twenty-six hostages, eleven women and fifteen babies. Putin refused to negotiate and ringed the school with police and Special Forces. On the stand-off's third day, two explosions erupted in the school and the roof caught fire. Some hostages tried to escape but were killed as police opened fire. Special Forces charged in, firing indiscriminately. The death toll was 334 hostages, including 186 children, ten Special Forces and thirty terrorists; one terrorist was captured, and then later tried and executed. Chechen military leader Samil Beslan announced that he had planned the attack and warned that Russians could expect more unless they granted Chechnya independence.

That evening Putin addressed Russia on television to explain that "a horrible tragedy happened in our land." He tried to diminish that horror by recalling the "many tragic pages and difficult trials in the history of Russia." He then blamed the attack on

> the disintegration of a huge, great country ... we managed to preserve the nucleus of that giant, the Soviet Union. We called the new country the Russian Federation. We all expected changes, changes for the better, but found ourselves absolutely unprepared for much that changed in our lives ... We live in conditions of aggravated internal conflicts and ethnic conflicts that before were harshly repressed by the governing ideology. We stopped paying due attention to the issues of defense and security. We allowed corruption to affect the judiciary and law enforcement systems.[16]

If so, the only obvious path to alleviate these worsening problems was a more powerful government.

Putin revealed what he had in mind ten days later when he decreed that henceforth the nation's mayors, governors and presidents of regions and republics would be appointed rather than elected. He eliminated the 225 seats of the Duma's 450 that were elected from districts. Later, before a group of foreign correspondents, Putin justified his actions because "the Russian people are backward. They cannot adapt to democracy as they have done in your countries."[17] As Putin implemented these latest authoritarian measures for Russia, he was also undermining democracy in a neighboring country.

With 50 million people, Ukraine is the second most populous former Soviet colony after Russia; no former Soviet colony has suffered more from the Kremlin.[18] Russia colonized Ukraine during the eighteenth century and began the process of ethnic cleansing to transform Ukrainians into Russians. That policy converted a portion of the population but provoked most Ukrainians into proudly retaining their identity. Ukrainian nationalists asserted what became a fleeting independence during the Russian Revolution in 1918 when they declared the People's Republic of Ukraine. Tragically, in 1920, the Red Army invaded, conquered and transformed Ukraine into the Ukrainian Soviet Socialist Republic. Stalin was determined to destroy Ukraine's identity and economic autonomy.

Perhaps as many as five million Ukrainians died from murder or starvation when the Kremlin nationalized all property and collectivized agriculture during the 1930s. Schools forced children to speak Russian rather than Ukrainian.

Conditions in Ukraine and elsewhere across the Soviet Union slowly improved after Stalin's death in 1953. On February 19, 1954 Premier Nikita Khrushchev decreed that Crimea would join Ukraine. He did so to curry the Ukrainian Communist Party's support for him as Soviet premier. The trouble was that historically Ukrainians had never populated Crimea. When the Russians conquered Crimea in 1783 they took it from Cossacks and Turks.

Ukrainians finally achieved independence with the Soviet Union's collapse in December 1991 and have struggled to retain their freedom ever since. President Leonid Kravchuk resisted Kremlin pressure for an economic and military alliance through the Commonwealth of Independent States. The Kremlin tried to bend Kiev to its will by cutting back gas and oil supplies and raising prices from 1992 to 1994, but Kravchuk still refused to yield.

When Ukrainians declared independence, they still had nuclear weapons, 800,000 Soviet troops on their territory and a Soviet fleet at Sevastopol in Crimea. Under a Trilateral Statement signed among Presidents Bill Clinton, Boris Yeltsin and Leonid Kravchuk on January 14, 1994 Ukraine agreed to transfer its nuclear weapons to Russia, which would dismantle them, and sign the Treaty on Non-Proliferation of Nuclear Weapons (NPT). As for the troops, the non-Ukrainian conscripts and non-commissioned officers could return to their home countries while officers could either go home or remain in the Ukrainian army after pledging allegiance to Ukraine. On December 5, 1994, by signing at Budapest the Memorial on Security Assurances, envoys of America, Britain, Russia, Ukraine, Belarus and Kazakhstan agreed to respect existing borders.

Ukraine was a highly illiberal democracy with rampant corruption and incompetence. Yet, there were independent newspapers and one independent television station, Channel 5, owned by billionaire chocolate mogul Petro Poroshenko. Journalists, however, told the truth at their peril. Georgy Gongadze was kidnapped, beheaded and dumped in a forest after he wrote a series of exposés on government corruption and incompetence in 2000. With financial and political backing from Moscow, Leonid Kuchma won the presidential election of 1994. Under Kuchma, Ukraine became increasingly corrupt. Kuchma won re-election with 57 per cent of the vote in 1999. In 1997 Yeltsin and Kuchma agreed to split the warships into separate national navies; the Russian fleet and 25,000 troops could remain at leased facilities at Sevastopol for twenty years.

Putin was determined to bend Ukraine to his will. From December 1999 to February 2000 Russia cut back its oil and gas exports to Ukraine. The price for resuming those exports and writing off a portion of the debt that Kiev owed Moscow was for Ukraine to give Russian oil and gas corporations commanding shares in Ukraine's equivalent corporations. Kuchma grudgingly agreed. As a result, the Russians control Ukraine's oil and gas infrastructure including refineries, pipelines, electricity plants and marketing. Russian corporations own huge shares of Ukraine's other industries, including banking, petrochemicals, and steel.

During a summit with Kuchma in Kiev in July 2004 Putin insisted that Ukraine reject any invitation from NATO to join. Putin and Kuchma established a new company called RosUkrEnergo with Gazprom and Raiffeisen International, an Austrian bank, each owning half; RosUkrEnergo would supply Ukraine with natural gas.

Like Russia, Ukraine also had a presidential election scheduled for 2004. Unlike that year's Russian election, Ukraine's future president could not be easily predicted for October 31, 2004. Kuchma decided not to run for re-election, opening the way for his ambitious prime minister. Viktor Yanukovych was from Donetsk in prominently Russia-speaking eastern Ukraine. Determined that Yanukovych would win the election, Putin nominated Dmitri Medvedev to lead that operation. Medvedev channeled around $600 million in campaign contributions to Yanukovych from Russian oligarchs, especially Gazprom and other energy corporations. This was an amount equal to 1 per cent of Ukraine's GDP.[19]

The liberal candidate was Viktor Yushchenko, who had established Ukraine's new currency, the *hyrvna*, when he worked at the Central Bank. He was an effective reform prime minister from 1999 to 2001, having rescheduled Ukraine's debt payments, cut middle-class taxes, enforced tax collection from the rich and called for Ukraine's membership in NATO and the European Union. He was married to a beautiful Ukrainian-American woman and allied with Yulia Tymoshenko, a beautiful and brilliant businesswoman who controlled an energy corporation. Tymoshenko generously funded his political movement, which adopted the color orange. Channel 5, the independent television station, endorsed Yushchenko. All of this placed him in the Kremlin's crosshairs.[20]

Yushchenko should have been wary of dining with General Ihor Smeshko, who headed Ukraine's Security Service of (SBU), and his deputy, Volodymyr Satsyuk on September 5. The next day he became violently sick with thousands of cysts erupting across his body and face. He was flown to Vienna for treatment. The doctors discovered that he had been poisoned with 8-Tetrachlorodibenzo-p-dioxin. They were able to save his life, but the poison grossly disfigured him. Yushchenko returned to Kiev on September 21 and resumed his campaign.

Putin repeatedly called on Ukrainians to vote for Yanukovych. He invited Kuchma and Yanukovych to his birthday party in Moscow on October 9, flew to Kiev to meet with Kuchma and Yanukovych on October 28, then stayed until election day on October 31. The three would not celebrate victory.

Yushchenko edged out Yanukovych with 39.87 per cent to 39.32 per cent of the vote while a score of other candidates split the rest. Rumors of government ballot stuffing to favor Yanukovych provoked mass protests by Yushchenko supporters. That did not deter Kuchma's operatives from even more outrageous vote rigging in the run-off election on November 21. The official total gave Yanukovych 49.5 per cent and Yushchenko 46.9 per cent. Two hundred thousand protesters packed Independence Square (*Maidan Nezalezhnostri*) to condemn the cheating and demand a new election. Yanukovych flew to Severodonetsk where a congress of pro-Russian leaders threatened to secede if Yushchenko took power. On November 27 a majority in Ukraine's parliament (*Rada*) voted for a resolution that condemned the election result. On December 3 the Supreme Court ruled that the election was fraudulent and called for a third election on December 26.

During this final election on December 26 Yushchenko decisively won with 51.99 per cent of the vote to Yanukovych's 44.20 per cent.

Yushchenko was inaugurated as president on January 23, 2005. The next day parliament unanimously voted by 373 to 0 for Tymoshenko as prime minister.

That democratic triumph became known as the Orange Revolution. Unfortunately, the initial elation among most Ukrainians steadily diminished as Yushchenko's government failed to develop the economy and diminish dependence on Russia. Yushchenko initiated talks with the European Union and NATO over Ukraine's future membership. Putin retaliated in late 2005 by having Gazprom raise the natural gas price to Ukraine from $50 to $160 per thousand cubic metres. When Yushchenko protested Putin informed him that the price would drop if Ukraine spurned the West and instead embraced Moscow. Yushchenko had the pipelines that ran through Ukraine tapped to serve his country's needs while reducing supplies for Austria, Slovenia, Italy, France, Moldova, Poland, Romania, Hungary and Slovakia. That provoked those countries to protest about Putin's bullying. Putin replied by raising the stakes. On January 1, 2006 Gazprom cut off shipments and demanded $230 per thousand cubic metres. Three days of intense negotiations between Kiev and Moscow led to a resumption of shipments for $95 per thousand cubic metres for a year subject to higher prices later in 2006. Kiev tried to lessen its energy dependence on Russia by building the Baku-Tbilisi-Ceyhan oil pipeline that pumps Caspian Sea region oil to Turkey's port of Ceyhan and then to Ukraine. Prime Minister Tymoshenko flew to Moscow for direct talks with Putin in October 2006. Putin gave Tymoshenko a stark choice: pay $230 per thousand cubic metres and develop closer ties with the West, or pay $130 and have its debt to Gazprom cut from $2.1 billion to $1.52 billion in return for renouncing any future EU and NATO membership and renewing Russia's lease for its naval base at Sevastopol. Tymoshenko tentatively agreed to shelve closer ties with the West.

Then Ukraine was walloped by the 2008 great recession when the economy plunged 15 per cent as bankruptcies, joblessness and desperation soared. To revive its economy Kiev borrowed heavily from the European Union in return for promises of reforms that could lead to membership. Once again Putin replied by threatening to impose higher costs and ultimately shut off shipments if Kiev did not reject the West. Ukraine's deep recession persisted through 2009 exacerbated by Russia's imposition of $300 per thousand cubic metres for gas. The next presidential election was scheduled for February 2010. Putin hoped that Ukrainians would be so disgruntled that they would reject pro-Western Viktor Yushchenko and embrace pro-Moscow candidate Viktor Vanukovych. Putin would get his wish.

Putin also got his wish for the results of the Duma election on December 2, 2007 when his United Russia won a resounding victory, garnering 64.30 per cent of the vote and 315 of the 450 seats, up from 223 seats. Once again, the next two largest opposition parties, the Communist and Liberal Democratic, with combined 20 per cent of the vote were both authoritarian. Only the A Just Russia Party espoused liberal principles and received a mere 7 per cent of the votes. The liberal Yabloko or Apple Party lost all its seats and was an outsider for the first time since its founding in 1993. This was the first Duma election since Putin abolished single-member districts. That made all candidates dependent on their place on the party list, which strengthened party leaders and thus strengthened Putin's power over them.

Table 5.4 Top Four Parties in the December 2007 Duma Election.[21]

	Share of Votes	*Share of Seats*
United Russia	64.30	315
Communist	11.57	57
Liberal Democratic	8.14	40
A Just Russia	7.74	38
		450

After consulting with key United Russia leaders, Putin choose Dmitri Medvedev to replace Viktor Zubkov as prime minister. Medvedev was then forty-three years old and, like Putin, a St Petersburg native. He earned a doctorate in jurisprudence and taught at Leningrad University before Putin selected him to be one of his advisors. Putin valued Medvedev for his integrity, moderation, intelligence and loyalty. A bonus was that Medvedev was as short as Putin, although he lacked his mentor's physical toughness and confidence. Putin entrusted Medvedev with a series of increasingly important posts, including deputy chief of staff, chief legal advisor, management committee's deputy chair, Gazprom Export's director general, prime minister and, finally, president.[22]

The Constitution prevented Putin from serving a third consecutive term so he cut a deal with Medvedev. After winning the presidency in 2008, Medvedev would appoint Putin as prime minister. They would collaborate for four years with the key task amending the 1993 Constitution to let Putin run in 2012. Putin announced his endorsement of Medvedev to replace him during the United Russia convention on December 10, 2007.

During the 2008 election campaign, Medvedev refused to debate with his key rivals, Gennady Zyuganov and Vladimir Zhirinovsky, the respective candidates of the Communist Party and Liberal Democratic Party, and Andrei Bogdanov, an independent liberal candidate. Medvedev got 71.2 per cent of the vote, with his closest rival Zyuganov getting only 18 per cent.

Medvedev was inaugurated as president on April 11, 2008. Over the next four years few people were fooled over who the real president was. Inevitably, Medvedev became the butt of jokes. Russians lampooned him for spending four years keeping the presidential chair warm for Putin or playing Robin to Putin's Batman or being Putin's "Mini-me". Among other powers and duties, Putin retained the critical role of managing the oligarchs.

Switching places with Medvedev was not Putin's only significant change in 2008. He and Lyudmila secretly divorced in February. The marriage had been dead for years but recently he had fallen in love with Alina Kabayeva, a beautiful gymnast who had won a bronze medal at the 2000 Sydney Olympics and a gold medal at the 2004 Athens Olympics before entering politics and being elected to the Duma.

Over the next four years, President Medvedev rhetorically tried to reassure the world that he was dedicated to a kinder, gentler Russian foreign policy, co-operative and mutually beneficial rather than aggressive and exploitive. After he took office he expressed his vision with these foreign ministry policy goals:

Creating favorable conditions for the modernization of Russia, transformation of its economy through innovation, enhancement of living standards, consolidation of society, strengthening of the foundation of the constitutional system rule of law and democratic institutions, realization of human rights and freedoms and, as a consequence, ensuring national competitiveness in a globalizing world.

A 2011 report of the Institute for Contemporary Development that Medvedev chaired expressed a version of his vision:

A country's greatness is above all determined by what it can offer the world and the extent of its attractiveness to foreign partners. Russia's basic position as a state with significant natural resources hardly exhausts our role in the world. International influence is above all a function of [a state's] internal condition .... Russia can exist as an active world power while taking renovative politics [at home]. But it should not be active merely for the sake of external effect, divorced from consideration for ... the domestic potential of its foreign policy.[23]

But all along Medvedev was bound by Putin's contrary Russian foreign policy ends and means. Thus, time after time, Medvedev had to violate his own principles and good will.

Just a few months into his presidency, Medvedev found himself in a worsening crisis that resulted in a war against Georgia.[24] Georgia is a small, poor country whose 5 million people averaged $10,600 in purchasing power parity in 2017. The largest ethnic groups are Georgians with 87.6 per cent followed by Azeris with 6.3 per cent, Armenians with 3.9 per cent and Russians with 1.2 per cent. As for religion, 83.4 per cent are Orthodox Christians and 10.7 per cent are Muslims.[25]

Georgia is among the oldest Christian countries, having converted in the 330s and retained that faith despite being conquered by Persians, Arabs, Mongols and Turks. Russia took over eastern Georgia in 1783 and western Georgia in 1810. Amidst the chaos and violence of Russia's communist revolution, Georgia declared independence on May 26, 1918. Tragically, that freedom was fleeting. The Red Army conquered Georgia along with

Armenia and Azerbaijan in 1921 and eventually incorporated them into the Soviet Union. Seventy years later, amidst the democratic revolution that demolished the Soviet Union, Georgia declared independence on April 9, 1991. After several years of political turmoil, Eduard Shevardnadze, a former Soviet foreign minister, was elected president in 1994. As in Russia, Georgia's transformation from communism towards democracy was beset by massive corruption, incompetence, worsening poverty and the rise of a super-rich set of oligarchs who bought privatized industries and companies at fire-sale prices.

A rigged parliamentary election in November 2003 provoked mass protests. When Shevardnadze tried to convene parliament on November 22, opposition leader Mikhail Saakashvili, holding high a long-stemmed red rose, strode into the hall followed by his supporters. Shevardnadze called Putin for help. Putin despatched Foreign Minister Igor Ivanov to mediate. Saakashvili refused to accept the election results. Shevardnadze resigned. Saakashvili won the presidential election on January 4, 2004 and his party won most seats in parliamentary elections on March 28. Georgia's democratic "Rose Revolution" was bloodless.

Seen from Washington and Brussels, the 2008 war between Russia and Georgia pitted an imperialistic Goliath against a peace-loving David resulting in Russia's conquest of two Georgian provinces, South Ossetia and Abkhazia.[26] It was more complex than that. Georgians are minorities in both those provinces. Georgia's South Ossetia is linked by tunnel through the central Caucasus Mountains to Russia's North Ossetia, while Abkhazia sprawls along the Black Sea. In 1990 a civil war erupted when the ethnically distinct Ossetians and Abkhazians declared independence from Georgia. More than 1,000 people died and 120,000 lost their homes before June 1992, when the Georgians agreed to a Russian brokered ceasefire and peacekeeping troops.

During the April 2008 NATO summit in Bucharest, the alliance extended invitations to Georgia and Ukraine to apply for membership. That emboldened Georgia President Saakashvili to announce his intention to recover Abkhazia and South Ossetia. During a meeting on July 10 Secretary of State Condoleezza Rice urged Saakashvili not to let Moscow "provoke you" to "get you to do something stupid" and "engage Russian military forces." If so "no one will come to your aid and you will lose."[27] Yet during the subsequent press conference, Rice declared that America was committed to Georgia's territorial integrity no matter what.

Tragically, Saakashvili did not heed that sensible advice. On August 8 he launched a war to recapture South Ossetia. The result was a catastrophe. Medvedev, Putin and other key ministers swiftly decided to drive the Georgians from South Ossetia. The Georgian army put up a spirited defense, capitalizing on its defensive positions and Russian blunders. Yet the overwhelming mass of Russian tanks and troops routed the Georgian army to within twenty-five miles of Tbilisi. Around 397 Georgians and seventy-four Russian troops died in the fighting, while 192,000 Georgians fled South Ossetia.[28]

French President Nicolas Sarkozy, who was also the European Union's rotating president, flew to Moscow where he met Medvedev and Putin on August 12. The Russian leaders played good and bad cop as Medvedev remained calm while Putin ranted against Saakashvili, threatening to capture and hang him by his balls. When Sarkozy asked why he would want to do that, Putin replied that the Americans had hanged Saddam Hussein. Sarkozy deflated Putin's rage by asking him if he wanted history to rank him with Bush as an aggressor.[29] He then assured Putin and Medvedev that NATO would freeze the membership applications of Georgia and Ukraine for the indefinite future. In return the Russian leaders agreed to halt their offensive, withdraw their troops and tolerate Saakashvili as Georgia's president.

Putin had decisively won his key goals. The Russian army had routed Georgia's army and humbled Saakashvili; Abkhazia and South Ossetia remained secure and, most importantly, NATO would not expand to Georgia and Ukraine. On August 26 Russia recognized the independence of South Ossetia and Abkhazia, citing as precedent the American and European Union recognition of Kosovo's declaration of independence from Serbia on February 17, 2008.

As usual, Putin happened to be in the right place at the right time. After serving two terms as president, he traded places with Medvedev just as eight years of Bush administration economic deregulations, tax cuts and worsening budget deficits that fueled speculative housing and stock bubbles imploded with the great recession. In September 2008, Lehman Brothers' declaration of bankruptcy triggered a domino effect across America and around the world. Russia's stock market lost 80 per cent of its value from June 2008 to January 2009; $130 billion was transferred to safe overseas havens; foreign reserves plummeted from $598 billion to $200 billion; oil prices dropped from $147 a barrel in July to $50 in November; and the economy and industrial output contracted 7.9 per cent and 10.8 per cent. The Kremlin tried to restore confidence and prop up the economy by promising $40 billion to banks and $50 billion to 295 other corporations, but that did little to stem the panic. The economy plunged another 8 per cent in 2009.[30] Russians blamed Medvedev rather than Putin for the soaring unemployment and plummeting living standards. Then a series of rebellions erupted across the Arab world, provoking fears by Russia's elite that something similar could engulf them.

One tragic incident in an obscure Tunisian town in December 2010 ignited revolutionary movements in a dozen countries in the Arab world and beyond, rendering dictators everywhere increasingly nervous. An impoverished street vendor had no money to pay a bribe demanded by police and was beaten when he protested. In despair and rage, he poured gasoline over himself and struck a match. He became a martyr to countless poverty-stricken, exploited people who, in country after country, vented their fury in mass protests against corrupt, autocratic oppressors in Tunisia, Egypt, Libya, Bahrain, Yemen and Syria. Of these democratic movements, dubbed the Arab Spring, only Tunisia's transformed the country from an autocracy into a democracy. Elsewhere, either the government crushed the movement as in Egypt and Bahrain, or the country dissolved into chronic civil war as in Libya, Yemen and Syria. Populist uprisings were not confined to the Arab world. Mass democratic movements eventually arose against dictators in Ukraine, Venezuela, Nicaragua and Mozambique with varying results.

That provoked a debate within the Kremlin over how to respond to each country's democratic movement and how to prevent a similar movement arising in Russia. President Medvedev was both sympathetic and worried. The lesson was clear:

When governments fail to keep up with social change and fail to meet people's hopes, disorganization and chaos ensue ... This is a problem of governments themselves and the responsibility they bear. Even if governments in power find many of the demands made unacceptable, they still must remain in dialogue with all the different groups because otherwise they lose their real foundation."[31]

The Arab Spring at once inspired and dismayed Russia's liberals. Just what, if anything, could they do about the Putin regime's worsening repression? Vice President Joe Biden provided an answer for them during a speech at Moscow University in March 2011:

Most Russians want to choose their national and local leaders in competitive elections. They want to be able to assemble freely, and they want a media to be independent of the state. And they want to live in a country that fights corruption. That's democracy ... So I urge all of you students here: Don't compromise on the basic elements of democracy. You need not make that Faustian bargain.[32]

A dispute between Putin and Medvedev over Russian policy nearly destroyed their relationship. Dictator Muamar Gaddafi had been a Moscow client since he took power in a coup in 1969. Yet he was no Kremlin puppet, often committing acts contrary to Soviet interests and advice, including reneging on payments for Russian weapons and other imports. So, the Russians had mixed feelings when a rebellion erupted against him in 2011. French President Nicola Sarkozy forged a consensus with other key NATO members, including a reluctant President Obama, to support the rebels against Gaddafi. Sarkozy and Obama pressured Medvedev to agree to abstain from a UN Security Council resolution on March 17, 2011 that authorized NATO to use military force to prevent Gaddafi's troops from slaughtering the rebels. Medvedev did not consult Putin beforehand.

Putin was enraged when Medvedev informed him. He tried to pressure Medvedev into giving up the presidency, arguing that: "The global situation is complex, Dima. You could end up losing Russia." When an alarmed Medvedev asked how that was possible, Putin replied, "Because the world is mixed up, Dima. Gaddafi thought he would never lose Libya, but the Americans tricked him." Putin then asserted:

In 2008, I was Russia's number one politician. I could have gotten reelected, but the Constitution didn't allow it. I played by the rules and handed power to you. But we agreed that when the day came, we'd sit down and decide what to do next. And now that day has come.

He told Medvedev not to run for re-election and instead support Putin's candidacy and after Putin won he would name Medvedev prime minister again.[33]

And that is what happened. Medvedev pushed a law through the Duma that extended presidential terms for six years and let presidents rule for two consecutive terms. Putin created the All Russian People's Front to include all the parties with himself at their head. The All Russian People's Front held a convention on September 24, 2011. Putin and Medvedev appeared side by side before the delegates and the president made a stunning announcement. Medvedev would not run for re-election but would nominate Putin as the presidential candidate. The delegates cheered wildly. Russian voters would have much more mixed feelings.

Officially the December 4, 2011 Duma election resulted in United Russia winning only 49.3 per cent of the vote or half compared to two-thirds in the 2007 election, and having its seats plunge from 315 to 238. Yet that result was artificially boosted by widespread and blatant ballot stuffing and multiple votes by busloads of supporters. Polls indicated that United Russia received only around 35 per cent of the vote.[34] The authoritarian Communist Party and Liberal Democratic Party won nearly one-third of the votes. The only bright spot was that the liberal A Just Russia Party gained 26 seats for 64 total.

Table 5.5 Top Four Parties in the December 2011 Duma Election.[35]

	Share of Votes	*Share of Seats*
United Russia	49.32	238
Communist	19.19	92
A Just Russia	13.24	64
Liberal Democratic	11.67	56
		450

In Moscow thousands of people protested the fraudulent election under the banner For Fair Elections. The Kremlin organized counter-demonstrations by the militant conservative youth groups, Nashi and United Russia's Young Guard. The resulting violence provoked ever larger anti-Kremlin protests that peaked on December 24, 2011 when over 100,000 people marched down Andrei Sakharov Avenue. Eventually more than 5,000 protestors were jailed, often for long stretches and on various charges.[36]

The most prominent protestor was Aleksei Navalny who is somewhat of an anomaly in Russian politics; he has been both a fervent liberal and nationalist since the 1990s. The Yabloko Party revoked his membership after he joined Russia March, an ultra-nationalist demonstration. Yet he buys stock in corporations just to exercise the right to attend shareholder meetings and ask pointed questions about where all the profits are going. In 2007, he revealed Transneft Corporation's diversion of hundreds of millions of dollars to Kremlin oligarchs. And that made him a target for Putin and his coterie. Police arrested and jailed Navalny several times on "hooligan" and other charges during anti-government protests.

Then there was Pussy Riot, a punk-rock girl band. On February 21, 2012 five members barged into the Cathedral of Christ the Savior and one of them filmed as the others danced and ranted for a minute until security guards expelled them. That footage was used for a music video called *Punk Prayer – Mother of God, Chase Putin Away*. Police soon arrested three members and charged them with religious hate crimes. The stunt backfired as most Russians were disgusted at what they believed was gratuitous blasphemy. The Sunday after Easter, 60,000 devotees attended mass at the Cathedral of Christ the Savior where Patriarch Kirill condemned such behavior. The three women received two-year sentences and were released in December 2013 after serving eighteen months.[37]

Secretary of State Hillary Clinton enraged Putin when she backed the demonstrators, declaring:

> Russian voters deserve a full investigation of all credible reports of electoral fraud and manipulation. The Russian people, like people everywhere, deserve the right to have their voices heard and votes counted.

Putin denounced Clinton for asserting that Russia's elections "were dishonest and unfair ... She set the tone for certain actors in this country – she gave them a signal. They heard that signal and, with the support of the U.S. State Department, began their active work."[38] Putin would avenge himself during America's 2016 election by unleashing hundreds of Russian cyber-trolls who extracted and posted on WikiLeaks information that embarrassed Democratic Party candidate Clinton while spreading lies through social media that denigrated her and celebrated her rival, Republican Party candidate Donald Trump.

The only question about the presidential election scheduled for March 4, 2012 was how big Putin's victory margin would be. Putin won with 63.6 per cent of the vote, with majorities in every district except Moscow where he got 47 per cent. His closest rival, Communist Party candidate Gennady Zyuganov received 17 per cent. During his inaugural address on May 7 Putin tried to be at once humble, conciliatory and inspirational: "We did not succeed in doing everything we hoped and did not manage to complete everything we planned. I see the whole sense and purpose of my life as being to serve our country and serve our people." And, despite the shortcomings, "the world has seen a Russian arisen anew."[39]

The day before Putin's inauguration, around 20,000 people packed Bolotnaya Square and protested Putin's election. After rioting erupted, police arrested 400 protesters including, once again, Navalny. The protestors gathered again on June 12, the anniversary of Russia's independence from the Soviet Union. More rioting and arrests occurred. Eventually judges sentenced thirty protesters to terms of up to four and a half years in prison. That was not harsh enough for Putin. He got the Duma to pass a law that raised the fines for illegal protests from around 5,000 rubles or $600 to 300,000 rubles or $10,000. Slander and libel laws received similar boosts in penalties.

The year 2014 should have been a triumph for Putin and Russian. Most Russians were exhilarated after several years of economic growth capped by the glories won by their nation's athletes at the Sochi Olympics. A March Levada Center opinion poll found that 63 per cent of Russians considered their country a superpower. Polls later that year revealed that most Russians believed themselves to be nicer than other nationalities and that their country was the best place to raise children, while 78 per cent considered themselves to be happy.[40]

Perhaps Putin's most exhilarating success as president was to host the 2014 Olympics in Sochi. That prestige cost Russia a lot of money. The Olympic Committee's decision came in Guatemaula City in July 2007. Putin made a speech in English directly before them while behind the scenes Russian agents dispensed bribes to officials with corrupt reputations. As a result, Sochi beat Salzburg, Austria, and Pyeongchang, South Korea, for the honor. Putin then marshalled $51 billion to spend on the Olympics, although at least half of that was stolen or resulted in shoddy, delayed construction. The Russians won most medals, thirty-three, with thirteen of them gold.[41]

Yet that national exhilaration soured after the western world's tough reaction to what Putin ordered the Russian army to do to Ukraine.[42] Putin was obsessed with Ukraine's political orientation. Ukraine had tilted westward after Viktor Yushchenko took power with his Orange Revolution in 2004. Unfortunately, his initial popularity steadily dwindled as his administration failed to develop the economy, culminating with its collapse during the global recession from 2008. Overwhelmed with political and health problems, he was in wretched shape for the January 17, 2010 election.

Pro-Russian Viktor Yanukovych, who Yushchenko had bested in the 2004 revolution, was determined to become president. Once again Moscow backed him massively with money and operatives. Since 2004 his political advisor was Paul Manafort, a Republican Party activist who had worked for Presidents Gerald Ford, Ronald Reagan, George H.W. Bush and George W. Bush. Manafort concocted a slick media campaign that remade Yanukovych with crowd-pleasing slogans, gestures and clothes. Yanukovych won the first round with 35.32 per cent of the vote, far ahead of the next candidate, Yulia Tymoshenko with 25.5 per cent, and thirteen others who split the other votes. Yushchenko received only 5 per cent of the vote. In the run off, Yanukovych beat Tymoshenko with 48.95 per cent to 45.47 per cent. Yanukovych was a sore winner. In 2010 he had Tymoshenko arrested on an array of mostly trumped-up charges and a court sentenced her to seven years in prison.

After taking power, Yanukovych was Janus-faced as he appealed for aid from both Moscow and the West, hoping to play them off against each other. His first summit was with Russian President Medvedev, during which he agreed to extend the Sevastopol naval base lease to 2042 in return for Moscow lifting a 30 per cent surcharge on natural gas sales and reducing the price from $300 to $230 per thousand cubic metres. That only slightly pulled Ukraine back from complete economic collapse.

To extract itself from the worsening recession, Ukraine needed a massive injection of money that could be obtained only from western sources. Yanukovych's threat to default on Ukraine's debt led to negotiations with the International Monetary Fund (IMF). A deal was struck whereby the IMF lent Ukraine $15 billion in exchange for economic reforms that cut subsidies and regulations to promote market efficiency. Yanukovych yielded to pressure from Ukraine's business corporations to put the country on track for EU membership.

An infuriated Putin got tough with what should have been Moscow's puppet in Kiev. He threatened to raise gas prices to $400 per thousand cubic metres or even cut off shipments if Yanukovych did not repudiate any notion of joining NATO or the EU; require Russian to be used equally with Ukrainian in the state's judicial, bureaucratic and school systems; and join Ukraine with the Eurasian Customs Union of Russia, Belarus and Kazakhstan. Putin sweetened that deal by having millions of dollars transferred to the secret bank accounts of Yanukovych and his cronies. Putin put direct pressure on Yanukovych during his visit to Kiev to celebrate Ukraine's 1,087th anniversary of converting to Christianity. During his speech Putin provoked controversy when he declared: "We, Russia and Ukraine, have always been united and our future lies in this unity …. The question is only one of how we go about agreeing on working together under absolutely equal, transparent and clear conditions."[43]

As Putin pulled Yanukovych toward Moscow, Brussels pulled him westward. The Europeans gave him a deadline to agree to sign an Association Agreement and release Tymoshenko from prison – November 21, a week before the EU's November 2014 summit in Vilnius, Lithuania. On that day Kiev announced that it would delay indefinitely any signing. At the summit on November 28 Yanukovych announced that Ukraine would reject the Association Agreement. Desperately he pleaded for the European leaders to understand that: "I'd like you to listen to me. For three and a half years I've been alone. I've been face-to-face with a very strong Russia on a very unlevel playing field."[44]

That provoked demonstrations in Kiev's Maidan Nezalezhnostri or Independence Square. Police beatings and arrests of protesters provoked ever more Ukrainians to pack the square. From prison, Tymoshenko urged all Ukrainians to resist. On December 8 the protesters demolished a huge statue of Lenin. Inspired by the pro-democracy movement, Senator John McCain flew to Kiev and for a day joined them to declare: "The free world is with you. Ukraine will make Europe better and Europe will make Ukraine better."[45] The EU tried to broker a deal whereby Yanukovych agreed to respect the 2004 constitution, turn over most powers to the prime minister, form a cabinet that included all major political factions and schedule a presidential election for December 2014.

Instead, Yanukovych flew to Moscow for a summit with Putin on December 17. Putin tried to undercut the pro-democracy movement by promising Yanukovych $15 billion to shore up Ukraine's economy and Gazprom gas price cuts from $400 to $268 per thousand cubic metres. An FSB team urged Yanukovych to crack down harder on the demonstrators. After returning to Kiev, Yanukovych followed that advice. By February 20 police had beaten and arrested hundreds of protesters, and that day murdered eighty-eight and wounded hundreds while suffering seventeen deaths in their own ranks.

The next day Yanukovych signed the opposition's "Agreement on Settlement of the Political Crisis in Ukraine," then lost his nerve and fled Kiev, eventually reaching safety in Russia. On February 24 Ukraine's parliament declared Yanukovych deposed, issued a warrant for his arrest on treason charges and set presidential elections for May 25, 2014. Meanwhile a vivid understanding of the billions of dollars that Yanukovych and his cronies had looted from Ukraine was revealed when his opulent palace outside Kiev was opened for public tours.

Putin and his Security Council agreed on February 23 to annex Crimea. Putin later explained the reasons for that critical decision:

I told my colleagues that the situation in Ukraine was developing in such a way that we had to start working on returning Crimea to Russia. We could not abandon this territory and the people who lived there to the mercy of fate, under the steamroller of nationalism.[46]

The operation began on February 27 as the 25,000 Russian troops already based at Sevastopol, reinforced by thousands of others from the nearby Russian city of Novorossiysk, bloodlessly took over. Faced with overwhelming odds, Ukrainian troops in Crimea surrendered without resistance. On March 2 Putin got Yanukovych to sign as Ukraine's president a letter, dated the previous day, that read:

Ukraine is on the brink of a civil war ... Under the influence of Western countries there are open acts of terror and violence. People are being persecuted for language and political reasons. So, in this regard I would call on the president of Russia, Mr Putin, asking him to use the armed forces of the Russian Federation to establish legitimacy, peace, law, and order, stability and defend the people of Ukraine.[47]

On March 6 Crimea's parliament voted to join Russia if a plebiscite approved. During the plebiscite on March 16, 83.1 per cent of eligible voters turned up and 96.77 per cent of them voted to join Russia.

Putin formally announced and justified Russia's takeover of Crimea in a televised speech on March 18, 2014, insisting that it was no different from Germany's re-unification in 1990:

I believe that even Europeans will understand me, and first and foremost Germans. I remember how during the political consultations for the unification of the FRB and the GDR ... the countries that then were ... allies of Germany, had their own ideals about unification. But our country ... unequivocally supported ... the irrepressible striving of Germans for national unity.

He then condemned America whose policies are:

guided not by international law, not by the law of force. They believe in their exceptionalism and exclusivity, in the fact that they are permitted to decide the fate of the world, that only they can ever be right .... It is alarming that military intervention in internal conflicts in foreign countries has become commonplace for the United States ... Millions around the world increasingly see America not as a model of democracy, but as relying solely on brute force, cobbling coalitions together under the slogan, 'you're either for us or against us.'[48]

In justifying Russian imperialism against Ukraine, he asserted the time-worn Russian belief that they are the true victims who are standing up against the true aggressions:

The Ukrainian crisis is not Russia's fault. It is the result of the attempts of the United States and its Western allies, who considered themselves 'winners' in the Cold War – to impose their will everywhere ... Notice how NATO's infrastructure is moving closer to Russia's borders; how it is ignoring Russian interests ... We have repeatedly warned the United States and its Western partners about the harmful effects of interference in the internal affairs of Ukraine.[49]

He told British Prime Minister David Cameron: "This is my backyard. The West has repeatedly humiliated me, over Libya, over Syria ... for the last ten years."[50] Foreign Minister Sergei Lavrov elaborated Putin's justifications:

Kiev is the mother of Russian cities. Russian language, Russian religion, Orthodox Christianity, [were] born on the territory of Ukraine ... We have been one nation for more than 300 years ... The Slavs brought their religion more than 1,000 years ago. It's absolutely impossible to miss the psychological, historical and family feeling.[51]

Washington and Brussels announced sanctions that barred travel, froze the accounts and forbade business with a list of Russian oligarchs. The Group of 8's seven original members – the United States, Britain, France,

Germany, Italy, Japan and Canada – expelled Russia which had been a member since 1998. Putin was going to host that year's G-8 summit at Sochi. Instead, the G-7 held their summit in Brussels. The sanctions sparked a stampede of money from Russia, at least $150 billion by the end of 2014, while the ruble nosedived. The result was a deep recession and inflation.

Meanwhile, Russian-speakers rebelled and declared independence in Ukraine's eastern provinces of Donetsk on April 7 and Luhansk on April 27. The Russian army supplied the rebels with troops, weapons and other critical supplies. Independence referenda in the "People's Republics of" Donetsk and Luhansk resulted in 89 per cent and 96 per cent of those respective voters in favor.

Amidst this crisis Ukraine held a presidential election on May 25. Billionaire Petro Poroshenko, known as the Chocolate King for the source of his wealth, won with 54 per cent of the vote. He promptly appointed Yulia Tymoshenko prime minister.

The crisis worsened on July 17, when Russian troops shot down a Malaysia Airlines flight with 283 passengers and fifteen crew aboard, apparently mistaking it for a military aircraft. Typically, the Kremlin blamed Ukraine for the atrocity, even concocting a false radar image of a fighter shooting down the jetliner. The Russian and separatist forces defeated each Ukrainian offensive. Negotiations led to a ceasefire on September 5 but fighting soon erupted again. Another ceasefire was announced on February 12, 2015 and that one has largely held with brief spats of fighting. To date about 10,000 Ukrainians and 2,000 Russians have died and more than 2.5 million have become refugees. Russian military and economic aid to its puppet regimes in Donetsk and Luhansk annually costs around $4.5 billion.[52]

In the face of swelling international condemnation of his blatant imperialism, Putin's rhetoric became increasingly belligerent. He warned Jose Manuel Barroso, the EU Commission chief: "If I want, I would take Kiev in two weeks." He boasted to Poroshenko: "If I wanted to, Russian troops could take in two days not only Kiev but also Riga, Vilnius, Tallinn, Warsaw and Bucharest."[53] That latter quote was even more disturbing because it was an absurd fantasy. If Putin really believed that then he was utterly deluded about Russian power. And if he acted on that delusion and invaded those NATO members, he would trigger the Third World War. Most likely, he was just blustering and was well aware that NATO would swiftly rout any Russian attack and then devastate Russia's military and economic infrastructure in a crippling counter-attack.

Putin and Poroshenko signed a truce in Minsk on September 5, 2015. In doing so, Poroshenko essentially wrote off Luhansk and Donetsk, implicitly acknowledging that Ukraine's military was too weak, the Russia-speaking population in those provinces was too pervasive and the Russian army was too formidable. Yet, ever since, firefights, sniping and planted bombs erupt between Russian and Ukrainian, and more commonly among Russian factions vying for power within those breakaway provinces. Atop that, the West's economic sanctions impose a chronic heavy penalty on Russian imperialism there.

Putin's imperialism toward Ukraine and the subsequent international sanctions inspired a rally-around-the-flag effect among Russians. To United Russia's advantage, Putin restored the single-member districts for the Duma election of September 18, 2016. United Russia won a stunning 203 of the 225 single member seats and with 54.7 per cent of the proportional vote took 343 of the 450 seats. One of four Russians voted for either of the two other authoritarian parties, the Communist and Liberal Democratic. The liberal A Just Russia Party suffered a devastating loss of 41 seats, emerging with only 23. Russia appeared to be more illiberal than any year since the communist regime was destroyed in 1991.

Table 5.6 Top Six Parties in the December 2016 Duma Election.[54]

	Share of Votes	*Share of Seats*
United Russia	54.20	343
Communist	13.34	42
Liberal Democratic	13.14	39
A Just Russia	6.22	23
Rodina	1.51	1
Civic Platform	0.22	1
		450

Two years later Vladimir Putin won a resounding re-election victory on March 18, 2018 with 76.69 per cent of the vote compared to Communist

Party nominee Pavel Grudinin with 11.77 per cent and Liberal Democratic Party Vladimir Zhirinovsky with 5.65 per cent. That gives Putin another six years in power, during which he most likely will have the constitution amended to let him be re-elected for as long as he desires.

Part III

Putin and the World

Chapter 6

Russia and America

Will he become my new best friend?

(Donald Trump)

In all free governments contention in elections will take place; and, whilst it is confined to our own citizens it is not to be regretted; but severely indeed ought it to be reprobated when occasioned by foreign machinations.

(George Washington)[1]

Vladimir Putin was indoctrinated by a regime, then trained by an organization that depicted the United States as an imperialist, materialistic superpower determined to destroy the Soviet Union and communism. Indeed, that happened and since then Putin, along with most Russians, perceives America as dedicated to toppling his regime and dismantling Russia. A 2014 Kremlin-backed study condemned America for imposing on Russia during the 1990s material and spiritual poverty; eroding its statehood, economy, science, education, and armed forces; preventing the revival of the country and turning it into a raw oil and gas appendage of the West; and making the country's security directly dependent on global oil and gas market prices, resulting in the flow of enormous Russian financial resources abroad.[2]

Scapegoating America for Russian failures did not start with Putin, but was integral to the Kremlin's Cold War strategy. Regardless, as president, Putin is doing all he can to undermine American power and revive the Russian empire amidst a second Cold War.

To date, Putin has dealt with four American presidents, Bill Clinton, George W. Bush, Barack Obama and Donald Trump. His relations varied with each.[3] From the Democrats, he provoked Clinton's wariness and Obama's loathing. From the Republicans, he inspired Bush's admiration and Trump's outright adoration and collusion. Although Putin has tried to manipulate each president differently, his multi-stranded tug-of-war with the White House for influence around the world has remained constant.

Vladimir Putin became Russia's president during President Bill Clinton's last year in power. Clinton and his advisors warily welcomed Putin as Boris Yeltsin's replacement, hoping that he would bring order, calm and predictability to Russia and its foreign relations that were often lacking under his erratic, volatile predecessor. Their only fear was that Putin might reverse the democratic reforms begun by Yeltsin. They would be right about both possibilities. Secretary of State Madeline Albright met Putin in Moscow in early February 2000, and found him "a very well-informed person, a good interlocutor, obviously a Russian patriot who seeks a normal position with the West."[4] Clinton met Putin three times before his presidency ended. He confided to Prime Minister Tony Blair that "Putin has enormous potential …. He's very smart and thoughtful. I think we can do a lot of good with him."[5] Yet, he had misgivings. To Yeltsin, Clinton observed:

> You've got the fire in your belly of a real democrat and a real reformer. I'm not sure Putin has that. You'll have to keep an eye on him and use your influence to make sure that he stays on the right path. Putin needs you … Russia needs you.[6]

Actually, Yeltsin and Putin had cut a deal. In return for not using his influence, Yeltsin would escape prosecution for any crimes that he and his family had committed.

In policy and personality, Clinton's successor was just as glaring a contrast as that between Yeltsin and Putin. Clinton was a "policy wonk" and realist whose policy toward Moscow was to integrate and develop Russia economically and politically within the global system while mutually reducing nuclear weapons. George W. Bush was an ideologue who saw politics as a moral struggle between good and evil. As a neo-conservative he was dedicated to expanding the military's budget and missile defense, policies that could only be justified by identifying ominous foreign dangers. The neo-conservatives identified Russia along with China, Iraq and Iran as adversaries to confront. Bush's national security advisor, Condoleezza Rice, typified the administration's attitudes toward Russia: "I believe Russia is a threat to the West in general and to our European allies in particular."[7]

Realists tried to explain that if Russia posed a threat it was from weakness rather than strength. Russia's worsening debt loomed ever larger over the global economy. A default could set off a financial domino effect that toppled the world's financial system. Even more frightening was the specter of "loose" nukes, chemicals, pathogens and radioactive materials possibly being sold to the highest bidder by ill-paid Russian scientists, engineers, technicians and guards at laboratories or warehouses packed with weapons of mass destruction. Clinton's policy of engagement and aid helped diminish that threat. Tragically, the Bush White House was ideologically deaf and blind to that potential threat along with a genuine threat that the outgoing Clinton administration's national security experts warned them about – Osama bin Laden's transnational terrorist group al Qaeda. Indeed, al Qaeda operatives had already committed a series of terrorist attacks against the United States including New York's World Trade Center in 1993, American-led peacekeeping forces in Somalia in 1993, the American embassies in Nairobi and Dar es Salaam in 1999 and the USS *Cole* in 2000.

The Bush administration soon found a way to depict Russia as an enemy. FBI agents arrested Robert Hanssen, a Russian counter-intelligence FBI agent, on espionage charges on February 18, 2001. Over twenty-two years Hanssen had pocketed $1.2 million from KGB handlers in return for critical secrets including Soviets spying for the CIA. The White House declared fifty Soviet diplomats *persona non grata*. The Kremlin reacted by expelling the same number of American diplomats from the Moscow embassy. Those tit-for-tat expulsions were typical Cold War political theater for a global audience. But, on May 1, 2001, the Bush administration detonated a political bombshell with far more ominous potential consequences.

The president announced his intention to withdraw the United States from the 1972 Anti-Ballistic Missile (ABM) Treaty. That treaty had limited the United States and Soviet Union initially to only two ABM sites each, which a protocol later reduced to one site each. Bush denounced the treaty "that prohibits us from pursuing promising technology to defend ourselves, our friends, and our allies." He then tried to placate Moscow by suggesting that "one day, we can even co-operate in a joint defense."[8] Russia Defense Minister Sergei Ivanov denounced that policy, arguing that it threatened to unravel "the entire existing system of arms control, some 32 treaties rested on the ABM Treaty's foundation. Destroy the ABM Treaty and those other treaties topple with it."[9]

The truth lay in between. The ABM Treaty had been important for three reasons. It saved both sides enormous amounts of money building unworkable ABM systems. That relatively easy agreement paved the way in mutual confidence and understanding to tackle more difficult disputes. Most vital was that it reduced tensions by removing the threat that one side could wield an ABM as a shield, however feeble, behind which to launch a devastating first strike on the other. Bush's repudiation of the ABM and development of missile defense revived Kremlin fears that the neo-conservatives were plotting a first strike against Russia. In a crisis that fear might have prompted Moscow to "use or lose" their nuclear arsenal, thus provoking a nuclear holocaust.

Then something extraordinary happened. Putin, with his black belt in judo and KGB training, flipped Bush psychologically from confrontation into co-operation. To wean Bush from his ideological straitjacket, Putin knew he had to appeal to his emotions rather than limited intellect. They first met at Ljubljana, Slovenia's capital, on June 15, 2001. Putin played Bush to the point where Bush later gushed:

> I looked the man in the eye. I found him to be very straightforward and trustworthy. We had a very good dialogue. I was able to get a sense of his soul; a man deeply committed to his country and the best interests of his country.[10]

Putin showed Bush an aluminum cross that his mother had given him to bless in Jerusalem which then had miraculously survived a fire that destroyed his dacha. Bush declared, "Vladimir, that is the story of the cross. Things are meant to be."[11]

Had a Democratic Party president expressed such dewy-eyed sentiments for a ruthless Russian leader, the conservative mass media would have mercilessly and justifiably excoriated his naiveté and ignorance. Instead, most conservatives bit their lips while the mainstream media pointed out how inappropriate Bush's feelings and words were. Rice later admitted, "We were never able to escape the perception that the president had naively trusted Putin and then been betrayed."[12]

Putin was not quite as smitten with Bush. When asked what he thought of his counterpart, he replied "It is the retinue that makes the king."[13] That cryptic statement undoubtedly harbored several related meanings. Perhaps the most important was his fear that the spell that he cast on Bush would wear off soon after the president re-immersed himself in the neo-conservative sea. Yet he dismissed the importance of the Bush administration's scrapping of the ABM Treaty and development of missile defense. He had reached the same conclusion that Mikhail Gorbachev had twenty years earlier toward Ronald Reagan's obsession with his Strategic Defense Initiative, dubbed Star Wars – it did not matter. If the Americans wanted to squander their wealth on an exorbitantly expensive system that would probably not work and could easily be neutralized, so much the better for Russia. He declared that if they want "the most excessive response to the least probable threat situation, that's ok." He did express concern that the neo-conservatives' zealotry deluded them into believing that "America is so strong that it does not need any negotiations and any agreements," an attitude that was "the most extreme" approach to international relations.[14]

The Bush administration's dismissal of al Qaeda as a threat most likely contributed to the devastating attacks against America on September 11, 2001. Had the neo-conservative Bush team instead vigorously targeted al Qaeda, could they have thwarted the attack? That, of course, is unknowable.

Regardless, ironically, Putin was the last in a long line of experts to warn Bush about a pending attack. Ahmad Shah Massoud was an anti-Taliban and anti-al Qaeda warlord whose stronghold was the Panjshir Valley in northeastern Afghanistan. The CIA had nurtured Massoud and his Northern Alliance fighters as an ally against the Taliban and al Qaeda. On September 9, 2001 two suicide bombers killed Massoud at his headquarters. Putin called Bush to warn him that Russian intelligence had concluded that Massoud's murder was the prelude to a terrorist attack against the United States. Tragically, Bush and his fellow neo-conservatives rejected that warning like numerous others that they had received since the election.[15]

The events of September 11 were a blessing in disguise for American-Russian relations. Now that the United States had a genuine enemy, the neo-conservatives could ease up on portraying Russia as a bogeyman. Putin was the first foreign leader to call Bush. He resisted the temptation to remind Bush that he had warned him about the imminent attack and instead re-assured him that: "Good will triumph over evil. I want you to know that in this struggle we will stand together." In a televised speech, he declared:

> Russia knows first-hand what terrorism is. So, we understand as well as anyone the feelings of the American people. Addressing the people of the United States on behalf of Russia, I would like to say that we are with you, we entirely and fully share and experience your pain.[16]

Putin supported the Bush administration's "Global War on Terrorism" in two vital ways. First, Moscow shared vital intelligence with Washington on the Taliban, al Qaeda and other terrorist groups within Afghanistan and elsewhere around the world. As importantly, it shared its Central Asian sphere of influence with the United States, encouraging those countries bordering Afghanistan – Turkmenistan, Uzbekistan and Tajikistan – to co-operate fully with Washington.

In return the Bush administration made one concession, although only after a heated debate between the dominant neo-conservatives and handful of realists like Secretary of State Colin Powell, Deputy Secretary of State Richard Armitage, CIA Director George Tenet and Counter-Terrorist Director Richard Clarke. Before September 11 Bush had condemned Russia for trying to crush an independence movement in its mostly Muslim province of Chechnya. Thereafter Bush supported that effort, finally understanding that Moscow's Chechnya policy indirectly aided his own global crusade against Jihadism while distracting the Russians from aggression further west.

Bush hosted Putin at the White House on November 13, then the next day they flew to Crawford, Texas, where they stayed at his ranch. The following morning the two leaders strode toward massed reporters and camera operators. Bush's most important announcement was his pledge to reduce America's nuclear arsenal from around 6,000 warheads to between 1,700 and 2,200 over the next decade. He then made several largely symbolic gestures. He promised to remove Russia permanently from the list of countries that could be penalized with trade sanctions for their restrictive emigration laws under the 1974 Jackson-Vanik amendment, a law that had not actually been invoked since the Cold War ended a decade earlier. He also avoided criticizing Kremlin restrictions on the mass media, simply suggesting that a "Russian-American Entrepreneurship Dialogue" be formed "to explore the conditions necessary for media to flourish as a business in Russia". Given the Bush administration's own post-September 11 attempts to muzzle America's print and electronic media, any complaints about how Moscow treated journalists would have appeared hypocritical. Finally, Bush promised swift inclusion of Russia in the World Trade Organization (WTO) with the logic that Russia's economic development aids American and global interests. Bush's only sour note concerned Putin's rejection of his demand officially to sign off on the administration's withdrawal from the ABM Treaty. Bush denigrated the ABM treaty as "a piece of paper that's codified a relationship that no longer exists. It codified a hateful relationship. And we have got a friendly relationship." Thus did Bush again spotlight his ignorance about fundamental principles of deterrence. Yet, in summing up the talks, Bush crowed that "the United States and Russia are in the midst of a transformationed relationship that will yield peace and progress".[17]

For his part, Putin had nothing but praise for his host, sincerely grateful that "I've never been to the home of another world leader," and perhaps less sincere when he described America as "fortunate at such a critical time in its history to have a man of such character at its helm."[18] He then announced that Russia would cut its nuclear arsenal from 5,800 to 1,500 over the next decade, and added that he intended that both nations' promises be codified in a treaty. The Russian president's commitment to a legally binding document riled Bush and his fellow neo-conservatives who ideologically opposed any arms control laws under domestic or international law. Bush petulantly quipped, "If we need to write it down on a piece of paper, I'd be glad to do that."[19]

Putin then flew to New York to visit the World Trade Center's ruins before heading home to Moscow. Putin's visit boosted Russia's image in countless American minds. The Russian leader clearly appeared articulate and dignified alongside Bush who was as usual tense and linguistically challenged. Senator Joe Biden, the Foreign Relations Committee chair, captured the positive feelings when he proclaimed that, "no Russian leader since Peter the Great has looked as far West as Putin seems to have."[20]

Actually, Putin's willingness to co-operate with Bush was limited to their common interests in combating terrorism. He was still committed to developing ties with long-standing Russian client states including those that Bush dubbed an "axis of evil" in his January 2002 State of the Union address. Bush singled out Iraq, Iran and North Korea for sponsoring terrorism and developing weapons of mass destruction, and that in turn justified America's missile defense program and regime change for all three countries. Putin defied Bush in early 2001, when he hosted first Iran President Mohammad Khatami in March and North Korean President Kim Jong Il in April. After Bush designated his "axis of evil," in a typical contradiction, he did not link, let alone condemn, the presumed ringleader of that "axis of evil," Putin. Actually, although the ties among those three countries were limited, they all variously depended on Russia for trade and aid. In July 2002 the Kremlin announced a five-year agreement with Iran to expand their economic and scientific relations, including Russian help in building five nuclear energy plants. On August 23, Putin met Kim Jong Il in Vladivostok and they agreed to connect North Korea with the trans-Siberian railroad and thus Europe's distant markets. But Russia's most extensive economic relations were with Iraq where more than 300 Russian firms did business. In 2001 alone Russia exported $1.4 billion worth of goods to Iraq under the UN's "oil for food" program and signed more than $4 billion in investment and trade deals. In 2002 Putin and Saddam Hussein agreed to a ten-year $60 billion deal that let Russian companies develop some of Iraq's most bountiful oil fields. Iraq owed Russia $8.5 billion in debts incurred during the Soviet era. The Russians would lose virtually all of that trade and investment after Bush launched his war against Iraq.[21]

The Bush administration warned Putin that Russia's relations with the United States would diminish the closer its ties with America's enemies. Defense Secretary Donald Rumsfeld was the bluntest:

> To the extent that Russia decides that it wants to parade its relationships with countries like Iraq and Syria and Libya and Cuba and North Korea, it sends a signal ... that is what Russia thinks is a good thing to do, to deal with terrorist states.[22]

The Kremlin replied with repeated explanations that while it shared the White House concern with terrorism and the proliferation of weapons of mass destruction, each of those states singled out for condemnation presented a different set of opportunities and challenges, and thus demanded different policies.

Meanwhile, Bush remained obsessed with getting Putin to agree to scrap the ABM Treaty. Powell flew to Moscow on December 11 for one last attempt to convince him. Putin, however, stood firm. On December 13 Bush made his repudiation official: "Today I have given formal notice to Russia ... that the United States is withdrawing from this almost 30-year-old treaty. I have concluded that the ABM Treaty hinders our people from future terrorist or rogue-state missile attacks."[23]

In a televised speech, Putin responded to Bush, the Russian people, and the world. He dismissed Bush's decision as "erroneous" and explained that the White House was barking up the wrong strategic tree: "Today, when the world has confronted new threats, one should not allow a legal vacuum in the sphere of strategic stability. One should not undermine the regime of nonproliferation of weapons of mass destruction." In a later press conference, Putin expressed his government's puzzlement about the Bush administration's refusal to discuss any change in the ABM treaty that would permit the testing they wanted:

We asked to be given specific parameters that stood in the way
of U.S. desires to develop defensive systems …. We were fully
prepared to discuss those parameters But nothing specific was given
to us. We heard only insistent requests for bilateral withdrawal from
the treaty. To this day I fail to understand this insistence, given our
position, which was fairly flexible.

Whether Russia's puzzlement was genuine or feigned is not publicly
known. Clearly, the Bush administration was ideologically driven to bury
rather than refine the treaty.[24]

Nonetheless, nuclear arms negotiations continued, based on the
preliminary agreement that the two presidents had reached. The Bush
and Putin administrations signed the Strategic Offensive Reduction
Treaty on May 24, 2002. Under the treaty each side agreed to reduce
its nuclear warheads to 2,200 by December 31, 2012. Bush boasted
that "This treaty will liquidate the legacy of the Cold War."[25] That
hyperbole aside, the three-page-long treaty was a vital step in reducing
nuclear weapons. Yet, not surprisingly, the neo-conservatives had woven
into the text a significant catch. The world would not necessarily be
rid of the dismantled warheads. Either side could warehouse them for
redeployment in an "emergency". Indeed Powell later admitted that the
Pentagon planned to hold 2,400 to 2,900 warheads in active reserve. Also
either state could repudiate the entire treaty with only three months'
notice, half the usual six-month limit. Finally, there were no verification
procedures; each had to trust the other without proof.[26]

Clearly, if Putin was willing to reduce Russia's nuclear forces so sharply
he lost no more sleep over Bush's version of Star Wars than Gorbachev
did over Reagan's original scheme. The reason was simple. Even in the
extremely unlikely event that Bush's missile defense worked and both
sides cut their missile forces by one-third, Russia's nuclear arsenal would
still be able to overwhelm it. Just to be sure, Putin unveiled in November
2004 a program eventually to make Russia's nuclear forces impervious to
any potential missile defense system. That program was part of a 27 per
cent increase in Russian defense spending for 2005.[27]

The satisfaction realists derived from that nuclear arms treaty was
diluted as conflicts between Washington and Moscow over other questions

worsened relations, none more than the Bush White House's pending war against Iraq. The neo-conservatives were obsessed with destroying Saddam Hussein's regime and enabling America's petroleum giants to control Iraq's oil. The Kremlin's close ties to Iraq began in 1958 after a military coup overthrew a pro-western regime. Thereafter Moscow sold Iraq massive amounts of military weapons, provided technological aid and shared intelligence. If a neo-conservative crusade destroyed Saddam's regime, then Moscow would not only lose a valued client state but billions of dollars that Iraq owed Russia.

Putin did not stand alone. French President Jacques Chirac and German Chancellor Gerhard Schröder joined him in condemning an American war against Iraq. On March 5, 2003 their foreign ministers issued a joint statement in Paris that they would reject any Security Council resolution that authorized the United States to war against Iraq. The Bush White House reacted with a policy of "punish France, ignore Germany, and forgive Russia". That attempt to play the Iraq War's leading opponents off against each other failed. The three, and scores of other, leaders stood firmly against the war.

The Bush administration launched its war against Iraq on March 19, 2003. The blitzkrieg overran most of Iraq and destroyed Saddam's army and regime within a month. The White House concocted a public relations stunt to announce what the neo-conservatives believed was the Iraq War's end. On May 1 George Bush dressed in a flight-suit and was flown to land on the aircraft carrier *Abraham Lincoln*. He emerged from the plane and, with a huge "Mission Accomplished" banner behind him, declared "major combat operations in Iraq have ended." In reality, the American troops and their allies in Iraq were enjoying the fleeting eye of a devastating hurricane. An insurgency soon began and worsened steadily for the next half dozen years. A shift in American strategy from search, destroy and withdraw to take, hold and build eventually quelled the insurgency for a few brief years.[28]

Meanwhile, Bush tried to mend relations with Putin. During a summit in St Petersburg on May 23, 2003 Bush proclaimed that their differences over Iraq: "will make our relationship stronger, not weaker. As we go forward we will show that friends can disagree, move beyond disagreements, and work in constructive and very important ways to maintain the peace."[29] That era of good feelings did not last long.

Two NATO policies enraged Putin.[30] First, NATO advanced eastward by admitting Bulgaria, Romania, Slovakia, Slovenia, Lithuania, Latvia and Estonia on April 2, 2004; Estonia's northeastern border was just sixty miles from St Petersburg. The Kremlin angrily denounced that enlargement for violating an understanding reached in 1990 between Moscow and Berlin that Germany could re-unite as long as NATO never expanded eastward. To Putin's fury, Mikhail Gorbachev repudiated that notion, saying that subject was never raised during talks over German re-unification. Then came Bush's announcement in 2007 that America would deploy a ballistic missile defense (BMD) system in Poland and a radar base in the Czech Republic. The Kremlin protested against that for attempting to negate Russia's nuclear deterrent. The White House claimed that the system was designed to counter a threat from Iran, not Russia.

Putin vented pent-up rage at NATO's enlargement and the proposed missile defense system during the February 2007 Munich Security Conference:

> It turns out that NATO has put its frontline forces on our borders, and we continue to strictly fulfill the treaty obligations and do not react to these actions ... [I]t is obvious that NATO expansion does not have any relation with the modernization of the Alliance itself or with ensuring security in Europe. On the contrary, it represents a serious provocation that reduces the level of mutual trust. And we have the right to ask: against whom is this expansion intended?[31]

"Against Russia, of course" was the obvious answer and for numerous rock-solid reasons, including the persistent threat of an autocratic, aggressive, nationalist Russian regime led by Vladimir Putin.

Putin elaborated his arguments during the April 2008 NATO summit in Bucharest:

> It is obvious that today there is no Soviet Union, no eastern bloc, and no Warsaw Pact. So, NATO exists to confront whom? We hear that it exists in order to solve today's problems and challenges.

Which ones? ... We have withdrawn our troops deployed in eastern Europe, and withdrawn almost all large and heavy weapons from the European part of Russia. And what happened? A base in Romania ... one in Bulgaria, an American missile defense area in Poland and the Czech Republic. That all means moving military infrastructure to our borders.[32]

During his last year in the White House, Bush was determined to end his relationship with Putin on a high note. On April 6, 2008, during their summit at his palace in Sochi, they issued this hopeful joint declaration:

We re-affirm that the era in which the United States and Russia considered one another an enemy of strategic threat has ended. We reject the zero-sum thinking of the Cold War when, "what was good for Russia was bad for America" and vice versa. Rather we are dedicated to working together, and with other nations, to address the global challenges of the twenty-first century, moving the US-Russia relationship from one of strategic competition to strategic partnership.[33]

Once again, those good feelings died hard, this time in August 2008, after Russia trounced Georgia during a short war, detached Georgia's provinces of South Ossetia and Abkhazia, and declared them independent countries. The Bush administration protested Putin's blatant act of imperialism but did not impose sanctions against Russia. In return, Putin gave Bush a going away gift in January 2009, just before he yielded the presidency to Barack Obama. He agreed to let the Americans and their NATO partnership move military supplies by land and air across Russia toward Afghanistan, thus easing Washington's reliance on routes across Pakistan, whose government was at once pro-Western and pro-Jihadist. The Northern Distribution Network eventually included Russia, Latvia, Uzbekistan, Kazakhstan, Tajikistan, Kyrgyzstan, Georgia and Azerbaijan.

President Barack Obama was determined to "reset" relations with Moscow by placing them in a historic context: "This is not another cold war that we are entering into. After all, unlike the Soviet Union, Russia leads no bloc of nations, no global ideology."[34] To spearhead that policy, he appointed as ambassador to Russia renowned expert Michael McFaul, a Stanford University political scientist who had lived and researched in Moscow and Leningrad.

Obama hoped to develop better relations with Russia through a series of summits with its president, then Dmitri Medvedev. They first met in London in April 2009, then Moscow in July 2009 during which they agreed to negotiate a START III Treaty, curb the nuclear ambitions of North Korea and Iran and fulfill Putin's pledge to allow ground routes across and air routes over Russia for American military supplies bound for Afghanistan. In September 2009 Obama made a major concession to Moscow by announcing that a Bush policy to deploy anti-ballistic missiles in Poland and a radar station in the Czech Republic would instead be moved to warships on the Black Sea near Iran. Their relationship peaked on April 8, 2010 when they signed the START III treaty at Prague. Under the agreement each side would reduce its nuclear weapons to 1,550 and determine the mix among land, sea and air-launched missiles.

Their third summit was a letdown. Obama hosted Medvedev in Washington in June 2010. Rather than treat Medvedev to an elaborate state dinner, he took the Russian president to Ray's Hell Burger in Arlington, Virginia. Medvedev then flew to Silicon Valley where he toured the headquarters of several high technology corporations. Then, on June 27, they met at the Group of 8 summit in Toronto during which the FBI announced the arrests of eleven Russian sleeper agents who had infiltrated America over the previous years and even decades, ideally to infiltrate key government and business positions. One spy escaped but the other ten pleaded guilty to espionage charges in July. Eventually they were exchanged for four Russian officials who had been caught spying for the CIA or MI6.

If Obama's relations with Medvedev were cordial and businesslike, his relations with Putin were the opposite. Indeed, Putin and Obama despised each other. Each meeting was frosty, starting with their first in Moscow on July 7, 2009, when Putin was prime minister. Their most awkward summit was at the G-20 meeting at San Jose, Mexico, on June 18 and 19, 2012 after Putin regained the presidency. After a perfunctory handshake, they sat stiffly side by side with each occasionally glancing warily at the other. Obama later described Putin as "looking like that bored kid in the back of the classroom" with "that kind of slouch."[35]

Secretary of State Hillary Clinton also had an acrimonious relationship with Putin. She first enraged him by refusing a request by Foreign Minister Sergei Lavrov that she grant a visa to Oleg Deripaska, a Russian mobster, money-launderer, oligarch and Putin supporter. In March 2010, when Clinton met Putin in Moscow, he disdained her and ranted against the United States and NATO expansion. She later observed that "Putin's claim that NATO's open door is a threat to Russia reflects his refusal to accept the idea that Russia's relations with the West could be based on partnership and mutual interest."[36]

Russian-American relations steadily worsened. Clinton infuriated Putin when she denounced Russia's 2011 Duma election for massive fraud that awarded most seats to United Russia, Putin's party. She asserted: "The Russian people, like people everywhere, deserve the right to have their voices heard and their votes counted. And that means they deserve fair, free, transparent elections and leaders who are accountable to them."[37] Putin would avenge himself in 2016 when Clinton campaigned to become America's president.

Meanwhile another issue arose that enraged both Moscow and Washington, although for opposite reasons. Bill Browder was the chief executive officer for Heritage Capital Management, an American corporation that invested billions of dollars in Russia, especially Gazprom. In 2005 Browder tried to wield his influence to pressure Gazprom's board of directors to open their books to public scrutiny. The Kremlin retaliated by barring Browder from Russia. Browder withdrew $4.5 billion from Heritage and two affiliates, leaving them shell companies. The Kremlin struck back by issuing Browder a multi-billion-dollar tax penalty and arresting many of Heritage's Russian employees. Browder engaged the Moscow legal firm Firestone Duncan. In 2008 police arrested Firestone Duncan's head lawyer, Sergei Magnitsky. Putin was determined to make a harsh example of Magnitsky who had revealed massive tax fraud by Gazprom and its affiliates and corruption by government officials. On November 16, 2009 Magnitsky died in prison after suffering beatings and being denied medical treatment. Congress retaliated by passing the 2012 "Sergei Magnitsky Rule of Law Accountability Act" that froze the financial assets and forbade visas for a list of top Kremlin officials implicated for confiscating Heritage's assets, imprisoning its employees and murdering Magnitsky.[38]

Bizarrely, Putin retaliated by barring Americans from adopting Russian children and canceling the Future Leaders Exchange (FLEX) program that brought 8,000 Russian teenagers to American high schools and homes over twenty-one years. His excuse was that fifteen teens had chosen to remain in America, of whom a gay couple adopted one, while an adopted small child had died after being left in a locked car for nine hours. That overlooked the reality that Americans had adopted more than 50,000 Russian children who needed loving families since 1999, while over 800,000 children remained in orphanages. Compounding the absurdity, Putin had not just Browder but the deceased Magnitsky tried in absentia for tax fraud; the court found both men guilty in 2013.

The Kremlin, along with other anti-American regimes, scored an immense intelligence and propaganda windfall in June 2013. Edward Snowden, a computer expert employed by the National Security Agency (NSA), defected after stealing and sending millions of top-secret documents to the Manchester Guardian, Washington Post and New York Times. Snowden's first choice was Cuba, but the State Department revoked his passport while he was at Moscow's Sheremetyevo airport on June 23. Putin gleefully rejected Obama's request to extradite Snowden and instead granted him asylum. Kremlin controlled or influenced media in Russia and around the world celebrated Snowden as a hero while the newspapers released the often-embarrassing secret reports, including one that revealed American intelligence tapped the telephones of western allied leaders like Angela Merkel. All Obama immediately could do was cancel his pending full state visit to Moscow that Putin had prepared. Instead, Obama would only attend the scheduled Group of Twenty meeting in St Petersburg.

Then in 2014 came the tough sanctions imposed by the United States, European Union and other allies to punish Russia for annexing Ukraine's Crimean peninsula and imposing puppet regimes on the two eastern provinces of Luhansk and Donetsk. Secretary of State John Kerry expressed the collective stunned outrage against the Kremlin's blatant imperialism: "It's really nineteenth century behavior in the twenty-first century. You just don't invade another country on phony pretexts in order to assert your interests."[39] The sanctions punished Putin's inner circle with bans on travel for a list of oligarchs and bans on business for a list of corporations complicit in Russian imperialism. Putin angrily protested those sanctions, then issued his own list of western people and products barred from entering Russia. Yet this policy, like his ban on foreign adoptions of Russian orphans, hurt Russia far more than the western world. Russian imperialism in Ukraine forced NATO to become stronger. In 2015 Obama increased America's commitment to Ukraine by sending 350 advisors and authorizing sales of military weapons and equipment.

During NATO's summit at Newport, Wales, in September 2014, all twenty-eight members agreed to devote at least 2 per cent of their respective economies to military spending by 2024. After brandishing that stick, they extended a carrot to Putin:

> We continue to believe that a partnership between NATO and Russia based on respect for international law would be of strategic value. We continue to aspire to a co-operative, constructive relationship with Russia, including reciprocal and confidence-building and transparency measures and increased mutual understanding of NATO's and Russia's non-strategic nuclear force postures in Europe, based on our common security concerns and interests, where each country freely chooses its future.[40]

Obama then flew to Tallinn, Estonia's capital, to declare: "We'll be here for Estonia. We will be here for Latvia. We will be here for Lithuania. You lost your independence once before. With NATO, you will never lose it again."[41]

As usual, the Kremlin could only denounce harshly what it could not prevent and could not admit that it had provoked. Meanwhile, the sanctions combined with a global oil glut to damage Russia's economy as the ruble plummeted in value, foreign exchange reserves dwindled, prices soared, capital fled and the Kremlin's budget deficit worsened.

During his eight years in the White House, Obama failed to achieve the "reset" for better relations with Russia that he had sought after he became president. Russian imperialism in Ukraine destroyed that possibility. Obama explained that Russia was "a regional power that is threatening some of its immediate neighbors – not out of strength, but from weakness".[42] The only way to deal with an insecure bully is to contain rather than appease him, which is what the Obama administration, along with NATO, the EU and allies elsewhere, did with tough economic sanctions against Russia. Ironically, Obama's characterization of Russia and by extension Putin as an insecure bully would just as aptly describe America's next president.

The man who followed Barack Obama into the White House clashed with him starkly in intelligence, integrity, temperament, knowledge and stands on the issues. Donald Trump beat sixteen contenders for the Republican Party's presidential nomination, then beat Democratic candidate Hillary Clinton. With the votes counted on November 8, nearly three million more Americans voted for Clinton than Trump. The final tally was 65,853,652 or 48.0 per cent for Clinton and 62,985,134 or 45.93 per cent for Trump. However, Trump racked up a decisive Electoral College victory with 304 to 227 votes. The key swing states favoring Trump were Michigan, Wisconsin and Pennsylvania which he won by 77,000 total votes or a 1 per cent margin.[43]

How did Trump do it?[44] By starring in his own so-called reality television show, *The Apprentice*, from 2004 to 2015, he exceeded in fame any of his Republican rivals. Yet that alone did not clinch his victory over them, let alone Clinton. Trump's character was critical to his victory because it mirrored that of countless other Americans. He won despite or, more likely, because of his non-stop bullying, lying, bellowing, narcissism, boasting, sexism and racism. His won despite or, more likely, because of his demagoguery and Midas-lifestyle that enflamed the prejudices, jealousies, fears, hatreds and hopes of nearly half of Americans who ranted and fantasized vicariously through him. He won despite or, more likely, because he warred against the truths of science, asserting that global warming was a hoax, and the truths of history, asserting that massive tax cuts for the rich would pay for themselves. He won despite or, more likely, because of his business incompetence that led to six bankruptcies; his refusal to reveal his tax returns; his links to organized crime, including the Russian mob; his stiffing of contractors; and the nineteen women who accused him of sexual assault. He rightly bragged that he could shoot someone in the middle of Fifth Avenue and his supporters would adore him even more. Trump's ability to manipulate the mass media into feeding frenzies with his outrageous stunts and statements earned him $2 billion in free exposure, twice what Clinton received, by the end of February 2016.[45] Yet Trump's deplorable character alone was not enough for his election to the White House.

Senator Bernie Sanders of Vermont also contributed to Trump's victory. Although he proudly asserts himself as an independent socialist, he tried to capture the Democratic Party's presidential nomination. After announcing that ambition on May 26, 2015, he spent the next fourteen months savaging Clinton, splintering the Democratic Party between liberals and socialists and forcing Clinton to embrace the political far left rather than sensible center. Yet Clinton would likely have still won despite Sanders' invective.

Ultimately FBI Director James Comey tipped the 2016 election in Trump's favor by publicly discrediting Clinton twice while hiding an active investigation of Trump's ties to Putin and Russia. In doing so, Comey violated FBI protocol and the Hatch Act that outlaws federal officials from interfering in elections. On July 5 he declared that the FBI had ended its investigation of Clinton's emails, having found no evidence of crimes but then vented a fifteen-minute tirade condemning her for alleged wrongdoing. During an appearance before the House Judiciary Committee on September 28, he refused to confirm or deny whether the FBI was investigating Trump campaign collusion with the Kremlin. Then, on October 28, just eleven days before the election, Comey announced that he was re-opening the Clinton investigation. That inflicted the coup de grâce to Clinton's campaign as her poll numbers dropped several percentage points, enough for Trump to win crucial swing states. Senator Harry Reid fired off a letter to Comey, condemning him for favoring Trump over Clinton and thus violating the Hatch Act: "As soon as you came into possession of the slightest innuendo related to Secretary Clinton, you rushed to publicize it in the most negative light possible." Meanwhile, Comey possessed: "explosive information about close ties and co-ordination among Donald Trump, his top advisors, and the Russian government. The public has a right to know this information."[46]

How important to Trump's victory was the massive cyber-assault against American democracy by Russia's intelligence agencies?[47] Just how many Americans voted for Trump or did not vote for Clinton because of Moscow's systematic cyber onslaught is unknowable. What is known is that, for America's 2016 election, the Kremlin had three related goals: discredit the electoral system, defeat Hillary Clinton, and elect Donald Trump. The Russians brilliantly advanced all three goals via two simultaneous campaigns. Cyber-trolls hacked and spearfished into state electoral systems, political parties, and campaign organizations to steal and reveal embarrassing secrets. They also created incendiary websites designed to exacerbate racial, class, ethnic, religious and political animosities that savaged Clinton and celebrated her opponents including Trump, Bernie Sanders and Green Party candidate Jill Stein.

Spearheading that assault was the Main Directorate (GU), Russia's military intelligence, seconded by the Foreign Intelligence Service (SVR). The operation actually began in 2014 when they despatched agents to the United States to perfect their English and understand the diversity, issues, acrimonies and extremes of American politics. Watching the television series *House of Cards* about corrupt American politicians was mandatory for the agents. The Russians created two types of websites and underwrote most of their operations with Bitcoin. Mainstream voters viewed innocuous sounding websites like Cozy Bear, Fancy Bear, Heart of Texas, Dukes, Smoking Gun and Guccifer. Radical leftists and rightists received incendiary appeals from Black Lives Matter, Woke Blacks, United Muslims of America, The South United, Guns4Life, Being Patriotic and Pray for America. The most prolific source was the Internet Research Agency located in St Petersburg with 400 cyber-trolls employed in three twelve-hour weekly shifts during which each was "expected to write five political posts, ten non-political ones, and at least 150 comments on fellow trolls' posts."[48] The Internet Research Agency was funded by a holding company owned by Yevgeny Prigozhin, among Putin's coterie of oligarchs. Each cyber-troll had multiple fake American personas and groups whose incendiary views appeared on

Facebook, Instagram, YouTube, Twitter, Reddit and other popular social media sites. The Russians especially targeted African Americans, hoping to discourage them from voting by inundating them with fake videos and texts that portrayed Clinton, the police and the electoral system as racist. On Facebook alone, the Russians fabricated 2,700 accounts and 80,000 posts that reached 126 million Americans, nearly as many as the 132 million who voted in the election; and on Instagram 170 accounts and 120,000 posts that reached 20 million Americans. In the ten weeks before the election the Russians flooded Twitter with 3,814 accounts and 50,258 bots.[49]

Two Russian attacks were especially damaging to Clinton. First came the computer hacking of John Podesta, her campaign manager, with a spearfish masked by a Google warning about his Gmail account's security. On March 19, 2016 Podesta clicked on the bait and followed instructions to click on a website and change his password. The Russians extracted thousands of emails, many with politically damaging messages that they later posted on WikiLeaks. More devastating was an attack on July 22, three days before the Democratic Party convention opened. WikiLeaks had earlier beseeched Guccifer: "If you have anything hillary [sic] related we want it in the next two days prefable [sic] because the DNC is approaching and she will solidify Bernie supporters behind her after."[50] WikiLeaks received and posted 19,252 emails and 8,034 attachments from the Democratic National Committee (DNC). Many of these emails revealed that the DNC had helped Hillary Clinton against her socialist rival Bernie Sanders. That enraged Sanders partisans and many did not vote for Clinton on Election Day.

The Russians also targeted state electoral systems and voting machine manufacturers. The Senate Intelligence Committee reported in May 2018 that, during the 2016 election Russian cyber-attacks penetrated the voting systems of at least twenty-one states to varying degrees, with the power to delete registered voters or change votes in at least six states, although no evidence revealed that the hackers had done so. They also penetrated at least one of the three largest voting machine manufacturers, embedding moles to gather information.[51]

News of Trump's victory provoked champagne- and vodka-soaked celebrations at the Kremlin, Russia's intelligence agencies and government-controlled mass media.[52] Why did the Russians back Trump? Putin saw in Trump two critical potential assets. First his easy to manipulate narcissism. Second someone who if he became president would devastate American national security, western civilization and the global system.

Trump has admired Putin for many years. During the 2013 Miss Universe contest that he held in Moscow, Trump was eager to meet Putin, tweeting "will he become my new best friend?" Trump was able to hold the contest there because one of his fixers, Rob Goldstone, had close ties with pop star Emin Agalarov and his father Aras Agalarov, a billionaire real estate developer known as "Putin's builder" and the pageant's sponsor. To Trump's disappointment, Putin did not meet him at that time. Yet that did not dampen his adulation. After Russia invaded Ukraine in 2014, Trump gushed incoherently about Putin:

> Well, he's done an amazing job taking the mantle. And he's taken it away from the president [Obama]. And you look at what he's doing. And so smart. When you see the riots in a country because they're the Russians, okay, "Let's go and take it over." And he really goes step by step by step, and you have to give him a lot of credit.[53]

Then, in December 2015, Trump was thrilled when Putin called him "a talent, without any doubt" and "brilliant," although the latter was a mistranslation that should have been "colorful." Trump marveled: "It is always a great honor to be so nicely complimented by a man so highly respected within his own country and beyond."[54]

Actually, the relationship between Trump and Putin is one-sided. Trump's adoration of Putin is unrequited. Undoubtedly, Putin is as contemptuous of Trump's ignorance, childishness, petulance and destructiveness as Trump is fawning of him. As a KGB officer, Putin exploited numerous willing or duped "useful idiots" like Trump. Putin has at times revealed his disdain for Trump. For instance, after their 2017 summit at Da Nang, Vietnam, he rejected any notion of an intimate relationship between them, insisting that Trump "is not my bride and I am not his groom." That choice of words designated Putin the dominant male and Trump the dependent female.[55]

What explains Trump's slavishness toward Putin?[56] Does he merely bear homage to a ruthless autocrat whose powers to steal billions of dollars, invade countries and assassinate opponents Trump fantasizes wielding for himself? While that may well be, Trump must be careful not to offend the supreme leader of a country whose organized crime syndicates may have lent or given him as much as a couple of billion dollars laundered through his real estate and casinos. That relationship goes back to 1984 when the Russian mob first laundered money through a shell company to buy five luxury apartments in Trump Tower. Since then, according to investigator Craig Unger, "Trump and his associates have had significant ties to at least fifty-nine people who facilitated business between Trump and the Russians, including relationships with dozens who have alleged ties to the Russian Mafia."[57] Investigator Thomas Frank revealed that Russian mobsters accounted for 1,300 or twenty per cent of Trump's 6,500 condominiums sold since the 1980s "in secretive, all-cash transactions that enable buyers to avoid legal scrutiny by shielding their finances and identities."[58] A typical transaction occurred in 2008 when Trump pocketed $54 million after mobster Dmitry Rybolovlev paid $95 million for a Palm Beach mansion that Trump originally bought for $41 million. Trump's biggest loan from Russian sources – $360 million – came via Deutsche Bank, whose owners are among the most notorious money launderers who eventually pleaded guilty and paid $7.2 billion in fines in a Justice Department trial.[59]

Yet another back channel to the Kremlin emanated from Trump's first wife, Ivana Zelnikova, whose family was linked to Czechoslovakia's Ministry of State Security (StB) and thus to the Soviet KGB.[60] After the democratic revolution overthrew Czechoslovakia's communist regime, the liberals revealed StB's secret files to the world. Among them was the file on the Trumps. The most intriguing passage revealed Trump's presidential ambitions: "Even though it looks like a utopia, D. TRUMP is confident he will succeed."[61] Just what communist agent received that confidence from Trump and what hold the agent had over him remains secret.

Atop all the illegal finance are rumors that the Kremlin has kinky sex videos of Trump during one or more of his Moscow sojourns in 1987, 1996 and 2013. If the Russians blackmailed Trump that most likely happened during his first two visits when the Kremlin entertained him in grand style in hopes of cutting joint venture development deals. Each time, Trump was tempted but ultimately declined because the Soviets insisted on a 51 per cent share. Yet did he reject all offers in Moscow, including those whispered by beautiful Russian girls who promised to fulfill all his fantasies? If not, perhaps one day the truth will surface. Regardless, shortly after returning from his first Moscow sojourn, Trump spent $100,000 for ads in the *New York Times*, *Boston Globe* and *Washington Post* calling on America to withdraw its military forces from the Persian Gulf, a top Kremlin foreign policy goal.[62]

The most salacious account of Trump's links with the Kremlin is the so-called "dossier," the product of collaboration between a journalist and a spy. Glen Simpson was a former *Wall Street Journal* reporter who founded Fusion GPS to conduct political research for whoever was willing to pay for it. Christopher Steele was a career British MI6 operative who specialized in Russia. After retiring in 2009, Steele formed a consulting company called Orbis Business Intelligence and passed critical intelligence on Russia to Justice Department prosecutor Bruce Ohr who specialized in the Russian mob. Fusion and Orbis collaborated on numerous investigations. Among Fusion's clients was Paul Singer, a billionaire conservative but anti-Trump. In early 2016 he contracted Fusion to find dirt on Trump but gave up after Trump appeared to have secured the nomination. In April the DNC and the Clinton campaign contracted the investigation via Marc Elias, a Democratic Party lawyer. In early June Simpson asked Steele to conduct that mission. Using his network of informants in Russia, Steele soon produced a preliminary three-page assessment that he eventually expanded to thirty-five pages.

The dossier's conclusions were stunning:

The Russian regime has been cultivating, supporting, and assisting TRUMP for at least 5 years. Aim, endorsed by PUTIN, has been to encourage splits and divisions in western alliance … TRUMP … and his inner circle have accepted a regular flow of intelligence from the

Kremlin, including on his Democratic and other political rivals ... Former top Russian intelligence officer claims FSB has compromised TRUMP through his activities in MOSCOW sufficiently to be able to blackmail him. According to several knowledgeable sources, his conduct in Moscow has included perverted sexual acts which have been arranged and monitored by the FSB.

The kinkiest passage read:

TRUMP's (perverted) conduct in Moscow included hiring the presidential suite of the Ritz Carlton Hotel where he knew President and Mrs OBAMA (whom he hated) had stayed on one of their official trips to Russia, and defiling the bed where they had slept by employing a number of prostitutes to perform a 'golden shower' (urination) show in front of him. The hotel was known to be under FSB control with microphones and concealed cameras in all the main rooms to record anything.

The result of Trump's "unorthodox behavior in Russia over the years had provided the authorities there with enough embarrassing material on the new Republican presidential candidate to be able to blackmail him if they so wished." The dossier also revealed that the Russians had "compromising material on Hillary CLINTON ... and mainly comprises bugged conversations she had on various trips to Russia ... rather than any embarrassing conduct." The dossier concluded that Russia's intervention achieved its goal:

of shifting the US political consensus in Russia's perceived interests regardless of who won. It basically comprised of pushing candidate CLINTON away from President OBAMA's policies. The best example of this was that both candidates now openly opposed the draft trade agreements, TPP, and TTIP, which were assessed by Moscow as detrimental to Russian interests.

Steele's findings so disturbed him that he shared his dossier with the FBI on July 5, 2016. In a revised report Steele submitted on July 30, he concluded that Trump's collusion with the Kremlin began at least eight years before.[63]

Conspiracy happens when two or more people plan an illegal act. The most serious national security allegation against Donald Trump is that he and his presidential campaign conspired with the Kremlin to subvert America's 2016 election. Although overwhelming evidence indicates that Trump and his coterie wanted and tried to do so, their fumbling efforts apparently fell short of convictable conspiracy. At least that was the conclusion of Special Counsel Robert Mueller's twenty-two-month investigation. That conclusion undoubtedly reflected political as much or more as legal calculations. Conspiracy as a crime does not depend on the conspiracy's success, only on seriously attempting it. And that certainly took place. But Mueller was straitjacketed by Justice Department rules that sitting presidents cannot be indicted, along with the political firestorm he would have ignited had he broken those rules.

George Papadopoulos was a Trump campaign advisor charged with developing relations with the Russians. In March, he traveled to Rome and in April to London to meet with Joseph Mifsud, a former Maltese diplomat and then professor at London's Academy of Diplomacy. Mifsud revealed that the Russians had "thousands" of potentially embarrassing Clinton emails that they would eventually release, and introduced him to Ivan Timofeev who directed the Russian International Affairs Council, and Olga Polonskaya who falsely claimed to be Putin's niece. Papadopoulos informed campaign headquarters that the Russians had "history-making" "dirt" on Clinton and wanted a meeting between Trump and Putin.[64] Then Papadopoulos committed an act that would have disastrous consequences for himself, other campaign members and Trump. In a swanky London bar he boasted that he knew about Russian "dirt" on Clinton to Alexander Downer, Australia's ambassador to Britain. Alarmed, Downer informed the American ambassador who passed that intelligence to the FBI, whose director, James Comey, launched an investigation. Had Papadopoulos been discreet, Trump and his coterie may have gotten away undetected with their array of national security, money-laundering, tax evasion and electoral campaign crimes.

Trump's campaign advisors were eager to seize that opportunity without rousing any suspicions from America's intelligence community or the Federal Election Commission (FEC). For their point man, they chose Carter Page, who had developed deep ties to Russian oligarchs from 2004 to 2015, first as Merrill Lynch's oil and gas portfolio investor, then with his own company Global Energy Capital. At some point, Russian intelligence recruited him, although it is unclear how cognizant he was of that. His primary SVR handler, Viktor Podobnyy, described Page as "an idiot" who "forgot who I am."[65] Page joined the Trump campaign in December 2015. The Trump campaign's excuse for Page to go to Russia came with an engineered invitation for him to deliver a speech at Moscow University's New Economic School on July 7. There he lambasted America and Europe for impeding "progress through their often hypocritical focus on ideas such as democratization, inequality, corruption and regime change" and for having "perpetuated Cold War tendencies." He lauded Putin for bringing to international relations "mutual respect, equality and mutual benefit and tolerance, and access to resources."[66] Among the high-ranking Russians he met were Deputy Prime Minister Sergei Prikhodko and Igor Sechin, a close Putin advisor and Rosneft Oil Company's chief. Among the subjects they discussed was the possibility of lifting sanctions if Trump became president.[67]

Paul Manafort joined Trump's campaign on March 29, 2016 and managed it from June 20 to August 19. His association with Trump goes back to 1980 when he and his law partners Charles Black and Roger Stone lobbied on his behalf. He was a long-time Republican Party operative, starting with Gerald Ford then Ronald Reagan, George H.W. Bush, Robert Dole and George W. Bush. He also advised such foreign thugs as Ferdinand Marcos of the Philippines, Mobutu Sese Seko of Zaire, Jonas Savimbi of Angola and Viktor Yanukovych of Ukraine. Manafort's tenure as first campaign manager and then advisor for Yanukovych from 2004 to 2014 was his most lucrative until the Ukrainian president fled to exile in Russia after a democratic revolution erupted against his autocracy. For his services, Manafort may have received and laundered $75 million through fifteen shell companies in Cyprus, the Cayman Islands, and St Vincent.[68]

Among Manafort's array of character flaws was spending beyond his means. A $15,000 ostrich leather suit symbolized his decadence and vulgarity. To cover his worsening debt, Manafort borrowed $17 million from Oleg Deripaska, an oligarch billionaire closely tied to Putin. He will never be able to repay that loan which makes him a target for assassination. Another business crony of Manafort was Konstantin Kilimnik, tied to Russian intelligence. On July 7, 2016 Manafort emailed Kilimnik a request to inform Deripaska that "If he needs private briefings" on Trump "we can accommodate."[69] Manafort passed polling data to Kilimnik. On August 19 Trump had to fire Manafort after a *New York Times* report revealed that he had pocketed $12.7 million from pro-Russian Ukrainian oligarchs.[70]

Meanwhile, another potential channel opened between Putin and Trump. Martina Butina was a twenty-nine-year-old Russian spy who enrolled at American University in Washington in January 2015. She used her university affiliation as a front to recruit Republicans as unwitting Russian agents through conservative organizations like the National Rifle Association (NRA) and Conservative Political Action Conference (CPAC), events like the National Prayer Breakfast and evangelical Freedom Fest, and meetings with prominent leaders like anti-taxation movement head Grover Norquist and NRA head David Keene. In speeches before various conservative groups she extolled Putin and denounced sanctions against Russia. At least $300,000 moved through her bank account to fund her operations. Often joining her during her first year of recruiting was Alexander Torshin, the deputy governor of Russia's central bank, known affiliate of Russian intelligence and crime gangs and attendee of NRA conventions since 2011. Butina's key target was Donald Trump. She tried and failed to arrange a meeting between Trump and Putin. In July 2015 she appeared at a Trump news conference and asked him what his Russian policy would be as president. He replied, "I know Putin and I'll tell you what, we'll get along with Putin. I don't think you need the sanctions."[71]

Sex was among Butina's tactics for getting what she wanted. She so beguiled Paul Erickson, a Republican leader and American Conservative Union board member, that he actually wrote many of her class assignments to free her for her spy duties.[72] In May 2016, Erickson fired off a stunning email entitled "Kremlin connection" to Rick Dearborn at Trump headquarters:

> Putin is deadly serious about building a good relationship with Mr Trump. He wants to extend an invitation to Mr Trump to visit him in the Kremlin before the election .... The Kremlin believes that the only possibility of a true reset in this relationship would be with a new Republican White House. Ever since Hillary compared Putin to Hitler, all senior Russian leaders consider her beyond redemption.[73]

Rick Clay, another conservative leader and Butina devotee, advocated a meeting between Trump and Torshin at an upcoming NRA conference in Louisville where Trump would speak. Torshin would then arrange for Trump and evangelical leader Franklin Graham, Billy Graham's son, to meet Putin in Moscow. He implored Dearborn to imagine:

> The optics of Mr Trump in Russia with Franklin Graham attending an event of over 1,000 World Christian Leaders addressing the Defense of Persecuted Christians accompanied by a very visible meeting between President Putin and Mr Trump would devastate the Clinton campaign's effort to marginalize Mr Trump on foreign policy and embolden him further with evangelicals.[74]

Although Torshin and Trump did meet in Louisville, they did not implement the second stage meeting with Putin in Moscow.

On June 6 Donald Trump Junior received an electrifying offer from Rob Goldstone, a British business ally, on behalf of billionaire Aras Agalarov, "Putin's builder" and sponsor of Trump's 2013 Miss Universe pageant in Moscow. Agalarov knew Russians who could:

> provide the Trump campaign with some official documents and information that would incriminate Hillary and her dealings with Russia and would be very useful to your father. This is obviously very high level and sensitive information but is part of Russia and its government's support for Mr Trump ... I can send this info to your father ... but it is ultra sensitive so wanted to send this to you first.

Trump fired back: "If it's what you say I love it especially later in the summer."[75]

Donald Trump Junior, Jared Kushner and Paul Manafort, the candidate's respective son, son-in-law and soon to be campaign manager met with four Russians, Natalia Veselnitskaya, a Kremlin-linked lawyer, Anatoli Samochornov, the translator, Rinat Akhmetshin, a Russian-American lobbyist, and Irakly Kaveladze, a businessman, at Trump Tower on June 9. Rob Goldstone, who set up the meeting, was also there. To the Trump team's disappointment, the Russians did not present any "dirt" on Clinton. Instead, Veselnitskaya implored candidate Trump to support the suspension of the Magnitsky Act that imposed sanctions on Russia. Trump Junior was non-committal, suggesting that his father would address that issue after he won election. At no point before or after did Trump, Kushner or Manafort inform the FBI of their meeting with the Russians. It is illegal for a political campaign to receive any financial, advertising or information aid from a foreign group or individual. On January 25, 2019 the Justice Department indicted Veselnitskaya for obstruction and money-laundering.

The meeting's outcome undoubtedly disappointed candidate Donald Trump. Two days earlier, during a campaign rally, he had boasted:

> I am going to give a major speech on probably Monday of next week and we're going to be discussing all of the things that have taken place with the Clintons. I think you're going to find it very informative and very, very interesting.[76]

That speech would have to wait, but not long.

As for collusion between the future American president and the Russian president, Trump was well aware that Putin backed his White House campaign and he in return protected Putin against criticism. His first notorious defense came during a television interview in December 2015, when he adamantly denied the charge that Putin had his opponents murdered: "In all fairness to Putin, you're saying he killed people. I haven't seen that. I don't know that he has. Have you been able to prove that? I think our country does plenty of killing also." He lauded Putin for "running his country and at least he's a leader, unlike what we have in this country." During a July 2, 2016 campaign rally, Trump revealed what a sucker he was for flattery and how much he was willing to concede in return when he boasted: "Then Putin said, 'Trump is a genius, he's going to be the next great leader of the United States .... Wouldn't it be nice if we actually got along with Russia?"[77] Trump issued this tweet on July 25: "The new joke is that Russia leaked the disastrous DNC emails, which should never have been written (stupid), because Putin likes me."[78]

Trump was partly right. Whether Putin actually liked him is moot. What was clear is that Putin wanted Trump to become president and was doing all he could to realize that, including releasing via WikiLeaks tens of thousands of emails that embarrassed Clinton and the Democrats.[79] Trump bellowed for more revelations during a speech on July 27: "Russia if you are listening, I hope you are able to find the 30,000 emails that are missing," referring to the personal messages that Clinton had deleted. Indeed Moscow was listening. Within hours, GU launched cyber-penetrations of seventy-six Clinton campaign websites and eventually targeted more than 300 people involved in her campaign.[80]

Trump's most blatant collusion with Russia during his campaign came at the Republican Party convention in Cleveland that acclaimed him the presidential nominee. The only change that Trump insisted upon for the Republican platform was to shift from condemnation to reconciliation toward Moscow over its imperialism in Ukraine. When asked about that during a television interview on July 31, Trump insisted that Putin is "not going into Ukraine, OK, just so you understand, he's not going into Ukraine, all right?" When asked if he realized that the Russians were already there, Trump replied, "Ok – well, he's there in a certain way." He then defended Russian imperialism: "You know, the people of Crimea, from what I've heard, would rather be with Russia than where they were."[81]

The question of Trump's collusion with Russia's cyber-offensive surfaced during the first of three presidential candidate debates on September 26. In response to the question of what to do to counter Russia, Clinton replied,

There is no doubt now of Russia cyberattacks against all kinds of organizations in our country ... I know Donald's very praiseworthy of Vladimir Putin, but Putin is playing a really tough, long game here. And one of the things he has done is to let loose cyber-attackers to hack into government files, to hack into personal files, hack into the Democratic National Committee. I was so shocked when Donald publicly invited Putin to hack into Americans. That is just unacceptable.

Trump angrily dismissed allegations of Russian cyber manipulation of America's election: "I don't think anyone knows it was Russia. It could be Russia, it could be China, and it could also be someone sitting on their bed that weighs 400 pounds."[82] They revisited that critical issue during their October 19 debate. After Trump insisted that Putin had no respect for Clinton, she quipped: "Well that's because he'd rather have a puppet as president of the United States." An enraged Trump could only bluster, "I am not a puppet! You're the puppet."[83]

America's intelligence community first became aware of the Kremlin's campaign to subvert America's political system in August 2015. The tip off came from the Netherlands' General intelligence and Security Service that had penetrated Russia's SVR and discovered that it had hacked the Democratic Party's National Committee (DNC). The Dutch informed the National Security Agency (NSA), which informed the FBI, which informed the DNC. Unfortunately, the DNC leaders failed to take precautions that might have prevented future hackings.

Throughout 2016 America's intelligence community amassed ever more alarming intelligence of how massive and systematic Moscow's campaign was to discredit and warp the presidential election. In July CIA Director John Brennan, FBI Director James Comey, NSA Director Mike Rogers and DNI Director James Clapper formed a joint working group to share information and assess the Russian assault. On August 4 Brennan called FSB Director Alexander Bortnikov and warned him that Russia would pay a high price if it did not end its assault on America's election; Bortnikov denied any wrongdoing. Actually, Brennan was bluffing. President Obama and his advisors initially agreed that the United States should not retaliate or even reveal that the Russians were trying to warp America's election system, discredit Clinton and elect Trump. They feared that doing so would itself discredit the election by appearing to make Clinton a martyr and Trump a lackey. After all, anticipating that he would lose, Trump was already denouncing America's electoral system by claiming that it was rigged against him. Obama and his advisors assumed Clinton would win despite Russia's machinations. Only after that would they expose and impose sanctions against Moscow. During the September Group of 20 summit Obama met privately with Putin and demanded that he end the assault, to which Putin angrily retorted, "I don't know anything about it."[84]

Meanwhile the mainstream media sporadically reported on Russia's assault against the electoral system and Clinton in Trump's favor. The *Washington Post*'s front page carried an alarming story on June 14 headlined: "Russia Government Hackers Penetrated DNC, Stole Opposition Research on Trump." On August 5 former CIA director Mike Morell wrote a *New York Times* opinion piece in which he described Trump as "an unwitting agent of the Russian Federation."[85]

The White House did try indirectly to sound the alarm without being alarming. Obama authorized Clapper to warn both political parties of Russian hacking and to encourage them to upgrade their malware. On August 15 he had Homeland Security Department Secretary Jeh Johnson encourage state electoral commissions to bolster their cyber security. Meanwhile he first had the CIA brief the Joint Intelligence Committee, then had Johnson brief the twelve top Republican and Democratic leaders of Congress. Finally, he invited to the White House Congressional Democratic leaders Nancy Pelosi and Harry Reid, and Republican leaders Paul Ryan and Mitch McConnell, shared the intelligence with them, and urged them to issue a joint denunciation of the Russian assault. Pelosi and Reid agreed to do so, Ryan was reluctant, and McConnell was fiercely opposed and accused Obama of trying to politicize the election; McConnell stonewalled until September 28 when he grudgingly agreed to sign a generic statement that did not mention Russia but simply warned state election committees to guard against malware.

Three Democratic leaders in Congress issued their own warnings. On August 27 Senator Reid had published a private letter to Comey in which he asserted:

the threat of the Russian government tampering in our presidential election is more extensive than widely known and may include the intent to falsify official election results …. The evidence of a direct connection between the Russian government and Donald Trump's presidential campaign continues to mount …. The prospect of a hostile government actively seeking to undermines our free and fair elections represents one of the greatest threats to our democracy since the Cold War.

Predictably, most Democrats expressed alarm at the Russian threat while the Republicans dismissed the idea as a Democratic political smear tactic. On September 22 Joint Intelligence Committee members Senator Diane Feinstein and Representative Adam Schiff issued this more restrained declaration: "Based on briefings we have received we have concluded that the Russian intelligence agencies are making a serious and concerted effort to influence the U.S. election." They demanded that Putin stop the machinations.[86]

Two other electrifying events obscured the White House's sole attempt directly to inform the public. During a press conference on October 7 the intelligence community's leaders announced that Russia was trying to influence America's election through 'cybertage'. Breaking news interrupted that message with an *Access Hollywood* recording of Trump boasting of sexually assaulting women, a revelation that would have crippled anyone's campaign but Trump's. WikiLeaks diluted that political bombshell by releasing the first tranche of 50,000 emails from John Podesta, Clinton's campaign advisor. October 7 also happened to be Vladimir Putin's birthday. The following day at a campaign rally Trump exclaimed, "I love WikiLeaks!" then led the crowd in the chant "Lock her up!" referring to his opponent Hillary Clinton for alleged and unproven crimes.[87]

The Trump team's attempts to collude with Putin did not end with the election victory. Trump's latest point man for Russia was General Michael Flynn who he named his national security advisor. Flynn had headed the Pentagon's Defense Intelligence Agency (DIA) but, in August 2014, was fired for insubordination, bad management and warping intelligence assessments. He started his own company, called Flynn Intel Group, which counted Russian oligarchs among its clients. In December 2015 Flynn actually sat beside Putin during a banquet celebrating the anniversary of Russia Today (RT) that broadcasts propaganda worldwide; the Kremlin had underwritten his trip's expenses and had given him $33,750 to appear. During the Republican Party convention, Flynn led the anti-Clinton chant "Lock her up!" In doing so, Flynn projected his own guilt for collusion onto a hated other.

Circumstantial evidence has Trump conspiring with the Kremlin after the election. He may have received secret word from Putin on November 12 when Arron Banks, the United Kingdom Independent Party's financier, Brexit leader and alleged Russian collaborator, met him at Trump Tower.[88] On December 1 Trump had Flynn and Jared Kushner, his son-in-law, meet Russian Ambassador Sergei Kislyak at Trump Tower. Flynn and Kushner stunned Kislyak by asking him to set up a secret channel with the Kremlin that would be undetected by America's intelligence community. As a former DIA director Flynn should have known how impractical that request was, let alone treasonous. Eventually the NSA would detect that back channel and a leak to the public would provoke catastrophic political and legal consequences. Kislyak informed Putin who saved the pending Trump administration from self-destruction by rejecting the request. Kushner met again with Kislyak along with Sergei Gorkov, an oligarch in charge of "Putin's slush fund," on December 13. Kushner negotiated a massive loan to stave off bankruptcy on a $1.2 billion Manhattan skyscraper his father had bought in 2008. His father was in prison after his conviction for committing numerous financial felonies.[89]

Meanwhile, Hamlet-like, Obama still debated what to do about Russia's assault on America's political system. During a press conference on December 16 he tried to hit Putin's psychological insecurities by declaring, "The Russians can't change us or significantly weaken us. They are a smaller country. Their economy doesn't produce anything that anybody wants to buy except oil, gas, and arms."[90] CIA Director Brennan finally convinced Obama to retaliate against the Kremlin. On December 29 the State Department announced that the United States would expel thirty-five known Russian spies, impose economic sanctions against Russia's intelligence agencies and their front companies, close the consulate in San Francisco and force Russians to evacuate compounds in New York and Maryland. The White House then braced itself for the Kremlin to inflict similar punishments against the United States. Those punishments never came.

Trump immediately authorized Flynn to call Kislyak and plead with him to forgo retaliation in return for a promise to revoke the sanctions after he became president. That plea worked. Putin promptly declared:

We regard the recent unfriendly steps taken by the outgoing U.S. administration as provocative and further weakening the Russia-U.S. relationship. Although we have the right to retaliate ... [we] will plan our future steps to restore Russian-U.S. relations based on the policies of the Trump administration.

On December 30 Trump lauded Putin with a tweet: "Great move on delay (by V. Putin)—I always knew he was very smart!"[91]

President-elect Trump received a high-level intelligence briefing by CIA director Brennan, DNI director Clapper, NSA director Rogers and FBI director Comey on January 6, 2018. They explained that America's intelligence community had concluded that Putin's regime had massively manipulated the 2016 election to discredit the system, defeat Clinton and promote Trump along with Bernie Sanders who fought Clinton for the Democratic nomination and Green Party candidate Jill Stein.[92] Comey recalled that Trump and his advisors "shifted immediately into a strategy session about messaging on Russia. About how they could spin what we'd just told them."[93] After his three colleagues left the room, Comey explained the Steele dossier that claimed the Kremlin had incriminating evidence against Trump that made him susceptible to blackmail.

To Comey then and thereafter with frequent public assertions, Trump vehemently rejected the idea of Russian manipulation on his behalf or embarrassing blackmail material on him. Instead, he accused America's intelligence community, or the "Deep State" as he called it, of trying to blackmail him. On January 10 he declared, "I think it was disgraceful – disgraceful that the intelligence agencies allowed any information [out] that turned out to be so false ... That's something that Nazi Germany would have done and did do."[94] Once again, Trump was projecting his own inner demons onto some scapegoat.

Donald Trump took the oath to protect America's Constitution on January 20, 2017. In doing so, he finally realized a dream that he had harbored most of his life and that included an aborted presidential run in 2000. His subsequent behavior as president would be the most controversial in American history.[95]

Never has a president's character more adversely affected his policies. Someone is pathological when he commits a crime repeatedly without remorse. By that definition, through his words and behavior, Trump parades pathological levels of lying, bullying, tax cheating, adultery and sexual predation.

Virtually everything about Trump is false and illicit. He always boasted that he turned a million-dollar loan from his father into a multi-billion-dollar corporate empire. Actually, his father gave him the equivalent of $413 million that he expanded through massive tax and business fraud. Trump blatantly cheated on his taxes, paying only $52.2 million or ten per cent of the $550 million that he actually owed.[96] He boasts of being the world's greatest businessman, yet blundered his way into six bankruptcies. As for sex, Trump is a chronic adulterer who paid at least two mistresses to remain silent during the 2016 election campaign with campaign funds, a felony. Nineteen women have formally filed sexual assault charges against him; countless others among his victims remained silent. Then there is Trump's pathological lying. He first acquired a national political following when he led the "Birther Movement" that propagated the lie that President Barack Obama was a foreign-born Muslim. The *Washington Post* has fact-checked Trump's daily spoken and written words ever since he entered the White House. Two years after taking power, Trump had committed 8,158 "false or misleading statements" during which averaged 5.9 daily his first year and 16.5 daily during his second year.[97] Finally, Trump is a vicious bully who, psychologically, projects his vilest characteristics onto hated others, at once scapegoating them and martyrizing himself. He is happiest when whipping campaign rallies of his adoring supporters into near lynch mob frenzies of hatred. Trump's pathological character flaws either inspire or do not trouble his zealous supporters, including many conservative Christians, who live vicariously through him. Trump's ability to personify the hatreds, fears, prejudices and hopes of nearly half of Americans is his greatest source of power. By autumn 2019 a dozen separate legal or congressional authorities were investigating Trump for conspiracy, obstruction of justice, campaign finance violations, tax fraud, witness tampering, emoluments and charity foundation violations.

After Vladimir Putin, Trump most admires and tries to emulate Roy Cohn, the lawyer who abetted Senator Joe McCarthy's right-wing political witch-hunts during the 1950s and afterwards an array of ultra-conservative politicians, Mafia bosses and rapacious corporate moguls until Cohn died of AIDS in 1986. He became close to Cohn in the 1970s when the latter helped Trump and his father get away with hundreds of millions of dollars of illegal business practices. One New York elite lawyer, Viktor Kovner, admitted, "You knew when you were in Cohn's presence you were in the presence of pure evil."[98]

Among Trump's more dangerous delusions as president is that he is the world's greatest negotiator, which he most exhaustingly boasted in his ghostwritten book *Art of the Deal*.[99] Trump is actually an awful negotiator because his narcissism and ignorance is so easy to manipulate. Flattery gains foreign leaders an advantage over Trump who subsequently gushes praise in return, along with often significant concessions. Michael McFaul, a former ambassador to Russia, explained Trump's deficient negotiating skills: "Trump sees a good meeting as a positive achievement. That's wrong! Good meetings are a means to an end."[100] Henry Kissinger explained, "It is dangerous to rely on personality or negotiating skills to break deadlocks; they cannot redeem the shortcomings of an ill-considered strategy."[101]

Trump's greatest skill is wielding mass media to project messages and images that excite his followers. His favorite form of communication is the tweet. Indeed, he boasts that he is the "Ernest Hemingway of one-hundred-forty characters."[102] Trump's obsession with tweets recalls Hillary Clinton's warning during the 2016 campaign that "A man you can bait with a tweet is not a man we can trust with nuclear weapons."[103] The far right Fox Broadcasting Corporation is at once Trump's bullhorn and fountain of misinformation. Trump gets many of his extreme ideas from the radical assertions of Fox pundits, especially on the morning show "Fox and Friends".

Trump's administration was split between an overwhelming number of conservative ideologues who egg on his far right views and a diminishing handful of pragmatists who try to restrain his more destructive behavior. The ideologues initially included Steve Bannon as political advisor, Michael Flynn as National Security Advisor, Jeff Sessions as Attorney General, Mike Pompeo as CIA director, Scott Pruitt as Environmental Protection Agency (EPA) director, Ryan Zinke as Interior secretary and Steve Mnuchin as Treasury secretary. Trump did fill some positions with intellectually and emotionally mature people who tried to blunt his narcissism, bullying, petulance and ignorance like Defense Secretary James Mattis, National Security Advisor Herbert McMaster, Secretary of State Tillerson, UN Ambassador Nikki Haley, Homeland Security Director Kirstjen Nielsen and John Kelly as chief of staff. Of this group, only Tillerson might have been suspected of being a Putin kingpin. As Exon-Mobil's CEO, he had received Russia's Order of Friendship from Putin in 2013 for a joint venture with Rosneft, headed by Igor Sechin. To his credit, Tillerson was not overtly pro-Russian. Trump also embedded in his administration at least twenty-five people who failed their background security checks for "foreign influence, conflicts of interest, personal conduct, financial problems, drug use and criminal conduct." His son-in-law Jared Kushner was among those whom Trump appointed despite his susceptibility to being blackmailed by foreign governments into espionage or sabotage against America.[104]

Under Donald Trump, the White House became an Alice in Wonderland realm presided over in this case by a mad king rather than queen. Trump has a bizarre ultimately self-defeating strategy of trying to obscure scandals by picking fights with domestic and foreign enemies. That strategy briefly shifts newspaper and television headlines at the long-term cost of proliferating his problems. Trump's ignorance, extreme views, tantrums and stunted intellect appalled the White House's handful of pragmatists. After an especially disturbing meeting, Tillerson exclaimed, "He's a fucking moron." Another bizarre encounter prompted Kelly to declare, "The president's unhinged. The president just really doesn't understand anything ... He doesn't know what he's talking about."[105] Trump was so spiteful and erratic that the pragmatists scrambled constantly to divert his "off with his head" type orders that would have devastating effects on America national power, wealth, prestige, morality and security. Former Trump advisor Rob Porter explained that "A third of my job was trying to react to some of the really dangerous ideas that he had and try to give him reasons to believe that maybe they weren't such good ideas."[106]

Pragmatists were a dwindling band within the Trump White House. In early 2018 Trump eliminated two and replaced them with hardline neo-conservatives, Secretary of State Tillerson with Mike Pompeo on March 13, and National Security Advisor McMaster with John Bolton on April 9, 2018. Fortunately, he replaced Pompeo as CIA director with Gina Haspel, a highly esteemed career CIA operative who immediately began restoring the agency's professionalism and pragmatism that avoids partisanship and ideology. On April 7, 2019 Trump fired Homeland Security Department Director Kirstjen Nielsen as a scapegoat for the surge in illegal refugees but also because she repeatedly tried to mobilize the administration to counter Russian cyber-offensives for the 2018 and 2020 elections. He replaced her with Kevin McAleenan, a hardliner on immigration and other issues. Nielsen was the administration's last prominent pragmatist.[107]

After entering the White House, Trump's most urgent business was to kill the Russian investigation, initially by trying to pressure FBI Director Comey into being his lackey. On January 27, 2017 Trump had Comey over for a private White House dinner during which he demanded loyalty several times. Comey replied, "You will always get honesty from me." Then, during an intelligence briefing in mid-February, Trump asked Comey to stay behind and, once they were alone, insisted that he stop investigating Flynn's ties with Russia. The FBI had interrogated Flynn and caught him in several lies. After that became public, Trump reluctantly accepted Flynn's resignation on February 13.

The investigation persisted and Trump was increasingly desperate to stop it. During testimony before the House Intelligence Committee on March 13 Comey stated that the FBI was investigating:

the nature of any links between individuals associated with the Trump campaign and the Russian government and whether there was any co-ordination between the campaign and Russia's efforts. This will also include an assessment of whether any crimes were committed.

On March 30 Trump summoned Comey, declared that he had nothing to do with Russia, and insisted that he "lift the cloud". He made the same demand to Comey in a telephone call on April 30.[108]

Comey found not just Trump's behavior but that of his administration profoundly disturbing:

> I had never seen anything like it in the Oval Office. As I found myself thrust into the Trump orbit, I once again was having flashbacks to my earlier career as a prosecutor against the Mob. The silent circle of assent. The boss in complete control. The loyalty oaths. The us-versus-them worldview. The lying about all things, large and small, in service to some code of loyalty that put the organization above morality and above the truth.[109]

Comey offered a penetrating psychological analysis of why bright people with strong resumes but weak characters lie and commit crimes for Trump:

> Accomplished people lacking inner strength can't resist the compromises .... It starts with your sitting silent while he lies, both in private and in public, making your complicit by your silence .... Trump makes everyone a co-conspirator in his preferred set of facts, or delusions ... building with his words a web of alternative reality and busily wrapping it around all of us in the room .... From the private circle of assent, it moves to public displays of personal fealty .... And then you are lost. He has eaten your soul.[110]

Trump finally had Deputy Attorney General Rod Rosenstein fire Comey on May 9, 2017 with the excuse that his two pronouncements about Clinton's emails during the 2016 election violated FBI protocols. Trump soon revealed publicly the true reason for getting rid of Comey. Later that day, at the Oval Office, he greeted Russian Foreign Minister Sergei

Lavrov and Ambassador Sergei Kislyak with the boast that "I just fired the head of the FBI, a real nut job. I faced real pressure on Russia. That's taken off." Atop that, he revealed to the Russians top-secret intelligence about laptop computer bombs that Islamic State was using and later revealed that the source was Israel. During a television interview on May 11 Trump admitted that he had fired Comey because "this Russia thing with Trump and Russia is a made up story. It's an excuse by the Democrats for having lost an election they should have won." Typically, Trump had utterly deluded himself. Firing Comey did not end the investigation but instead provoked an even more systematic and comprehensive version.[111]

A dark ethical and legal cloud hung over Attorney General Sessions. During his confirmation hearing he committed perjury when he denied under oath that he had had any encounters with Russians. In fact he twice met Russian Ambassador Kislyak during the 2016 campaign. Unlike Flynn, Sessions did not resign but, on March 2, he did accept Justice Department legal advice to recuse himself from the Russia investigation. That transferred the responsibility to Deputy Attorney General Rosenstein. On May 17 Rosenstein hired Robert Mueller as a special counsel to investigate "any links and/or co-ordination between the Russian government and individuals associated with the campaign of President Donald Trump," and to that end empowered him to subpoena people, testimony and records "for any matters that arose or may arise directly from the investigation." That of course includes evidence of other crimes like obstruction of justice, money-laundering, campaign finance violations, foreign interference in elections and tax fraud.

Mueller was an all-American hero. He got an undergraduate degree from Princeton University, joined the marines to fight in Vietnam, where he won a Bronze Star for courage and a Purple Heart, got a law degree at Princeton, became a public prosecutor, served as the FBI director from 2001 to 2013, then returned to private practice. For his special counsel team, Mueller assembled fourteen brilliant lawyers renowned for their prosecutorial prowess and discretion, backed by fifteen support staff. Then there were allied judicial bodies like grand juries, the United States Attorney General for the Southern District of New York and the New York Tax Court, to which Mueller handed mountains of evidence for uncovered crimes not directly under his mandate.[112]

Mueller's investigation proceeded quietly, steadily and professionally to determine whether Trump and anyone associated with his campaign committed such felonies as conspiracy, obstruction of justice, money-laundering, witness tampering and election campaign violations. It is illegal for Americans to solicit or receive any money or "thing of value" from foreigners in an American election. That "thing of value" can be information. The most serious charge was conspiring with foreign adversaries to subvert American democracy. The key to proving a conspiracy is "corrupt intent," or determining whether the conspirators were serious or just talking. The Mueller team eventually subpoenaed 1.4 million pages of documents from the Trump campaign and 20,000 from the Trump White House, while interviewing hundreds of witnesses or suspects. By May 2019 they had won eight guilty pleas or convictions, twenty-six indictments of Russians and three indictments of Russian organizations.

The largest number of indicted Russians came on July 13, 2018, appropriately on the eve of a summit between Trump and Putin. Deputy Attorney General Rosenstein announced charges against twelve Russian GU officers on eleven felony counts for hacking the Democratic National Committee, the Clinton presidential campaign and state election boards. Rosenstein called for vigilance in protecting America's electoral system from its enemies:

> Free and fair elections are hard fought and contentious, and there will always be adversaries who work to exacerbate domestic differences and try to confuse and conquer us. So long as we are united in our commitment to shared values enshrined in our Constitution, they will not succeed.[113]

So far Maria Butina is the only Russian to be arrested, jailed and convicted for subverting American democracy. After being charged with being an unregistered foreign agent and conspiracy on July 15, 2018 she was not only denied bail as a flight risk, but placed in solitary confinement and only allowed contact with her lawyers. Unfortunately, Alexander Torshin, her supervisor, was beyond apprehension since he was on a list of Russian officials previously sanctioned by the federal government.

On December 10, 2018 she pleaded guilty and promised to tell all in exchange for her release for time served. On April 26, 2019 she received an eighteen-month prison sentence.[114]

The next indictment of a Russian came on October 9, 2018 when the FBI charged Russian Elena Khusyaynova for defrauding the United States. From January 2016 she led a $35 million cyber-troll campaign, codenamed Project Lakhta, that sowed hatred among Americans via thousands of vicious lies strewn across Twitter, Facebook and Instagram. Unfortunately, like her comrades, she was beyond the FBI's reach in Russia.[115]

Mueller negotiated plea deals with an array of American criminals whereby they received lesser sentences in return for providing evidence against others. He won two key guilty pleas in 2017. On July 27 the FBI arrested George Papadopoulos on charges of lying to them during a January 27, 2017 interview. Papadopoulos agreed to co-operate in return for a lighter sentence. Michael Flynn pleaded guilty to charges of lying to the FBI on November 30, 2017; he then became a co-operating witness through scores of hours of interviews with investigators.

Sam Patten was a Trump campaign advisor who, through a straw purchaser, brokered $50,000 for four seats to pro-Russian Ukrainian oligarch Serhiy Lyovochkin to attend Trump's inauguration; it is illegal for foreigners to contribute to presidential inaugurations, election campaigns or political action committees. Patten also arranged meetings between Lyovochkin and congressional conservatives. Patten is linked with Rinat Akhmetshin who was with the Russian team that attended the Trump Tower meeting and promised to deliver damaging information about Hillary Clinton. He collaborated with Cambridge Analytica to aid Trump's campaign. On September 1, 2018 Patten pleaded guilty for failing to register as a foreign agent. On April 12, 2019 he received a sentence of three years' probation and a $5,000 fine.[116]

Mueller's office announced charges against Paul Manafort and his deputy Paul Gates on October 30, 2017. When his trial opened in Alexandria, Virginia on July 31, 2018 Manafort faced thirty-two charges of fraud, tax evasion and money-laundering. The FBI found evidence that Manafort hid at least $16 million in income and fraudulently solicited $20 million in bank loans. If convicted, Manafort faced as many as thirty years in prison that, since he was then sixty-nine years old, would amount to a life sentence. Although none of the charges directly related to the Trump campaign's conspiracy with Russians to subvert America's 2016 election, the trial revealed plenty of evidence for that conspiracy. The most disturbing was Manafort's decade-long relationship with Konstantin Kilimnik, a Russian intelligence agent and also indicted by Mueller. On August 2 Manafort met with Kilimnik to share polling data and discuss Trump's recognition of Russia's conquest of eastern Ukraine if he won the presidency.[117] The key witness against Manafort was Paul Gates, his deputy since 2006. Gates turned against Manafort after a plea bargain with Mueller that reduced his own potential number of years in prison.

Yet Manafort nearly got away with all his crimes. The judge, T.S. Ellis, was a Reagan appointee who repeatedly castigated the prosecutors "for going after President Trump," even though they almost never mentioned Trump's name. Then a Trump supporter among the jurors did what she could to derail the process. In the end, the jury found Manafort guilty on eighteen counts for financial fraud, tax fraud and conspiracy to obstruct justice, but Ellis once again aided Manafort and Trump by throwing out ten of the convictions. Manafort appealed his convictions, then agreed to co-operate fully with the Mueller investigation in return for pleading guilty and receiving a lighter sentence. Instead, over the following months, Manafort typically lied repeatedly while his lawyers colluded with Trump's lawyers to reveal how the investigation was proceeding and plot a common strategy including a future presidential pardon. On November 26 the Mueller team declared Manafort had violated his agreement and was now liable to the harshest possible punishment for his crimes. Yet at Manafort's sentencing hearing on March 5, 2019 Ellis rejected the federal guidelines of nineteen to twenty-four years for his crimes. Instead, Ellis lauded Manafort as "otherwise blameless" and slapped him on the wrist with forty-seven months, minus the nine months he had already served.[118]

That blatant coddling of a Russian stooge and Trump crony provoked outrage among patriotic Americans. Fortunately, on March 13, Judge Amy Berman Jackson upheld justice in a separate trial for Manafort's conviction on other crimes by imposing a three-year prison term atop his earlier sentence. Although Jackson's punishment was also below federal sentencing guidelines, she found Manafort's crimes as appalling as Ellis found them inconsequential, stating that "It is hard to overstate the number of lies and the amount of fraud and the amount of money involved." That same day, the Manhattan district attorney for New York State indicted Manafort on sixteen felony charges that could keep Manafort in prison for another quarter of a century. Presidents can pardon criminals for their federal crimes but not their state crimes, which trumped Trump's power to spring Manafort.[119]

Michael Cohen was Trump's executive vice president from 2007 to 2017. His specialty was helping Trump evade the law by acting as his "fixer." He boasted:

> If somebody does something Mr Trump doesn't like I do everything in my power to resolve it to Mr Trump's benefit. If you do something wrong, I'm going to come at you, grab you by the neck and I'm not going to let you go until I'm finished.[120]

His best-known fixes were obeying Trump's orders to use campaign funds to pay off two of Trump's former mistresses to be silent during the 2016 campaign. His links with organized crime preceded his relationship with Trump; his uncle owned the El Caribe country club in Brooklyn, which catered to Russian and Italian Mafiosi. On August 21, 2018 Cohen pleaded guilty to eight felonies including tax, finance and election campaign crimes and agreed to co-operate fully with the Mueller investigation.[121]

Among Cohen's most serious admissions was that he met repeatedly with Russian officials for permission to build a Trump Tower in Moscow amidst Trump's presidential campaign until June 16, 2016. To sweeten the deal, Trump had Cohen convey his promise to give Putin a $50 million penthouse in the tower. Trump reluctantly ended the haggling after he won the Republican Party nomination. All along Trump's denials of negotiating with the Russians gave the Kremlin blackmail power over him because they could reveal the truth. On December 12, 2018 Cohen received a three-year sentence for pleading guilty to felonies that included election campaign violations, tax evasion and perjury, charges asserted by both Special Counsel Robert Mueller and the United States Southern District for New York. Before the court he apologized for his crimes and explained that he committed them from his "weakness and blind loyalty" to Trump and "his dirty deeds."[122] On February 27, 2019, during a hearing before the House Oversight and Reform Committee, Cohen condemned Trump: "He is a racist. He is a con man. And he is a cheat." As for Russia, Trump

> directed the Moscow negotiations throughout the campaign and lied about it … because he never expected to win … [and] because he stood to make hundreds of millions of dollars on the Moscow real estate project …. Trump would often say, this campaign was going to be 'the greatest infomercial in political history'.

Trump reimbursed Cohen for paying off his mistresses when he was in the White House. Trump also knew beforehand about both the Trump Tower meeting and the WikiLeaks dumps. Trump's denials of all that in written testimony to Mueller opens him to perjury, obstruction of justice and campaign finance law felonies.[123]

Michael Flynn was Trump's initial national security advisor who eventually pleaded guilty to lying to the FBI about his meetings with Russians during and after the campaign. In return for agreeing to co-operate, he avoided charges on a litany of other crimes that could have led to fifteen years in prison. During Flynn's court appearance on December 17, 2018, Judge Emmet Sullivan declared that he was "not hiding my disgust … [that] undermines everything this flag … stands for …. Arguably you sold your country out."[124]

Roger Stone is among the Republican Party's most esteemed masters of political dirty tricks and influence peddling. He began his machinations with Richard Nixon, then served a series of Republicans who won or ran for the presidency. He also championed the Trump Institute along with the National Rifle Association, Tobacco Institute and Rupert Murdoch's News Corporation. Among his first partners was Paul Manafort. Stone worked for Trump's campaign in 2015 and advised it throughout 2016. His most critical role was trying to co-ordinate with Julian Assange and WikiLeaks the release of embarrassing Clinton campaign and Democratic

Party emails. He also exchanged Twitter emails with Guccifer 2.0, a Russian cyber-troll. One of his go-betweens with WikiLeaks was Jerome Corsi, a rabid right-wing conspiracy theorist who authored a "birther" book that claimed that Barack Obama was a Muslim born in Kenya.[125] On January 24, 2019 Mueller had Stone arrested and issued a seven-count indictment for obstruction, perjury and witness tampering. The indictment referred to a "senior campaign official," presumably then campaign chair Steve Bannon, who was directed by an unnamed person, presumably Trump himself, to work with Assange and WikiLeaks.[126]

Then Assange himself received a Justice Department indictment on April 11, 2019, after Ecuador's embassy in London finally expelled him and British police arrested him on bail-jumping charges. Assange had sheltered in the embassy for seven years after fleeing there to escape extradition to Sweden on rape charges. Ecuador's radical leftist President Rafael Correa granted him honorary citizenship but his successor, President Lenin Moreno, finally succumbed to American and British pressure. The Justice Department charged Assange for helping Private Chelsea Manning hack and steal top secret Pentagon documents on March 8, 2010; Assange was not charged for conspiring with Russian to warp America's 2016 election. A British court sentenced Assange to fifty weeks in prison for bail-jumping. After being released Assange faces being extradited to the United States.[127]

Trump enjoyed a critical ally during his first two years in power, a Republican-dominated Congress whose committees refused seriously to investigate any allegations of wrongdoing by him or his coterie. That changed after Democrats won a majority in the House of Representatives in the November 2018 election. In early March 2019, five committees – Judiciary, Intelligence, Oversight and Reform, Ways and Means and Foreign Affairs – launched wide-ranging investigations of the spectrum of criminal allegations against Trump. On March 4 the Judiciary Committee alone issued eighty-one letters requesting information from individuals, businesses and organizations associated with Trump. Any impeachment of Trump would begin with the Judiciary Committee. The committees have the power to subpoena and interview under oath anyone, including the president.[128]

Trump's mendacity prevented him from engaging a world-class law firm. No reputable firm wanted to risk sullying itself by representing a pathological liar and narcissist who refused to follow advice. Trump ended up hiring and firing a series of second-rate lawyers. In April 2018 he hired Rudolf Giuliani, once renowned as a tough federal prosecutor and New York mayor. Giuliani proceeded to reveal that his best legal days were far behind him. Every few days he appeared on cable news shows to blurt embarrassing and legally compromising revelations about Trump. He admitted but dismissed the importance that his client had committed collusion, obstruction of justices, financial improprieties and election law violations. At one point, he proclaimed that "Truth isn't truth." Another time, Giuliani insisted that "there is nothing wrong with taking information from Russians."[129]

Like Trump and Putin, Giuliani backed illiberal rather than liberal democracy and thus promoted Russian interests. Among his clients was Romanian oligarch Gabriel Popoviciu who, in 2017, received a seven-year prison sentence for real estate fraud. Romania is a member of NATO and the EU. On August 22, 2018 Giuliani lambasted Romanian President Klaus Iohannis for his administration's crackdown on corruption through tougher laws and prosecutions. This, of course, was sweet music for Putin and all other authoritarians, especially presidents Victor Orban of Hungary and Andrzej Duda of Poland, who are transforming those EU and NATO members from liberal into illiberal democracies.[130]

Trump lawyers repeatedly rebuffed Mueller's requests to interview him. If one had occurred, Mueller and his colleagues might have extracted massive evidence from Trump that he had committed conspiracy, obstruction of justice, perjury, money-laundering, tax fraud and other crimes. Instead, the Trump team agreed to answer written questions submitted by the Mueller team. Two months after receiving a list of questions, they submitted Trump's "take home exam" answers on November 20, 2018.

Rather uncharacteristically, political rather than legal reasoning shaped Mueller's decision not to interview Trump. He believed that the subpoena process to force Trump to do so would be too prolonged and divisive. Besides, he explained, an interview was not vital to the investigation because Trump has repeatedly, unwittingly, and publicly admitted his "criminal intent" to obstruct justice to kill the Russia investigation. He did so with the Russian ambassador and foreign minister at the Oval Office on May 9, 2017. He did so in a television interview with NBC anchor Lester Holt on May 11, 2017. Several times, he declared that he would never have named Jeff Sessions attorney general if he knew he would recuse himself from the Russia investigation, implying that he wanted someone who would fulfill his demand to obstruct rather than promote justice.[131]

Trump's most potentially damaging attempt to derail the Mueller investigation came on September 8, 2018 when he ordered the declassification and public release of FBI evidence against his former aides. In doing so, Trump once again, consciously or not, played Putin's stooge. Not just the Russians but all American adversaries would benefit from the exposure of the intelligence community's espionage sources and methods. That provoked concerted efforts by the intelligence community and America's allies for Trump to reverse that order. Fortunately, Trump angrily yielded on September 22 before he could betray any actual top-secret American intelligence sources and methods.[132]

Then, the day after the November 2018 mid-term election, Trump fired Sessions and named Matthew Whitaker as acting attorney general. Sessions had enraged Trump for excusing himself from overseeing the Russian Special Consul Investigation. Trump later confessed if he had known that would happen "I would have picked someone else."[133] In admitting that, Trump unwittingly admitted his "intent" to commit "obstruction of justice. In picking Whitaker, Trump elevated someone who had not been approved by the Senate above Deputy Attorney General Rosenstein, who should have been named acting attorney general according to administrative protocol. Whitaker was committed to subverting the Mueller investigation that he condemned as a "witch hunt" and "lynch mob" because "the Trump campaign did not conspire with the Russians and the Russians never interfered in America's election." Whitaker's moral and legal character was as repellent as his denial of reality. He was an executive director of World Patent Marketing that a federal judge fined $26 million for bilking customers of millions of dollars of their wealth. White House chief of Staff John Kelly admitted that Whitaker was Trump's "eyes and ears" in the Justice Department and would "rein in" the Mueller investigation.[134] Although an attorney general's duty is to protect the office of the presidency from presidents who commit "high crimes and misdemeanors," Whitaker insisted that his job was to "jump on a grenade" for Trump.[135]

Trump finally found an attorney general willing to absolve him of any wrong-doing in William Barr, whose nomination the Senate confirmed by 54 to 45 votes on February 24, 2019. Barr has an impressive legal career, including a previous stint as George H. W. Bush's attorney general from 1991 to 1993. However, contrary to the Founding Fathers' original intent, Barr shared Trump's belief that, as the chief executive, the president is above the law and has virtually unlimited power, including "complete authority to start or stop a law enforcement proceeding," and thus cannot obstruct justice. Barr argued that in a nineteen-page memo he sent Assistant Attorney General Rod Rosenstein on June 8, 2018. That belief contradicts the original intent of the Constitution's framers who insisted that the law applies equally to everyone, especially the president; that no one can be a judge in his own defense; and that obstructing justice is a serious crime. Barr characterized the intelligence community's surveillance and investigation of Russia's attempt to subvert America's 2016 election as illegal "spying" on Trump's campaign. Barr's protection of Trump violated his duty as attorney general to uphold the constitution, the law and the presidency, and to persecute anyone who violates that, including any sitting president. And, in defending Trump, Barr also obstructed justice.[136]

Special Counsel Robert Mueller concluded his investigation on March 21, 2018 when he handed his 448-page report to Attorney General William Barr.[137] Two days later, Barr issued his own three and a half-page summary that said the Mueller team did not find convicting evidence that Trump and his associates conspired with Russians to distort the 2016 election; as for obstruction of justice, Mueller decided not to decide, thus neither condemning nor exonerating Trump. Some members of Mueller's team complained publicly that Barr had understated and distorted their findings while refusing to release Mueller's own summary intended for the public. Muller wrote Barr a letter accusing him of mischaracterizing the Report's "context, nature, and substance."[138]

An unrepentant Barr publicly released an 8 per cent redacted version of Mueller's Report on April 18, 2019. The Report presented overwhelming evidence for several related key conclusions. The Russians systematically and extensively tried to undermine America's electoral system to defeat Hillary Clinton and elect Donald Trump president. The Kremlin did so because it "perceived it would benefit from a Trump presidency and worked to secure that outcome." The Trump campaign "expected it would benefit electorally from information stolen and released through Russian efforts." There were: "multiple links between Trump campaign officials and individuals tied to the Russian government. Those links included Russian offers of assistance to the campaign." However, the "evidence was not sufficient to charge any" Trump campaign official with conspiracy. The Mueller team understood conspiracy "to require an agreement – tacit or express – between the Trump campaign and the Russian government on election interference. That requires more than the two parties taking actions that were informed by or responses to the other's actions or desires." Nonetheless, Trump apparently committed obstruction of justice on at least ten occasions but Mueller was straitjacketed by the Justice Department rule that a sitting president cannot be indicted, contrary to the founders' original intent. Mueller did offer this re-assuring support for America's democratic political system: "The conclusion that Congress may apply the obstruction laws to the president's corrupt exercise of the powers of office accords with our constitutional system of checks and balances and the principle that no man is above the law."[139]

As such, the Mueller Report presented a powerful legal roadmap either to Trump's impeachment while he remains president or his indictment after he leaves office. Beginning on May 6, 2019 and for several days thereafter nearly 1,000 former federal prosecutors, around half Republicans, signed a public statement that "the conduct of President Trump described in Special Counsel Robert Mueller's Report would, in the case of any other person "than a sitting president result in multiple felony charges for obstruction of justice."[140] On May 29, 2019, Robert Mueller broke his silence by publicly declaring, "If we had confidence that the president clearly did not commit a crime we would have said so."[141]

The Special Counsel's twenty-two-month investigation included nineteen lawyers, forty FBI agents, and more than 230 communication record demands and 2,800 subpoenas to 500 witnesses and thirteen foreign governments. That led Mueller and other federal and state prosecutors to 199 charges against thirty-four people, including twenty-six Russians and three organizations. The convictions or guilty pleas to an array of felonies of five Trump advisors – Michael Flynn, Michael Cohen, Paul Manafort, Rick Gates and George Papadopoulos, and the pending trial of Roger Stone; sentences or pending trials for another nine people; and revelations that Trump and eighteen of his coterie held 140 meetings with Russians while another twenty members knew about the meetings during the campaign and transition. In addition, there were fourteen other secret ongoing criminal investigations, of which Mueller transferred two to the Justice Department and twelve to other courts.[142]

A number of Trump associates could still be indicted by other prosecutors for various felonies. Among the more prominent is former Attorney General Jeff Sessions. He was the first senator to endorse Trump for president and then join his campaign. He had practiced law before serving as a senator from Alabama for twenty-four years. In gratitude, Trump named him attorney general. During testimony before Congress, Sessions clearly committed perjury when he claimed that he had never met any Russians during the campaign. In reality, Sessions met Russian Ambassador Sergei Kislyak twice, once in April and then in July, when they discussed campaign and policy matters.

Felix Sater is among the more colorful characters in Trump's entourage. He is a Russian-born immigrant to New York who made a fortune in real estate with his Bayrock Group. He also served time in prison for assault and was an FBI informant whose evidence helped convict a score of Russian Mafiosi. He and Trump collaborated on some big deals that included laundering Russian mob money and trying to erect a Trump Tower in Moscow. Most vitally, Bayrock was the conduit for Russian loans that rescued Trump from bankruptcy. Sater's links with Moscow were so tight that in November 2015 he was allowed to give Ivanka Trump a Kremlin tour that climaxed when she sat in Putin's chair. He assured Michael Cohen that:

I will get Putin on this program and we will get Donald elected … Buddy our boy can become president of the USA and we can engineer it. I will get all of Putin's team to buy in on this. I will manage this process.[143]

And so he did. Sater set up meetings for Michael Cohen with an array of Russian officials and oligarchs including GU General Evgeny Shymkov.

Steve Bannon achieved national prominence as the publisher of the alt-right *Breitbart News* and Trump campaign and White House advisor. He employed Cambridge Analytica, a right-wing data-mining firm, to provide likely voting patterns for the 2016 election. Cambridge Analytica's CEO, Alexander Nix, had close ties with WikiLeaks' CEO Julian Assange. They exchanged information on the pilfered DNC and Podesta emails.

Donald Trump Junior and Jared Kushner also evaded indictments on a potential array of felony charges, including perjury and conspiracy. Trump Junior's setting up of the notorious Trump Tower meeting on June 9, 2016 was only his most blatant conspiracy act. He and Kushner met together or separately with Russian officials or go-betweens numerous times. Trump Junior also communicated with Assange and WikiLeaks. Yet Mueller apparently did not consider those convictable acts of conspiracy for reasons that may never be publicly revealed. Other prosecutors may reach the opposite conclusion.

Of course, Donald Trump is the key so-far unindicted co-conspirator. Trump has repeatedly denied that Russia tried to influence the 2016 election and repeatedly denounced the Mueller Investigation as "a rigged witch hunt."[144] Nonetheless, the Trump team's defense shifted with time. When reports of collusion first emerged, they denied any contacts with Russians. Then, after overwhelming evidence emerged of the Trump Tower meeting, they claimed that it merely concerned adopting Russian children. Finally, after overwhelming evidence revealed that they met specifically to obtain unsavory information on Clinton, the argument became "collusion is not a crime." That defense of admitting to collusion was bizarre since collusion is the same as conspiracy, which is a felony.[145] Trump's most astonishing assertion came during a television interview in the Oval Office on June 12, 2019. He found nothing wrong with accepting "dirt" on one's political rivals from foreigners and not informing the FBI even though doing so blatantly violates federal law. Once again, Trump green-lighted the Kremlin and other adversaries that he welcomed their gross manipulation of the pending 2020 American election to favor him and attack his opponent as they had the 2016 election.[146]

A mountain of evidence rose steadily that Trump committed an array of other felonies, including obstruction of justice, tax fraud, money-laundering, emoluments and election campaign violations that may eventually result in a long prison term after he leaves the White House. For instance, damning evidence of election campaign violations came from Michael Cohen in return for a lesser sentence and David Pecker, the president of American Media, which owns the *National Enquirer* tabloid. Within a few weeks of the 2016 election Trump had Cohen use campaign finance funds to pay off one Trump mistress, Stephanie Clifford, also known as Stormy Daniels, for $130,000, and funnel $150,000 to Pecker to "catch and kill" a story by another mistress, Karen McDougall.[147]

As the investigations by Mueller and others deepened, broadened and proliferated, President Donald Trump daily committed acts that made him a dream come true not just for Putin's regime but for any anti-American government or movement. Trump's outrageous statements, behavior and policies have perverted America's democratic laws, institutions and mores; alienated America's economic and military allies; bolstered America's enemies and adversaries; and thus corroded America's power, wealth, influence, prestige and security. Trump's impact can be divided among damage confined to the United States, damage extended to American allies and damage inflicted on all of humanity.

Trump has inflicted possibly irreparable harm to American democracy's institutions, laws and mores. He has purged experts from government departments and agencies, especially scientists, and either left the posts open or filled them with right-wing ideologues. He and his coterie have repeatedly violated federal laws and mores. He has repeatedly denounced and thus undermined the legitimacy of America's intelligence community, judicial system, scientific community and mass media, each a vital watchdog of American national security and democracy. By February 14, 2019 Trump had publicly attacked the Russian investigation nearly 1,200 times, including the FBI and Justice Department 277 times, former FBI Director James Comey 148 times, former Attorney General Jeff Sessions fifty-seven times and the news media for reporting the investigation, 151 times. Meanwhile, Trump defended Russian President Vladimir Putin sixty-one times.[148]

Trump condemned America's intelligence community, often declaring "I don't trust human intelligence and these spies."[149] He spurned even the most fundamental advice, including the CIA's Presidential Daily Brief (PDB). For instance, in March 2018, National Security Advisor McMaster warned Trump not to congratulate with either spoken or written words Putin on his re-election as president but instead to condemn him for the attempted assassination of defector Sergei Skripal earlier that month. Typically, Trump did the opposite. He failed to mention the attempted murder but instead congratulated Putin.[150] Former National Intelligence Director Clapper expressed the dismay of America's intelligence community and its foreign allies at being targeted by Trump's attacks: "There's a difference between skepticism and disparagement. Public trust and confidence in the intelligence community is crucial .... I've received many expressions of concern from foreign counterparts about … the disparagement of the U.S. intelligence community."[151] After the Mueller Report appeared, Trump ordered Barr to investigate those in the intelligence community who had initiated the investigation of Russia's manipulation of the 2016 election and ties with the Trump campaign.[152]

The Intelligence Community's "Worldwide Threat Assessment," issued in January 2019, decisively refuted virtually all of Trump's deluded and dangerous assertions about the world. That enraged Trump, who denounced the Intelligence Community as "extremely passive and naïve" and said they "should go back to school." Douglas Wise, a former top CIA and DIA official, unofficially spoke for the Intelligence Community when he condemned Trump's rant as "a consequence of narcissism" and:

strong and inappropriate political pressure to get the intelligence community's leadership aligned with his political goals. The existential danger to the nation is when the policymaker corrupts the role of the intelligence agencies, which is to provide unbiased and apolitical intelligence to inform policy.[153]

Trump repeatedly savaged the mainstream media as "the enemy of the people" perpetuating "fake news". During a campaign rally in October 2018, he actually lauded as "my kind of guy" Republican congressman Greg Gianforte who was convicted of assaulting a reporter.[154] In October 2018, Cesar Sayoc, among Trump's more ardent supporters, mailed pipe bombs to people that Trump had repeatedly smeared. The targets included such prominent Democratic Party leaders as Bill and Hillary Clinton, Barack Obama, Joe Biden, Nancy Pelosi, Corey Booker, Eric Holder, Maxime Waters and Tom Steyer, former intelligence directors John Brennan and James Clapper, billionaire philanthropist George Soros and even actor Robert de Niro. The FBI captured Sayoc and charged him with a litany of federal crimes.

A fundamental maxim of international power is that one only negotiates contentious issues with friends behind firmly-closed and guarded doors; to outsiders an alliance displays nothing but unity, resolve and common purpose. As for one's foes, one negotiates with some mix of private talks and public assertions depending on circumstances. One's bargaining power obviously swells with the number of other governments one rallies to one's side. Trump has repeatedly violated those maxims. He has insulted and alienated America's friends, and weakened America's alliances, while bolstering America's adversaries. Meanwhile, Trump lauds murderous dictators like Russia's Vladimir Putin, North Korea's Kim Jong-un, Saudi Arabia's Mohammad bin Salman and the Philippines' Rodrigo Duterte. This Trump behavior reached a crescendo during the Group of 7 Quebec Summit in June 2018 when he insulted the host Canadian Prime Minister Justin Trudeau along with German Chancellor Angela Merkel, announced new sanctions in the trade war he started and refused to sign the communiqué that called for unity. Atop all that, as usual, Trump had nothing but praise for Putin, denied that the Russians interfered in the 2016 election and called for lifting sanctions on Russia and bringing it back into the Group of 7, making it again eight.

American prosperity and security are synonymous with global prosperity and security. To that end, during the Second World War, President Franklin Roosevelt laid the diplomatic groundwork for establishing international organizations that developed and regulated the global system like the International Monetary Fund (IMF), International

Bank for Reconstruction and Development (IBRD or World Bank) and United Nations (UN). Subsequent presidents helped lead or supported the establishment of new international organizations that further bolstered the global system, including the General Agreement on Trade and Tariffs (GATT) later renamed the World Trade Organization (WTO), the North Atlantic Treaty Organization (NATO), the Organization of America States (OAS), North American Free Trade Association (NAFTA), the Asia Pacific Economic Co-operation (APEC), the International Panel on Climate Change (IPCC), International Criminal Court (ICC) and Trans-Pacific Partnership (TPP), in which the United States was a member, and others like what became the European Union (EU) and the Association of Southeast Asian Nations (ASEAN) in which it was not a member. As Defense Secretary James Mattis put it, "The great gift of the greatest generation to us is the rules-based, international democratic order. This global architecture brought security, stability, and prosperity."[155]

Trump was determined to destroy the global system. In a debate with Gary Cohn, his economic advisor, Trump insisted that "The World Trade Organization is the worst organization ever created! We lose more cases than anything." To that, Cohn replied that in reality the United States wins 85.7 per cent of its WTO cases. But Trump clung to his delusion.[156] Throughout his presidency he issued various "off with their heads" commands that inflicted varying degrees of damage on international organizations and bilateral economic partnerships. He launched a trade war by imposing 25 per cent tariffs on steel imports and 10 per cent tariffs on aluminum imports on March 7, 2018. On August 27, 2017 he declared: "We're talked about this ad nauseum. Just do it ... Get out of NAFTA. Get out of KORUS. And get out of the WTO. We're withdrawing from all three."[157] Fortunately, this time cooler heads prevailed.

Trump nearly wrecked the North American Free Trade Association (NAFTA), established among the United States, Canada and Mexico in 1993. One Trump criticism of NAFTA was true. The United States did suffer perennial trade deficits with Mexico as American consumers and investors took advantage of labor priced 10 per cent of what the average American made along with lax anti-pollution enforcement. Yet cheap parts imported from Mexico and assembled into final products like automobiles helped keep those American industries internationally competitive. In violation of NAFTA, Trump initiated a trade war with Mexico and Canada by raising tariffs on their products. Negotiations began in 2017 and ended in October 2018 when diplomats announced that they had revised the treaty. Trump crowed that he had won a great trade victory. In fact, the changes were modest with the most significant changing the domestic content requirement for automobiles made in America from 62 per cent to 75 per cent. Typically, Trump tried to paper over the lack of substance with a brand change. Henceforth, NAFTA will be USMCA or the United States, Mexico, Canada Association. Trump's trade war and nasty denigration of Prime Minister Justin Trudeau caused favorable Canadian views of America to plummet to 39 per cent, the lowest since the Pew Research Center began polling in 2002. Once again Trump played Putin's game of breaking up or weakening alliances with acrimony.[158]

The Obama administration had a brilliant strategy for enhancing American and global security but, typically, failed to champion it. The United States would be the centerpiece of two grand alliances, explicitly economic and implicitly military, with one spanning the Pacific basin and the other the Atlantic basin. Obama did not explain, let alone boast, about his success in forging the first and that failure led to its eventual demise under his successor. Under the Trans-Pacific Partnership (TPP) the United States and eleven other countries, which together amounted to 45 per cent of the global economy, agreed to cut or eliminate 18,000 tariffs and other trade barriers to establish a free trade zone. To varying degrees and ways, that would have accelerated the creation and distribution of wealth in each member. Pointedly, the TPP left out China. Indeed China's economic nationalism had largely inspired TPP's creation. If wielded, TPP's collective power could have forced Beijing to end its economic and military aggression. A Trans-Atlantic Trade and Investment Partnership (TTIP) between the United States and the European Union that established a massive free trade zone would also have boosted its members' economic development and potentially forced Russia to end its own aggression. Trump destroyed that vast expansion of American and global security by withdrawing the United States from TPP and leaving TTIP stillborn diplomatically, thus inspiring joy in Beijing and Moscow.[159]

Trump's attempts to destroy the western alliance, European Union and global trade system provoked the Europeans to redouble their efforts at improving their trade relations with others. On July 17, 2018 European and Japanese envoys signed a treaty that would reduce trade barriers between them on January 1, 2019. The Europeans also had negotiations with Australia, New Zealand, Chile, China, Tunisia, Indonesia, India, Mexico, Vietnam, Singapore and the Mercosur countries Argentina, Brazil, Paraguay and Uruguay.[160]

Rhetorically and diplomatically, Chinese President Xi Jinping has filled the global leadership void that Trump abandoned for the United States. Shamelessly, Xi has called on all countries to promote free trade and curb global warming, even though China is the world's worst protectionist, intellectual property thief and polluter. He also tried to establish an alternative Regional Comprehensive Economic Partnership (RCEP) that embraced the TAP countries for which Trump abdicated leadership; RCEP pointedly snubbed American membership. Xi and Japanese Prime Minister Shinzo Abe have developed an especially close relationship between themselves and their countries on trade and investments.

The parallel policies of Trump and Xi may shift the Pacific basin's power balance decisively from America to China. By one estimate, the Chinese have stolen and capitalized on $600 billion worth of American intellectual property. China is surpassing America in one innovative technology and manufacturing industry after another. Atop that, Beijing is asserting domination over the East and South China Seas by constructing and fortifying islands, using them to claim sovereignty over the surrounding waters and airspace and forbidding access to warships and warplanes from the United States and other nations.[161]

Trump, initially, was nearly as reluctant to confront China as he was Russia. At one point, when his advisors tried to convince him to single out and retaliate against China as America's worst economic threat, he replied, "No, no. no. I don't want to make it China-specific. Let's just do it for the whole world."[162] It was not until the summer of 2018 that Trump launched a trade war against China by imposing tariffs on imports. Beijing retaliated with tariffs on American imports. In October 2018 Vice President Mike Pence accused China of interfering in America's pending mid-term election so egregiously that "what the Russians are doing pales in comparison to what China is doing across the country," and "China wants a different American president."[163] The trouble with Pence's accusation was that he did not support it with facts. In doing so, Trump deluded himself in believing he would dilute Mueller's investigation into Russia's machinations by diverting attention to China; instead, typically, he exacerbated an already fraught relationship with the world's largest economy.

Trump's potentially most damaging policy was to withdraw the United States from the United Nations Convention on Climate Change whose draft treaty was finished at Paris on December 12, 2015 and signed in New York by 195 countries on April 22, 2016. That treaty requires each country to reduce greenhouse chemical emissions to levels that will prevent the earth from heating more than 1.5 degrees Celsius. The consequences of failing to do so will be catastrophic as prolonged droughts, devastating storms, and rising seas destroy the livelihoods and lives of ever more people around the world, including in the United States.

The Korean peninsula is potentially one of the world's deadliest places. A war between the Koreas with the United States backing the South and China the North could result in millions of casualties just with conventional fighting and tens of millions if nuclear weapons detonate. The United States has allied with South Korea since June 25, 1950 when President Harry Truman and his advisors chose to defend that country against a massive communist North Korean invasion backed by China. The result was a three-year war in which 38,000 Americans died before an armistice ended the fighting. In the six decades since then, America's military and economic alliance with South Korea has deterred another North Korean invasion and, in recent years, a nuclear missile attack against American cities. The 28,500 American troops deployed in South Korea ensure that the United States will war against North Korea if it attacks South Korea. The American Theater High Altitude Area Defense (THAAD) system deployed in South Korea can detect a North Korean nuclear missile within seven seconds of its launch, compared to fifteen minutes for the THAAD deployed in Alaska. Obviously the sooner a missile attack is detected, the greater the chance for a THAAD to be fired and intercept it. That in turn better deters the North Koreans from ever launching a missile attack.[164]

Trump nearly wrecked America's alliance with South Korea. He was angered to learn that the United States suffered an $18 billion trade deficit while spending $3.5 billion to deploy 28,500 American troops there and another $1 billion to deploy THAAD. He threatened to withdraw American forces and abandon the United States-Korea Free Trade Agreement (KORUS). Defense Secretary Mattis tried to reason with him, arguing that: "Kim Jong Un poses the most immediate threat to our national security. We need South Korea as an ally. It may not seem like trade is related to all this, but it's central." To that Trump angrily replied, "I don't care. I'm tired of these arguments! I don't want to hear about it anymore. We're getting out of KORUS ... Why is the U.S. paying $1 billion a year for an anti-missile system in South Korea?" To that, Mattis explained, "We're doing this in order to prevent World War Three ... Forward-positioned troops provide the least costly means of achieving our security objectives and withdrawal would lead our allies to lose confidence in us." That very basic logic and facts were lost on Trump. Then, on September 5, 2017, two of his advisors, literally took the world's fate in their hands. Gary Cohn and Rob Porter pre-empted a national security crisis when they managed to distract Trump and steal the written order off his desk before he could sign it. With his child-like attention span, Trump never noticed that he had been hoodwinked.[165]

Meanwhile, as Trump attacked a key American ally, North Korea steadily developed its nuclear weapons and intercontinental ballistic missiles (ICBMs). On July 3, 2017 Pyongyang launched the Hwasong-14 that was capable of hitting America's west coast cities. China had supplied the missile's eight-axle mobile launch platform. On September 3 Pyongyang conducted its sixth nuclear bomb test, this one seventeen times larger than the atomic bomb that destroyed Hiroshima. Typically, in response to these alarming nuclear advances, Trump could only engage in schoolyard name-calling by taunting Kim as "Little Rocket-man" in a speech before the UN General Assembly on September 19. Later Trump replied to a threat from Kim by bragging that "I too have a Nuclear Button, but it is a much bigger & more powerful one than his, and my

Button works!"[166] Trump's insults and boasts did not deter the North Koreans from conducting more bomb and missile tests. Eventually that prompted Trump to change his tune. He authorized UN Ambassador Nikki Haley to negotiate a Security Council resolution that imposed economic sanctions on North Korea to force it to give up its nuclear weapons and ICBMs; the subsequent 15 to 0 vote for that resolution passed on December 22, 2017.

The worse the sanctions hurt North Korea, the greater the chance that Pyongyang would be forced to yield. Typically, Trump squandered that power. North Korean dictator Kim Jong Un snookered Trump during their summit at Singapore on June 12, 2018. Trump spent a few hours chatting with Kim then jetted back to Washington where he proclaimed, "North Korea is no longer a nuclear threat." Within a month Kim had denounced "the unilateral and gangster-like demand for denuclearization."[167] Meanwhile, the North Koreans continued deploying more nuclear bombs and missiles at multiple underground sites in remote mountain valleys. The United States lacks satellites capable of constantly watching all those sites. Nonetheless, Trump bizarrely declared that Kim "wrote me beautiful letters and they're great letters. We fell in love."[168] He defended Kim again after a summit at Hanoi on February 28, 2019. Once again, Trump failed to get Kim to begin dismantling his nuclear arsenal, although he did refuse to give up the sanctions against North Korea. But then, on March 21, 2019, Trump weakened the economic sanctions against North Korea even as Pyongyang refurbished its nuclear testing and launch complex.

Trump's most stunning concession to communist North Korea came on June 11, 2019, when he angrily denounced revelations that the CIA had recruited as an informant Kim's half-brother, Kim Jung-Nam, who the regime had assassinated in Singapore, and promised that "I wouldn't let that happen under my auspices." Recruiting high-ranking foreigners is critical to learning the plans and motives of one's adversaries and enemies, and enticing someone in that country's inner circle is a priceless asset. Trump's rejection of that fundamental role of intelligence-gathering inflicted a potentially devastating blow to American national security.[169]

Kim is not the only foreign dictator that obsesses or manipulates Trump.

To Vladimir Putin's glee, Trump has repeatedly declared that the North Atlantic Treaty Organization (NATO), established in 1949 to deter a Soviet attack on Western Europe, is obsolete and should be abolished and that the United States should withdraw from NATO. He was surprised that the United States still keeps 35,000 troops in Germany and threatened to withdraw them. He became obsessed with member military spending levels, repeatedly castigating those who fell short of the commitment they made at their Wales summit meeting in 2014 to spend 2 per cent of their respective economies on defense by 2024. Trump wrote a public letter to Merkel warning:

> The United States continues to devote more resources to the defense of Europe, when the Continent's economy, including Germany's, are doing well and security challenges abound. This is no longer sustainable for us. Growing frustration is not confined to our executive branch. The United States Congress is concerned as well.[170]

Trump unleashed his fury against NATO during the summit at Brussels on July 11 and 12, 2018 when he denounced the alliance as "obsolete," castigated its members as "deadbeats" for not reaching the 2 per cent ratio of military spending to GDP target, and threatened that the United States "would go it alone" if they did not pay up. Then, after the members reiterated their 2014 commitment to reaching the 2 per cent level by 2024, Trump took credit for that, demanded that they instead increase spending to 4 per cent of GDP, and described himself as "a stable genius". He then insisted: "Germany, as far as I am concerned, is captive to Russia because it's getting so much of its energy from Russia. So, we are supposed to protect Germany, but they're getting their energy from Russia." Germany does receive from Russia about 70 per cent of its natural gas, 40 per cent of its oil, and 30 per cent of its coal, but only 9 per cent of its total energy needs.[171]

Fortunately, Defense Secretary Mattis and National Security Advisor Bolton had anticipated Trump's assaults against NATO and behind his back worked out a carefully worded *communiqué* that alleviated some of his poisonous words. The *communiqué* that Trump signed, without reading it, committed the alliance to invite Macedonia to be a member, establish a headquarters at Norfolk, Virginia and designate thirty mechanized battalions, thirty air squadrons and thirty warships to be ready within thirty days by 2020 if war erupted with Russia, a plan known as the "Four Thirties Initiative".[172]

In reality, despite Trump's attempts to undermine the alliance, NATO and its members continue to enhance forces, bases and strategies to deter or defeat a Russian attack. For instance, during the first six months of 2018, NATO deployed 4,500 troops as trip-wires in Lithuania, Latvia, and Estonia, and designated a "special rapid strike force" of 30,000 troops to respond to any attack on any member. Poland allocated $2 billion to build a base for American troops and surveillance drones on its territory. Norway doubled to 700 the number of American marines training in its territory. Over 10,000 special forces from ten members including the United States conducted training in Poland and the three Baltic States. An American armored brigade of 950 vehicles drove 840 miles from its base in Germany to a base in Lithuania in a few days. Lithuania increased its army from 7,500 to 10,000 troops. Defense Secretary James Mattis announced his "thirty-thirty-thirty-thirty Plan" whereby NATO would muster thirty land battalions, thirty aircraft squadrons and thirty warships within thirty days against any attacker.[173] As for spending, by 2024, eighteen of the twenty-eight NATO will reach or surpass the 2 per cent spending goal. America's 2018 defense budget was $602 billion, of which $31 billion contributed to NATO. As for NATO's administration costs, Washington paid 22 per cent of the total.[174]

Typically, Putin demonstrated why NATO was still vital to western civilization's security. In 2018, on the painfully symbolic date of September 11, he launched Russia's largest military exercise since 1981 after Ronald Reagan became president. The Russians fielded more than 300,000 troops, 1,000 aircraft, 900 tanks and even a Chinese contingent of 3,200 troops.[175]

Trump cancelled the 2019 summit in Washington that would have celebrated NATO's seventy-year history, similar to President Clinton's fiftieth anniversary summit. Instead, the foreign ministers gathered and there was no parade. Some diplomats were relieved at the switch, fearing that Trump would ruin the celebration with his latest attacks on NATO.[176]

Trump's assaults have weakened the alliance. Former German foreign minister Sigmar Gabriel explained Europe's Trump dilemma and a possible way to finesse it:

> The truth is that we can't get along with Trump and we can't get along without the United States. We therefore need a dual strategy, clear, hard, and above all common European answers to Trump. Any attempt to accommodate him … only leads him to go a step further … from trade to NATO.[177]

To bolster NATO, Secretary General Jens Stoltenberg committed an extraordinary and unprecedented act. He journeyed to Washington in mid-September 2018 and spent days trying to convince conservative members of Congress and lobby groups like the Heritage Foundation that NATO was critical to the security of not just Europe but the United States. As for spending, he explained that "Last year, NATO allies across Europe and Canada boosted their defense budgets by a combined 5.2 per cent." As for espionage, "America's NATO allies employ tens of thousands of intelligence personnel, many of them working with their American counterparts, giving the United States better eyes and ears than you would otherwise have." Finally, as for western principles, "NATO has helped to spread democratic values, free enterprise, and stability to millions of people in the eastern part of Europe. This represents a historic geopolitical shift that has benefited the United States and the world."[178]

After the Brussels summit, Trump flew to Britain where he committed a series of diplomatic blunders with Prime Minister Theresa May and Queen Elizabeth II. With May, he condemned her handling of the Brexit negotiations with Brussels, urged her to 'sue the EU' and endorsed Boris Johnson, who had just resigned as foreign minister, to replace May as prime minister. Although he tried to take back his comments the next day, the political damage lingered. With the Queen, Trump violated etiquette by keeping her waiting then walking quickly beside her and cutting ahead before her. He re-assured the world that "I am doing a great job; that I can tell you."[179]

Trump once again played into Putin's hands when, on October 23, 2018, he declared that the United States would withdraw from the

Intermediate-Range Nuclear Forces (INF) Treaty that was signed between President Ronald Reagan and Premier Mikhail Gorbachev on December 8, 1987. The INF was the nuclear arms race's watershed. Under the INF the United States and Soviet Union openly dismantled 2,692 land-based nuclear missiles, 846 American and 1,846 Soviet, with a range of between 311 and 3,420 miles. Eliminating an entire class of missiles gave the Americans and Russians the confidence subsequently to conclude four strategic arms reduction treaties (START) that reduced each side's nuclear weapons to 1,550.[180]

What explains Trump's decision to end such a critical treaty? His excuse was that in 2014 the Russians violated the INF by deploying the SSC-8 while the Chinese were not signatories and have an array of intermediate range nuclear missiles that compose 95 per cent of all their nuclear forces. Typically, Trump's threat to match Russia's SSC-8 with American land-based intermediate-range missiles posed a potentially catastrophic threat to American national security. Land-based missiles are vulnerable "first-strike" weapons that in war impose a "use 'em or lose 'em" psychosis on each side, thus making nuclear war more likely. In contrast, sea- and air-launched missiles are much less vulnerable "second strike" weapons to be used only to retaliate against a first strike by the other side, which is why the INF allowed them. At the very least, Trump's repudiation of INF would provoke an expensive arms race that undermined each side's economies.[181]

The worst immediate effect of Trump's withdrawal was to inflict another blow to NATO unity. Putin issued this dark warning to the Europeans: "The main question is, if the United States does withdraw from this treaty, what will it do with these newly emerging missiles?" Any European nation that provides bases for new missiles: "will have to understand that they put their own territory under the threat of possible counterstrike. I don't understand whether Europe should be put in a situation of such a high level of danger." NATO Secretary General Stoltenberg replied, "We don't want a new Cold War. I don't foresee that allies will deploy more nuclear weapons in Europe as a response to the new Russian missile."[182]

As Trump tried to destroy America's economic and military alliances, he was just as eager to develop a friendship with Vladimir Putin. They first met during the Group of 20 meeting in Hamburg on July 7, 2017. Film of their handshake revealed Trump offering his palm up, a subconscious sign of submission, as Putin's came down and grasped it.[183] They then met for more than two hours during which Trump asked Putin about Russian interference in America's election and accepted his vociferous denial. That evening, during the state dinner, he left his own table to sit down at Putin's table. The two spoke for half an hour accompanied only by Putin's translator. The next day Trump announced that he and Putin had agreed to form a joint cyber-security force to prevent any future hacking. That obvious Trojan Horse Russian ploy provoked protests by Democratic and even some Republican members of Congress.

Later that month Congress passed with veto-proof majorities the Countering America's Adversaries through Sanctions Act that targeted a list of Russian oligarchs and corporations, with separate sections for Iran and North Korea, and prevented the president from easing or eliminating those sanctions without congressional approval. Trump protested the bill but signed it anyway. Later he refused to implement it.[184] In a tweet, Prime Minister Dmitri Medvedev taunted Trump for revealing "complete impotence in the most humiliating manner, transferring executive power to Congress." [185] Putin reacted with far harsher measures that forced the Americans to slash 755 of 1,279 personnel from their embassy and three consulates in Russia and close two annexes. Trump not only refused to retaliate but thanked Putin "because we are trying to cut down on payroll … We'll save a lot of money."[186]

Trump and Putin met again during the Asia Pacific Economic Co-operation summit at Da Nang, Vietnam, on November 12, 2017. When asked about Russia's assault on the 2016 election, Trump blurted:

He said he didn't meddle. He said he didn't meddle. You can only ask so many times. Every time he sees me, he says, 'I didn't do that.' And I believe. I really believe, that when he tells me that, he means it. I think he is very insulted by it.[187]

Their third summit took place at Helsinki, Finland, on July 16, 2018. Before that meeting, Trump issued pro-Russian and anti-European comments. He again called for bringing Russia back into the Group of 7. When asked whether he should demand that Putin hand over twelve indicted Russian GU agents, he replied, "I hadn't thought of that." He then declared that the European Union was the primary threat facing the United States: "Now you wouldn't think of the European Union, but they're a foe. Russia is a foe in certain respects. China is a foe economically, certainly a foe." Finally, he identified an enemy within America itself: "Much of our news media is indeed the enemy of the people."[188]

Trump and Putin met privately for two hours then appeared before journalists. Once again Trump rejected the American intelligence community's overwhelming evidence of Russia's assault on America's 2016 election:

> They said they think it's Russia. I have President Putin; he just said it's not Russia. I will say this. I have great confidence in my intelligence people, but I will tell you that President Putin was extremely strong and powerful in his denial today.

Trump condemned the Mueller investigation into the Russia cyber-assaults and Trump's conspiracy and obstruction of justice as "a disaster for our country." He lauded Putin as "a competitor" and "a good competitor he is. And I think the word competitor is a compliment."[189]

When asked whether he had wanted Trump to win and helped him win the 2016 election, Putin replied, "Yes, I did because he talked about bringing the U.S.-Russian relationship back to normal." At one point Putin actually said what Trump should have said but did not, that he had objected to Russia's takeover of Crimea. Putin offered a teasing possibly revealing reply to a question over whether he had recordings of Trump's alleged sexual romps in Moscow. He laughed and at no point denied such a recording existed. Instead, he explained that hundreds of foreign businessmen visit Russia: "Do you think we try to collect compromising material on each and every one of them?" Then he falsely claimed that he was unaware that Trump was in Moscow during the Miss World pageant.[190]

Perhaps most disturbing of all was Trump twice declaring "an incredible offer" when Putin said he would let Mueller's team interview the twelve indicted GU agents in Moscow. In return Trump would ensure Putin American co-operation in persecuting people "who have something to do with illegal actions on the territory of Russia," then singled out William Browder, an American-born British national and billionaire committed to promoting democracy in Russian, and Michael McFaul, the former ambassador to Russia. That offer would have been disastrous for America in two ways. First, letting the Russians supervise any American interrogations would give them insights into American sources and methods of intelligence gathering. Then, the White House would collaborate with the Kremlin in bolstering Putin's autocracy by persecuting an American citizen and former American and now British citizen.[191]

The press conference concluded with Putin tossing a soccer ball to Trump and declaring "the ball is now in your court". That symbolized both Russia's triumphs in the propaganda war, in hosting the world soccer cup and co-opting Trump. In all, the summit was a brilliant propaganda victory for Russia and against America and western civilization. Yet Putin did not gain any concrete concessions like Trump's recognition of Russia's take-over of Crimea. Within a week of the summit, Trump and Putin each invited the other to his country for another summit. They agreed to postpone any summit until after the November election.

Meanwhile a chorus of experts lambasted Trump's latest appeasement of Putin. Alina Polyakova, a Brookings Institute Russian expert, noted, "Putin took the role not only of grand statesman but even a ventriloquist." Former CIA director John Brennan wrote, "Donald Trump's press conference performance in Helsinki rises to & exceeds the threshold of 'high crimes and misdemeanors.' It was nothing short of treason." National Security Advisor Dan Coats dared to contradict the president, explaining:

We have been clear in our assessments of Russian meddling in the 2016 election and their ongoing efforts to undermine our democracy … The warning lights are blinking red again. Today the digital infrastructure that serves this country is literally under attack. These actions are persistent, they are pervasive, and they are meant to undermine America's democracy.

Trump's embrace of Putin was so blatant that even some Republicans denounced it. Senator John McCain declared, "no prior president has ever abased himself more abjectly before a tyrant." Senator Jeff Flake went further in lambasting Trump, "By choosing to reject objective reality in Helsinki, the president let down the free world by giving aid and comfort to an enemy of democracy." Representative Will Hurd wrote:

> Over the course of my career as an undercover officer in the C.I.A., I saw Russian intelligence manipulate many people. I never thought I would see the day when an American president would be one of them .... By playing into Vladimir Putin's hands, the leader of the free world actively participated in a Russia disinformation campaign that legitimized Russian denial and weakened the credibility of the United States to both our friends and foes abroad.[192]

Deputy Attorney General Rosenstein announced that the Justice Department would assert more efforts to apprehending or countering foreign agents threatening national security: "The Russian effort to influence the 2016 presidential election is just one tree in a growing forest. These actions are persistent, they are pervasive, and they are meant to undermine American democracy."[193]

Yet nearly all other Republicans supported Trump and his pro-Russian policies. In Congress the Republicans killed two Democratic proposals. One would have forced Trump to impose stronger sanctions against Russia and deliver to Congress any notes taken by the American translator during Trump's two-hour meeting with Putin. The other would have called on Trump to work closely with America's allies against Russian aggression. The Senate did vote ninety-eight to zero for a resolution that rejected Putin's demand that Trump deliver former ambassador McFaul for questioning by Russian officials.[194]

Nonetheless, the United States did impose sanctions against Russia for its failed attempt to assassinate defector Sergei Skripal in Salisbury, England, on March 4, 2018. At first Trump angrily rejected any retaliation against Russia, dismissing it as a European problem. When British Prime Minister Theresa May asked Trump to join sanctions against Russia, he retorted, "Why are you asking me to do this?"[195] Finally, on April

6, he grudgingly agreed to sanctions against seven Russia oligarchs and seventeen high-ranking officials. That immediately hit Russia's economy as the ruble plunged twenty percent within a few days.

The United States imposed stronger sanctions against Russia on August 22, 2018 after a laboratory confirmed that the Russians had used the deadly chemical Novichok against Skripal. Trump opposed those sanctions as well but could do nothing to stop them. The sanctions were automatically triggered because Russia's use of Novichok violated the 1991 Chemical and Biological Weapons Control and Warfare Elimination Treaty. The sanctions forbade Americans from purchasing Russian high-technology equipment except any needed for the international space station.[196]

The latest sanctions caused Russia's ruble and stock to drop sharply in value as investors sought safer havens in dollars or euros. A weaker currency does boost exports if there are willing buyers, problematic with the tightening trade sanctions on Russia. In August 2018 the Kremlin had $458 billion in gold and hard currency but did not intervene to prop up the ruble. The drooping economy caused Putin's popularity rating to fall from 79 per cent to 64 per cent, while just 45 per cent would vote for him again and 35 per cent did not trust him.[197]

In an attempt to forestall pending tough bipartisan sanctions, Trump issued an executive order on September 12, 2018 that empowered National Intelligence Director Coats to investigate for forty-five days any allegations of foreign interference in America's 2018 election. That gave enough pro-Trump Republicans political cover to oppose a sanctions bill that might have crushed Russia's economy jointly sponsored by Robert Menendez, a New Jersey Democrat, and Lindsey Graham, a South Carolina Republican. Once again Trump protected Russia and Putin from serious harm.[198]

Then, on September 20, 2018, more than a year and a half after taking power, Trump grudgingly succumbed to the chronic appeals by the Pentagon and Intelligence Community that he authorize the United States Cyber Command to conduct retaliatory cyber-attacks against any aggressive country including Russia. General Paul Nakasone, Cyber Command's director, explained that America suffered unrelenting attacks because the White House had failed promptly to counter-attack in ways that inflicted more damage than was sustained: "I would say right now they do not think much will happen to them. They don't fear us."[199]

Nonplussed, Moscow expanded its cyberwar fronts in 2018 from subverting America's democracy to subverting its infrastructure, especially the electrical grid, by implanting malware that could destroy those systems. Meanwhile, the Russians became more adept at masking their penetrations. During the summer new reports revealed that Russian hackers had entered the computer systems of two politicians, both Democratic senators, of whom one was Claire McCaskell, an outspoken critic of the Kremlin, and the other who remained anonymous. Russian cyber trolls also targeted American conservative groups like the Republican Party, International Republican Institute, Hudson Institute, Eurasian Group, Center for a New American Security and National Rifle Association. Finally, they tried to penetrate centrist think tanks like the Council on Foreign Relations and the Brookings Institute, along with Transparency International based in London. Facebook reported that it had scrubbed thirty-two pages of 652 fake accounts that often mentioned actual extremist groups like "Unite the Right" and "Black Lives Matter". That scrubbing came only after Facebook's value plummeted a record-breaking $120 billion when investors bailed because Russian hackers continued to exploit Facebook as a propaganda vehicle while CEO President Mark Zuckerberg dithered on acting decisively against the infestation.[200]

Five national security chiefs held a dramatic press conference on August 2, 2018. The National Intelligence Directorate's Coats, Federal Bureau of Investigation's Christopher Wray, Homeland Security Department's Kirstjen Nielsen, Cyber Command's Paul Nakasone and National Security Council's Bolton took turns warning that Russia's cyber-war threat to America's democracy and electrical grid was constant and worsening. Each pledged to do anything possible to counter that threat. Ideally, the president would have headlined that press conference. Instead, Trump was at a political rally in Wilkes-Barre, Pennsylvania, where he once again dismissed the Russian threat as a hoax.

Bolton soon backed off his tough stand and instead gave Putin a milk toast message on October 22, 2018 when he met with him in Moscow:

I told our Russian colleagues I don't think their meddling in our election process had any real effect. But something else is important. The very desire to meddle in our affairs creates mistrust toward Russians, toward Russia. I consider it intolerable .... This cold-blooded, blatant intrusion into our electoral process will be discussed with American legal entities.[201]

That statement was all but a green light for the Kremlin to redouble its efforts not just to meddle but to degrade and discredit American democracy, and exacerbate existing racial, ethnic, class, political and ideological differences.[202]

The United States will remain vulnerable to Russia's continuing hybrid war. Two-thirds of Americans, three-fourths of non-white Americans, 55 per cent of those aged over fifty, and 80 per cent of those younger than fifty get their "news" from social media. Russian cyber-trolls generated 414 million fake news stories on Facebook and Twitter alone from 2015 to 2017. Social media corporations and the Republican Party have blocked Democratic Party proposals to regulate that industry to minimize the fake news. The Federal Election Commission (FEC) is supposed to enforce the law that prohibits foreigners without green cards from making campaign contributions. The Republicans on the board of directors have prevented the FEC from enforcing that law.[203]

Meanwhile, CIA sources in the Kremlin stopped giving critical information about Putin's strategy. Although none were thought to have been killed, they apparently lay low both because Russian intelligence redoubled its efforts to identify and eliminate them along with the fear that Trump might somehow expose them; one key source, Oleg Smolenkov, an agent for over a decade, was extradited to safety.[204]

Vladimir Putin has had a Rasputin-like effect on two of the four presidents whose years in power have so far overlapped with his own. Republicans George W. Bush and Donald Trump at times fawned over the Russian dictator. Yet Putin not only failed to either intimidate or charm Democrats Bill Clinton and Barack Obama, but instead provoked a deep wariness from both and loathing from Obama.

Congressional Democrats and Republicans are just as split over Putin and Russia. Democrats unite in denouncing Putin as an imperialist and autocrat. Republicans are Janus-faced. Most condemn his imperialism yet silently laud his beliefs. After all, Putin's conservative values differ little from those of American conservatives with their emphasis on nationalism, authority, religion and family, while condemning free thinkers and sexual "deviants". Oligarchs close to Putin like Oleg Deripaska have entangled some prominent Republicans in money schemes like Mitch McConnell, Bob Dole, Haley Barbour, Trent Lott, Marco Rubio, John Kasich and Lindsay Graham, along with former FBI directors Louis Freeh and William Sessions.[205] Yet, all those collaborators combined fell far short of one American in value to the Kremlin.

Donald Trump has been a priceless "useful idiot" not just for Vladimir Putin's regime but for all anti-American governments around the world. Trump has harshly corroded the institutions, laws and norms of American democracy by his incessant savage attacks on the constitution, legal system, election system, intelligence community, mass media, scientific community and Special Counsel Robert Mueller's investigation. Then there are Trump's assaults on the international organizations that enhance the security and prosperity of America and its allies like NAFTA, NATO, EU, WTO and TPP; atop all that was his withdrawal from the 2015 Paris Global Warning accord that will slow climate change's worsening catastrophic effects if all governments fulfill their promises. Trump's belligerence and bullying has provoked favorable views by foreigners of the United States to plummet in all countries except Russia, Israel and Kenya. For instance, Mexicans who held favorable views of America nose-dived from 66 per cent in 2016 to 32 per cent in 2018.[206]

No American president has ever been more psychologically transparent than Trump who parades his pathologies by publicly projecting them onto hated others. For instance, a November 15, 2018 Trump tweet that attacked the Mueller investigation instead vividly reflected the chaos, viciousness, and dishonor that characterized his presidency:

The inner workings ... are a total mess. They are screaming and shouting at people, horribly threatened them to come up with the answers they want. They are a disgrace to our Nation and don't ... care how many lives they ruin. These are Angry people.[207]

Trump has done whatever he could to derail any attempts within his administration and beyond to develop a tough policy toward Russia. In December 2017 National Security Advisor McMaster presented Trump with a National Security Strategy that confronted Russian along with Chinese aggression. Trump had his speechwriter purge anything critical of Russia from his speech that announced the strategy on December 18. Trump resisted convening a special cabinet national security meeting on Russia's threat to America's elections until July 27, 2018, then said little, decided nothing, and left after an hour to go play golf.[208]

Symbolically, Trump's most offensive behavior came during the solemn commemorative ceremonies in France surrounding November 11, 2018, the hundredth anniversary of the First World War's armistice that ended the fighting on the western front. That should have been a time of sober humility and unity among the nations that fought in that horrific war, in which sixteen million people died. Instead, as always, Trump's egomania triumphed as he insulted French President Emmanuel Macron, demanded that NATO members pay more for defense, skipped one ceremony, was late for another and refused to sign the "Paris Call for Trust and Security in Cyberspace" that was signed by fifty-one countries, more than 130 companies and ninety universities and non-governmental organizations.[209] Trump's nasty attacks provoked both Macron and Merkel to discuss the need for Europeans to develop their own army independent of the United States and NATO. Merkel declared: "The day where we can unconditionally rely on others is gone. That means that we Europeans should take our fate more in our own hands if we want to survive as a European community."[210] Putin, who attended, could not have been happier at the latest deep fissures that Trump inflicted on western civilization.

Then Trump gave Putin two Christmas presents in December 2018 that enhanced Russian and diminished American power. The Treasury Department lifted sanctions against multi-billionaire and Putin crony Oleg Deripaska after a face-saving gesture whereby he promised to reduce his share of his corporate empire to less than half. That enriched

Deripaska by hundreds of dollars in debt and likely saved him from bankruptcy. Trump then announced that he was withdrawing 2,000 American troops who backed the Kurds against Islamic State in eastern Syria, thus ceding that ground and those people to domination by Syrian President Bashar al-Assad, Russia and Iran.[211]

Every year a security conference among Americans, Europeans and Russians takes place in Munich. During the February 2019 conference, relations between the Trump administration and Europe's leaders were so acrimonious that Russian Foreign Minister Sergei Lavrov celebrated, "We see new cracks forming, and old cracks deepening."[212] The longer that Trump remains president the worse he will damage American security, wealth, power and prestige that may take years and even decades to repair, if ever.

Chapter 7

Russia and Europe

Putin has a very clear agenda of modernizing Russia. When he talks of a strong Russia, he means strength not in a threatening way but in a way that means the country economically and politically is capable of standing up for itself, which is a perfectly good aim to have.

(Tony Blair)

Russia is part of the European culture. And I cannot imagine my own country in isolation from Europe and what we often call the civilized world. So it is hard for me to visualize NATO as an enemy.

(Vladimir Putin)

Russia faced daunting political and economic challenges when the European Union's leaders adopted a "Common Strategy of the EU on Russia" at their Cologne summit on June 4, 1999. During his then eight years as president, Boris Yeltsin had imposed a constitution that established a liberal democratic political system but also tolerated and benefited from massive corruption that culminated with Russia's financial collapse in 1997. Europe's leaders committed themselves to helping consolidate Russian democracy, integrating Russia economically with the European Union and working together on common interests like energy, drug and human trafficking, nuclear safety, money-laundering, organized crime and environmental problems. The Kremlin replied with its "Medium Term Strategy for the Development of Relations between the RF and EU (2000–2010)" that accepted the EU's eastward expansion while guaranteeing civil rights for Russian speakers in European countries, migration and border security. When Yeltsin ceded the presidency to Prime Minister Vladimir Putin on New Year's Eve 1999, most Europeans welcomed the new leader as a technocrat who would bring political stability and economic prosperity to Russia. They got that, along with Putin policies that undercut better relations with Europe.

For Vladimir Putin, Russian national interests demand the following: the European Union's destruction; the transformation of liberal democracies into illiberal democracies; the transformation of illiberal democracies into autocracies; the deepening dependence of each European country on Russian oil and natural gas corporations; the deepening dependence of Europe's political and corporate leaders on Russian petrodollars; and, ultimately, Moscow becoming Europe's political, economic and cultural capital. To those ends the Kremlin is doing whatever it can get away with.

The result is a new cold war between Russia and Europe. The fiercest battles are the tugs-of-war between Moscow and Brussels over the eastern European countries liberated as the Soviet empire imploded from 1989 to 1991. Brussels wants to complete their liberation by integrating them in the European Union. Moscow wants them back. So far the Kremlin has lost most of its attempts to block countries from joining the European Union. The European Union became neighbors with Russia with Finland's membership in 1995. The European Union's largest expansion came in 2004, with the addition of Cyprus, the Czech Republic, Estonia, Hungary, Latvia, Lithuania, Malta, Poland, Slovakia and Slovenia. Estonia was not only a Russia neighbor but its north-eastern border was just sixty miles from St Petersburg. Since then, Bulgaria and Romania joined in 2007 and Croatia in 2013.

Brussels' policies for recruiting new members who meet the democratic and market criteria have included the "Wider Europe Program" of 2003, the "European Neighborhood Policy" of 2004, the "European Neighborhood Policy Plus" of 2006, the "Black Sea Synergy" of 2007 and the "Enhanced European Neighborhood Policy" of 2008. In February 2018, Brussels issued a report that called for expanding the European Union's membership by extending invitations to Serbia, Montenegro, Macedonia, Albania, Bosnia and Kosovo to apply and begin the process of meeting the political, economic and legal qualifications. The earliest possible new members would be Serbia and Montenegro in 2025.

The European Union's expansion policy has provoked controversy within its own ranks. Many Europeans have mixed feelings about that policy. They want to expand membership but worry that possible candidates may be too illiberal, poor and corrupt, and thus ultimately corrode rather than strengthen the Union. Norbert Rottgen, who chairs the German Bundestag's foreign affairs committee, explained:

> The argument is that only by taking in the Balkan states are we assured to strengthen stability. But is that true? If we import fragile states in the E.U. we import fragility. If we compromise on conditions, we let in fragile countries open to foreign influences, and so we have to be tough on entrance requirements.[1]

Those problems were among the reasons why, in July 2016, a majority of Britons voted to leave the European Union. Thereafter the United Kingdom's prolonged exit transformed the power balance among its members. Formerly, Britain had joined Germany and France in leading the European Union. Since then German Chancellor Angela Merkel and French President Emmanuel Macron have co-operated in leading the making and assertion of common European Union policies, including those that counter Russia. But that dual leadership will soon disappear. Merkel will retire as chancellor and leader of her Christian Democratic Union (CDU) party regardless of the results of the next general election in 2021. Macron is increasingly unpopular and may not win re-election in 2023.

Meanwhile, the Kremlin has deepened Europe's dependence on Russian oil and natural gas.[2] Despite decades of trying to diversify its sources, the Europeans buy half their oil and gas from Russia, a share that varies greatly for each country:

> Germany, Europe's largest economy, is most dependent. It receives thirty-six per cent of its natural gas from Russia, followed by Italy (twenty-seven per cent), and France (twenty-three per cent). Half of Poland's gas imports, and roughly two-thirds of the Czech Republic's come from Putin. Slovakia, Hungary, Serbia, Bulgaria and Moldova are nearly entirely dependent. Finland and the Baltic States are one hundred per cent dependent on Russia for their energy."[3]

Brussels has tried to lessen the European Union's energy dependence on Russia with anti-trust, diversification and conservation policies. Those policies have halted if not reversed Europe's growing dependence.

Obviously, Russian power swells with Europe's dependence and the Kremlin does everything it can get away with to deepen that dependence. The Russians seek to dominate every link in the energy industry including production, transportation, refining and marketing by buying or forming joint ventures with local companies. Russia's political influence over Europe deepens with Europe's energy dependence as corporate giants like Rosneft and Gazprom shamelessly try to corrupt European politicians and bureaucrats with stacks of petro-dollars. Co-ordinating these policies are Russia's ministries of Finance, Energy, and Natural Resources.

Moscow is trying to expand its web of oil and gas pipelines to entangle more countries. Diversifying routes and customers strengthens Russia. The Kremlin is especially eager to bypass Ukraine through which around 80 per cent of its oil and gas flowed to Western Europe. Nord Stream I and Nord Stream II run from Russia under the Baltic Sea and surface in Germany, thus bypassing Eastern Europe. South Stream will run from Russia under the Black Sea to surface in Bulgaria where one branch will run through Greece then under the Adriatic Sea to Italy; another will run through Serbia, Croatia and Slovenia to Austria; and the third will run through Romania to Hungary. Those pipelines were routed to bypass Ukraine, Belarus, Latvia, Lithuanian, Estonia and Poland.

Gazprom is Russia's natural gas giant, 51 per cent owned by Russia's government, and accounts for 40 per cent of Europe's natural gas. It is trying to diversify from mostly pumping and delivering to marketing natural gas by buying or partnering with distributors in each country. It has not hesitated to hike prices or cut supplies to countries whose governments and corporations try to limit its power. In each pipeline, Gazprom is the dominant partner in consortiums with European firms. Putin ensured that former German chancellor Gerhard Schroder chaired Nord Stream's board of directors. Former Italian Prime Minister Romano Prodi turned down an offer for the same powerful position in South Stream.

Oil and gas are not the only products whereby the Kremlin seeks to deepen the European Union's economic and political dependence. The Russian corporation PhosAgro is the world's largest producer of phosphates, a key fertilizer ingredient. PhosAgro is also among the corporations whose directors Andrei Guryey and Vladimir Litvinenko are among Putin's inner coterie of oligarchs. That giant has lobbied Brussels to raise its standards restricting cadmium, a toxic chemical attached to phosphates. That would normally be a progressive act except that it would give PhosAgro a near monopoly over sales to Europe since its phosphates have much lower portions of cadmium compared to other suppliers.[4]

Dependence is not just an expanding set of one-way streets emanating from the Kremlin. Russia depends on Europe to buy 80 per cent of its oil and gas exports. Russia also depends on Europe for innovative technologies. In 2014 alone Russia concluded 524 technology imports from and 208 exports to Germany, 219 from and 53 to Britain, 145 from and 70 to France, 111 from and 61 to the Netherlands, 94 from and 48 to Finland, and 92 from and 39 to Italy.[5]

As with America, the Kremlin nurtures ties with European leaders and groups that are anti-American, anti-EU, and/or anti-NATO including most prominently Nigel Farage's UK Independent Party, French Marine Le Pen's National Front, Italian Luigi di Maio's Five Star Movement, Italian Matteo Salvini's Lega Nord, Hungarian Viktor Oban's Fidesz Party, Polish Jaroslaw Kaczynski's Law and Justice Party, Bulgarian Volen Siderow's Ataka Party, Austrian Heinz-Christian's Freedom Party and Dutch Geert Wilder's Freedom Party. Like Trump, Farage has nothing but praise for Putin, lauding him as "brilliant" for repeatedly outwitting the West and the world leader he most admired.[6] As for wooing national leaders, Putin's greatest successes were with Gerhard Schroder, Germany's chancellor from 1998 to 2005, and Silvio Berlusconi, Italy's prime minister from 1994 to 1995, 2001 to 2006 and 2008 to 2011.

Another way the Kremlin insidiously infiltrates and undermines Europe is through regional organizations that by one count included:

Euroregion Baltic (Russia, Denmark, Lithuania, Poland and Sweden); Barents Euro-Atlantic Council (Russia, Finland, Norway and Sweden); Euroregion Karelia (Russia and Finland); Neman Euroregion (Russia, Belarus, Lithuania and Poland). Some regions do not include the European countries: Yaroslavna (Russia and Ukraine), Slobozhanshchina (Russia and Ukraine), and Dnepr (Russia, Belarus and Ukraine).[7]

The Kremlin's most important and problematic membership is with the Organization for Security and Cooperation in Europe (OSCE), established in 1975. That organization's Office of Democratic Institutions and Human Rights has investigated and issued reports critical of Russian human rights violations during its elections and in Chechnya. In 2005 Putin accused the institution of double standards and trying to undermine Russia's political system. He retaliated by blocking approval of the institution's budget and forbidding it from observing future Russian elections.

As the Kremlin's diplomacy unfolds so too do ever more concerted and outrageous cyber-assaults by hackers, trolls, automated bots and semi-automated cyborgs. In 2016 alone, Russian cyber-campaigns disrupted nineteen European countries.[8] Those attacks are increasingly effective. Pro-Russian candidates won nine of sixteen elections in 2016 and 2017.[9] To defend Europe against cyber-espionage and outright cyberwar, Brussels established the EastStratCom Task Force in April 2015. That organization monitors Russian fake news and tries to combat it with facts distributed by the weekly publications *Disinformation Review* and *The Disinformation Digest*.

Vladimir Putin naturally feels more comfortable dealing with Germany than any other foreign country. He spent five mostly pleasant years in Dresden as a KBG officer, speaks fluent German, enjoys German culture and respects German power with Europe's largest population and economy. And topping all that are Germany's share of "useful idiots" or outright "agents of influence" aligned with the Kremlin. Putin nurtured the two most prominent.

Gerhard Schroder was Germany's chancellor from 1998 to 2005. The relationship between Putin and Schroder did not start out well. Schroder insisted that Russia repay every penny of the billions of dollars it owed the Paris Club of public lenders and London Club of private lenders. If not, he threatened to block Russia's full membership in the group, which it joined as an associate member in 1997. Putin continued to pay interest on those debts while pressing Schroder to write-off a substantial amount of the principal. The London Club eventually canceled one-third of Russia's debt but the Paris Club insisted on full repayment. For Putin half a loaf was better than none.

Meanwhile, Putin and Schroder bonded. Like Putin, Schroder rose through hard work and often ruthless means from rags to riches. Putin found his friend a lucrative powerful corporate post just three months after his party lost the 2005 election and he retired from politics. Schroder is one of the directors of Nord Stream that built a natural gas pipeline from Russia along the Baltic Sea's bottom to Germany.

An even more powerful collaborator is Dresdner Bank director Matthias Warnig, who forged closer ties with Russia, most powerfully through its 33 per cent share of Gazprombank that it purchased in August 2005. Warnig was a former Stasi intelligence officer with whom Putin worked when the KGB posted him to Dresden. Warnig and Putin have re-established a relationship aimed at undermining the West while expanding their own wealth.

Moscow's key political party ally is the Alternative-fur-Deutschland (AfD) which opposes the EU and immigration, although the Social Democrat Party (SDP) also faces accusations of having numerous Russian collaborators in its ranks. Front groups include the German Federation of Industry's Eastern Committee, Petersburger Dialogue, German-Russian Forum, Dialogue of Civilizations Institute and Yakunin Foundation. The Kremlin nurtures an array of German mass media collaborators including RT-Deutsche, Sputnik-Deutsche and NewsFront-Deutsche.

Steadfastly resisting Putin's pull was Angela Merkel, Germany's chancellor from 2005 to 2019. No western leader was better positioned to understand Putin and his authoritarian regime than her. She is two years younger than him, grew up in communist East Germany, speaks fluent Russian, studied at the Academy of Sciences in East Berlin, joined the mass democratic movement that drove the communists from power and then rose through the ranks of the conservative Christian Democratic Union (CDU) until she became chancellor. One biographer argued that Putin and Merkel "followed similar paths in life, almost as if they were mirror images".[10] That is superficially true to a point. With intelligence, flexibility, determination, connections and luck, each developed a career in a harshly repressive regime. Although each has a rather taciturn, dour and methodical personality, the similarities end there. Merkel helped transform East Germany from communism into liberalism and re-unite it with democratic West Germany. Putin witnessed the Soviet Union's break-up and Russia's re-emergence with an illiberal democracy. Then, after becoming president on New Year's Eve 1999, Putin transformed Russia into an autocracy. As for character, they could not differ more. Merkel is a model of probity. Putin became a multi-billionaire through titanic corruption and had many of his rivals murdered.

Twice Putin pulled a mean trick on Merkel during her visit to his palace near Sochi. Merkel is terrified of dogs, having twice suffered attacks. Knowing her fear, Putin brought his labrador into two meetings with her. Those acts revealed a cruel streak in Putin's character. Of course, such behavior backfires when it provokes contempt, loathing and resistance rather than intimidation and compliance by the victim for the bully.

Nonetheless, Merkel does not let her feelings warp her realistic understanding of German, EU and NATO interests in the face of Russia's multiple threats. As the EU's de facto leader, she asserted Germany's power eventually to overcome Greece's financial defaults, the 2008 Great Recession, integration of new members and sanctions against Russia for annexing Crimea. Meanwhile, she firmly opposed NATO membership for Ukraine and Georgia, recognizing that those distant, corrupt, poor, unstable, volatile, authoritarian countries would be gross liabilities rather than assets. She might have paraphrased and updated one of Otto von Bismarck's more renowned quips, that neither Kiev nor Tbilisi is worth the bones of a single German soldier. She bluntly told Georgian President Mikhail Saakashvili, who was about to meet Bush, that "Whatever Bush says, I will not allow a NATO track for Georgia and Ukraine." When Saakashvili shared that with Bush, he replied, "You take care of your own business. Leave that woman to me."[11] Bush failed to convince Merkel to fast-track Ukraine and Georgia for NATO membership. Instead, he grudgingly agreed to Merkel's compromise proposal that NATO issue a vague statement that it was open to future membership by Ukraine and Georgia without any specific process or timetable.

Merkel became western civilization's de facto leader after Trump became America's president on January 20, 2017 and essentially abdicated that role. She has done what she could to deter or repair Trump's damage to NATO, the EU and the global economy. The trouble is that her power has slipped steadily since 2015, when she announced that Germany would accept one million Syrian refugees. Conservatives condemned that influx of a million mostly Muslim Arabs into Germany. During the election on September 24, 2017 her center-right Christian Democratic Party (CDP) lost seats after winning only a third of the vote, the right-wing Alternative for Deutschland (AfD) Party won seats, and it took Merkel half a year to cobble together a coalition government that eventually included the center-left Social Democratic Party (SDP). At least the Russians did not directly warp that election's outcome because the system uses paper ballots counted by an encrypted network detached from the internet.

Instead, for years but with worsening intensity, Russian cyber-trolls have spewed false incendiary messages designed to cleave and embitter Germans along ethnic, class and religious lines. For example, in January 2016 they launched the "Our Lisa" campaign, a fabricated story that three Arab Muslims had kidnapped and raped a Russian-German girl. That sparked anti-foreigner demonstrations in German cities including before the chancellery in Berlin. At times Russian cyber-trolls have directly attacked Germany's government. In January 2015 CyberBerkut actually shut down much of the government's computer network during a visit by Ukrainian Prime Minister Arseniy Yatsenyuk; CyberBerkut posted a message that called on Berlin to sever aid to "the criminal government in Kiev". In April and May 2015, Fancy Bear, a GU front, attacked the parliament (Bundestag) for weeks, eventually infecting 5,600 computers and 12,000 users, including Merkel's office.[12]

Merkel's government has responded by boosting its cyber defenses by establishing the Cyber Defense Center, a quick response team within the Federal Office for Information Security, and the Cyber and Information Space Command with 13,500 personnel as the military's sixth branch, while hardening all public sites against cyber attacks. The think tanks Global Public Policy Institute and German Council on Foreign Relations have set up cyber-warfare sections.

Merkel provoked concern not just among most Germans but informed people worldwide when, after her party lost heavily in the October 2018 state elections, she announced that that would be her last election as chancellor or the CDU's leader. She felt that was the only proper act after her party's Bundestag share had fallen to 27 per cent from 41 per cent as recently as the 2013 election. Although the CDU still has the largest share of seats for any party, coalitions will be increasingly difficult to forge. The good news was that the next general German election would not be until October 2021. That gives the CDU three years to find a worthy successor. Meanwhile, the Russians will do everything they can to thwart that possibility.

When Putin took power, Prime Minister Tony Blair saw his relationship with him as similar to that of Margaret Thatcher with Mikhail Gorbachev. Both Putin and Gorbachev were intelligent, pragmatic Russian nationalists with whom one could "do business" as Thatcher put it. Blair first met Putin for two days in March 2000. The highlight was them seated side-by-side in the presidential box seat at the Mariinsky Theater for Sergei Prokofiev's opera *War and Peace*. Back in Britain, Blair lauded Putin's "future" as:

> one that we would feel comfortable with. Putin has a very clear agenda of modernizing Russia. When he talks of a strong Russia, he means strength not in a threatening way but in a way that means the country economically and politically is capable of standing up for itself, which is a perfectly good aim to have.[13]

Blair invited Putin to London for talks in April. During their joint press conference, Blair praised Putin for being "ready to embrace a new relationship with the European Union and the United States, who wants a strong and modern Russia and a strong relationship with the West."[14] In an interview with David Frost, Putin re-assured people in Britain and beyond that

> Russia is part of the European culture. And I cannot imagine my own country in isolation from Europe and what we often call the civilized world. So it is hard for me to visualize NATO as an enemy.[15]

Putin and Blair met three more times that year alone.

To date, Putin's most successful foreign trip came during four days in Britain in June 2003. Blair set up an official state visit and reception with Queen Elizabeth, the first time a British monarch had received a Russian leader since Tsar Nicholas in 1896. The trip's practical high points were two contracts, one that established a 50–50 joint venture between Russia's Tyumen Oil Company and British Petroleum, and the other that established the North European Gas Pipeline, later renamed Nord Stream that would link Russia and Britain. Yet Putin did not let those diplomatic and economic triumphs obscure a broad vision of Russia interests. During a speech in Edinburgh, he warned:

> Russia is undoubtedly part of Europe ... We should make sure that no new dividing lines appear in Europe, that people are able to communicate with each other, that the rules of the Schengen zone are not perceived as something similar to the Berlin Wall, which divided Europe until a few years ago. We must do everything to enable Russia and Europe to help each other to develop in a harmonious and stable way. We have a mutual interest in each other because even the structures of the Russian and European economies mutually complement each other.[16]

Putin's key goal with Britain was estranging it from the European Union. That was not a stretch. London's relations with the European Union and its predecessors have always been troubled. During the 1950s London rejected membership with, first, the European Coal and Steel Community (ECSC) and, then, the European Economic Community (EEC). During the 1960s French President Charles de Gaulle blocked Britain's two attempts at EEC membership. Britain did not become an EEC member until 1973. As prime minister from 1979 to 1990, Margaret Thatcher distanced Britain from the EEC, insisting on behalf of Britain to Brussels that "I want my money back". Indeed, Britain did contribute more in dues to Brussels than it received in development aid. Nonetheless, economically the benefits of British membership in the European Union far exceeded the costs.[17]

The trouble was that most Britons did not understand that. Instead, they perceived that membership was draining Britain financially while inundating the country with immigrants who displaced Britons in jobs by working for less money and longer hours. The UK Independence Party was founded as an anti-European union and anti-immigrant party in 1991 but for a quarter century was nothing more than a fringe political gadfly. Then, under Nigel Farage's populist leadership, the party attracted ever more voters in Britain's 2013 local, 2014 European and 2015 general elections. In 2015, the UK Independence Party received 12.9 per cent of the vote but only one seat because of Britain's first-past-the-post electoral system.

The UK Independence Party's gains largely represented losses for the Conservative Party. In response, Prime Minister David Cameron took an enormous gamble when he placated the Conservative Party's separatist wing by promising a referendum on British membership in the European Union. Cameron favored remaining in the European Union, but only if Britain began taking as many benefits as it conferred.

The referendum on whether Britain should exit the Europe Union, known as "Brexit," gave the Kremlin an enormous opportunity to advance Russian interests. Russian cyber-trolls spent only around $2 million backing Britain's exit from the European Union, yet that interference may have been decisive. During the months leading up to the vote, *Russia Today* and *Sputnik* published 261 articles that called for Britain's withdrawal from the European Union. In the days before the vote, 150,000 Russian-linked Twitter accounts tweeted propaganda. Arron Banks, the UK Independence Party's financier, met repeatedly with Russian ambassador Alexander Yakovenko and diplomat Alexander Udod who was among twenty-three spies later expelled for the attempted murder of defector Sergei Skripal; Banks spent more than £8 million pounds promoting Brexit. Unfortunately, not just nearly all British voters but even British intelligence was largely oblivious to those meetings at the time. And, as with Russian attempts to corrode democracy in America and other countries, the exact impact can never be known.[18]

As a result, the emotional arguments for exit trumped the rational arguments that European Union membership enriched Britain and withdrawal would diminish Britain. The standard estimate was that leaving the European Union will cost Britain 3 per cent of GDP and a million jobs in 2020. In the June 23, 2016 referendum, the votes for and against leaving the European Union were 51.89 per cent and 48.11 per cent respectively.[19]

Cameron resigned as prime minister and after an election within the Conservative Party, Theresa May took his place. Thereafter, May tried to negotiate a "soft" exit that preserved Britain's economic advantages while eliminating membership costs. Brussels was determined to make a harsh example of Britain's withdrawal by insisting on a huge financial penalty while revoking its trade advantages. Brexit bitterly split the British people and their animosities worsened with the worsening economic, political and social costs of leaving the European Union. And Putin could not have been more triumphant.[20]

As if Russia's violation of Britain's referendum was not egregious enough, there are murders. Since Putin took power, assassins have twice violated Britain's sovereignty to target former intelligence officers who defected there. In 2005 they murdered Aleksander Litvinenko with Plutonium-210 coated on his bedside reading lamp. In 2018, they nearly murdered Sergei Skripal and his daughter with the chemical Novichok smeared on their home's front door-knob. The victims spent weeks in the hospital while a British woman died who handled the discarded vial that held the Novichok. Each time, the British government retaliated by expelling Russian spies under diplomatic cover.

Putin responded by denying that Russia was involved and expelling British diplomats. After the British government released to the mass media photos of the two suspected Skripal assassins, Igor Kostyukov and Vladimir Alexseyev, Putin claimed they were innocent and had RT, Russia's English language propaganda television network, interview them. The suspects claimed to be just two regular blokes interested in gothic architecture who journeyed to Salisbury to visit the cathedral. Their cover story's trouble was that public video cameras, which are ubiquitous in British cities and towns, revealed that they did not tour the cathedral but instead left the railway station toward Skripal's suburban neighborhood. Britain's mass media described the interview as Monty-Pythonesque in its utter absurdity. On January 21, 2019 the European Union sanctioned the two GU would-be assassins and their two immediate commanding officers.[21]

Yet, Russia's assaults on democracy in Britain and elsewhere are no laughing matter. As in America, the Russian threat bitterly splits Britain politically both among and within parties. Like America's Republican Party, the Conservative Party harbors accusers and deniers. Prime Minister May issued this warning to Moscow: "I have a very simple message for Russia. We know what you are doing. And you will not succeed." Foreign Minister Boris Johnson undercut that message by spouting the Kremlin's line that no "sausage of evidence" exists that the Russians interfered with Britain's elections. To that Russia's foreign ministry blamed the victim: "It is understandable that an external enemy is direly needed to distract public attention for which role Russia has been chosen. It is deeply regrettable."[22]

France was been a political anomaly in Europe since its 2017 national election. Emmanuel Macron, a thirty-nine-year-old former investment banker and finance minister, created and led to a decisive victory a populist centrist movement he called *"En Marche!"* or Forward! He trounced five contenders in the first presidential election round on April 23 and won the second round with 66.1 per cent of the vote to 33.9 per cent for his opponent, National Front candidate Marine Le Pen on May 7. Meanwhile, his party won 350 of the National Assembly's 577 seats while the National Front took merely eight seats. Those astonishing results for a new political movement that captured the political center could be a model for similar movements elsewhere, most importantly for the United States. Macron and *En Marche!* are also models for how to defeat a right-wing populist party backed by Moscow with a massive cyber-assault on a nation's political system.

The National Front, which opposes the European Union and immigration, is France's most powerful political party allied with Russia. In December 2014 the National Front received a $9.8 million loan from a Russian oligarch linked to the Kremlin. For the upcoming 2017 presidential election, Russia's cyber-trolls launched a massive cyber-assault to denigrate center-left, centrist and center-right candidates while celebrating National Front candidate Marine Le Pen. Russia's Fancy Bear hackers inflicted the most audacious coup when they retaliated against critical reports by Tele5Monde, France's most powerful television network; they posed as Islamic State, took over the network, and broadcast Jihadist propaganda for two days in February 2017.

Yet Russia's cyber-war against France's electoral system and democracy was far less effective than its offensives the previous year in America and Britain. The reason was that Macron's campaign anticipated and pre-empted that attack and thus decisively deflated its impact. A team of eighteen cyber warriors led by Mounir Mahjoubi secured the Macron campaign's sites, then asserted a counter-measures strategy known as cyber-blurring. Mahjoubi explained that:

> We created false accounts, with false content, as traps. We did this massively, to create the obligation for them to verify, to determine whether it was a real account .... During all their attacks we put in phony documents. And that forced them to waste time.[23]

Silvio Berlusconi is Italy's version of Donald Trump, a narcissistic corrupt billionaire and philanderer who is inordinately fond of and beholden to Vladimir Putin. He diverted some of his wealth to creating and leading the *Forza Italia!* (Forward Italy!) Party, and served as prime minister from 1994 to 1995, 2001 to 2006 and 2008 to 2011. Like Trump, he has faced an array of legal charges including bribery, corruption, conflicts of interest, tax fraud, money-laundering and sex with an under-age girl. After becoming prime minister in 2001, he and Putin became close friends. Over the years Putin has hosted Berlusconi in Moscow or his Sochi palace numerous times. Berlusconi, who made his fortune developing a mass media empire, gave Putin political advice that he found invaluable: "What is on TV does not exist."[24] Putin interpreted that Zen-like maxim to mean that truth is relative to one's power to get others to believe one's assertions that may be utterly false. Berlusconi has repeatedly called for Russia's membership in the European Union while condemning the American and European sanctions against Russia for its imperialism against Ukraine in 2014.

Two of Italy's largest political parties are anti-European Union and anti-American. In 1991 Umberto Bossi founded the Northern League to promote federalism and regional autonomy for northern Italy; Matteo Salvini became the party's leader in 2013. In 2009, satirist Beppe Grillo founded the anti-immigrant, anti-EU Five Star Movement; Luigi di Maio became the party's leader in 2017. In the March 2018 election those parties won the most seats and, with several smaller parties, formed a government with Salvini and di Maio as deputy prime ministers, and Giuseppe Conte, a law professor at the University of Florence, as prime minister, chosen because of his intelligence, integrity and lack of party affiliation.

Conte shunned the anti-Washington, anti-Brussels rhetoric of the Five Star and League politicians. Instead, his government reached an agreement with a consortium to build a 545 mile, $5.2 billion gas Trans-Adriatic Pipeline from Azerbaijan on the Caspian Sea to Italy. That would significantly reduce Italy's dependence on Russia with the South Stream Pipeline then being built.[25] Nonetheless, Conte's government expanded spending and borrowing that exceeded EU standards. In 2018, Italy's budget deficit and national debt reached 2.4 per cent and 131 per cent of the economy; the $2.6 trillion national debt is the world's fifth largest. Moody's Investors Service downgraded Italy's debt rating to just a notch above "junk".[26] On October 23 Brussels warned Rome that it had three weeks to comply with EU standards. Conte, Savimbi and di Maio issued angry defiant replies that included condemning the EU as "the enemy of the people". Yet nearly two months later, Conte made a concession in the face of crippling sanctions. He promised to cut the budget deficit from 2.40 to 2.04 per cent of the economy, although that was still above the 1.6 per cent EU standard. Negotiations deadlocked. Salvini bolstered Italy's bargaining power when he got parliament unanimously to approve a resolution that Italy adopt Mini-Bills of Currency or a parallel currency for the government and citizens to pay their debts. Not only did that violate EU law that permits only the European Central Bank to issue currency for Eurozone members but it would flood financial markets with junk money precipitating inflation and a speculative boom that would inevitably implode.[27]

Italy's economy is too big to fail. It is the Eurozone's third largest and ten times larger than that of Greece, whose bailout so far has cost $300 billion. An Italian default or creation of an alternative currency would be an economic catastrophe for Europe and the world beyond. It would shatter not just the Eurozone but quite likely the European Union while fueling the expansion of far left and far right populist movements across the continent. Putin and his regime reveled in the stand-off and crisis between Brussels and Rome.

Meanwhile, Salvini and di Maio undercut Conte's constructive policies by openly criticizing French President Macron and egging on the Yellow Vest (Gilets Jaune) anarchist movement that rioted in Paris and other cities from November 2017 into 2018. Indeed, di Maio actually met in

France with Yellow Vest leader Christophe Chalencon and pledged his support. On February 7, 2019 Macron withdrew France's ambassador from Italy in protest. The motivations for the agitation by Salvini and di Maio were ideological and political. As right- and left-wing populists, they hated that Macron's centralist policies of liberalizing markets and spending austerity were slowly expanding the economy and reducing unemployment. They also wanted to divert attention from their own fiscally irresponsible policies that provoked condemnation by Brussels. Finally, as European Union opponents, they exacerbated political fissures. And, in doing all this, they advanced Putin's goals.[28]

No European countries face a more chronic Russian threat than the three Baltic States, Lithuania, Latvia and Estonia. Russia has deep ties in each country having conquered them in the late-sixteenth century. The Baltic States asserted their independence in 1920, but the Soviets re-conquered them in 1939. They declared independence in 1991 and have maintained it ever since. In 2004 they joined NATO on March 29 and the EU on May 1.

Nonetheless, Moscow has varying degrees of influence over each country, especially through the Russian-speakers who, of those populations, comprise 8 per cent of Lithuania, 29 per cent of Estonia and 33 per cent of Latvia. The Kremlin asserts power by underwriting ethnic Russian parties, businesses and interest groups, along with communist and socialist parties. EU and NATO membership did not prevent Gazprom, Transneft, Lukoil, Yukos and other Russian energy corporations from buying controlling shares of the gas and oil industries of Lithuania, Latvia and Estonia, nor does it prevent those Russian corporations from cutting energy supplies and raising prices in attempts to bully those states to comply with Kremlin demands. Yet EU and NATO membership has empowered those countries to resist Moscow's demands.

Of the Baltic states, Estonia is geographically the closest to Russia, which places it in a Kremlin geopolitical bullseye. In February 2002 Moscow issued these demands to Tallinn: ease naturalization rules and annually grant Estonian citizenship to as many as 30,000 Russians; subject Estonian's Orthodox church to Moscow's Patriarch; make

Russian an official language with Estonian; fund Russian language programs; provide social security to former KGB and other security personnel who settled in Estonia; and end any investigation of crimes against humanity against former Soviet military and intelligence forces. Estonia's government bluntly rejected all these demands and accelerated its efforts to join the EU and NATO. In April 2007 Putin launched a cyber blitzkrieg against Estonia after the government removed a Soviet war memorial from central Tallinn. One of the cyber war launch pads was traced back to Putin's presidential palace. Meanwhile, Putin's militant youth group Nashi protested outside Estonia's embassy in Moscow.[29] Russian commercial and military aircraft periodically violate Estonia's airspace, most notoriously when President Putin's jetliner flew for fifty seconds above Estonia on the way to a summit with President Trump in Helsinki in July 2018.[30]

Moscow's greatest victory in the Baltic States occurred during Latvia's election on October 7, 2018, when the Harmony Center Party, affiliated with Putin's United Russia Party, won a plurality with nearly 20 per cent of the vote. Next with 14.1 per cent of the vote was the Who Owns the State Party, led by Artuss Kaimins, known as Latvia's Donald Trump for his wealth and ties to Putin. Third place went to the New Conservative Party with 13.6 per cent of the vote.[31]

Lithuania was the only Soviet colony that suffered violence as its people struggled to free themselves from Moscow's tyranny. On January 13, 1991 the Kremlin authorized Soviet troops to take over Vilnius's television station, leading to fifteen deaths and scores of wounded. The Lithuanian resistance forced the Kremlin to withdraw Soviet troops. Lithuania has rejected periodic Moscow demands that it open a free corridor between Belarus and the Russian enclave of Kaliningrad on the Baltic Sea. In January 2017 Russian cyber-trolls spread the lie that German troops stationed in Lithuania during a NATO training exercise had raped a girl. With only 8 per cent of its population Russia, Lithuania is less vulnerable than Latvia and Estonia.

Hungarian Prime Minister Viktor Orban is among Putin's kingpins. He was a liberal reformer during his first stint as prime minister from 1998 to 2002, but cynically discarded that for anti-immigrant and anti-

EU populism after he lost power. After leading his nationalistic Fidesz Party to victory in the 2010 election, Orban systematically transformed Hungary from a liberal into an illiberal democracy by monopolizing the press, muzzling protesters, gerrymandering electoral districts, worsening corruption, packing the courts with judges from his followers, and scapegoating Muslim, liberals and billionaire philanthropist George Soros for all of Hungary's problems. Through buyouts and bullying, he expanded the number of pro-Fidesz news outlets including newspapers, television stations, internet sites and radio stations from thirty-one to more than 500! According to Freedom House, Hungary's Press Freedom Index ranking among countries plummeted from forty to eighty-seven between 2010 and 2017, while its democracy index changed from "consolidated democracy" to "semi-consolidated democracy."[32]

Orban's authoritarianism has provoked increasing tension with western European leaders. Relations are especially strained between Orban and German Chancellor Merkel. Like other populists, Orban opposes immigration while Merkel supports it, having pledged that Germany would accept one million Syrian refugees in 2015. The focus of that conflict is the European Parliament where the European People's Party is a coalition of center-right parties that includes Orban's Fidesz and Merkel's Christian Democratic Party. On September 13, 2018 the European Parliament voted 448 to 197 for a resolution that Hungary's democracy was endangered because its government violated democratic norms, the first time such a resolution had ever been asserted. The resolution required the support of at least two-thirds of representatives. That is the first step toward punishing Hungary's government for its violation of the EU requirement that all members be liberal democracies. Of the European People's Party, 115 voted against Orban's government, fifty-seven supported it and twenty-eight abstained. Then, on March 20, 2019, the European People's Party suspended Fidesz's membership until a three-person monitoring panel determines that it complies with democratic standards.[33]

Poland is another eastern European country in which a populist party has won power and attempted to transform the political system from a liberal into an illiberal democracy. The Law and Justice Party first governed

Poland in 2005, when twin brothers Lech and Jaroslaw Kaczynski were elected president and prime minister. Initially, the Kaczynskis were openly pro-American and anti-Russia, supported NATO's expansion eastward to Ukraine and Georgia and denounced Russian aggression against those countries. Then, in the 2007 election, the Law and Justice Party came in second to the Civic Platform, went into opposition for the next eight years and retook power as populists and authoritarians.

Although Civic Platform leader Donald Tusk became prime minister, Lech Kaczynski remained president. In 2008, Kaszynski signed an agreement whereby the United States would base a missile defense system in Poland. Tusk and Putin first met at the Davos gathering of the world's elite in February 2009, during which Tusk agreed to ease the transit across Poland for Russian traffic to and from its Kaliningrad enclave. In return, Putin invited President Kaczynski to a commemorative ceremony at the Katyn Forest where the Soviets massacred 22,000 Polish prisoners-of-war during the Second World War.[34] Tragically, on April 10, 2010, the plane carrying Kaczynski and ninety-five other passengers crashed en route with no survivors. The sincerity with which Putin and Medvedev expressed their sorrow at that horrific tragedy actually strengthened relations between Poland and Russia. Catholic Archbishop Stanislaw Dziswiz, who had opposed closer ties, was so moved by the Russian leaders that he now supported *détente*.

The Law and Justice Party made a comeback in November 2015 with Andrzej Duda as president and Beata Szydlo as prime minister. Thereafter Duda's attempt to pack the Constitution Tribunal, which determines whether new laws are constitutional, with Law and Justice Party justices has provoked controversy within Poland and in Brussels. His first step was to transfer the position of prosecutor general from the independent National Council of the Judiciary to the Justice Ministry. His next step came on July 3, 2018 when the Constitutional Tribunal issued a ruling that lowered the mandatory retirement age from seventy to sixty-five, thus forcing twenty-seven of seventy-two justices to resign. Those who did not want to resign could appeal to Duda, who is solely empowered with determining whether they can stay. Duda and his supporters claimed that this change was designed to curb corruption. Opponents argued that this was the Duda regime's blatant attempt to pack the courts with right-wing justices. Most judges refused to resign while mass protests erupted against the new law. Seven of the Tribunal's fifteen justices signed a letter condemning Tribunal President Julia Przylebska for improper leadership.[35]

The European Union was essentially powerless to prevent these changes. Although authoritarian measures by a member state violate Europe's constitution and can result in the suspension of that state's voting rights in Europe's parliament, it requires the unanimous vote of all twenty-eight members. Justice Minister Zbigniew Ziobrow insisted:

> I am convinced that the Court of Justice of the European Union is neither competent nor proper and thus may not make statements on the judiciary reform in Poland, or any other EU country for that matter.[36]

Nonetheless, on October 19, 2018 the European Court of Justice ruled that Poland's government had violated judicial independence and ordered it to suspend a law whereby it purged twenty-seven judges and instead restore them to the court. On December 17, 2018 the Polish government finally and grudgingly agreed to obey the order. The Kremlin was delighted over the European Union's latest acrimonious stand-off.[37]

The one bright spot with Poland was its deep-rooted anti-Kremlin attitudes, the result of centuries of being victimized by Russian imperialism. The Poles are especially eager to cut their reliance on Russian natural gas, spurred by Gazprom's three-week cut-off in 2009. After that, Warsaw invested a billion euros to develop a natural gas port at Swinoujscie and named it Lech Kaczynski, after the former president who died in a mysterious plane crash in Russia. Liquefied natural gas – American, Norwegian and Qatari – through that port has reduced Russia's market from two-thirds to half and it will steadily diminish further.[38]

The Kremlin considers the Balkans a traditional Russian sphere of influence that NATO and EU expansion have grossly violated. Russia does share Slavic ethnicity and Orthodox Christianity with most people in the Balkans, although there are exceptions. Romania's people mostly speak a Latin-based Romance language or Hungarian. Albania and Kosovo are mostly Muslim. The Greeks speak an unrelated language. What the Balkan countries share are varying degrees of poverty and corruption.

Greece is the European Union's most irresponsible member and among its most corrupt. During the 1990s into the twenty-first century, Greece's political parties got in a bidding war for votes by promising ever more welfare benefits. They fulfilled that promise as each coalition of parties expanded pensions, health care, vacation days, cash for poor people and earlier retirement. The only trouble was that Greece's economy generated only a fraction of the revenues to pay for its Swedish-style welfare programs. So Athens borrowed ever more money from the internet and banks to pay for its commitments but fell further behind in servicing the interest on that debt.

Athens first threatened to default on its debt payment in 2009, leading to a crisis alleviated only when negotiations with Brussels led to more loans in return for promises to cut back government programs and spending. But that was just the first of several Greek threats and essentially shake-downs of the European Union for more money at cheaper rates to be repaid over more years.

With its lax banking laws, Greece is among the countries where Russian oligarchs and mobsters launder their money. Relations between Russia and Greece go beyond the latter's promiscuous financial standards. Greek Prime Minister Alexis Tsipras led the neo-communist Syriza Party. In 2015, Tsipras actually denounced and refused to participate in European Union sanctions against Russia for annexing Crimea and invading eastern Ukraine.

Yet even Tsipras has his limits. In July 2017, Greek police arrested Russian oligarch Aleksandr Vinnik for laundering $4 billion of bitcoin through Greek banks. Vinnik was linked to bitcoin transactions that financed Russia's cyber troll offensive to savage America's 2016 election. In 2018, a Greek court rejected an American extradition request and instead freed Vinnik to return to Moscow.

The worst clash between Russia and Greece was over Macedonia. The Kremlin views Macedonia with its mostly Slavic, Orthodox Christian population as an integral part of the greater Russian world. For those same reasons, Athens had long objected to their Slavic neighbor calling itself Macedonia. They bitterly resented that the Slavs, centuries ago, had invaded and displaced the original Greek inhabitants, taking the name along with the land.

The Macedonian government was committed to joining both NATO and the EU. The trouble was that Greece vetoed Macedonia's memberships until it officially became North Macedonia. Skopje agreed to submit the proposed name change to a referendum on October 5, 2018. The Russians did what they could to prevent that referendum from approving the change. Ivan Savvidis, a Russian-Greek billionaire, openly led that campaign while the Kremlin targeted Macedonia for a massive cyber assault that spewed exaggerations and lies and provoked violent street protests through hundreds of troll websites and payments by Savvidis to protesters in Athens and Skopje. Upon learning of those machinations in July 2018, Greek Prime Minister Tsipras expelled two Russian spies with diplomatic cover and barred two others from coming to Athens. In retaliation Moscow expelled two Greek diplomats.[39] On the referendum's eve, American Defense Secretary James Mattis journeyed to Macedonia to encourage the name change. In the referendum, 91 per cent favored the name change, although only 36.5 per cent of eligible voters bothered to turn out. Macedonia's parliament approved the name change on October 19, 2018. North Macedonia's future NATO and EU memberships were only a matter of time.[40]

Cyprus has become an all but outright Russian colony for tens of billions of dollars' worth of illicit Russian oligarch, mob and espionage transactions, and thousands of residents. By 2012, Russian money filled around half of all Cyprus financial accounts. Then calamity struck in March 2013. Years of irresponsible Cypriot government spending, corruption and mismanagement led to a default on its international debt. The International Monetary Fund (IMF) made a 10-billion-euro loan, contingent on government cutbacks in public spending and a tax on financial transactions. The Kremlin protested but actually increased its funds there. Cyprus was too valuable an asset to abandon just because the cost of doing business there suddenly jumped.[41]

Montenegro declared independence from Serbia in 2006 even though nearly all its citizens speak Serbian and are Orthodox Christians. And for those Slavic and Orthodox characteristics the Kremlin considers Montenegro a natural part of the greater Russian world and promotes that with an array of nefarious acts. Moscow supports financially the anti-NATO and anti-EU Serbian Nationalist Party and wields cyber-tryyolls to spew propaganda. But the most blatant operation that Putin authorized was during Montenegro's election on October 16, 2016 and amidst its negotiations to join NATO. The plan was for agents in police uniforms to attack the parliament, murder as many legislators as possible, including Prime Minister Milo Djukanovic, and replace him and his cabinet with pro-Russian politicians. Security forces thwarted the coup by arresting fourteen conspirators, twelve Montenegrins and two Russian GU agents, Vladimir Popov and Eduard Shishmakov, who with diplomatic immunity were expelled, rather than prosecuted.

The aborted Russian coup galvanized Montenegrins to vote for pro-NATO and pro-EU candidates who dominated the parliament. Montenegro became NATO's twenty-ninth member on June 5, 2017. Although only 2,000 of 650,000 Montenegrins are in the army, a small contingent serves with NATO forces in Afghanistan.

In a typically bizarre anti-NATO rant, President Trump condemned Montenegro during the NATO summit in July 2018. When asked why America should defend Montenegro if it were attacked, Trump uttered this insane reply: "I've asked myself the same question. Montenegro is a tiny country with very strong people. They have very aggressive people. They may get aggressive and, congratulations, you're in World War Three."[42] Of course, the answer that promotes rather than degrades American national security is that NATO's Article 5 requires all members to defend any member or members that have been attacked. That "one for all and all for one" commitment has helped preserve peace in Europe for the last seven decades by deterring first the Soviets and then the Russians from attacking.

Under the 1996 Dayton Accord that ended the civil war, Bosnia-Herzegovina has a federal government that presides over an autonomous Serb region and a Croatian-Muslim federation. Three presidents, one each for Serbs, Croats, and Muslims, share power with the chair among them rotating every eight months. Elections have occurred every four years since 1996. Although corruption in both the elections and governance is high, violence has been limited. The country is Europe's poorest.

The biggest threat to Bosnia is Serb President Milorad Dodik who wants to break away and either form a separate country or join Serbia. Dodik has close ties with Vladimir Putin. A corruption scandal cut Dodik's appeal among Serbs but not decisively. Dodik won the Serbian presidential seat in the election held on October 7, 2018. He stated just what he would do with his power: "I don't care who the other two representatives in the presidency are. I am going there, to the presidency, to work above all and only for the interests of Serbs." Whether Dodik will break Serbian Bosnia from the rest of that country remains to be seen.[43]

The Kremlin got its latest pro-Russian leader when Bulgarians elected Rumen Radev to the presidency in November 2016. The Russians assisted Radev with cyber trolls spewing thousands of propaganda pieces extolling him and denigrating his rivals while massively financing his campaign. Yet revelations of that Russian support discredited him. During the parliamentary election in March 2017, voters brought back as prime minister pro-EU Boyko Borisov, whom Radev had ousted.

Even Switzerland has not escaped Russian aggression. In September 2018 Dutch police caught two Russian operatives who were plotting to sabotage a Swiss laboratory that was conducting tests that might prove that Putin's government was guilty of murder. The British government had sent the lab traces of the Novichok that Russian agents used against defector Sergei Skripal in Salisbury, resulting in the hospitalization of him and his daughter, and the murder of an unrelated woman who handled the discarded vial. The Swiss lab is one of two designated to test allegations of chemical attacks by the Organization for the Prohibition of Chemical Weapons. Because the Russians had diplomatic immunity, the Dutch expelled rather than indicted them.[44]

So far, Putin's goal of breaking up the European Union and re-aligning those countries with Moscow has remained largely a dream. His greatest victory was Britain's vote to leave the European Union, although the impact of Russia's cyber assault on the result is impossible to determine.

Elsewhere, cyber-assaults to shift elections in Moscow's favor have been far less successful. Beyond that, Hungary and Poland have pro-Russian governments that have transformed their liberal democracies into increasingly illiberal ones.

The Kremlin's machinations failed to stop or later reverse European Union sanctions against Russia for its annexation of Ukraine's Crimea and unofficial takeover of the provinces of Donetsk and Luhansk in 2014. Meanwhile, Russian views of the European Union have declined steadily from 2003 to 2017, with sharp drops after the West's reaction to Russia's wars against Georgia in 2008 and Ukraine in 2014. In December 2003 Russians were 9 per cent very positive and 63 per cent positive, 17 per cent hard to say, and only 9 per cent negative and 2 per cent very negative. By August 2017 Russians were 38 per cent negative, 10 per cent very negative, 15 per cent hard to say, and 35 per cent positive and 3 per cent very positive.[45] Putin wants to entice Europe toward Moscow. Instead, Putin's aggressive policies have steadily distanced Russia from Europe. And that violates the interests of Europeans and Russians alike.

Putin promotes Eurasianism to counter and, ideally, replace America's Atlanticism. He envisions Moscow as the capital of an economic, political and military association of European and Asian states. Eurasianism faces daunting problems. One is cultural. Only Russia geographically and culturally can be considered a Eurasian culture. All the other countries that Russia hopes to reduce to satellites are much smaller with distinct cultures. Another is economic. All the countries that Moscow is trying to dominate are economically stunted like Russia. In contrast, the countries that embrace Atlanticism tend to be economically developed.

Atlanticism is another name for western civilization that began around 2,700 years ago. The civilization's core value is humanism or enlightened individualism that developed independently in ancient Greece, Rome and Judea, then mingled along with Christianity around 1,900 years ago. Those values were obscured but never died during the Middle Ages, then re-emerged and spread across Europe through the Renaissance, Reformation and Enlightenment. English colonists carried those values to the New World where, eventually, America's Revolution personified them in the late eighteenth century. By the mid-twentieth century, the United States helped western civilization economically, militarily and culturally through victory first in the Second World War and then the Cold War. After 1945, to protect and develop western civilization, Washington joined with Europeans in NATO and encouraged Europeans to develop what became the EU.

Given western civilization's deep roots and development, Putin's dream of destroying it and enticing the shards into his Eurasian association is likely a chimera. Nonetheless, the Kremlin's attacks on western unity have clearly damaged it by assisting Trump's election to the White House, Britain's exit from the European Union, the transformation of Hungary and Poland into illiberal democracies and growing populist authoritarian movements across Europe and America.

Chapter 8

Russia and the World Beyond

At last! Now we are not alone in the battle against the American empire! Now we have Russia on our side!

(Hugo Chavez)

You don't understand, George, Ukraine is not even a state. What is Ukraine? Part of its territories is eastern Europe, but the greater part is a gift from us.

(Vladimir Putin)

Putin's foreign policy beyond America and Europe is as diverse as the array of countries, regions and international organizations. Yet the goal is constant, expanding Russian political, strategic and economic influence by whatever mix of means works best. With notable exceptions, the relative importance of a country or region usually depends on its distance from Moscow. As with America and Europe, the Russians have at times misjudged what was appropriate and actually undercut rather than promoted their interests. Yet overall, the Kremlin racks up far more advances than setbacks.

As during Soviet times, Putin's Russia has nurtured ties with a rogues' gallery of brutal anti-American dictators notorious for looting and ruining their countries. Among these are Kim Jong Un of North Korea, Fidel Castro then Raul Castro of Cuba, Hugo Chavez then Nicolas Madura of Venezuela, Daniel Ortega of Nicaragua, Bashar al-Assad of Syria, Muamar Gaddafi of Libya, Slobodan Milosevic then Vojislav Kostunica of Serbia and Robert Mugabe of Zimbabwe. What does Moscow get out from such bad company? These rogue leaders usually support the Kremlin's policies. For instance, following Russia's war with Georgia, the rogues recognized the "independence" of Georgia's breakaway states of South Ossetia and Abkhazia that were actually Russian puppets. The same happened in 2014 after Russia's annexation of Crimea and "independence of Ukraine's breakaway provinces of Luhansk and Donetsk. Yet the catcalls emanating from that rogues' gallery does nothing to relieve the economic pain inflicted by the sanctions imposed by America and Europe against Russia and its allies.

The Kremlin uses international organizations as forums to showcase and, ideally, assert Russian interests. Foreign Minister Sergei Lavrov explained that through international organizations Russia can develop "network diplomacy" (*setovaya diplomatiya*) of informal understandings and relations among appropriate partners.[1] From the United Nations' inauguration in 1945, Moscow has wielded its permanent membership and veto power on the Security Council to assert its interests. During the Cold War most international organizations shunned the Soviet Union but, since the collapse, have welcomed Russia. For instance, Russia became a "full dialogue partner" of the ten-member Association of Southeast Asian Nations (ASEAN) in 1997 and joined the twenty-one-member Asia Pacific Economic Cooperation (APEC) in 1998. During the 2000 APEC summit at Brunei, Putin declared, "Russia always felt itself a Eurasian country."[2] Vladivostok hosted APEC's 2012 summit.

Thanks largely to American sponsorship, Russia finally formally joined the World Trade Organization (WTO) in August 2012 after nearly a decade of negotiations. In 2009, then Prime Minister Putin nearly derailed that effort when he insisted that Russia would join only if Kazakhstan and Belarus were also admitted simultaneously with the same terms because the three countries had set up a customs union. In doing so, Putin trumped the strategy of his theoretical boss, President Dmitri Medvedev, of getting membership for Russia first and its partners later. A month later Medvedev made the face-saving announcement that Russia would join independently but parallel to Kazakhstan and Belarus. The conflicting statements revealed deeper tensions between the two men.

Moscow has not hesitated to thwart an international organization's purpose when it was in its interests to do so. For instance, in 2017, the United Nations created a Joint Investigative Mechanism to partner with the Organization for the Proliferation of Chemical Weapons to determine who used chemical weapons in Syria. The Russians wielded every procedural device to dilute and delay the report that concluded Syria was responsible. In November 2017, the Russians vetoed that program's renewal. Britain then tried to get the Organization for the Proliferation of Chemical Weapons to investigate the attempted murder with a deadly chemical of former FSB agent Sergei Skripol and his daughter Yulia in Salisbury. Once again, the Russians obstructed decisive action.[3]

Putin was instrumental in arranging a summit among the BRIC countries of Brazil, Russia, India and China to offset American power in 2009. South Africa's admission in 2010 transformed that organization into BRICS. Putin's attempts to get BRICS to represent Russian interests often fail. For instance, during a BRICS summit in July 2014, he proposed that they form their own development bank capitalized with $50 billion by 2020 and doubled within five years. That bank's primary purpose would not be economic, but political to offset Washington's dollar power and headquarters for the International Monetary Fund (IMF) and World Bank. He has yet to convince his colleagues to fulfill that vision.

World sports provide yet another set of arenas where Russians battle with their rivals for dominance. The Kremlin blatantly conspires with Russian athletes to cheat in various international sporting events, including the drug tests required to participate. Bribes to key Olympic and World Cup officials let Russia sponsor the Winter Olympics in 2014 and World Cup in 2018. During the 2014 Winter Olympics in Sochi, FSB operatives swapped contaminated urine samples with clear ones in the testing laboratory. The discovery led the Olympic Committee to suspend Russia's drug-testing organization, though, in September 2018 the World Anti-Doping Agency absolved Russia of any wrongdoing.

Russia's most important international organization began as an attempt to reconstitute the Soviet Union. Moscow formed first the Commonwealth of Slavic States (CSS) among Russia, Belarus and Ukraine on December 8, 1991, and then changed the name to the Commonwealth of Independent States (CIS) and invited all the other Soviet republics to join.[4] Azerbaijan and Moldova joined as associate rather than full members. The three Baltic states – Lithuania, Latvia and Estonia – along with Georgia, spurned the invitation. Turkmenistan dropped out in 2005.

The Commonwealth serves the Kremlin by preserving Russian hegemony and co-ordinating relations among its former colonies. Although the Warsaw Pact was dissolved in June 1991 and the Soviet Union in December 1991, Moscow took several years to withdraw all its troops from its former empire. For instance, the last Russian soldiers did not leave East Berlin, Estonia and Latvia until August 31, 1994. General Igor Rodionov, the Chief of Staff, explained Russia's key security elements in May 1992:

> The neutrality of East European countries or their friendly relations with Russia; free Russian access to seaports in the Baltics; the exclusion of 'third country' military forces from the Baltics and non-membership of the Baltic states in military blocs directed at Russia; the prevention of the countries that constitute the CIS from becoming part of a buffer zone aimed at separating Russia from the West, South or East; maintaining the CIS states under Russia's exclusive influence.[5]

Russians occupy the Commonwealth secretariat's key positions. Commonwealth policy is developed through the Council of the Heads of State that meets twice yearly, and the Council of Heads of Government that meets four times annually. Each council's presidency rotates. The Russians have repeatedly tried and failed to transform the Commonwealth into an outright military alliance and economic union. At best, they have managed to forge closer military and economic links with a few of the members. Unlike the Soviet "republics," Commonwealth members are genuinely sovereign, and their participation is purely voluntary.

The Kremlin forged a Collective Security Treaty signed by Russia, Armenia, Kazakhstan, Kyrgyzstan, Tajikistan and Uzbekistan at Tashkent on May 15, 1992; Azerbaijan, Belarus and Georgia joined in 1993. Under the Tashkent Treaty, an attack on one member would be considered an attack on all. Then, in March 1996, those states upgraded their relations with the Tashkent Treaty on Collective Security that set up a general staff in Moscow to co-ordinate military relations. In May 1999 the alliance renamed itself the Collective Security Treaty Organization (CSTO). One key requirement of CSTO membership is not to join any other military alliance.

That alarmed most Commonwealth members. Georgia, Uzbekistan, Azerbaijan and Moldova joined with Ukraine to form their own alliance with the acronym GUUAM in November 1997. They denounced any Russian military or economic aggression, including oil and gas pipeline blackmail, and called for closer ties with NATO. NATO reciprocated by inviting those states to form associate relationships. GUUAM transformed itself into the Organization for Democracy and Economic Development with a secretariat at Kiev on May 23, 2006.

Nonetheless, Putin and the presidents of Belarus, Kazakhstan, Kyrgyzstan and Tajikistan agreed that Russia would be their military leader in October 2000. That relationship took two major steps toward a formal alliance after the al Qaeda attacks on September 11, 2001 and America's war against al Qaeda in Afghanistan and elsewhere around the world. In October 7, 2002 Putin got those countries along with Armenia to negotiate a Collective Security Treaty that came into force in April 2003. Georgia left the alliance after Russia's invasion in August 2008.

Meanwhile, economic ties among the Commonwealth states grew, although often more symbolically than substantively. Russia, Belarus, Kazakhstan, Kyrgyzstan and Tajikistan signed a treaty in February 1999 that formed the Customs Union and Common Economic Space. They transformed themselves into the Eurasian Economic Community at Minsk in October 10, 2001. The Commonwealth's International Exchange Association issued a statement in July 2001 that called for a "single financial space," although just what that meant has never been clearly defined, let alone realized. In April 2003 Russia, Ukraine, Belarus and Kazakhstan announced their commitment to a "unified economic zone," although here again they asserted principles rather than practices, then formed the Joint Economic Space in September 2003. The members renamed themselves the Eurasian Economic Union on January 1, 2015.

Russia's war against Georgia in August 2008 prompted the European Union to retaliate. In 2009 Brussels inaugurated its Eastern Partnership (EaP) Program to entice former Soviet "republics" like Moldova, Ukraine, Belarus, Georgia, Armenia and Azerbaijan. Brussels would sign a "Deep and Comprehensive Trade Agreement" (DCFTA) and "Association Agreement" (AA) with any country that achieved EU market opening, transparency, human rights, free election and anti-corruption standards.

Putin expressed Russian policy ideals toward the Commonwealth during an April 2005 speech:

> In asserting Russia's policy interests, we aim to achieve economic development, strengthen the international authority of our neighbors' counties, and synchronize the pace and parameters of the reform process in Russia and the CIS states. We are willing to adopt the best practices of our neighbors and share with them our ideas and results.[6]

From a national security viewpoint, Russians feel most vulnerable when they look westward. Most alarming are NATO's Baltic members with Estonia and Russia sharing a border. Although Russians can take solace in having Belarus as an ally, they also face Ukraine currently as a foe. Russia's most exposed region is an enclave within the EU and NATO; Kaliningrad faces the Baltic Sea squeezed between Poland and Lithuania. Kaliningrad is notorious for its poverty, corruption, crime, smuggling and disease, especially Klaipeda its seedy capital and port. Although Moscow designated Kaliningrad a free economic zone in September 1991, few foreign businesses have invested in such a dismal setting. The Kremlin periodically demands a special corridor from Belarus to Kaliningrad but the Polish and Lithuanian governments firmly reject that notion.

No former Soviet state has closer ties with Russia than Belarus.[7] Following the Soviet Union's break-up in December 1991, Belarus President Stanislau Shushkevich sought closer economic ties with the West while remaining militarily neutral and asserting control over Soviet troops, weapons and bases in his country. At first he resisted signing the Commonwealth's collective security treaty in 1992 but finally yielded to unrelenting pressure from Moscow and pro-Kremlin Belarussians in June 1994. The following month, Alexander Lukashenko became president and enthusiastically forged closer ties with Moscow. Yeltsin and Lukashenko signed treaties that eliminated border controls in April 1996 and all economic barriers in May 1997. The Kremlin sweetened the latter deal by writing off a billion dollars that Belarus owed Russia for energy supplies. In March 2003 Putin and Lukashenko agreed to a Constitutional Act of the Belarus-Russian Union whereby each country retained its sovereignty and separate government while sharing a common flag, currency, market, economic policies and 300,000-man military dominated by the Kremlin.

Belarus is dependent on Russia for 90 per cent of its exports and 80 per cent of its imports, including nearly all its oil and gas. Although Moscow does give Belarus cut-rate energy prices, those are subject to change parallel to swings in global prices. Starting in April 2002 Gazprom tried to use Belarus debt to acquire more than half of the shares in that country's Beltranshaz Corporation and its monopoly over natural gas pipelines, refineries, electricity plants and marketing. Beltranshaz resisted until January 2004 when Gazprom cut supplies and tripled prices to Belarus. Beltranshaz soon agreed to a price for Gazprom's takeover. Gazprom cut supplies again in 2007. That did the trick. Belarus has been compliant ever since.

Since the Soviet Union's collapse Ukraine has been a wishbone between Europe and Russia while Kiev has been Janus-faced toward Brussels and Moscow. That reflects the cleavage between the mostly Ukrainians in the center and west versus the mostly Russians in the east. During their 2008 summit Putin expressed to Bush a common Russian view of Ukraine: "You don't understand, George, Ukraine is not even a state. What is Ukraine? Part of its territories is Eastern Europe, but the greater part is a gift from us."[8] As "evidence," Putin and other Russian spokesmen cite the word Ukraine which means frontier.

Presidents Boris Yeltsin, Bill Clinton and Leonid Kuchma and Britain's Prime Minister John Major met in Budapest on December 5, 1994 to sign the Memorandum on Security Assurance that respected "the independence and sovereignty and the existing borders of Ukraine" and "refrain from the threat or use of force against the territorial integrity or political independence of Ukraine."[9] Twenty years later, in February 2014, Putin violently broke this legal promise after Ukrainians overthrew the pro-Kremlin government of Viktor Yanukovych. In retaliation, Putin ordered the army to invade Ukraine's mostly Russian-speaking provinces of Crimea, Donetsk and Luhansk, annex Crimea and impose puppet regimes on the "independent" People's Republics of Donetsk and Luhansk. Although the United States, European Union and other concerned states asserted painful economic sanctions against Russia, Putin remains determined to keep those conquests no matter what.

The so-called Minsk II Peace accord of 2015 brought not peace but a truce between Russia and Ukraine, often broken by sporadic low-level violence. These days more people die from power struggles among gangs within Donetsk and Luhansk than between Russian and Ukrainian troops along the frontier. No one is immune. Most likely rival factions killed separatist commanders Arsen Pavlov in 2016 and Mikhail Toltec in 2017. On August 31, 2018 a bomb blew up Donetsk's president Aleksandr Zakharchenko, a Kremlin hand puppet, while he was dining at his favorite restaurant. Although Russia's foreign ministry blamed Kiev, Putin's condemnation actually targeted the rebel factions warring against each other, although he did not cite them:

> The despicable murder of Aleksandr Zakharchenko is once again evidence that those who chose the path of terror, violence and fear don't want to find a peaceful, political resolution to the conflict. They are making a dangerous bet on destabilizing the situation.[10]

Ukraine is trapped in a vicious cycle of economic stagnation, massive corruption, political instability and a stalemated war with Russia over its eastern provinces. Only European Union membership could help transform that vicious cycle, but Ukraine must first meet the stringent requirements and is incapable of doing so. Although, on December 23, 2014, Ukraine's parliament, the Rada, voted 303 to 8 to pursue NATO membership, for now the alliance's members have no intention of issuing an invitation to what would be an enormous strategic liability.

Russia's imperialism in 2014 inadvertently split Ukraine religiously as well as linguistically. Since 1686 Ukraine's Orthodox Christian patriarch was autonomous but subordinate to Russia's patriarch. That is no longer true. On October 15, 2018 Patriarch Bartholomew I, who heads around 300 million Orthodox Christians in about 12,000 congregations from his cathedral in Istanbul, gave permission for Ukraine's church to become independent, known as autocephaly, from Moscow's Patriarch Kirill I. He acted in response to pressure from Ukraine's congregations to free themselves from Moscow's meddling. He also did so despite, or perhaps partly because, the Kremlin bullied him not to do so with social media attacks, thefts of tens of thousands of emails and denunciations of him as a stooge of Washington and the Vatican. Kirill refused to recognize Ukraine's autocephaly. President Petro Poroshenko explained that now Ukrainian Orthodox services no longer must include "prayers for the Russian government and Russian military."[11]

All along Moscow tightened the screws on Kiev. Prime Minister Dmitri Medvedev announced on November 1, 2018 that Russia would sanction sixty-eight Ukrainian businesses and 322 individuals, including freezing their financial assets in Russian banks. The excuse was similar: Ukrainian sanctions against Russian firms and businessmen the previous year, although undoubtedly the Orthodox split was the real catalyst.[12]

Tensions soared on November 26, 2018 when Russian warships captured two Ukrainian gunboats and a tugboat manned by twenty-four sailors, wounding three of them, in the Kerch Strait linking the Azov Sea with the Black Sea, then asserted a blockade to prevent any ships from sailing to or from the Ukrainian ports of Mariupol and Berdyansk in the Azov Sea. The Kremlin justified its acts of war by claiming that it was protecting the twelve-mile-long bridge spanning the Kerch Strait that cost $7.5 billion to build. But the gunboats posed no threat while the attacks and blockade violated a 2003 treaty between Russia and Ukraine that guaranteed equal access to that strait through which around seven per cent of Ukraine's exports flow. Since Russia's 2014 invasion the number of ships docking at Mariupol fell from 1,417 to 532 in 2017. President Poroshenko pleaded for NATO to pressure Russia to return Ukraine's vessels and re-open the strait. NATO Secretary General Jens Stoltenberg condemned the attack and declared that the alliance "fully supports the sovereignty of Ukraine and its territorial integrity, including the right to navigation in its own territorial waters." More disturbingly, Poroshenko also responded by declaring martial law that suspended any pending elections, strikes or demonstrations. Ukraine's parliament upheld the imposition by a vote of 276 to 30. Once again, Putin provoked a foreign leader into undermining his own country's liberties.[13]

By 2019, Russian imperialism in eastern Ukraine had inflicted more than 13,000 deaths, tens of thousands of wounded, hundreds of thousands of refugees and billions of dollars' worth of destroyed infrastructure, businesses and homes. But Ukrainians do not suffer all the costs. The West's sanctions annually deprive Russia of wealth that it would otherwise garner. Atop that Moscow annually expends billions of rubles in economic and military aid to the rebel provinces. Overall, Crimea and eastern Ukraine financially and politically drain rather than enhance Russian power. Those conquests symbolize Putin's commitment to unifying the Russian diaspora regardless of the cost. On April 25, 2019 Putin announced that the 3.7 million inhabitants of Donetsk and Luhansk would be eligible for Russian citizenship and thus passports.[14]

Moldova is Europe's poorest country, landlocked between Ukraine and Romania. The Russians conquered Moldova in 1815. Moldova did not become independent until 1991 when the Soviet Union collapsed. During the colonial era the Russians forced the Moldovans to switch their alphabet from Latin to Cyrillic while Russians dominated the government and economy. Around 65 per cent of the population speaks a Romanian dialect, 14 per cent Ukrainian, 13 per cent Russian and the rest mostly Turkish. Chisinau is the capital.

Moldova's Transnistria region is split almost equally among Romanian, Ukrainian and Russian speakers. When Moldova declared independence from the Soviet Union, Transnistrian separatists declared independence from Moldova. Moscow pressured Chisinau to establish a Join Control Commission with Moldavan, Russian and Transnistrian representatives and let a Russian peacekeeping force occupy Transnistria, with most deployed in its capital Tiraspol. Those Russian troops abet rather than suppress the rampant criminal gangs that smuggle arms, narcotics, alcohol, tobacco and sex slaves; extract protection money from businesses; and bribe politicians and bureaucrats for lucrative deals, or just look the other way.

Putin forced Moldova to sign a treaty in 2001 that required Russian to be taught in schools. Then in 2003 he tried to bully Chisinau into federalizing the country with autonomous Moldovan and Transnistrian regions and Russia empowered to intervene militarily to maintain order. The Moldovans appealed to the Organization for Security and Co-operation in Europe (OSCE). In 2005, a deal was struck that allowed observer contingents of American and European troops to join the peacekeeping mission. In 2013, the Kremlin boycotted Moldova's usual

$100 million worth of wine sales and Moldovan labor immigrants to Russia after Chisinau declared its interest in joining the European Union. Refusing to be bullied, Moldova's government signed an Association Agreement with Brussels later that year.

That relationship may take years, if ever, before Moldovans discern any concrete economic benefits. There is not much demand in Europe for cheap Moldovan wines. And, for the foreseeable future, Moldova will remain dependent on Russian oil and gas. As elsewhere, Russia's energy giants bullied Moldova's government into ceding them control over the country's oil and gas industry in return for moderate prices, steady supplies and some debt relief.

Russian interests in Serbia are linguistic, religious and strategic. The countries share a Slavic language and Orthodox faith while Serbia's geography can enhance Russian power with a friendly regime in Belgrade. During the mid-nineteenth century Moscow helped win Serbia its eventual independence from the Ottoman Empire in 1878. Up until 1918, Moscow valued Serbia as a strategic impediment to Austrian expansion in southeastern Europe and ally in the First World War. Serbia became the core country for Yugoslavia, created in 1919 with Slovenia, Croatia, Bosnia-Herzegovina, Montenegro and Macedonia. Starting in 1991, Moscow tried to prevent Yugoslavia's break-up by giving Serbia vast military and economic aid in its failed attempts to crush the independence of the other members and its own province, Kosovo. More recently, the Russians treasure Serbia's location as a rock in the garden of the EU and NATO, west of Romania and Bulgaria, south of Hungary, east of Croatia, Montenegro and possible future member Bosnia-Herzegovina and north of future member Macedonia and possible future member Kosovo.

That Russian interest suffered a setback in 2014 when Serbian President Aleksandar Vucic applied for EU membership although he declared his intention never to join NATO. In doing so Vucic, walked a political tightrope. Serbia is dependent on the EU for 82 per cent of its foreign investments and two-thirds of Serbia's exports. Yet Serbia's economy has an Achilles Heel. Serbia's dependence on Russian natural gas and oil to supply most of its energy needs along with Russian economic and military aid are sensible economic reasons for good relations with the Kremlin. Atop that, with Slavs and Orthodox Christians comprising 85 per cent of the seven million Serbs, the vast majority of people culturally and sentimentally align with Russia. A 2014 survey found that 50 per cent of Serbs have a positive view of Russia, 82 per cent view NATO negatively, only 46 per cent favored EU membership and only 30 per cent believe liberal democracy is the best form of government. Politically, Serbia is a mini-version of Russia with its powerful president, weak parliament, massive corruption and human rights violations. Moscow asserts soft power in Serbia through its propaganda organization, Sputnik, which began broadcasting to Serbia in January 2015 and is an umbrella for more than a hundred other media outlets. Moscow reinforces its mass media message that celebrates Russia and denigrates the EU, NATO and, especially, America with scores of organizations, many operating on university campuses to sway students. The Russian Institute for Strategic Studies sponsors conferences with international "scholars" that promote pro-Moscow themes. Although Putin enjoys friendly relations with Vucic, he does threaten to raise gas and oil prices whenever debates arise over whether Serbia should join NATO.[15]

Vucic not only rolled out the red carpet but organized a massive rally of 100,000 people for his "big friend" Putin and had billboards celebrating his visit on January 17, 2019. Putin-mania swept Serbia as fans bought t-shirts, mugs and even underwear displaying the Russian president. Serbia's Orthodox Church was closely aligned with Russia's Orthodox Church. For his part, Putin announced a $1.4 billion investment to improve the pipeline that brings Russian gas to Serbia, atop $4 billion of existing Russian investments. Putin also maintained his refusal to recognize Kosovo's independence. Although the tug-of-war between Brussels and Moscow over Serbia remains a draw, Putin is clearly the Serbian crowd's favorite.[16]

The Caucasus region is the mostly mountainous land between the Black and Caspian Seas that includes Georgia, Armenia and Azerbaijan. The Red Army conquered those countries in 1921, imposed communist dictatorships and designated them "republics" within the Soviet Union. Those three Moscow puppets achieved independence with the Soviet Union's collapse in 1991. Since then, the Kremlin has done whatever it could get away to re-impose its domination.

Putin's most blatant imperialism in the Caucasus came in 2008, when he launched a war against Georgia to "liberate" and recognize the "independence" of two autonomous provinces, South Ossetia and Abkhazia. Russia had kept peacekeeping troops in both provinces since the early 1990s when separatist rebels fought for their independence. Then Georgian President Eduard Shevardnadze had acquiesced to that Russian presence when Georgia's army was incapable of crushing those revolts. President Mikhail Saakashvili attempt to crush the renewed separatist revolt in South Ossetia prompted the Russian invasion.

Armenia is the oldest Christian nation, having officially embraced that faith in the fourth century. Armenians kept that faith despite being conquered and split between the Persian and Turkish empires. With the rise of the Russian empire, Armenians looked to Moscow to liberate them from Muslim rule. That partly came true with the Treaty of Adrianople and Congress of Berlin in 1829 and the 1878 Treaty of San Stefano that followed victorious Russian wars against Persia and Turkey. Armenians continued to pay a heavy cultural price for being subjects of another imperial power. Russians dominated the government, economy and schools, and tried to ethnically cleanse Armenians of their language, culture and history. Tragically, millions of Armenians still lived under Turkish rule. The Turks murdered a million and a half Armenians during the First World War. The Russian Empire collapsed after the Communist takeover in November 1917 and subsequent civil war. The surviving Armenians formed a government and army and declared independence. The 1920 Treaty of Sevres recognized Armenia's independence. Turkey repudiated that treaty and warred against Armenia. The Armenians once again appealed to Moscow, this time ruled by the Communists. The Red Army expelled the Turkish army. Under the 1921 Treaty of Kars, Turkey recognized Armenia as the Soviet Union's Transcaucasian region.[17]

The Kremlin takes full advantage of the continuing conflict and at times violence between mostly Christian Armenia and mostly Muslim Azerbaijan over the latter's Nagorno-Karabakh province which is 95 per cent Armenian. War erupted between Armenia and Azerbaijan after Nagorno-Karabakh declared independence in 1994.[18]

Armenia is thoroughly tied to Russia as a member of the Commonwealth of Independent States (CIS), the Collective Security Treaty Organization

(CSTO) and the Customs Union. Russian corporations dominate Armenia's energy industry. Gazprom controls 80 per cent of Armenia's ArmRosGazprom.

Moscow swiftly suppresses any Armenia attempts, however tentative, to forge better relations with Europe. During the April 2014 European Union-Eastern European summit President Serzh Sargsyan simply stated, "We do not want to choose between friends – we want to have as many friends as possible."[19] That prompted Putin to warn that Russia would tilt toward Azerbaijan if Sargsyan turned westward. That was enough to force Armenia to spurn an Association Agreement with the European Union and instead join the Customs Union with Russia. In keeping the peace, Armenia sacrificed the potential development that it might have achieved by integrating with Europe.

Like its neighbors Azerbaijan suffered conquest by the Russians, asserted independence during the Civil War from 1918 to 1920, then conquered by the Red Army and eventually transformed into a Soviet "republic".[20] Oil gives Azerbaijan an economic edge over Armenia and Georgia but, as for all other petro-states, that has proven to be a double-edged sword. Baku hosts both the national government and energy corporate headquarters. As with other former Soviets, the Russians dominate Azerbaijan's oil and gas industry as Gazprom, Transneft, Yukos and others took controlling shares of the local companies.

Although Azerbaijan remains a Commonwealth member it has not joined the Customs Union, Common Economic Space or Eurasian Economic Community. Azerbaijan took a major step in reducing Moscow's influence by withdrawing from the Collective Security Treaty Organization (CSTO) in 1999. Putin talked President Ilham Aliyev into signing a Declaration of Friendship and Strategic Partnership in 2008. Although the duties of that partnership were vague, Putin hoped that it would encourage Azerbaijan to return to CSTO. Meanwhile, Azerbaijan has diverted billions of petro-dollars to purchase such cutting-edge Russian weapons as advanced T-90 tanks, SA-10 Grumble long-range surface-to-air missiles and Tor-2ME anti-aircraft missiles, along with attack and transport helicopters and artillery.[21]

Although conflicts abound among Azerbaijan, Armenia and Georgia, they share an interest in reducing their dependence on Russia. One way has been to invite in western corporations to compete with the Russian giants. Exon-Mobil, British Petroleum and Chevron have invested heavily in the region, especially Azerbaijan, and most importantly by developing the Baku-Tbilisi-Erzerum gas pipeline and the Baku-Tbilisi-Supsa and Baku-Tbilisi-Ceyhan oil pipelines from the Caspian Sea to European markets via Turkey.

Central Asia includes the five Muslim countries of Kazakhstan, Turkmenistan, Uzbekistan, Kirgizstan and Tajikistan.[22] Russia conquered this vast, diverse region through a series of treaties and wars during the eighteenth and nineteenth centuries. During the late nineteenth century Russian expansion was spurred by British advances northward from India, especially the conquest of Afghanistan in 1887 three decades after the catastrophic defeat of their first attempt from 1839 to 1842. The rivalry between Russia and Britain for Central Asia was known as the "Great Game," a cold war struggle in which each side wielded all means to advance except directly warring against each other. In no region are Moscow's geopolitical and geo-economic interests more thoroughly mingled than in Central Asia. Since the 1990s Jihadism has been the worst threat that Russia has faced in Central Asia. Jihadism's appeal in a Muslim population rises with its poverty, corruption, exploitation and despair. Economic development that is widely shared alleviates those problems. So, Moscow has a geo-political interest in assisting that development, just as Russian businesses see each Central Asia country as a market in which they can potentially buy and sell an array of products. Turkmenistan and Kazakhstan have enormous oil and gas reserves that Moscow has managed to dominate through joint ventures and buyouts of local firms by Russian corporations. Pipelines carry that oil and gas from the wellheads across Russia to European markets. Rendering Moscow's interests more complex are the indigenous Russian immigrants, who accompanied each country's colonization and who retain political and economic influence.

As in other regions, Putin has tried to swell Russian influence by entangling countries in international treaties and organizations. With Moscow's guidance, diplomats of Russia, Kazakhstan, Turkmenistan, Azerbaijan and Iran signed the "Convention on the Legal Status of the Caspian Sea" on August 12, 2018. That split the Caspian Sea into national and international sections for mineral exploitation, regulated oil and gas pipeline construction and forbade non-regional countries from any access. Each state's territorial waters extend fifteen nautical miles and fishing monopoly ten more miles. The treaty also recognized the Russian navy's domination by ensuring that its vessels can sail throughout the sea beyond the territorial limits of the others. The Russian flotilla's destroyers armed with cruise missiles dwarf any foreign warships.

Since the Soviet Union's break-up Russia has faced a growing rivalry with China for power in Central Asia. The Chinese value that region for its markets, oil, gas and other natural resources. They have built oil and gas pipelines from fields across that region to refineries in China. Beijing also has a significant geo-political interest in each of those Turkic Muslim countries whose Islamists and Jihadists have varying links to Turkic Uighur Muslims in China's north-west province of Xinjiang.

To help manage that rivalry, Russia and China, along with Kazakhstan, Kyrgyzstan and Uzbekistan, formed the Shanghai Five in 1996, then renamed themselves the Shanghai Co-operation Organization (SCO) at Shanghai in June 2001 when Tajikistan joined them. They dedicated their association to "non-interference and non-alignment" and "a new economic and political order," although they never defined clearly any of those terms. During the Tashkent summit in June 2004, they set up the Regional Anti-Terrorist Structure (RATS) and relocated their secretariat from Shanghai to Tashkent. The highlights of the July 2005 Astana summit were to demand that the United States withdraw all its troops from Central Asia and grant Iran, India, Pakistan and Mongolia observer status.

In Central Asia, Russia's closest ties are with Kazakhstan. One reason is that one of five Kazakhs is Russian, the largest proportion among the five Central Asia countries. Kazakhstan has loyally joined every international organization that Moscow has sponsored, including the Commonwealth of Independent States, Eurasian Economic Community, Shanghai Co-operation Organization, Regional Anti-Terrorist Structure and Collective Security Treaty Organization. Russia uses the Baikonut space base, built during Soviet times, for satellite launches. President Nursultan Nazarbayev was a faithful partner with Boris Yeltsin and

Vladimir Putin. Nazarbayev received this backhanded compliment from Putin: "Kazakhs never had their statehood. He created it."[23]

In contrast, Russia's relations with Kyrgizstan have been the most problematic. Like most leaders of former Soviet colonies, Kyrgizstan President Kurmanbek Bakiyez had mingled economic and political reasons to maintain ties with Moscow while diversifying relations with other countries, regions and international organizations. He agreed to lease bases for Russian military forces at Kant in 2003 and Osh in 2009. In 2009, he also agreed to end an American lease for a base at Manas that was used for operations against Jihadists in Afghanistan. He did so after President Medvedev promised a $2 billion loan atop a $150 million grant to build a hydro-electric dam. But, rather than evict the Americans, Bakiyez tripled the lease price for Manas. The White House paid that price and officially described the base as "a transit center" that let Bakiyez insist that he had kept his side of the deal with Medvedev.

Bakiyez's double-dealing enraged the Russians. The Kremlin raised prices for oil and gas exports to Kyrgizstan that crippled the economy. Russian operatives helped organize mass protests against Bakiyez that caused him to flee the country in 2010. Moscow then returned oil and gas prices to their former levels. The new president, Almazbek Atambayev, is pro-Russian.

Moscow is Janus-faced, sternly looking eastward as well as westward, nowhere more suspiciously than toward Beijing. Russia and China share some critical experiences and interests.[24] Both suffered catastrophic periods under totalitarian communist rule – Russia from 1917 to 1991, and China from 1949 to 1978. Both abandoned communism for an authoritarian government and a mostly privatized economy. Their governments do not hesitate to violate human rights and prosecute anyone who appears to threaten their rule. They share a 2,615–mile frontier, the world's second longest after the 3,987–mile border between America and Canada. They have a common interest in undermining America's global hegemony. However, their worst common threat is each country's large, restless Muslim minorities susceptible to Islamism – the regions of Chechnya and Dagestan for Russia, and Xinjiang for China. Moscow and Beijing have cracked down harshly on Islamist rebellions. Russia fought two wars against Chechnyan rebels, lost the first, then crushed resistance during the second. China has imprisoned over a million Uighurs, Xinjiang's Turkic-speaking Muslim majority, many of whom joined the East Turkistan Islamic Movement or Hizb-ut-Tahrir.

Yet beneath those common interests are animosities that go back to the seventeenth century when Russian settlements and expeditions spread across Siberia, reaching the Pacific Ocean in 1639. The Chinese bitterly resented that Russian intrusion into their traditional sphere of influence. Although the 1689 Treaty of Nerchinsk delineated the frontier between their empires, the Russians would violate Chinese sovereignty and punch back its borders with increasing frequency over the next three centuries. The communist brotherhood between dictators Joseph Stalin and Mao Zedong was fleeting. After Stalin died in 1953, Mao sought to replace him as head of the communist world. Mao tried to achieve complete communism with his so-called Great Leap Forward of 1957 to 1958, but tens of millions of people either starved to death or were murdered when they resisted. Mao then broke relations with the Soviets after the Kremlin castigated those disastrous policies. Tension rose steadily until the Soviets and Chinese fought a short war along the Amur River in 1969. At one-point, Premier Leonid Brezhnev actually sent a message to President Richard Nixon, asking approval for a nuclear strike against China. After Nixon rejected that request Moscow and Beijing negotiated a truce.

Mikhail Gorbachev initiated *détente* between the Soviet Union and China during his visit to Beijing and summit with Deng Xiaoping in June 1989. When Boris Yeltsin was in Beijing in April 1996, he and Deng announced their establishment of a bilateral "strategic partnership." On July 16, 2001 Putin bolstered that relationship by signing with President Jiang Zemin a Treaty of Good Neighborly Friendship and Co-operation." The terms bound Russia and China to the peaceful resolution of problems, troop reductions along their frontier, "one-China" with Taiwan a province, expanded trade and investment, non-intervention in each other's internal affairs, common efforts to combat drug-smuggling and terrorism, and opposition to America's hegemonic pretension. In October 2004 Putin and Jiang signed a treaty that resolved a longstanding territorial dispute along the Amur River. Starting in 2005, Russia and

China have annually conducted joint military training operations. Russia and China are among the UN Security Council's five permanent members and usually vote together on issues. They also collaborate as members of CSTO, BRICS, APEC and the Group of 20. Of their seven official summits, the most important visit came from June 7 to 9, 2019, when Xi led a thousand person delegation to the International Economic Forum that Putin hosted in St. Petersburg. During one public meeting, Xi called Putin his "best friend."[25]

Their economies complement rather than compete with each other; Russia sends oil, gas, and other natural resources along with advanced weapons to China in return for consumer goods and machinery. In February 2009, Beijing agreed to invest $25 billion in a branch of the Russia's Eastern Siberia-Pacific Ocean oil pipeline to run to Daqing. Rosneft received a $15 billion loan to finance its debts and Transneft received $10 billion to construct the pipeline in return for guaranteeing China a twenty-year oil flow. The relationship was advancing so well that Putin marveled in 2004 that "we have overcome all the tensions and disagreements that existed in the past. Today there is not a single problem we cannot openly and in an absolutely friendly manner discuss and find a mutually acceptable solution."[26]

For now, Putin's optimism may be warranted. Presidents Vladimir Putin and Xi singing have cordial and co-operative relations, with no serious disputes. They orchestrate their diplomacy in the United Nations Security Council to undercut the United States whenever opportunities arise. They have repeatedly condemned American sanctions against both their countries. Meanwhile bilateral trade and investments expand steadily. In 2018, on the deliberately chosen date of September 11, 3,200 Chinese troops joined Russia's largest military exercise since 1981 after Ronald Reagan became president.[27] Russians generally have a high regard for China with a January 2018 poll typical: 9 per cent of Russians had a very positive view and 61 per cent positive compared to 9 per cent negative and 4 per cent very negative. In a December 2017 poll only 2 per cent considered China an enemy.[28]

Yet the long-term relationship between Russia and China inspires a comparison to that between a rabbit and a boa constrictor.[29] They can co-exist peacefully inside the cage until the boa becomes hungry. In

2017, China's economy was \$23.160 trillion, nearly six times larger than Russia's \$4,000-trillion economy, although the average Russian had a \$27,800 income and the average Chinese only \$16,700 in 2017. China's 1.4 billion people are ten times more numerous than Russia's 140 million people, and demonstrably far more industrious and enterprising. China's economy continues not just to grow, but to diversify into increasingly sophisticated industries led by cutting-edge technologies, including a weapons industry largely based on improving original Russian designs. Over the decades Moscow has agreed to license production of some of its most advanced weapons systems including Su-27 Flanker interceptors, Su-30 MKK fighter-bombers, Varshavyanka- or Kilo-class diesel submarines and Sovremenny-class destroyers and an aircraft carrier, the former *Admiral Kuznetsov*, now the *Liaoning*, and has sold advanced weapons like SU-35 fighter-bombers and S-400 surface-to-air (SAM) missiles. In contrast, Russia remains a plodding petro-state straitjacketed to the oil and gas price roller-coaster. Their trade and, thus, power relationship is asymmetrical: China is Russia's largest trading partner, while Russia is only number nine or ten in trade importance to China. Russia imports high technology, machinery, and consumer products in exchange for energy, wood, and other raw materials. Underpopulated Siberia with its abundant minerals, wood and water beckons north of overpopulated China. Ever more Chinese are immigrating, legally or not, into Russia's Far East and Siberia beyond the Urals. Beijing competes with Moscow for influence in the Central Asian states. China's "One Belt, One World" strategy is to establish dynamic trade and investment relations across Central and Southwest Asia through countries that were formerly part of Russia's empire. The Kremlin is increasingly concerned that China is neo-colonizing Russia and that it can do nothing to prevent that.

Russia has fought two wars against Japan, disastrously from 1904 to 1905, and decisively in August 1945. An unresolved dispute from that latter war has troubled the relationship ever since.[30] Moscow and Tokyo dispute who should possess the Kurile Islands that the Japanese call their Northern Territories, including Habomai, Iturup (Etofu), Kunashiri and Shikotan. Under an 1855 treaty Russians and Japanese could jointly occupy and exploit Sakhalin Island. Twenty years later, Moscow and Tokyo agreed that Russia would exclusively own Sakhalin while the Japanese took sole possession of the Kurile Islands. Under the 1905 Treaty of Portsmouth that ended the Russo-Japanese War, the Russians took the south Kurile Islands while the Japanese took Sakhalin's southern half. During the closing days of the Second World War the Soviet Union attacked Japanese forces in northeastern Asia and overran all of Sakhalin and the Kurile Islands. During a 1955 Joint Declaration, the Soviets agreed to give Shikotan and Habomai to Japan with a peace treaty but reneged after Tokyo renewed its alliance with Washington in 1960. The dispute has deadlocked there ever since. Tokyo actually withdrew its ambassador from Moscow after President Medvedev visited the Kurile Islands in 2012.

Nonetheless, relations between Moscow and Tokyo have generally been constructive. Putin and Japanese Prime Minister Shinzo Abe have forged a deep relationship through twenty-five summits. Economically, Russia's trade and investment patterns with Japan resemble those with China. Russia exports raw and semi-finished materials and imports consumer goods, sophisticated equipment and high technology. Russia runs trade deficits with Japan. Those deficits would worsen if Moscow ever gave back the Kurile Islands that are rich sources of wood, fish and 90 per cent of the world's rare mineral called rhenium, used for jet engines running on high-octane fuel.

North Korea has the world's last totalitarian communist system and the only one ever ruled by a dynasty, with Kim Il Sung the tyrant from 1945 to 1992, Kim Jong Il to 2011, and Kim Jong Un through to the present. North Korea's totalitarianism has been as genocidal as that of the Soviet Union under Stalin and China under Mao. Perhaps one in ten North Koreans starved to death or was murdered during the 1990s alone.

North Korea's totalitarian communist regime exists because of a Faustian bargain that President Franklin Roosevelt made with Joseph Stalin during the Second World War. Although the United States was making steady progress developing a nuclear bomb, the scientists and technicians could not be certain that they would eventually create one. Thus Washington had to prepare to invade Japan after fighting from island to island across its Pacific empire. Estimates were that Americans would suffer at least a quarter million casualties to overrun most of Japan, although the remnants of enemy forces might fight a guerrilla war for years or even decades in the mountainous, forested countryside. So Roosevelt got Stalin to promise to join the war against Japan within three months after Germany's defeat. Although Stalin played hard to get, warring against Japan to expand the Soviet empire in the Far East was exactly what he wanted to do. The Americans successfully tested an atomic bomb near Alamogordo, New Mexico, on July 16, 1945 but President Harry Truman did not inform Stalin that America no longer needed the Red Army to help defeat Japan. An atomic bomb destroyed Hiroshima on August 6. The Soviet offensive against the Japanese in Northeast Asia began on August 8. An atomic bomb destroyed Nagasaki on August 9. Japan agreed to surrender unconditionally on August 14. The surrender ceremony took place aboard the battleship USS *Missouri*, part of a vast American fleet anchored in Tokyo Bay on September 2.

Meanwhile, the Red Army overran much of northeastern China and Korea down to the forty-second parallel, where Moscow and Washington agreed to draw the line between a Soviet-occupied north and American-occupied south. Each placed his own dictator in power on his half, Moscow with Kim Il Sung heading a communist regime from Pyongyang, and Washington with Syngman Rhee heading a government in Seoul. Backed by Stalin and Mao, Kim launched an invasion of South Korea on June 25, 1950. Truman responded by getting the UN Security Council to authorize the United States to lead a military coalition that drove the invaders back to the north. The American-led offensive routed the North Koreans and advanced deep into the north. That provoked the Chinese to send the Red Army into Korea. The result was a three-year blood-soaked stalemate that finally ended with an armistice in July 1953.

No peace treaty followed. Instead, the Kim dynasty maintained itself in power through a totalitarian communist system that repressed and exploited the population, and imprisoned or executed anyone who resisted. Meanwhile, after several decades of dictatorship and poverty, South Korea adopted democracy and a Japanese-style neo-mercantilist strategy that developed the economy to ever more sophisticated levels and transformed an impoverished population into mass prosperity.

All along, Moscow supported North Korea's Kim dynasty and communist regime with massive economic and military aid. The Russians have written off billions of dollars in North Korean debt. Most ominously, they were instrumental in helping the North Koreans eventually develop nuclear weapons, starting in 1965 when Russians constructed the Yongbyon nuclear reactor.

Although Putin agreed to pressure Kim Jong Un to limit his nuclear weapon and intercontinental missile development, he authorized secret Russian trade and weapons transfers to North Korea. For instance, the Security Council sanctions permit North Korea to import annually 500,000 barrels of petroleum. In the first nine months of 2018 alone, American intelligence observed 148 instances when Russian oil tankers filled empty North Korean oil tankers. Nikki Haley, America's ambassador to the United Nations, condemned that blatant violation of the embargo. Moscow denied any wrongdoing. On April 24 Putin and Kim held a summit at Vladivostok in which they agreed to expand trade and Russian aid. Most ominously, Putin announced his support for Kim's position on nuclear weapons: that Pyongyang could keep them as a deterrent until the United States completely lifted sanctions and guaranteed North Korea's security.[31]

For nearly three centuries Russia and Turkey were distant neighbors until the Soviet Union's collapse. Historically animosity characterized their relationship as Russia's expanding empire fought a dozen wars against the contracting Ottoman Empire during the eighteenth and nineteenth centuries. Although the First World War was the last time Turkey and Russia fought each other, Turkey joined NATO during the Cold War and remains a member. A key Russian foreign policy goal is to convince Turkey to switch sides. That just may happen.

Tayyip Recep Erdogan has ruled Turkey since 2003, as prime minister until 2014 and as president since. During those years Erdogan became increasingly autocratic, Islamist and anti-western. He deeply resents the European Union for freezing Turkey's membership application. He rejected the Bush administration's request to launch one of their 2003 invasions of Iraq from Turkey. Erdogan and Putin have much in common. Each is a populist who, after gaining power in democratic elections, suspended ever more civil liberties and democratic institutions. Erdogan far surpassed Putin in political oppression. After a failed 2016 coup against him, he had more than 100,000 liberals arrested. Each tries to cover up his mistakes by blaming Washington and Brussels. That alignment is likely to become ever closer.

Of the pariah states that Moscow nurtures, none is more important than Iran for compelling geopolitical and geo-economic reasons. Iran has 90 million people, vast oil and gas reserves and an Islamist revolutionary regime. It represents both a huge market and a huge threat. Russian businessmen can profit there. Secret Iranian Islamist agents can stir rebellion among Russian Muslims. Tehran is just as eager to nurture close ties with the infidel regime in Moscow. The Russians happily evade America's economic sanctions against Iran.

As with Turkey, imperialism and war characterized Russia's early relations with Persia, Iran's previous name. Russia's late-eighteenth-century expansion to the Caucasus Mountains region collided with Persia's declining empire. Russia defeated Persia in wars from 1804 to 1813 and from 1826 to 1828, each time taking more territory. Russia and Persia split Azerbaijanis and other ethnic populations between their empires. In 1925 General Reza Pahlavi took power in a coup, had himself crowned the shah or king, and renamed Persia, Iran. During the Second World War Iran tilted toward but did not openly ally with Germany. That was the excuse for Stalin to order the Red Army to invade Iran and depose Pahlavi, who ceded the throne to his son, Mohammad Reza Pahlavi. Prime Minister Winston Churchill then sent British troops into southern Iran to counter the Soviets and ensure that the coup did not precede a communist revolution. President Franklin Roosevelt despatched a small contingent of American troops to Tehran to bolster the British.

After the Second World War, each side withdrew its forces, the Americans and British within six months, the Soviets after a year of pressure by Washington and London. A growing communist movement capped by socialist Prime Minister Mohammad Mossadegh's nationalization of British Petroleum's investments provoked Washington and London. In 1953 President Dwight Eisenhower and Prime Minister

Churchill authorized their intelligence agencies to overthrow Mossadegh and install the until then figurehead shah as the supreme leader.

For a quarter of a century Iran was a critical American ally for containing the Soviet Union. During that time the Americans sold Iran tens of billions of dollars' worth of military equipment. Then, in February 1979, an Islamist revolution led by Ayatollah Mohammad Khomeini overthrew the shah, imposed a fundamentalist regime and, in November, invaded the American embassy and held fifty-two diplomats hostage for 444 days. Ever since then the United States has embargoed trade with Iran.

Moscow filled the void by selling the Iranians weapons and equipment, including advanced aircraft, tanks and anti-aircraft missile systems. Russians also assisted Iran's nuclear development program. Moscow and Tehran made a deal in December 2005 for Russia to supply Iran with $800 million worth of S-300 surface-to-air missiles (SAMs), a deadly threat should the Israelis or Americans ever launch an air war against Iran.

Then, having aided Iran's nuclear programs, Moscow joined those who wanted to shut it down. Under pressure from Washington, Brussels and Jerusalem, Putin delayed implementing that SAM deal before canceling it in June 2010 after agreeing to join a UN Security Council resolution imposing sanctions on Iran for its nuclear program. In 2011 Putin called for easing sanctions if Iran agreed to talks aimed at dismantling its nuclear program. After moderate Hassan Rouhani replaced hardliner Mahmud Amadinejad as president, he agreed to talks with the Security Council's five permanent members, America, Russia, France, Britain and China, along with Germany. Tightening sanctions forced the Iranians to sign an agreement on July 14, 2015, whereby they agreed to give up 98 per cent of their enriched uranium, dismantled 66 per cent of their centrifuges that refine uranium, destroy their largest nuclear reactor and accept inspections by the International Atomic Energy Agency (IAEA) in return for the lifting of sanctions. Since then the Iranians have fulfilled those promises.

Among Donald Trump's priorities upon coming president was to repudiate the Iran nuclear deal and re-impose sanctions against not just Iran but more than 700 foreign companies and individuals currently doing business with Iran. Those sanctions came into force on November 5, 2018.

Their bark was worse than their bite. Trump allowed waivers for eight countries to continue to buy Iranian oil, including China, India, South Korea and Japan. Typically, America's key western allies Germany, Britain and France were not on the exception list. Nonetheless, since Trump announced that deadline half a year earlier, Iran's economy contracted, the *rial* lost two-thirds of its value and daily oil exports plummeted from 2.5 million to 1.5 million barrels. Trump promised that the sanctions would force the Iranians to end their support for the revolutionary Islamist movements Hezbollah, Hamas and Houthi, and give up their missile program. President Rouhani vowed that Iran would overcome the sanctions. Regardless, Putin was delighted at Trump's latest blows to the western alliance.[32]

Moscow's relations with Syria go back to 1946 when it became independent, but did not become close until 1963 when the Socialist Ba'ath Party took power in a coup. Moscow began supplying what became tens of billions of dollars-worth of military weapons and equipment to Syria. In 1971 Damascus let the Soviets establish a naval base at Tartus.

Vladimir Putin and Bashar al-Assad officially became the presidents of their respective countries in 2000. Since then Putin has done what he could to protect Assad's regime, especially from 2011 when Syria's civil war erupted. Russia, along with China, vetoed any UN Security Council resolutions that condemned the Syrian regime's human rights abuses or use of chemical weapons and, in 2015, Putin sent Russian troops to fight with Assad's army against the rebels. All along Iran supplied Syria with weapons and troops from its own Revolutionary Guards and the affiliated Hezbollah revolutionary movement based in Lebanon.

After the Syrian uprising erupted, President Barack Obama was leery of getting sucked into the latest Middle East quagmire, seeing no American interests on either side to support. But Assad's use of chemical weapons against the rebels provoked international outrage and pressure on Obama to do something. On August 11, 2011 Obama demanded that Assad resign as president and warned that the United States would retaliate if his regime conducted any more chemical attacks. Ten days later a chemical attack killed more than 1,400 people. Rather than fulfill immediately his pledge to retaliate, Obama asked Congress for permission to do so, knowing that it would not grant it. He also sought a united front with NATO but his reluctance to get involved in Syria's civil war was echoed by British Prime Minister David Cameron and German Chancellor Angela Merkel.

The question of Syria chemical attacks was high on the agenda of the G-20 meeting hosted by Putin in St Petersburg on September 5 and 6, 2013. Putin proposed convincing Assad to surrender his chemical weapons as required under international law. Obama agreed. Assad agreed to give up 1,300 tons of chemical weapons to the United States which would destroy them in special ships. The diplomacy between Obama and Putin led to an extraordinary achievement. On October 1, 2013 inspectors began to inventory then transfer the arsenal. The last revealed chemicals were eliminated on June 23, 2014. Tragically, Assad's regime retained some chemical weapons that they would later use.

Until 2014 a bloody stalemate persisted between Assad's regime and the array of rebel factions known collectively as the Syrian Free Army. Meanwhile, Islamic State, an al Qaeda affiliate and Jihadist Sunni revolutionary movement headquartered in Raqqa, Syria, amassed fighters, weapons and equipment. In 2014 Islamic State launched offensives that overran much of northern Syria and Iraq. The Obama administration sent massive aid to Iraq and began a bombing campaign that gradually, over the next two years, drove back Islamic State in Iraq and Syria.

Fearing that the United States would first destroy Islamic State, then turn its guns on Assad's regime, Putin despatched ground and air forces to Syria in the summer of 2015. On September 15 Russia launched its first assault against Syrian rebels by a bomber squadron based at Latakia. The Russians unleashed a barrage of cruise missiles against rebel positions on October 7, Putin's birthday; that attack was risky because the missiles were fired from warships in the Caspian Sea and flew over Iran and Iraq before hitting their targets. Islamic State struck back. On October 31, 2015 a planted bomb destroyed in mid-air a jetliner packed with 224 mostly Russian tourists returning from Sharm-el-Sheik, Egypt. But neither Islamic State nor the Free Syrian Army could withstand Moscow's campaign of carpet bombing followed by a Russian-led Syrian ground offensive. The most important offensive was to retake Aleppo, Syria's largest city and once home to 2.5 million people.

Putin announced on March 14, 2016 that the offensive against Syria's rebels had succeeded, so he would begin withdrawing Russian forces. A richly symbolic celebration of that victory occurred on May 5, 2016 when a Russian orchestra conducted a concert in the amphitheater of Palmyra, an ancient Roman city that Islamic State had taken over and destroyed before Russian-led forces drove them out. But that victory came at an enormous cost in lives. As the Russians had done to subdue Chechnya, their carpet-bombing of rebel positions killed tens of thousands and forced millions of Syrians to abandon their homes.

Washington and Moscow designated spheres of influence in Syria and channels for managing conflicts between them. The chiefs of staff, generals Joseph Dunford and Valery Gerasimov, met to discuss Syria and other security matters. A hotline links the two defense bureaucracies, although it is rarely used. The most critical demarcation is that Russian and American aircraft not stray from airspace west or east, respectively, of the Euphrates river. Another is to give warning when attacks may kill troops from the other side. For instance, Washington warned Moscow to clear its personnel from a Syrian chemical plant before American Tomahawk missiles destroyed it. The most serious incident occurred on February 7, 2018 when a force of 500 Syrian troops and Russian mercenaries attacked an American Special Operations base east of the Euphrates. The Americans nearly wiped out the attackers. Then, on December 19, 2018, President Donald Trump announced that "we have won against ISIS" and so he would withdraw the 2,000 troops in Syria that protected, trained and equipped the mostly Kurdish troops against both Islamic State and the Syrian-Russia-Iranian-Hezbollah coalition. In doing so, Trump once again betrayed an American ally against American enemies or adversaries. [33]

Moscow and Tehran share an interest in defending Syrian President Bashar al Assad and his regime. In September 2018 Iranian President Rouhani hosted Putin and Turkish President Erdogan in Tehran to forge a strategy for ending the war in Syria. Erdogan pressed for an immediate ceasefire that Putin and Rouhani rejected since the allied Syrian, Russian and Iranian Hezbollah forces were steadily crushing the rebel forces. They did agree that Syria's civil war ultimately could be ended only with a diplomatic settlement.[34]

To his credit, Putin does not appear to share the anti-Semitism that afflicts many Russians. His image of Jews was shaped by the kindhearted elderly Jewish couple who often took care of him when he was a boy while his parents were working. Atop that were the bonds he forged with several Jews during his years of practising judo in St Petersburg.

Putin traveled to Israel to dedicate a monument to the Red Army of the Second World War in June 2012. During his visit he invited Israeli President Simon Peres to Moscow to dedicate the new Jewish Museum and Center of Tolerance in November 2012. In their dedication speeches, each emphasized the struggle against their common enemy. Putin noted:

> We in the Soviet Union, in Russia, you know had enormous sacrifices during the Second World War ... But we will never forget the sacrifices made by the Jewish people in the fight against Nazism, and we will never forget the holocaust.

Peres thanked Russians "for giving Jews the possibility to live here over the course of a thousand years, and for making it possible for our people to have not just a past but also a future."[35] Of course, each diplomatically avoided mentioning that discrimination and pogroms by Russians against Jews darkened that history.

Israel covertly supported the uprising against Bashar al-Assad's regime in Syria in 2011. Mossad, Israel's foreign intelligence agency, backed anti-Assad forces and fought Iran's Quds Force and Hezbollah fighters who supported Assad. Israel's air forces conducted several hundred precision bombings of Quds and Hezbollah positions and supply columns. After Putin despatched Russian forces to rescue Assad and eventually destroy the rebel forces, Prime Minister Benjamin Netanyahu and Putin met nine times to prevent any inadvertent clash between their troops. Their most important summit came in July 2018, when Putin agreed to try to pressure Tehran not to deploy its forces near the Israeli border. A crisis erupted in September 2018, when a Syrian anti-aircraft unit shot down a Russian spy plane with a fifteen-man crew. Israeli jets had conducted a bombing mission earlier that day and the Syrians thought they had targeted an Israeli aircraft. Putin and Netanyahu spoke tersely by telephone. Putin agreed not to publicly repeat the Assad regime's claim that Israeli jets were shadowing the Russian plane when it was downed. Nonetheless, Putin did announce that he would sell Syria sophisticated mobile S-300 surface-to-air-missiles with a 150-mile range that, for those deployed around Damascus, would reach high over Israel's airspace.[36]

Among Russia's rivals is Saudi Arabia. For decades Saudi Arabia has had close ties with the United States and been the Organization for Petroleum Exporting Countries (OPEC) price leader. Riyadh usually kept oil prices stable and relatively moderate while annually buying tens of billions of dollars-worth of American weapons and equipment. Moscow would like to displace Riyadh as OPEC's price leader, moderate with high oil prices and Washington as Saudi Arabia's arms merchant. In October 2018 two of those goals briefly appeared possible after a vicious murder.

Jamal Khashoggi was a dissident, *Washington Post* journalist and American resident. Saudi Crown Prince Mohammad bin Salman had Khashoggi enticed to the Saudi embassy in Ankara, Turkey, then murdered and dismembered. Turkish intelligence recorded the murder and Turkey's President Tayyip Erdogan condemned Saudi Arabia. That put pressure on President Donald Trump to retaliate with economic sanctions against Saudi Arabia that included suspending arms sales. The Saudi foreign ministry warned that it would retaliate against sanctions by raising the price of an oil barrel to over $200 while turning to other countries for its arms.

Trump dashed the Kremlin's hopes for sky-high oil prices and arms sales. He accepted Salman's story that Khashoggi was accidently killed when he fought the security personnel who were trying to arrest him. Neither the United States nor any other countries imposed sanctions against Saudi Arabia. Riyadh continued to keep oil prices at moderate levels and buy American arms.

Moscow's interest in Africa varies with its erratic distribution of oil, gas and other mineral deposits and to exploit any governments eager to buy Russian arms. Russian corporations have invested heavily in Algeria, Libya, Nigeria, Angola, Niger, Mali, Chad, Burkina Faso, Mauritania, Guinea, Madagascar, Eritrea, Sudan, Burundi, Senegal, Cote d'Ivoire, Uganda, Libya, South Africa and Egypt.[37] The murder of three Russian journalists in the Central African Republic in July 2018 threw a fleeting spotlight on the Kremlin's ties with that country, which was touted as a model to entice other African dictatorships. The journalists were investigating Russian arms, equipment and training by Wagner Group paramilitary forces linked with GU to that government's military. The program began after a meeting between President Faustin-Archange Touadera and Foreign Minister Sergei Lavrov at Sochi in October 2017. Numerous Russian transport planes unloaded Russian weapons and equipment after dark at the airport near Bangui, the capital, between January 26 and February 7, 2018. Those shipments violated a United Nations arms embargo imposed in 2013 for massive human rights violations by Touadera's government. The Russians violated that embargo after Touadera yielded a large stake for Russian firms to exploit valuable mineral deposits.[38]

Putin's policy toward Latin America differs little from communist times.[39] While the Kremlin seeks better relations with every country, it instinctively seeks special ties with anti-American authoritarian regimes in Cuba, Venezuela and Nicaragua, and anti-American illiberal democracies in Peru and Bolivia.

In February 2015, Defense Minister Sergei Shoigu visited Cuba, Nicaragua, and Venezuela to forge stronger anti-American military ties. That is good business for Russian weapon and military equipment manufacturers who, under Putin, have signed billions of dollars-worth of long-term contracts for those three countries along with Brazil, Mexico, Peru and Argentina. Aside from military products, the Russians cannot compete economically with the Americans in Latin America, so they do what they can to undermine political ties between Washington and each country. Foreign Minister Sergei Lavrov has spearheaded that public diplomacy. Between 2008 and 2012 alone he conducted twenty-two summits and sixty high-level meetings and signed seventy bilateral agreements worth billions of dollars in new trade and investments.[40]

Although the Cold War ended in 1991, Moscow continues to do what it can to prop up Cuba's economically and morally bankrupt communist regime. Putin first visited Cuba for a summit with Fidel Castro in December 2000. Putin's most generous act came in December 2013, when he wrote off 90 per cent of Cuba's $32 billion debt to Russia. That came eleven years after January 2002, when he pulled the plug on an operation that aided Cuba but drained Russia's coffers with little payback. From 1964 Moscow paid $200 million in annual rent to maintain a base with 1,200 personnel deployed over twenty-eight square miles at Lourdes, Cuba, that eaves-dropped on American telecommunications. The trouble was that the base was expensive to maintain while American counter-measures blocked most Russian listening efforts.

Hugo Chavez was the quintessential Latin American populist, thug and dictator who loots his country in the name of the people and anti-Americanism. He tried and failed to overthrow Venezuela's government with a military coup in 1992. Nonetheless, his machismo image and populist socialist message won him the presidency in the 1998 election. After taking power, he nationalized the oil industry and raised taxes on the rich and middle classes, kept most of the billions of dollars for himself and his cronies, gave the Castro dictatorship a billion or so dollars and spread what little was left in subsidy programs for the poor. A military coup briefly ousted him in 2002, but he regained power and, to secure it further, corrupted high-ranking military officials by putting them in charge of nationalized corporations and the illegal drug trade.

Putin naturally supported Chavez as a thorn in the heel of America's hegemony in Latin America. He had hoped that Chavez's regime would inspire other would-be populist dictators to overthrow Latin America's illiberal democracies and install themselves in power. Instead, as Venezuela's economy imploded, it became a cautionary tale for petro-state dictators around the world, including Putin himself. In August 2008 Putin despatched Igor Sechin, one of his closest advisors, to present Chavez with a "bailout". Chavez was grateful for the support, exclaiming, "At last! Now we are not alone in the battle against the American empire! Now we have Russia on our side!"[41]

What did Moscow get in return? The Chavez regime nationalized Venezuela's oil industry, purging foreign and especially American shareholders. Without foreign expertise and maintenance, the productivity of Venezuela's oil and gas industry steadily declined. Desperate for investments, the Venezuelans turned to the Russians. Rosneft acquired a controlling stake in Venezuela's oil industry. Of course, in doing so, the Venezuelans exchanged innovative foreign partners for laggards. The Russians sold the Venezuelans billions of dollars-worth of equipment and technologies that often fell far below the standards of American or European petro-companies. They also sold Venezuela billions of dollars' worth of weapons and other military equipment. Finally, they got Caracas to recognize the "independence" of Ossetia and Abkhazia, Georgia's breakaway provinces and Russia's puppet regimes.[42]

Although Chavez died in 2013, tragically his regime did not perish with him. His successor, Nicolas Maduro, may lack Chavez's charisma but is just as authoritarian, corrupt and inept. Venezuela's socialist revolution mirrored Cuba's in which the communists destroyed the rich and middle classes by confiscating their wealth and driving them into exile. By 2019 over 5 million Venezuelans or one in nine had fled, most to neighboring Colombia but some found refuge in the United States, Europe and Brazil. Beyond the regime's coterie, life was increasingly hellish for the Venezuelans who stayed, with mass joblessness, homelessness, malnutrition, empty stores, soaring crime, electricity blackouts and hyperinflation that reached a mind-boggling one million per cent in 2018 while the economy contracted 18 per cent![43]

Mass protests erupted in January 2019 after Maduro's second presidential inauguration following a rigged May 2018 election. Juan Guaido, who ran against Maduro, declared himself Venezuela's legitimate president. Canada and a dozen Latin-American countries including Argentina, Brazil, Chile, Colombia, Costa Rica, Paraguay, Peru, Ecuador and Guatemala, recognized Guaido on January 4; the Trump administration did not do so until January 23. That lag reflected the American economy's dependence on Venezuela for half a million barrels of oil daily or 3 per cent of its total, while Venezuela buys 100,000 barrels of American light crude oil to mix with its heavier oil. Secretary of State Mike Pompeo urged the thirty-five-member Organization of American States (OAS) to back Guaido and declared Maduro's regime: "illegitimate … morally bankrupt … economically incompetent and … profoundly corrupt. It is undemocratic to its core."[44]

Moscow warned the United States against overthrowing Maduro. Dmitri Peskov, Putin's spokesman, stated: "Any external intervention is very dangerous. We consider the attempt to usurp the top power in

Venezuela as going against the foundations and principles of international law." That was richly ironic given Russian imperialism against Georgia and Ukraine. Russia's stake in Venezuela has deepened steadily in the two decades since Chavez first took power, including $10 billion in financial aid and $11 billion in arms contracts capped by an S300 air defense system, two Tu-160 bombers theoretically capable of carrying nuclear missiles, and several hundred military and intelligence advisors. The Chinese have even more to lose should the Maduro regime be overthrown – $65 billion in economic aid. Both the Russians and Chinese receive oil in payment for Venezuela's debts to them. They will also wield their vetoes against any American resolution in the UN Security Council that targets Maduro's regime for overthrow. In addition, the Cubans have hundreds of military and intelligence officers embedded in Venezuela's government who would be purged if Maduro is deposed. Finally, Hezbollah, the Islamist movement allied with Iran, has a foothold via Tareck el Aisami and his clan that originated in Syria. Aisami was Venezuela's former spy chief and vice president, and current industry minister. Washington has indictments against him and others in his clan for drug-trafficking and money-laundering, a vital source of Hezbollah finance. So not just Russia, but its allies China, Cuba, Iran and Syria work together to keep Maduro in power because they would suffer huge financial, political and strategic losses if he and his regime are overthrown.[45]

That nearly happened on April 30, 2019 when President-elect Juan Guaido appeared at an air force base outside Caracas and demanded that Maduro resign. Apparently, Guaido believed that enough officers and troops had shifted from supporting Maduro to supporting him that he could oust the dictator. And, apparently, Maduro thought so too. He had readied a jet to fly him to exile in communist Cuba when the Kremlin convinced him to defend the presidential palace. That prompted Secretary of State Mike Pompeo to warn Russian Foreign Minister Sergei Lavrov that "interference by Russia and Cuba is destabilizing for Venezuela and the U.S.-Russian bilateral relationship."[46]

Trump hastened to undercut the secretary of state and the intelligence community in an hour long telephone call with Putin the next day. Just as during their infamous Helsinki summit Trump accepted Putin's denial that Russia interfered in America's 2016 election, the "Russia hoax" as they called it, he now accepted Putin's assurance that Russia "is not at all to get involved in Venezuela." When asked by a reporter if he warned Putin not to interfere in America's 2020 election, Trump said he did not raise the issue.[47] And meanwhile, Maduro and his cronies clung to power as Venezuela collapsed around them.

A similar tragedy unfolded in Nicaragua, but without oil. Nicaragua has always been among Latin America's poorest countries. Those conditions worsened after 1979 when Daniel Ortega and his Sandinista movement overthrew Anastasio Somoza's dictatorship and imposed a communist dictatorship. The communists further impoverished the country by destroying the rich and middle classes. Meanwhile, President Ronald Reagan's administration backed an anti-communist insurgency known as the "Contras". In 1990, Ortega agreed to democratic elections that swept him and his communist party from power. Conditions did not markedly improve. Ortega and the Sandinistas won the 2007 election and have kept power ever since. Ortega's first trip was to Tehran, Iran, to summit with anti-American and anti-Western President Mahmud Ahmadinejad. Just like the Chavez regime, Ortega and his cronies looted the treasury and shook down foreign investors. The socialists locked Nicaragua into a worsening vicious cycle of corruption, incompetence, mass protests, violence, repression and refugees. Police arrested thousands of protesters. More than 500,000 Nicaraguans or one in ten people fled to neighboring countries or to America if they had enough money and connections. That influx of refugees exacerbated poverty elsewhere in Central America, including Costa Rica, the region's least worse-off country.[48]

So what can Ortega's neo-communist regime do for Russia? On July 13, 2014 Putin met with Ortega in Managua. Ortega gushed, "It is like a ray of light … This is the first time a Russian president has visited Nicaragua."[49] Their summit came as the western sanctions for Putin's imperialism against Ukraine bit deeper into Russia's economy. Desperate for support from any anti-American regime, Putin included Managua on his itinerary along with Havana and Caracas.

Putin's global ambitions provoke chains of questions of which one is perhaps the most critical – do they enhance Russian power or exceed and thus undermine it?

Chapter 9

Russia and the Future

As to some problematic pages in our history, yes, we have had them. But what state hasn't … All sorts of things happened in the history of every state. And we cannot allow ourselves to be saddled with guilt.

(Vladimir Putin)

Russia under Putin remains frozen between the past they can't let go of and the future they can't bring themselves to embrace.

(Hillary Clinton)

Winston Churchill famously expressed this insight into Russia: "I cannot forecast to you the action of Russia. It is a riddle, wrapped in a mystery, inside an enigma; but perhaps there is a key. That key is Russian national interests."[1] That does indeed reflect Russian's current leader and those who came before him. Vladimir Putin is the latest outer Matryoshka doll in a receding line of scores of leaders that began with Viking chief Rurik twelve centuries ago. In his own ways for his own time, each asserted Russia's core values, interests and institutions of autocracy, xenophobia, nationalism and imperialism.

That political culture makes perfect sense in light of Russian history. As the saying goes, just because someone is paranoid does not mean that enemies are not out to get him. For nearly twelve hundred years Russians faced a succession of actual or would-be conquerors, including, most prominently, Mongols, Poles, Swedes, Turks, French and Germans. The Russians responded by establishing an autocratic state with a supreme leader capable of mobilizing people and raw materials into armies that defeated invaders and expanded the state's territory to engulf more subjects, natural resources and defensible frontiers. Andrei Amalrik explained Russian autocracy's cultural foundation in his 1969 book, *Will the Soviet Union Last Beyond 1984?*:

The Russian people, by virtue of their historical traditions ... are almost completely unable to understand the idea of self-governance, equality of the law, and personal freedom – and the related responsibility ... The very word 'freedom' is understood by most people as a synonym for 'disorder'.[2]

Russian culture values keeping or recovering order and eliminating or avoiding chaos. It emphasizes rigid conformity and equates individualism with selfishness.

Russian autocratic instincts were bolstered during the decade of worsening economic conditions and political chaos following the Soviet Union's collapse in 1991. Economist Evgeni Yasin explained:

Russians consider democracy, accompanying the market economy in our country as defective, and the retirees generally oppose it, believing that it leads to anarchy and banditry. At the same time, many of them would like to see a tsar as the head of the country.[3]

In western minds the most disturbing manifestation of Russia's cultural norm of autocracy is the Joseph Stalin cult. Various public opinion polls find that Stalin is either the most or among the most popular Russian leaders despite or perhaps because he was a genocidal tyrant. In a 2015 poll 82 per cent of Russians believed that Stalin was either "unconditionally positive" (52 per cent) or "positive" (30 per cent) for Russia.[4] Not surprisingly, Russia's Stalin cult has flourished under Putin, with the tyrant's popularity soaring from 19 per cent in 1998 to 53 per cent in 2003.[5] Whenever the subject arises Putin downplays Russia's millennium-long dark autocratic shadow with Stalin its most horrific stretch. In a 2007 speech before a history teacher convention, he declared:

As to some problematic pages in our history, yes, we have had them. But what state hasn't ... All sorts of things happened in the history of every state. And we cannot allow ourselves to be saddled with guilt.[6]

The Stalin cult is part of a broader cultural amnesia for the horrors of Soviet communism synonymous with mass genocide, enslavement and exploitation. In his brilliant book *It Was a Long Time Ago, and It*

Never Happened Anyway: Russia and the Communist Past, David Satter explained the consequences:

> Failure to memorialize the victims of Communist terror has contributed to the moral corrosion of Russian society. Disregard for human life exists in many countries, but in Russia it is unsurprising to see it carried to grim extremes.[7]

Certainly, Russia can never be politically or culturally part of western civilization if Russians persist in admiring Stalin. As long as Putin and other autocrats rule, Russians will not purge themselves of their adoration for Stalin as Germans long ago purged themselves of their adoration for Hitler.

The first critical symbolic step in that long hard road to liberation would be removing Vladimir Lenin from his tomb in Red Square and burying him in some remote, obscure, unmarked site. Putin has continually rejected liberal Russian appeals to so. Putin's views on the Soviet Union are complex. In 2005, during his annual address to the Federal Assembly, he declared, "The collapse of the Soviet Union was the biggest geo-political catastrophe of the century."[8] Yet, in 2009, he was more ambivalent, "Anyone who does not regret the collapse of the Soviet Union has no heart. And anyone who wants to see it recreated in its former shape has no head."[9]

Nonetheless, Putin at once reflects and reinforces Russian cultural values. He shares with many of his predecessors the psychology of the bully in the playground. Plagued with insecurities and self-doubts, Putin asserts his manhood to disprove them but, of course, in doing so actually parades them. By evoking deep-rooted Russian xenophobia, he enhances his own power by diverting Russian anxieties, anger and frustrations against hated foreigners who he claims threaten Russia. A 2014 Levada Center poll found that 84 per cent of Russians believed that their country was surrounded by enemies, 79 per cent believed the West posed the worst threat, 59 per cent did not care if Russia was isolated from the West, 48 per cent preferred Russia being a great power rather having high living standards, and 84 per cent supported Putin's policies.[10]

After becoming president on New Year's Eve 1999 Putin developed his own personality cult. He presents himself as a model Russian man – wise, decisive, athletic, sexy and unflappable. The mass media daily shows photos and film of him, often shirtless, practicing judo, fly-fishing, stalking Siberian tigers, flying planes, horseback-riding, downhill skiing or meeting ordinary people. Apparently, countless women and teenage girls adore him. For nearly all Russians, Putin represents a reassuring continuity between the nation's Soviet and post-Soviet eras.

Perhaps more than most nationalities, Russians wrestle with existential questions of identity.[11] What is Russia and what does it mean to be Russian? These questions provoke soul-searching in countless Russians. According to expert Richard Sakwa, "Russia had never before been (and still is not) a classical nation-state focused on a titular nationality, but remains a 'state-nation' – a multinational entity focused on the institutions of the state."[12] Legally there are ethnic *Russkii* and non-ethnic but still citizen *Rossiyanin* within the country.

Most Americans think of themselves as belonging to an "exceptional" country, surpassing all others because of its ideals and achievements. Most Russians feel their country is just as exceptional, as the leader of Orthodox Christians and Slavic nations. Tsar Peter the Great complicated Russian identity when he attempted to transform Russia from an Asiatic into a European nation. Since then, for more than three centuries, Slavophiles and westernizers have struggled to assert their competing visions for Russian identity and interests. Former Foreign Minister Andrei Kozyrev explained that dynamic struggle:

> Historical analysis brings out a certain cyclical pattern in the evolution of Russia: major periods of modernization were always brought about by a brutal collision with the outside world, which only tended to underscore the inadequacy of a backward and xenophobic Russia.[13]

Russian political analyst Peter Chaadayev insisted in his *Philosophical Letter*: "We do not belong to any of the great families of humanity, to either the West or the East, and have no traditions of either. We exist outside of time."[14] Eurasianists (*Evraziistvo*) assert a third way between

Westernizers and Slavophiles. Putin and most other Russians see their nation as standing at the crossroads between Europe and Asia, representing a superior version of both, and thus having the compelling duty, right and national interest to lead both civilizations.

Communism's bankruptcy and abandonment left a vast political and psychological void that Putin is determined to fill by defining and developing Russian nationalism. He reinforces Russian nationalism by celebrating the religion that communism had persecuted for seventy-five years. He elevated Orthodox Christianity and its patriarch to be a key pillar of political cultural power. That effort culminated in 2014 with the All-Russia People's Sobor that produced the Declaration of Russian Identity. A Russian is anyone "who considers himself/herself a Russian; has no other ethnic preferences; speaks and thinks in Russian; recognizes Orthodox Christianity as the basis of national spiritual culture; and has conscious solidarity with the Russian people."[15]

Putin transformed how Russians view themselves. When Yeltsin named him prime minister in August 1999 only 12 per cent of Russians believed their nation was on the right development path and 54 per cent believed it was on the wrong path. Eighteen years later those portions were nearly reversed as 59 per cent believed their nation was following the right path and only 29 per cent the wrong path. All along Putin has enjoyed high popularity ratings with two in three to more than eight in ten approving his actions as president. In contrast, as prime minister and president, Dmitri Medvedev's popularity varied from a high of 76 per cent in August 2008 to a low of 42 per cent in March 2017. Russians distinguish between the actions of their leaders and the government, and feel freer to criticize that impersonal latter. Since Putin took power, approval of government actions varied from a low of 32 per cent in August 2004 to highs of 59 per cent in August 2008 and 62 per cent in August 2014 after Russia's imperialist wars against Georgia and Ukraine. For Russians the Duma is a convenient lightning rod for discontent because it essentially serves as a rubber stamp for Putin's polices. The Duma's nadir came in March 2005 with 18 per cent approval and 68 per cent disapproval, and its height in August 2014 with Russians equally split between 49 per cent approval and 49 per cent disapproval.[16] Russian views of themselves as a European nation dropped after the Western sanctions imposed after Russia's imperialist wars against Georgia in 2008 and Ukraine in 2014.

Table 9.1 Russian Views of Themselves as a European Nation.[17]

	December 2008	*September 2009*	*October 2015*	*August 2017*
Fully Agree	17%	13%	6%	7%
Somewhat Agree	39%	34%	26%	37%
Somewhat Disagree	23%	27%	39%	35%
Fully Disagree	9%	9%	20%	13%
Hard to Say	12%	16%	9%	9%

Russia's political system is a hybrid of superficial democratic and deep-rooted authoritarian elements. One scholar explained: "The Russian state under Putin is more responsible to its population but not more accountable."[18] Putin and his coterie describe and justify themselves as a "security cabal" (*siloviki*) that dominates Russia's political system (*sistema*).

Creating an ideology to explain and justify Russian autocracy has been challenging. Vladimir Surkov explained: "We must have our own political language .... If we do not have our own discourse, public philosophy and ideology acceptable to most (but preferably all) of our citizens."[19] To that end, Putin and his advisors have asserted and discarded a series of labels for their system, starting with the "vertical of power" and "dictatorship of the law" then "sovereign democracy" and recently "conservative modernization". None of these is catchy, let alone meaningful. Unfortunately, the Kremlin rejects calling their ideology what it is, "Putinism," as the twenty-first century manifestation of twelve centuries of autocracy, xenophobia, nationalism, Orthodox Christianity, Slavism and imperialism. The Kremlin officially rejects and unofficially promotes Putinism.[20]

One way to divide the world's countries is between the centrally- and federally-run. In a centralized state, the national capital determines the bulk of national laws, regulations and policies. In a federal state, the provincial governments do. Officially, Russia is a federation that includes twenty-one republics, forty-nine oblasts, special status oblast cities of Moscow and St Petersburg, six krais, ten okrugs, and one autonomous oblast. Many of these units have ethnic or religious groups. For instance, Chechyna and Dagestan are primarily Muslim while there is a Jewish oblast in the Far East on the Chinese border. Russia is territorially the world's largest country, so vast that a traveler traversing its 6,000 east-west miles must pass through eleven time zones. Russia has 193 recognized ethnic groups. Like many countries, Russia's north is less conservative than its south.

Yet how federal is Russia? How much autonomy do its administrative units have in raising taxes, passing laws, enforcing regulations and pursuing policies different from others? As usual in Russia, appearances are misleading. Russia may be federally organized, but is centrally governed.

Russia's State Duma and Federal Council either fail to do or do poorly the duties of a democratic legislature. There is little or no lawmaking or oversight. Elections, however, are mostly free for parties and independent candidates. A spectrum of parties with different outlooks and agendas vie for voters and seats. Putin's party, United Russia, is populist and nationalist, and dominates Russia's legislature. The next two largest parties, the Communists and Liberal Democratics, espouse far right statist and nationalist views. Liberal parties usually receive only around 5 to 10 per cent of the votes. A free, competitive and professional press is critical to any liberal democracy. In Russia, that "fourth branch of democratic government" is withered and intimidated. A few prominent liberal organizations exist in Russia like the Carnegie Moscow Center, Institute of World Economic and International Relations at the Russian Academy of Sciences and Institute of Contemporary Development, but have no influence on policy. According to Freedom House, Russian autocracy worsened under Putin.

Table 9.2 Freedom House Ratings of Putin's Russia.[21]

	1999	2002	2006	2010	2014	2018
Freedom	4.5	5	5.5	5.5	5.5	5.5
Civil Liberties	5	5	5	5	5	5
Political Rights	5	5	6	6	6	6
Status	Partly Free	Partly Free	Not Free	Not Free	Not Free	
The scale is from 1 to 7, with 1 most free.						

Russia is a petro-state whose oil and gas giants like Gazprom, Rosneft and Transneft dominate the economy. Being a petro-state is more a curse than a blessing for Russia because its warps and stunts the economy. Russia's economy expands and contracts with oil and gas prices but fails to diversify and develop. By one account, Russia received "$1.6 trillion from oil and gas exports from 2000 to 2011" but "was not able to build a single multi-lane highway during this time," while "China, another top down authoritarian regime has built 4,360 miles of modern highways annually for the last ten years."[22] Russia is among the world's least technologically innovative countries. In 2014 Russia ranked 124th in the availability of new technologies and 126th in the absorption of technologies by companies.[23]

Table 9.3 Global Economic Powers, 2017.[24]

	Population	*Economic Size (PPP)*	*Average Income (PPP)*
China		$23.160,000,000,000	$16,700
European Union		$20,850,000,000,000	$40,900
United States		$19,390,000,000,000	$59,500
India		$9,459,000,000,000	$7,200
Japan		$5,429,000,000,000	$42,800
Germany		$4,171,000,000,000	$50,400
Russia		$4,008,000,000,000	$27,800
PPP: Purchasing Power Parity			

Since the Soviet empire's collapse, Russia has suffered a chronic brain drain with over a million and a half people, many highly educated and skilled, emigrating to Europe, America and other places with better futures. Of course, that worsening void of talent at home exacerbates economic conditions and renders more people desperate to get out or to obliterate themselves. Deaths have risen from murder, drinking, smoking, driving accidents, drug overdose, air and water pollution, radiation exposure and suicide. Most women endure lower pay, menial jobs and high rates of violence at the hands of men. That vicious socio-economic cycle has also encouraged a low birth rate. As a result, Russia's population shrank from 148 million in 1992 to 142 million in 2018.

An enduring legacy of the communist era is literally toxic. For seven decades Moscow imposed factory, food and mining production quotas with no regard for the deadly chemical, biological and radioactive poisons spewed into water and air, and thus into "the people's" bodies and brains. Stalin expressed the communist attitude toward nature: "We cannot expect charity from nature. We must tear it from her."[25] The Kremlin's policies of industrializing and collectivizing at any price devastated nature. Cocktails of toxic chemicals foul rivers, lakes and aquifers whose waters cannot be safely drunk, or its fish eaten. Over-irrigation and climate change transformed the once vast Aral Sea into a desert. Clearcutting and overgrazing have destroyed vast swaths of Russian forest and soil. Consuming caviar processed from Caspian Sea sturgeon can harm one's health as well as income. The 1986 Chernobyl nuclear meltdown epitomized the communist system's utter depravity, incompetence and ruthlessness, both in causing and cleaning the catastrophe. Chernobyl was only the worst nuclear disaster. Nuclear weapons tests and nuclear power plant leakages have spewed dangerous levels of radiation across regions of Russia and other former Soviet lands. Nuclear waste steadily accumulates at energy facilities and on bases with often faulty security and maintenance. Theft and contamination are worsening concerns.

In a classic case of "be careful what you wish for," Russia will pay a chronic worsening surcharge atop the international economic sanctions for annexing Crimea. In September 2018 a brown chemical fog of titanium dioxide that corrodes metal and lungs descended on swaths of Crimea and Ukraine, forcing thousands of people to flee their homes. For decades that chemical, among many others, had been dumped into a canal linked to the Dnieper river. Since the canal dried up, winds whip that titanium dioxide cocktail into dust storms that engulf countless humans.

Regardless, under Putin the super-rich have definitely become super-richer. When he was elected president in 2000 no Russian billionaires existed; in 2018 Russia's ninety-six billionaires ranked number five in the world behind China's 619, America's 585, India's 131, and Germany's 114.[26] Putin effectively controls those billionaires and lesser oligarchs, rewarding those who conform and punishing those who defy him. The result is that Putin's Russia is a kleptocracy or government of the thieves, by the thieves and for the thieves. That kleptocracy enriches the elite while trapping the Russian people in a vicious economic and political cycle. Dishonest and honest entrepreneurs alike invest their money in safe overseas havens rather than gamble it at home. Around 10 per cent of the economy annually bleeds from around $300 billion in bribes and $350 billion in capital flight.[27] Transparency International has a corruption scale with number one for the least corrupt country: Russia ranked 82nd in 1999 when Putin took power and 135th in 2017.[28]

Yet despite, or perhaps because of, Russia's autocracy and kleptocracy, Putin remains popular. Indeed, although his popularity has varied, even his lowest rating might provoke envy in countless other national leaders, including the American president. Since he took power, usually around eight in ten Russians back him. That support dropped to around six in ten as economic sanctions bit hard after the 2014 invasion of Ukraine but has resumed its former level.

Putin's enduring high popularity would appear to mean that his regime has rock-solid legitimacy. But Russians are more ambivalent about the system. A Levada Center study of Russian opinion from 2000 to 2015 found that only 23 per cent considered the existing system best for Russia, while far more, or 37 per cent, preferred the communist Soviet system and only one in five, or 21 per cent, wanted a liberal democracy.[29] Given how split Russians are about what kind of system they want to live under, Putin's autocracy dominates the middle ground between liberalism and totalitarianism. That in turn leaves those at either end to shrug fatalistically and be grateful that the worse alternative does not prevail.

Russians have many complaints with their list's contents varying over time. In August 2017 inflation was the worst worry with 61 per cent followed by poverty with 45 per cent, joblessness and corruption each with 33 per cent, declining factory and farm production with 28 per cent, limited healthcare with 26 per cent, extreme gap between rich and poor with 25 per cent, moral and cultural crisis with 15 per cent and environmental crisis with 14 per cent. Tyrannical government officials and western sanctions against Russia were numbers 13 and 15 with 12 per cent and 11 per cent respectively.[30]

Putin dominates Russian foreign policy-making as he discusses ends and means with his inner circle of security advisors (*siloviki*) and the more diverse Security Council, while the foreign, defense, finance and intelligence ministries feed them critical information, then implement his decisions. Just what are Putin's foreign policy ends and means?

Putin is the only Russian leader other than Peter the Great and Lenin who actually lived in Europe. Like them, he carried back to Russia mingled feelings of jealousy, inspiration, resentment, inferiority and, above all, zeal to lead Russia eventually to surpass the West in power. Putin's attempts to realize that ambition does threaten America, Europe and the global system but mostly by Russian cybertrolls subverting liberal democracies. As during the previous Cold War, Putin is committed to wielding every strategy except militarily invading Europe to undermine and break up NATO, the EU and the global system. Yet Henry Kissinger warned against exaggerating Putin or the threat his policies pose:

> Putin is not a Stalin who feels obliged to destroy anyone who might potentially at some future point disagree with him. Putin is somebody who wants to amass the power needed to accomplish his immediate task.[31]

He further observed that "the demonization of Vladimir Putin is not a policy; it is an alibi for one."[32]

Putin's foreign policy is best understood as emanating from a nineteenth-century-type realist armed with twenty-first-century nuclear and cyber power. Traditionally, realists were pragmatists who did what they could to defend or expand their nation's related economic and security interests. That often involved a choice between two diametrically opposed strategies. In the face of a powerful rival country or coalition, one could either "bandwagon" by joining it or "balance" by forming a rival alliance. More often than not, Putin has tried to counter America which, with its allies, is still the world's dominant military, economic and cultural power. Foreign Minister Sergei Lavrov explained the Kremlin's foreign policy as: "Russia will continue playing its balance role in global affairs. It will never be part of any new 'holy alliance' against anybody."[33]

Shortly after Putin became president in 1999, the Kremlin issued a boilerplate declaration of Russian foreign policy's goals, called the National Security Concept:

Promoting the interests of the Russian Federation as a great power and one of the most influential centers in the modern world [by] assuring the country's security, preserving and strengthening its sovereignty and territorial integrity and its strong and authoritative position in the world community [in order to promote] the growth of its political, economic, intellectual and spiritual potential.[34]

Who could find fault let alone danger in as innocuous a statement at that? Are those not the goals of any country, great power or not?

As for the military option, Defense Minister Sergei Ivanov declared in October 2003 that: "We cannot absolutely rule out the preventive use of force outside Russia's borders if Russia's interests or its obligations as an ally make this necessary."[35] Actually, since the Soviet empire's collapse, the Russian army has fought wars in Chechnya twice, Georgia, Ukraine and Syria. Russia lost its first war against Chechnya, but won each subsequent war. Indeed, with imperialism the conquest and colonization of one people by another, Vladimir Putin has been the world's most imperialistic leader since the Second World War. Since Putin took power in 1999 Russia re-conquered the breakaway province of Chechnya, annexed Crimea from Ukraine and detached and imposed puppet regimes on the "independent sovereign republics" of Donetsk and Luhansk from Ukraine, South Ossetia and Abkhazia from Georgia and Transnistria from Moldova. Russians paid a high price for those conquests as American and European sanctions deprived them of wealth they might otherwise have enjoyed. Most Russians put soaring national pride before drooping incomes. Nearly all Putin's imperialist ventures provoked rally-around-the-flag phenomena and spikes in his popularity.[36]

The Kremlin has no timetable or priority list for conquest. Russian foreign policy has always been opportunistic. Moscow either carefully manufactures ways to advance its interests or exploits them when they arise. That opportunistic strategy is often compared to a thief slipping down a hotel corridor trying each door till he finds one that is open, then entering and taking what he can. For instance, Moscow seized opportunities to snatch Abkhazia and South Ossetia from Georgia in 2008 and Crimea, Luhansk and Donetsk from Ukraine in 2014. For many different reasons, the reaction of Washington and Brussels was relatively muted in 2008 and retaliatory in 2014. Nonetheless, Putin kept the gains of both blatant acts of imperialism, despite the higher costs Russia paid for the latter than the former.

What most of Putin's conquests share are Russian-speaking minorities. The Russian diaspora includes more than 25 million *Russkoyazychnye* or people who speak Russian as their first language scattered across the former Soviet republics. The Kremlin seeks at once to protect them against discrimination while promoting them broadly as a political and economic force, and elements of them as criminal and intelligence forces, within those countries.

Table 9.4 Russia's Diaspora and Imperialism's Legacy.[37]

	1989			2017		
	Population	*Dominant Nation Share*	*Russian Share*	*Population*	*Dominant Nation Share*	*Russia Share*
Russia	147,385,000	82.5	82.5	142,257.519	77.7	77.7
Estonia	1,573,000	61.5	30.3	1,251,581	68.7	24.8
Latvia	2,618,000	52.0	34.0	1,944,643	62.0	25.4
Lithuania	3,690,000	79.6	9.4	2,823,859	84.1	5.8
Moldova	4,340,000	64.5	13.0	3,474.121	75.1	4.1
Belarus	10,200,000	77.9	13.2	9,549,747	83.7	8.3
Ukraine	51,704,000	72.7	22.1	44,033,874	77.8	17.3
Armenia	3,283,000	93.3	1.6	3,045,191	98.1	0.7*
Azerbaijan	7,029,000	82.7	5.6	9,961,386	91.6	1.3
Georgia	5,449,000	70.1	6.3	4,926,330	86.8	2.3*
Kazakhstan	16,538,000	39.7	37.8	18,556,698	63.1	23.7
Kyrgyzstan	4,291,000	52.4	21.5	5,789,122	73.2	5.8
Tajikistan	5,112,000	62.3	7.6	8,468,555	84.3	2.0*
Turkmenistan	3,534,000	72.0	9.5	5,351,277	85.0	12.0
Uzbekistan	19,906,000	71.4	8.3	29,748,859	80.0	5.5

*includes Russians and other minorities

Putin's imperialist threat is geo-politically limited but virtually global, although there is a clear set of priority countries and regions with America and Europe cross-haired. In recent years, Russian cyber-warriors helped elect Donald Trump president, get Britain to abandon the European Union, and bring the radical Five Star and league movements to power in Italy. They were less successful in French and German elections. Nonetheless, Russian cyber trolls exacerbated chronic political, class, religious, ethnic and racial divisions.

Until January 2017 American and Russian foreign policies were diametrically opposed, especially towards Europe. The White House and the Kremlin offered Europe two very different primary foreign relationships. Washington's "Atlanticist" vision prevailed as expressed through its leadership of NATO and encouragement of the EU's development. After the Cold War ended in 1991, NATO and the EU expanded eastward into countries liberated after the Soviet empire imploded. NATO's treaty article 5 asserts that an attack on any one member will be considered an attack on all members. Article 10 offers membership to any European country "in a position to further the principles of this Treaty and to contribute to the security of the North Atlantic area."

In stark contrast, Moscow's Eurasianist vision has inspired no prominent western adherents. Indeed, Putin has failed to understand that his tough talk and acts to prevent NATO and EU expansion actually provoke it, thus acting as a self-fulfilling prophecy. He has failed to understand that imperialism literally and figuratively does not pay. Russia's economy suffered devastating blows after Russia's wars against Georgia in 2008 and Ukraine in 2014 as sanctions stampeded massive capital flight and crimped the oligarchs.

Animosities between Russia and America are deep-rooted and multi-faceted. After meeting with Premier Nikita Khrushchev in June 1961, President John Kennedy observed: "We have wholly different views of right and wrong, of what is an internal affair and what is aggression, and, above all … of where the world is and where it is going."[38] That was true throughout the Cold War and then post-Cold War years until Donald Trump became president and muddied those distinctions. Georgi Arbatov, a Russian expert on the bilateral relationship, explained why the post-Cold War honeymoon was so short-lived:

Towards the end of the Soviet Union there was virtually no anti-American sentiment in Russia. But then these rosy expectations changed into doubts, disappointment and suspicion. What was actually inevitable has now become clear: that the political interests of Russia and America are different and rarely coincide in reality.[39]

Russian anti-Americanism mostly results from more than a century of Kremlin propaganda that projects the often catastrophic consequences of its own policies onto a convenient scapegoat. Nonetheless, the United States enjoyed a mostly positive image during the 1990s amidst the collapse of the Soviet communist empire, emergence of Russia and its embrace of democracy and markets, with the sole large spike of disapproval amidst NATO's bombing of Serbia in 1999. During Putin's first eight years in power the gap between approval and disapproval narrowed with a negative spike after the United States invaded Iraq in 2003. Russian opinion of America became permanently negative after the condemnations of Washington and Brussels for Moscow's war against Georgia in 2008, and vastly more so after the West's condemnation and sanctions for Moscow's war against Ukraine in 2014.[40]

Then, in 2016, disapproval dropped sharply after Donald Trump won the White House. In a November poll 10 per cent of Russians believed that bilateral relations would improve greatly and 44 per cent somewhat, 27 per cent that they would remain the same, while only 2 per cent that they would worsen and only 1 per cent that they would worsen significantly. As for Kremlin tampering in America's election, 37 per cent thought it probably had not and 35 per cent that it definitely did not, 16 per cent that it was difficult to say, while only 10 per cent that it probably had and 2 per cent that it definitely had.[41]

Russian negative views of America climbed as Democrats prevented Trump from giving Putin all he desired. A January 2018 poll revealed that 33 per cent of Russians viewed the United States negatively and 13 per cent very negatively, while 29 per cent had a positive view, 22 per cent found it hard to say, and only 3 per cent had a very positive view. The most common reasons that Russians disliked America were that "they want to run the world, are aggressors, think they own the world, start wars" (44 per cent) and "aggressive against Russia, are our enemy" (35 per cent). Those Russians who liked America did so for many reasons, of which the top five were "it's a rich country with a strong economy, people have good lives" (19 per cent), "developed and technologically advanced with many achievements" (16 per cent), "the people are just like us" (13 per cent), "the people are good" (12 per cent) and "the United States has never done anything bad to us" (10 per cent).[42]

The United States regularly tops Russia's enemy list. A December 2017 poll found that more than two in three Russians or 68 per cent believed America was the worst enemy followed by 29 per cent for Ukraine, 14 per cent the European Union, 10 the former Soviet republics, only 6 per cent each for Germany, NATO, and Britain and only 2 per cent for China. As for internal enemies, only 4 per cent cited the Putin regime, 3 per cent each for terrorists and corruption, 2 per cent for oligarchs and only 1 per cent for Putin. Russians narrowly split over whether they were surrounded by enemies (23 per cent) or the most dangerous were hidden within the country (21 per cent), 16 per cent thought they provoked enemies, 13 per cent hard to say and a comparative majority (27 per cent) believed that any revitalizing country will have enemies.[43]

Nonetheless, the Kremlin acquired a priceless asset who asserted Russian national interests after Trump became president. During Putin's career as a KGB officer, he probably never recruited and manipulated someone as easily as he has Trump with his bundle of pathologies. Trump is a narcissist, obsessed with himself and thus a sucker for false praise and adoration. He personifies the psychological trait of projection. People like Trump with deep unresolved emotional problems deny them and instead project their vilest characteristics onto some hated other. Every time that Trump hurls invective at someone, he reveals depraved dimensions of his own character. Trump is a pathological liar who, according to the *Washington Post*'s fact checkers, has averaged ten daily lies since he put his hand on the Bible and swore to defend the constitution on January 20, 2017.

Trump has inflicted severe damage to American democracy, national security, western civilization and the global economy. He launches savage nearly daily attacks on such key foundations of American democracy as the mainstream media, the intelligence community, the justice system, the electoral system, the scientific community and the constitution. By spring 2019 a score or so federal and New York state legal authorities were investigating Trump and his coterie for conspiracy with Russia, obstruction of justice, tax fraud, witness tampering, emoluments and violations of campaign finance and charity foundation laws. Despite or probably because of his destructive behavior, Trump retains the zealous support of around 45 per cent of Americans and 90 per cent of Republicans. Trump's demagoguery at once reflects and shapes the hatreds, fears, prejudices and hopes of a hundred and fifty million or so Americans. Living in Trump's America is like stepping into the twisted world of George Orwell's novel, *1984.* Rudy Giuliani, Trump's lawyer, personified Trumpism when he asserted that "Truth isn't truth."[44]

Is the damage that Trump and his followers have inflicted permanent? That of course depends on the outcome of the 2020 election. Certainly, the rot will spread and deepen if Trump is re-elected but might be mitigated if Trump is replaced by a realist committed to repairing America's ravaged democracy, environment and morality, and leadership over western civilization and the global system.

America may still have the capacity to change for the better, but does Russia? Hillary Clinton captured the dilemma, "Russia under Putin remains frozen between the past they can't let go of and the future they can't bring themselves to embrace."[45] Russians themselves humorously capture how the state manipulates history with a common saying: "The future is known. It is the past that keeps changing." Not just Russians but Americans and the rest of humanity can expect Putin to persist in trying to undermine and break up the EU, NATO and the global system while transforming liberal democracies into illiberal democracies or outright autocracies in Russia's image. And most likely that policy will be carried forward by his successors. After all, Russian leaders are all guided by twelve hundred years of history in which xenophobia, autocracy and aggression prevailed.

Vladimir Putin and Donald Trump warmly greeted each other at the 2019 Group of 20 summit at Osaka, Japan. When a reporter asked Trump if he would warn Putin not to interfere in the 2020 election, he turned to the Russian president, grinned, and did so with a mocking tone and wagging finger as if what the Kremlin did in the 2016 election was some harmless schoolboy prank. As Putin chuckled, Trump pointed to the reporters and said, "Get rid of them. Fake news is a great term, isn't it?" He exclaimed, "it is a great honor to be with President Putin … We have had a very, very good relationship … A lot of very positive things going to come out of the relationship. "Later, Putin was coldly serious when he declared that the liberal world order "had outlived its purpose … The liberal idea has become obsolete. It has come into conflict with the interests of the overwhelming majority of the population."[46] Putin may be dead right about that.

Notes

Introduction

1. For the best Putin biography, see: Steven Lee Myers, *The New Tsar: The Rise and Reign of Vladimir Putin* (New York: Vintage, 2015). See also: Peter Truscott, *Putin's Progress: A Biography of Russia's Enigmatic President* (London: Simon and Schuster, 2004); Richard Sakwa, *Putin: Russia's Choice* (New York: Routledge, 2007); Masha Gessen, *The Man Without a Face: The Unlikely Rise of Vladimir Putin* (New York: Riverhead Books, 2012); Angus Roxburgh, *The Strongman: Vladimir Putin and the Struggle for Russia* (London: I.B. Tauris, 2012); Clifford Gaddy, *Mr. Putin: Operative in the Kremlin* (Washington D.C.: Brookings Institute, 2013); Anna Arutunya, *The Putin Mystique: Inside Russia's Power Cult* (Northampton, Mass.: Olive Branch Press, 2014).

2. Helena Goscilo, *Putin as Celebrity and Cultural Icon* (New York: Routledge, 2012); Ben Judah, *Fragile Empire: How Russia Fell In and Out of Love with Vladimir Putin* (New Haven, Conn.: Yale University Press, 2013).

3. Hill and Gaddy, *Mr. Putin*, 7.

4. Alex Marshall, "On State TV, Putin Tames the Wildest of Beasts," *New York Times*, September 5, 2018.

5. Hill and Gaddy, *Mr. Putin*, 10–11.

6. Karen Dawisha, "The Putin Principle: How It Came to Rule Russia," *World Affairs*, vol. 178, no. 1 (May-July 2015), 20, 13–22.

7. Dawisha, *Putin's Kleptocracy*, 9.

8. David Hoffman, *The Oligarchs: Wealth and Power in the New Russia* (New York: Public Affairs, 2003); Andrew Jack, *Inside Putin's Russia* (New York: Oxford University Press, 2002); Peter Baker and Susan Glasser, *Kremlin Rising: Vladimir Putin's Russia and the End of Revolution* (New York: Scribner, 2005); Allen Lynch, *How Russia Is Not Ruled: Reflections on Russian Political Development* (New York: Cambridge University Press, 2005); Steven Fish, *Democracy Derailed in Russia* (New York: Cambridge University Press, 2005); Lilia Shevtsova, *Putin's Russia* (Washington D.C.: Carnegie Institute for International Peace, 2005); Alena Ledeneva, *How Russia Really Works* (Ithaca, N.Y.: Cornell University Press, 2006); Joel Ostrow, Georgiy, and Irina Khakamada, *The Consolidation of Dictatorship in Russia: An Inside View of the Demise of Democracy* (Westport, Conn.: Praeger, 2007); Thomas Gomart, *Russian Civil-Military Relations: Putin's Legacy* (Washington D.C.: Carnegie Institute for International Peace, 2008); Mikhail Myagkov, Peter Ordeshook, and Dmitry Shaikin, *The Forensics of Election Fraud: Russia and Ukraine* (New York: Cambridge University Press, 2009); Steve LeVine, *Putin's Labyrinth: Spies, Murder, and the Dark Heart of the New Russia* (New York: Random House, 2008); Andrei Soldatov, and Irina Borogan, *The New Nobility: The Restoration of Russia's Security State and the Enduring Legacy of the KGB*

(New York: Public Affairs, 2010); Brian Taylor, *State Building in Putin's Russia: Policing and Coercion after Communism* (New York: Cambridge University Press, 2011); Stephen Blank, ed., *Can Russia Reform?: Economic, Political, and Military Perspectives* (Washington D.C.: U.S. Army War College Strategic Studies Institute, 2012); Mendras, Marie, *Russian Politics: The Paradox of a Weak State*, New York: Columbia University Press, 2012; J.V. Kochiw, *The Abuse of Power: Corruption in the Office of the President* (Reading, U.K.: Artemia Press, 2013); Alena Ledeneva, *Can Russia Modernise? Sistema, Power Networks, and Informal Governance* (New York: Cambridge University Press, 2013); Andrey Makarychev, and Andre Mommen, *Russia's Changing Economic and Political Regimes: The Putin Years and Afterwards* (New York: Routledge, 2013); Stephen, Wegner, *Return to Putin's Russia: Past Imperfect, Future Uncertain* (New York: Rowman and Littlefield, 2013); Richard Sakwa, *Putin and the Oligarchs* (London: I.B. Taurus, 2014); Samuel Greene, *Moscow in Movement: Power and Opposition in Putin's Russia* (Stanford, Calif.: Stanford University Press, 2014); Karen Dawisha, *Putin's Kleptocracy: Who Owns Russia?* (New York: Simon and Schuster, 2014); Richard Sakwa, *Putin Redux: Power and Contradiction in Contemporary Russia* (New York: Routledge, 2014); Mikhail Zygar, *All the Kremlin's Men: Inside the Court of Vladimir Putin* (New York: Public Affairs, 2016); Angela Stent, *Putin's World: Russia against the West and with the Rest* (New York: Twelve Books, 2019).

9. Gessen, *Man Without a Face*, 261.
10. Richard Staar, *Foreign Policy of the Soviet Union* (Stanford, Calif.: Hoover Institute Press, 1991), 79–88; Vladimir Bukovsky, "The Peace Movement and the Soviet Union," *Commentary*, May 1982; Dawisha, *Putin's Kleptocracy*, 37; Christopher Andrews and Vasili Mitrokhin, *The Sword and the Shield: The Mitrokhin Archives and the Secret History of the KGB* (New York: Basic Books, 1999).
11. "Grease My Palm," *Economist*, November 27, 2008.
12. For Putin and Russian nationalism, see: Marlene Laruelle, ed., *Russian Nationalism and the Nationalist Assertion of Russia* (New York: Routledge, 2009); Alexander Verkhovsky, ed., *Xenophobia and Radical Nationalism in Russia* (Moscow: Sova Center for Information and Analysis, 2013); Pal Kolsto and Helge Blakkisrud, eds., *The New Russian Nationalism: Imperialism, Ethnicity, and Authoritarianism, 2000–2105* (Edinburg: Edinburgh University Press, 2016). For Putin's foreign policy, see: Robert Legvold, *Russian Foreign Policy in the Twenty-First Century and the Shadow of the Past* (New York: Columbia University Press, 2007); Keith Crane et. al., *Russian Foreign Policy: Sources and Implications* (Santa Monica, Calif.: RAND, 2009); Allen Lynch, *Vladimir Putin and Russian Statecraft* (Washington D.C.: Potomac Books, 2011); Jeffrey Mankoff, *Russian Foreign Policy: The Return of Great Power Politics* (New York: Roman and Littlefield, 2012); Andrei Tsygankov, *Russia's Foreign Policy: Change and Continuity in National Identity* (New York: Rowman and Littlefield, 2013); Magda Leichtova, *Misunderstanding Russia: Russian Foreign Policy and the West* (London: Ashgate, 2014); Bruce Nalbandov, *Not by Bread Alone: Russian Foreign Policy Under Putin* (Lincoln: University of Nebraska Press, 2016). For Putin's Cold War, see: Alexis Arbatov, Karl Kaiser, and Robert Legvold, eds., *Russia and the West: The 21st Century Security Environment* (Armonk, N.Y.: M.E. Sharpe, 1999); Janusz Bugajski, *Cold Peace: Russia's New Imperialism* (Westport, Conn.: Praeger, 2004); Mark MacKinnon, *The New Cold War: Revolutions, Rigged Elections, and Pipeline Politics in the Former Soviet Union*

(New York: Carroll and Graf, 2007); Edward Lucas, *The New Cold War* (New York: Palgrave Macmillan, 2008).

13. Nalbandov, *Not By Bread Alone*, 117.

14. For democracy's vulnerabilities and subversion, see: John Keane, *The Life and Death of Democracy* (New York: W.W. Norton, 2009); Ross Rosenfeld, *The Slow Death of Democracy* (New York: Resistance Books, 2018); Steven Levitsky and Daniel Ziblatt, *How Democracies Die* (New York: Crown Publishers, 2018).

15. Janusz Bugajski, *Cold Peace: Russia's New Imperialism* (Westport, Conn.: Praeger, 2004), 223.

16. Marlene, Laruelle, *Russian Eurasianism: An Ideology of Empire* (Baltimore: Johns Hopkins University Press, 2008); Glen Diesen, *Russia's Geoeconomic Strategy for a Greater Eurasia* (New York: Routledge, 2018); Toni Mileski, "Identifying the New Eurasian Orientation in Modern Russian Geopolitical Though," *Eastern Journal of European Studies*, vol. 6, no 2 (December 2015), 177–87.

17. Craig Unger, *House of Trump, House of Putin* (New York: Dutton, 2018), 68.

18. Hill and Gaddy, *Mr. Putin*, 337.

19. Hill and Gaddy, *Mr. Putin*, 339.

20. Margarita Balmaceda, *Energy Dependency, Politics, and Corruption in the Former Soviet Union: Russia's Power, Oligarch's Profits, and Ukraine's Missing Energy Policy, 1995–2006* (London: Routledge, 2008); Marshall Goldman, *Petrostate: Putin, Power, and the New Russia* (New York: Oxford University Press, 2010); Vagit Alekperov, *Oil of Russia: Past, Present, and Future* (Minneapolis: East View Press, 2011); Thane Gustafson, *The Wheel of Fortune: The Battle for Oil and Power in Russia* (Cambridge, Mass.: Harvard University Press, 2012).

21. John Carlin and Garrett Graff, *Dawn of the Code War: America's Battle against Russia, China, and the Rising Global Cyber Threat* (New York: Public Affairs, 2018); David Sanger, *The Perfect Weapon: War, Sabotage, and Fear in the Cyber Age* (New York: Random House, 2018); Andy Greenburg, *Sandworm: A New Era of Cyberwar and the Hunt for the Kremlin's Most Dangerous Hackers* (New York: Doubleday, 2018).

22. For an excellent article, see: David Graham, "Is WikiLeaks a Russian Front Organization?" *The Atlantic*, November 29, 2018.

23. Conradi, *Who Lost Russia?*, 317.

24. For Trump's attacks on American democracy and western civilization, see: Arthur Paulson, *Donald Trump and the Prospects for American Democracy* (New York: Lexington Books, 2018); Greg Sargent, *An Uncivil War: Taking Back Our Democracy in an Age of Trumpian Disinformation* (New York: Custom House, 2018); Bob Woodward, *Fear: Trump in the White House* (New York: Simon and Schuster, 2018); Donald Frum, *Trumpocracy: The Corruption of the American Republic* (New York: Harper, 2018); Marvin Kalb, *Enemy of the People: Trump's War on the Press, the New McCarthyism, and the Threat to American Democracy* (Washington D.C.: Brookings, 2018). For Trump and Russia, see: Michael Isikoff and David Corn, *Russian Roulette: The Inside Story of Putin's War on America and the Election of Donald Trump* (New York: Hachette Group, 2018); Greg Miller, *The Apprentice: Trump, Russia, and the Subversion of American Democracy* (New York: Custom House, 2018); Seth Abramson, *Proof of Collusion: How Trump Betrayed America* (New York: Simon and Schuster, 2018); Malcom Nance and Rob Reisner, *The Plot to Destroy America: How Putin and His Spies Are Undermining America and Dismantling the West* (New York: Hachette, 2018); Stephen Cohen, *War with*

Russia?: From Putin and Ukraine to Trump and Russiangate (New York: Hot Books, 2018); Seth Hettena, *Trump/Russia: A Definitive History* (New York: Melville House, 2018); Craig Unger, *House of Trump, House of Putin: The Untold Story of Donald Trump and the Russian Mafia* (New York: Dutton, 2018).

25. Gustav Gessel, "Fellow Travelers: Russia, Anti-Westernism, and Europe's Political Parties," *European Council on Foreign Relations* (2018). See also: Michael Orenstein, "Putin's Western Allies: Why Europe's Far Right Is on the Kremlin's Side," *Foreign Affairs*, May 25, 2014; Casey Michel, "The Kremlin's California Dream: Why the Russian Government Cultivates Foreigners on the Far-Right and Far-Left," *Slate*, May 4, 2017; James Kirchick, "How the GOP Became the Party of Putin," *Politico Magazine*, July 18, 2018; Nick Noack, "The European Parties Accused of Being Influenced by Russia," *Washington Post*, November 17, 2017.

26. For books, see: Peter Foot, *The Protesters: Doubt, Dissent, and British Nuclear Weapons* (Aberdeen: Centre for Defense Studies, 1983); James Dougherty and Robert Phaltzgraff, *Shattering Europe's Defense Consensus: The Anti-Nuclear Movement and the Future of NATO* (Washington D.C.: Pergamon-Brassey's, 1985); Peter Hennessey, *The Secret State: Whitehall and the Cold War* (London: Allen Lane, 2002); Ronald Rychiak and Ion Mihai Pacepa, *Disinformation: Former Spy Chief Reveals Secret Strategies for Undermining Freedom, Attacking Religion, and Promoting Terrorism* (Washington D.C.: WND Books, 2013); Oscar Martin Garcia and Rosa Magnussorie, eds., *Rethinking the Cold War: Machineries of Persuasion* (Berlin: Oldenbourg-De Gruyter, 2019); For articles, see: Andrea Kendall-Taylor and David Shullman, "How Russia and China Undermine Democracy: Can the West Counter the Threat?" *Foreign Affairs*, October 2, 2018; Laura Rosenberger and Thomas Morley, "Russia's Promotion of Illiberal Populism: Tools, Tactics, Networks," *Alliance for Securing Democracy*, March 11, 2019; Geir Karlsen, "Divide and Rule: Ten Lessons about Russian Political Influence activities in Europe," *Palgrave Communications*, February 8, 2019.

Chapter 1

1. James Billington, *The Icon and the Axe: An Interpretative History of Russian Culture* (New York: Knopf, 1966); Hugh Ragsdale, *The Russian Tragedy: The Burden of History* (Armonk, N.Y.: M.E. Sharpe, 1996); Richard Pipes, *Russian Conservatism and Its Critics: A Study in Political Culture* (New Haven, Conn.: Yale University Press, 2005); Thomas Ambrosio, *Authoritarian Backlash: Russian Resistance to Democratization in the Former Soviet Union* (Burlington, Vermont: Ashgate, 2009); Julie Fedor, *Russia and the Cult of State Security* (New York: Routledge, 2011); Catherine Merridale, *Red Fortress: History and Illusion in the Kremlin* (New York: Metropolitan Books, 2013).

2. Nalbandov, *Not By Bread Alone*, 65.

3. Fyodor Dostoyevsky, *A Writer's Diary, Volume 1, 1873–1876* (Evanston, Il.: Northwestern University, 1994), 161–2.

4. David Satter, *It Was a Long Time Ago and It Never Happened Anyway: Russia and the Communist Past* (New Haven, Conn.: Yale University Press, 2012), 304–5.

5. Richard Pipes, *Russia Under the Old Regime* (New York: Charles Scribners' Sons, 1974); Paul Bushkovitch, *A Concise History of Russia* (New York: Cambridge University Press, 2013); Nicholas, Riasanovsky, and Mark Steinburg, *A History of Russia* (New York: Oxford University Press, 2018).

6. William Fuller, *Strategy and Power in Russia, 1600–1914* (New York: Free Press, 1992); Orlando Figes, *Natasha's Dance: A Cultural History of Russia* (New York: Picador, 2003); Simon Montefiore, *The Romanovs, 1613–1918* (New York: Vintage, 2017).

7. Evgenii Anisimov, *The Reforms of Peter the Great: Progress through Coercion in Russia* (New York: M.E. Sharpe, 1993); John LeDonne, *The Russian Empire and the World, 1700–1914* (New York: Oxford University Press, 1997); James Cracraft, *The Revolution of Peter the Great* (Cambridge, Mass.: Harvard University Press, 2003).

8. Barbara Jelevich, *St Petersburg and Moscow: Tsarist and Soviet Foreign Policy, 1814–1974* (Bloomington: Indiana University Press, 1974); William Fuller, *Strategy and Power in Russia, 1600–1914* (New York: Free Press, 1992); John LeDonne, *The Russian Empire and the World, 1700–1914* (New York: Oxford University Press, 1997).

9. William Blackwell, *The Beginnings of Russian Industrialization* (Princeton, N.J.: Princeton University Press, 1968); William Blackwell, ed., *Russian Economic Development from Peter the Great to Stalin* (New York: New Viewpoints, 1974).

10. Sakwa, *Russian Politics and Society*, 446.

11. Figes, *Revolutionary Russia*, 13; Salisbury, *Black Nights, White Snow*, 252.

12. Alexander Mikhailovich Romanov, *Once a Grand Duke* (New York: Farrar and Rinehart, 1932), 168–69.

13. Harrison Salisbury, *Black Night, White Snow: Russia's Revolutions, 1905–1917* (New York: Doubleday, 1977); Richard Pipes, *The Russian Revolution* (New York: Knopf, 1990); Martin Malia, *The Soviet Tragedy: A History of Socialism in Russia, 1917–1991* (New York: Free Press, 1994); Orlando Figes, *A People's Tragedy: A History of the Russian Revolution* (New York: Viking, 1996); Richard Pipes, *The Formation of the Soviet Union: Communism and Nationalism, 1917–1923* (Cambridge, Mass.: Harvard University Press, 1997); Arno Mayer, *The Furies: Violence and Terror in the French and Russian Revolutions* (Princeton, N.J.: Princeton University Press, 2000).

14. Christopher Clark, *The Sleepwalkers: How Europe Went to War in 1914* (New York: HarperCollins, 2014).

15. Niall Ferguson, *The Pity of War Explaining World War I* (New York: Basic Books, 1999); Peter Hart, *The Great War: A Combat History of the First World War* (London: Profile Books, 2015).

16. Peter Gatrell, *Russia's First World War: A Social and Economic History* (New York: Routledge, 2014); Dominic Lieven, *The End of Tsarist Russia: The March to World War I and Revolution* (New York: Penguin, 2015); David Stone, *The Russian Army in the Great War: The Eastern Front, 1914–1917* (Topeka: University Press of Kansas, 2015).

17. Salisbury, *Black Nights, White Snow*, 254–5.

18. Ferguson, *Pity of War*, 295.

Chapter 2

1. Konstantin Simis, *USSR: The Corrupt Society, The Secret World of Soviet Capitalism* (New York: Simon and Schuster, 1982); Mary McAuley, *Soviet Politics, 1917–1991* (New York: Oxford University Press, 1992); Stephen Cohen, *Soviet Fates and Lost Alternatives: From Stalinism to the New Cold War* (New York: Columbia University Press, 2009); Orlando Figes, *Revolutionary Russia, 1891–1991* (New York: Metropolitan Books, 2014).

2. Figes, *Revolutionary Russia*, 117.
3. Leon Trotsky, *Terrorism and Communism: A Reply to Karl Kautsky* (New York: Verso, 2017), 63.
4. Figes, *Revolutionary Russia*, 107.
5. Figes, *Revolutionary Russia*, 114.
6. Ferguson, Pity of War, 393.
7. Figes, *People's Tragedy*, 773; Malia, *Soviet Tragedy*, 137; Ferguson, *Pity of War*, 391–2; G.F. Krivosheev, *Soviet Casualties and Combat Losses in the Twentieth Century* (London: Greenhill, 1997).
8. Figes, *Revolutionary Russia*, 129.
9. Isaac Deutscher, *Stalin: A Political Biography* (New York: Oxford University Press, 1967), 248–61.
10. Bushkovitch, *History of Russia*, 357.
11. Alexander Solzhenitsyn, *The Gulag Archipelago, 1918–1956*, vols 1–2 (New York: Harper and Row, 1974); Anne Applebaum, *Gulag: A History* (New York: Doubleday, 2003); Oleg Khlevniuk, *The History of the Gulag: from Collectivization to the Great Terror* (New Haven, Conn.: Yale University Press, 2004).
12. Arch Getty, Oleg Naumov, and Benjamin Sher, *The Road to Terror: Stalin and the Self-Destruction of the Bolsheviks, 1932–1939* (New Haven, Conn.: Yale University Press, 2010); Michael Ellman, "Soviet Repression Statistics: Some Comments," *Europe-Asia Studies*, vol. 54, no. 7 (November 2002), 1151–72.
13. Veljko Vujacic, "Stalinism and Russian Nationalism: A Reconceptualization," Marlene Laruelle, ed. *Russian Nationalism and the Nationalist Assertion of Russia* (New York: Routledge, 2009), 51.
14. Robert Conquest, *Harvest of Sorrow: Soviet Collectivization and the Terror-Famine* (New York: Oxford University Press, 1986); Robert Conquest, *The Great Terror: A Reassessment* (New York: Oxford University Press, 2007); Paul Hagenloh, *Stalin's Police: Public Order and Mass Repression in the USSR, 1926–1941* (Baltimore: Johns Hopkins University Press, 2009); Anne Applebaum, *Red Famine: Stalin's War on Ukraine* (New York: Doubleday, 2017).
15. Figes, *Revolutionary Russia*, 221; G.F. Krivosheev, *Soviet Casualties and Combat Losses in the Twentieth Century* (London: Greenhill, 1997).
16. Paul Hollander, ed., *From the Gulag to the Killing Fields: Personal Accounts of Political Violence and Repression in Communist States* (Wilmington, Del.: Intercollegiate Studies Institute, 2007); Paul Gregory, *Terror by Quota: State Security from Lenin to Stalin* (New Haven, Conn.: Yale University Press, 2009); David Satter, *It Was a Long Time Ago and It Never Happened Anyway: Russia and the Communist Past* (New Haven, Conn.: Yale University Press, 2012).
17. Allen Paul, *Katyn: Stalin's Massacre and the Triumph of Truth* (Urbana: Northern Illinois University Press, 2010).
18. Figes, *Revolutionary Russia*, 2.
19. *Lend Lease Shipments: World War II* (Washington D.C.: War Department Chief of Finance, December 31, 1946); John Deane, *The Strange Alliance: The Story of Our Efforts at Wartime Cooperation with Russia* (New York: Viking, 1947); Albert Weeks, *Russia's Life Saver: Lend Lease Aid to the U.S.S.R. in World War II* (Lanham, Maryland: Lexington Books, 2009).
20. Richard Langworth, *Winston Churchill, Myth and Reality: What He Actually Did and Said* (Jefferson, N.C.: MacFarland and Company, 2017), 91.

21. Glen Diesen, *Russia's Geoeconomic Strategy for a Greater Eurasia* (New York: Routledge, 2018), 31.

22. Greg Behrman, *The Most Noble Adventure: The Marshall Plan and How America Helped Rebuild Europe* (New York: Free Press, 2008); Benn Stell, *The Marshall Plan: Dawn of the Cold War* (New York: Simon and Schuster, 2018).

23. John Lewis Gaddis, *Strategies of Containment: A Critical Appraisal of American National Security Policy during the Cold War* (New York: Oxford University Press, 2005); John Lewis Gaddis, *The Cold War: A New History* (New York: Penguin, 2006); Donald Miller, *The Cold War: A Military History* (New York: Thomas Dunne, 2015).

24. Max Hastings, *The Korean War* (New York: Simon and Schuster, 1988); Bruce Cummings, *The Korean War: A History* (New York: Modern Library, 2010); George Herring, *America's Longest War: The United States and Vietnam, 1950–1975* (New York: McGraw-Hill, 2013); Max Hastings, *Vietnam: An Epic Tragedy, 1945–1975* (New York: Harper, 2018).

25. Richard Rhodes, *Arsenals of Folly: The Making of the Nuclear Arms Race* (New York: Vintage, 2006); David Hoffman, *The Dead Hand: The Untold Story of the Cold War Nuclear Arms Race and Its Dangerous Legacy* (New York: Anchor, 2009).

26. Gaddis, *Strategies of Containment*, 310.

27. Frances Fitzgerald, *Way Out There in the Blue: Reagan, Star Wars, and the End of the Cold War* (New York: Simon and Schuster, 2000); Nate Jones, *Able Archer 83: The Secret History of the NATO Exercise That Almost Triggered Nuclear War* (New York: New Press, 2016).

28. Gaidar, *Collapse of Empire*, 75, 95.

29. Ibid., 73–4.

30. Ibid., 73.

31. Dusko Doder and Louise Branson, *Gorbachev: The Heretic in the Kremlin* (New York: Penguin, 1990); Archie Brown, *The Gorbachev Factor* (New York: 0xford University Press, 1996); Mark Galeotti, *Gorbachev and His Revolution* (London: Palgrave Macmillan, 1997); William Taubman, *Gorbachev: His Life and Times* (New York: W.W. Norton, 2017).

32. Stephen Cohen, *Soviet Fates and Lost Alternatives: From Stalinism to the New Cold War* (New York: Columbia University Press, 2009), 85.

33. Stephen Cohen, *Soviet Fates and Lost Alternatives: From Stalinism to the New Cold War* (New York: Columbia University Press, 2009), 132.

34. Jonathan Aitken, *Margaret Thatcher: Power and Personality* (New York: Bloomsbury, 2013), 485.

35. Brown, *Gorbachev Factor*, 93.

36. Ostrovsky, *Invention of Russia*, 59–60.

37. Ibid., *Invention of Russia*, 64.

38. "The Costs of Soviet Intervention in Afghanistan" (CIA: Office of Soviet Assessments, released 2000). Vladislav Tamarov, *Afghanistan: Soviet Vietnam* (New York: Mercury House, 1992); Roderic Braithwaite, *Afghantsy: The Russians in Afghanistan, 1979–89* (New York: Oxford University Press, 2011).

39. Serhil Plokhy, *Chernobyl: The History of a Nuclear Catastrophe* (New York: Basic Books 2018).

40. Gaidar, Collapse of Empire, 137; "Average Annual OPEC Crude Oil Prices from 1960 to 2018," *Statistica* website.

41. Leon Aron, *Yeltsin: A Revolutionary Life* (New York: St. Martin's Press, 2000); Timothy Colton, *Yeltsin: A Life* (New York: Basic Books, 2011).

42. John Dunlop, *The Rise of Russia and the Fall of the Soviet Empire* (Princeton, N.J.: Princeton University Press, 1993); David Remnick, *Lenin's Tomb: The Last Days of the Soviet Empire* (New York: Random House, 1993); Jack Matlock, *Autopsy of an Empire: The Ambassador's Account of the Collapse of the Soviet Union* (New York: Random House, 1995); Fred Coleman, *The Decline and Fall of the Soviet Empire* (New York: St. Martin's Press, 1996); Robert Strayer, *Why Did the Soviet Union Collapse?: Understanding Historical Change* (Armonk, N.Y.: M.E. Sharpe, 1998); Yegor Gaidar, *The Collapse of an Empire: Lessons for Modern Russia* (Washington D.C.: Brookings Institute, 2007); Leon Aron, *Roads to the Temple: Truth, Memory, Ideas, and the Ideals in the Making of the Russian Revolution, 1987–1991* (New Haven, Conn. Yale University Press, 2012); Serhii Plokhy, *The Last Empire: The Final Days of the Soviet Union* (New York: Basic Books, 2014).

43. Jeff Chinn and Robert Kaiser, *Russians as the New Minority: Ethnicity and Nationalism in the Soviet Successor States* (Boulder, Colo.: Westview, 1996), 75.

44. Avis Bohlen, William Burns, Steven Pifer, and John Woolworth, *The Treaty on Intermediate Range Nuclear Forces: History and Lessons Learned* (Washington D.C.: Brookings Institute, 2012).

45. Gaddis, *Strategies of Containment*, 367.

46. Gaidar, *Collapse of Empire*, 162, 190.

47. Sakwa, *Russian Politics and Society*, 22.

48. Christopher Maynard, *Out of the Shadows: George H.W. Bush and the End of the Cold War* (College Station: Texas A & M University Press, 2008), 107.

49. Mikhail Gorbachev, *The August Coup: The Truth and the Lessons* (London: HarperCollins, 1991), 20–21.

50. Christopher Wren, *The End of the Line: The Failure of Communism in the Soviet Union and China* (New York: Simon and Schuster, 1990); Zbigniew Bzezinski, *Grand Failure: The Birth and Death of Communism in the Twentieth Century* (New York: Collier Books, 1990).

51. Both quotes from Ostrovsky, *Invention of Russia*, 14, 15.

52. Ostrovsky, *Invention of Russia*, 16, 17.

53. William Walker, ed., *America in the Cold War: A Documentary History* (Santa Barbara, Calif.: ABC-CLIO Books, 2014), 237.

Chapter 3

1. Myers, *New Tsar*, 17.

2. Dawisha, *Putin's Kleptocracy*, 43.

3. Hill and Gaddy, *Mr. Putin*, 113.

4. Hill and Gaddy, *Mr. Putin*, 114, 118.

5. Gessen, *Man without a Face*, 69.

6. Michael McFaul, *Russia's Unfinished Revolution: Political Change from Gorbachev to Putin* (Ithaca, N.Y.: Cornell University Press, 2001); Stephen Kotkin, *Armageddon Averted: The Soviet Collapse, 1970–2000* (New York: Oxford University Press, 2001); Brown, Archie, and Lilia Shevtsova, eds., *Gorbachev, Yeltsin, and Putin: Political Leadership in Russia's Transition* (Washington D.C.: Carnegie Endowment for International Peace, 2001); Padma Desai, *Conversations on Russia: Reform from Yeltsin to Putin* (New York: Oxford University Press, 2006); David Katz, and Fred Weir, *Russia's Path from Gorbachev to Putin: The Demise of the Soviet System and*

the New Russia (New York: Routledge, 2007); Lilia Shevtsova, *Russia—Lost in Transition: The Yeltsin and Putin Legacies* (Washington D.C.: Carnegie Institute for International Peace, 2007); Richard Sakwa, *Russian Politics and Society* (New York: Routledge, 2008); David Treisman, *The Return: Russia's Journey from Gorbachev to Medvedev* (New York: Free Press, 2011).

7. Stephen Solnick, *Stealing the State: Control and Collapse in Soviet Institutions* (Cambridge, Mass.: Harvard University Press, 1998); Alena Ledeneva, *Russia's Economy of Favors: Blat, Networking, and Informal Exchange* (New York: Cambridge University Press, 1998); Chrystia Freeland, *Sale of the Century: Russia's Wild Ride from Communism to Capitalism* (New York: Crown, 2000); Stephen Cohen, *Failed Crusade: America and the Tragedy of Post-Communist Russia*, New York: W.W. Norton, 2000); Paul Klebnikov, *The Godfather of the Kremlin: The Decline of Russia in the Age of Gangster Capitalism* (New York: Harcourt, 2000); Peter Reddaway, and Dmitri Glinski, *The Tragedy of Russia's Reforms: Market Bolshevism against Democracy* (Washington D.C.: United States Institute of Peace, 2001); Amy Chua, *World on Fire: How Exporting Free Market Democracy Spreads Ethnic Hatred and Global Instability* (New York: Doubleday, 2003); Marshall Goldman, *The Privatization of Russia: Russian Reform Goes Awry* (New York: Routledge, 2004).

8. Dawisha, *Putin's Kleptocracy*, 25.

9. William Thompson, "Putin and the 'Oligarchs': A Two-Sided Commitment Problem," in Alex Pravda, ed., *Leading Russia: Putin in Perspective, Essays in Honor of Archie Brown* (New York: Oxford University Press, 2005), 181.

10. Ostrovsky, *Invention of Russia*, 134–5.

11. Ibid., *Invention of Russia*, 208.

12. Sakwa, *Russian Politics and Society*, 299; "Russia," *World Bank*, website.

13. Dawisha, *Putin's Kleptocracy*, 33.

14. Celestine Bohlen, "U.S. Company to Help Russia Track Billions," *New York Times*, March 3, 1992.

15. Oksana Antonenko, *The New Russian Analytical Centers and Their Role in Political Decisionmaking* (Cambridge, Mass.: Harvard University Press, 1996); Clifford Gaddy, *The Price of the Past: Russia's Struggle with the Legacy of a Militarized Economy* (Washington D.C.: Brookings Institute, 1996); David Remnick, *Resurrection: The Struggle for a New Russia* (New York: Random House, 1997); Herbert Ellison, *Boris Yeltsin and Russia's Democratic Transformation* (Seattle: University of Washington Press, 2006).

16. Ostrovsky, *Invention of Russia*, 151.

17. Sakwa, *Russian Politics and Society*, 50–1.

18. Ibid., 64.

19. Ibid., 170.

20. Carlotta Gall, and Thomas de Waal, Chechnya: Tragedy in the Caucasus (New York: New York University Press, 1998); Anatol Lieven, *Chechnya: The Tombstone of Russian Power* (New Haven, Conn.: Yale University Press, 1998).

21. Gaidar, *Collapse of Empire*, 245.

22. Louis Sell, *Slobodan Milosevic and the Destruction of Yugoslavia* (Durham, N.C.: Duke University Press, 2002).

23. James Goldgeier, and Michael McFaul, *Power and Purpose: U.S. Policy toward Russia after the Cold War* (Washington D.C.: Brookings Institute, 2003), 184.

24. Mankoff, *Russian Foreign Policy*, 156.

25. George Kennan, "A Fateful Error," *New York Times*, February 5, 1997; Thomas Friedman, "Foreign Affairs; Now a Word from X," *New York Times*, May 2, 1998.

26. Sakwa, *Russian Politics and Society*, 173.

27. Conradi, *Who Lost Russia*, 71.

28. Sakwa, *Russian Politics and Society*, 175.

29. Allen Lynch, *How Russia Is Not Ruled: Reflections on Russian Political Development* (New York: Cambridge University Press, 2005), 89–90.

30. Louis Sell, *Slobodan Milosevic and the Destruction of Yugoslavia* (Durham, N.C.: Duke University Press, 2002), 299.

31. Wesley Clark, *Waging Modern War: Bosnia, Kosovo, and the Future of Combat* (New York: Public Affairs, 2001), 394.

32. Dawisha, *Putin's Kleptocracy*, 11, 137.

33. Ibid., 17.

34. Ibid., 122.

35. Myers, *New Tsar*, 108–9.

36. Ibid., 113.

37. Ibid., 114–15.

38. Matthew Evangelista, *The Chechen Wars: Will Russia Go the Way of the Soviet Union?* (Washington D.C.: Brookings Institute, 2002); Andrew Meier, *Chechnya: To the Heart of a Conflict* (New York: W.W. Norton, 2004); Valery Tishkov, *Chechyna: Life in a War-Torn Society* (Berkeley: University of California Press, 2004).

39. Padma Desai, *Conversations on Russia: Reform from Yeltsin to Putin* (New York: Oxford University Press, 2006), 82.

40. Myers, *New Tsar*, 186.

41. John Dunlop, *The Moscow Bombings of September 1999: Examination of Russia Terrorist Attacks at the Onset of Vladimir Putin's Rule* (Stuttgart: Ibidem-Verlag, 2012).

42. Nataliya Gevorkyan, Natalya Timakova, and Andrei Kolesnikov, *First Person: An Astonishing Frank Self-Portrait by Russia's President Vladimir Putin* (New York: Public Affairs, 2000), 143–44.

43. Sergey Kovalev, "Putin's War," *New York Review of Books*, February 10, 2000.

44. Timothy Colton and Michael McFaul, *Popular Choice and Managed Democracy: The Russian Elections of 1999 and 2000* (Washington D.C.: Brookings Institute Press, 2003); Vicki Hesli and William Reisinger, eds., *The 1999–2000 Elections in Russia: Their Impact and Legacy* (New York: Cambridge University Press, 2003).

45. "Putin's Approval Ratings," *Levada Survey*, website.

46. Sakwa, *Russian Politics and Society*, 178.

47. David Johnson, "Note on Election Result's," *Johnson's List*, February 1, 2000; http://www.russialist.org/4082.html.

48. Gessen, *Man Without a Face*, 30.

49. Arkadi Vaksburg, Toxic Politics: The Secret History of the Kremlin's Poison Laboratory (Santa Barbara: ABC-CLIO, 2011), 182.

50. Ostrovsky, *Invention of Russia*, 264.

51. Sakwa, *Russian Politics and Society*, 179.

52. Yevgeniya Borisova, "Baby Boom or Dead Souls?" *Moscow Times*, September 9, 2000.

53. Ostrovsky, *Invention of Russia*, 255.

54. Vladimir Putin, "Inaugural Speech," BBC, May 7, 2000.

Chapter 4

1. Hill and Gaddy, *Mr Putin*, 69–70, 56, 49, 97.
2. Ostrovsky, *Invention of Russia*, 264–5.
3. Kolsto and Blakkisrud, *New Russian Nationalism*, 17.
4. Hill and Gaddy, *Mr Putin*, 130.
5. Ibid., 136.
6. Sergey Medvedev, "Power, Space, and Russian Foreign Policy," Ted Hopf, ed., *Understandings of Russian Foreign Policy* (University Park: Pennsylvania State University Press, 1999), 42.
7. Leon Aron, "Putinology," *The American Interest*, July 30, 2015.
8. Pal Kolsto and Helge Blakkisrud, *The New Russian Nationalism: Imperialism, Ethnicity, and Authoritarianism, 2000–2015* (Edinburgh: University of Edinburgh Press, 2016).
9. Chen, *Return of Ideology*, 82.
10. Sakwa, *Russian Politics and Society*, 197.
11. Ibid., 80.
12. Ibid., 76–8.
13. Peter Pomerantsev, *Nothing Is True and Everyone Is Possible: The Surreal Heart of the New Russia* (New York: Public Affairs, 2014); Marc Bennetts, *Kicking the Kremlin: Russia's New Dissidents and the Battle to Topple Putin* (London: Oneworld, 2014); Garry Kasparov, *Winter Is Coming: Why Vladimir Putin and the Enemies of the Free World Must Be Stopped* (New York: Public Affairs, 2015).
14. "Russia," Amnesty International, 2018, website.
15. Unger, *House of Trump*, 174.
16. Andrew Kramer, "Activist Freed and Arrested in Seconds," *New York Times*, September 25, 2018; Andrew Kramer, "Prosecution of Putin's Top Critic Was Political, European Rights Court Rules," *New York Times*, November 16, 2018.
17. Hill and Gaddy, *Mr Putin*, 167.
18. Gevorkyan, *First Person*, 157.
19. Chen, *Return of Ideology*, 92.
20. Peter Pomerantsky, "The Hidden Author of Putinism: How Vladislav Surkov Invented the New Russia," *The Atlantic Monthly*, November 7, 2014.
21. Craig Unger, *House of Trump, House of Putin* (New York: Dutton, 2018), 75–6.
22. Richard Sakwa, *Putin and the Oligarch: The Khodorkovsky Affair* (London: I.B. Tauris, 2014), xviii; Richard Sakwa, *The Quality of Freedom: Khodorkovsky, Putin, and the Yukos Affair* (New York: Oxford University Press, 2009).
23. Dawisha, *Putin's Kleptocracy*, 335.
24. Paul Klebnikov, *Godfather of the Kremlin: The Decline of Russia in an Age of Gangster Capitalism* (New York: Mariner Books, 2001); David Satter, *Darkness at Dawn: The Rise of the Russian Criminal State* (New Haven, Conn.: Yale University Press, 2003); Joseph Serio, *Investigating the Russian Mafia* (New York: Carolina Academic Press, 2008); Robert Friedman, *Red Mafiya: How the Russian Mob Invaded America* (New York: Little Brown, 2009); Laura Radanko, *The Russian Mafia in America* (Gainesville: University of Florida Press, 2011); Mark Galeotti, *The Vory: Russia's Super Mafia* (New Haven, Conn.: Yale University Press, 2018).
25. Sakwa, *Russian Politics and Society*, 92.
26. Ibid., 84–5, 91.
27. Chen, *Return of Ideology*, 80.
28. Unger, *House of Trump*, 114–17.

29. Robert Cottrell, "Putin's Trap," *New York Review of Books*, December 4, 2003.

30. Peter Truscott, *Kursk: The Gripping Story of Russia's Worst Submarine Disaster* (London: Simon and Schuster, 2004).

31. Zygar, *All the Kremlin's Men*, 27–8.

32. Ibid., *All the Kremlin's Men*, 28–9.

33. Garry Kasparov, *Winter Is Coming: Why Vladimir Putin and the Enemies of the Free World Must Be Stopped* (New York: Public Affairs, 2015), 184.

34. Unger, *House of Trump*, 18.

35. Paul Klebnikov, *Godfather of the Kremlin: The Decline of Russia in an Age of Gangster Capitalism* (New York: Mariner Books, 2001).

36. Anna Politkovskaya, *Putin's Russia: Life in a Failing Democracy* (New York: Metropolitan, 2005).

37. Andrew Higgins and Ivan Nechepurenko, "In Africa, Murder of Journalists Put Spotlight on Kremlin's Reach," *New York Times*, August 8, 2018.

38. Yevgenia Albats, *The State within the State: The KGB and Its Hold on Russia—Past, Present, and Future* (New York: Farrar, Straus, and Giroux, 1994); Amy Knight, *Spies without Cloaks: The KGB's Successors* (Princeton, N.J.: Princeton University Press, 1998); Pete Early, *Comrade J: The Untold Secrets of Russia's Master Spy in America after the End of the Cold War* (New York: G.P. Putnam's Sons, 2007); Yuri Felshtinskiy and Vladimir Pribylovskiy, *The Corporation: Russia and the KGB in the Age of President Putin* (New York: Encounter Books, 2008); Edward Lucas, *Deception: The Untold Story of East-West Espionage Today* (London: Walker Books, 2012).

39. Andrew Higgins and Ivan Nechepurenko, "In Africa, Murder of Journalists Put Spotlight on Kremlin's Reach," *New York Times*, August 8, 2018.

40. Alexander Litvinenko and Yuri Felshtinsky, *Blowing Up the Kremlin: The Secret Plan to Bring Back KGB Terror* (New York: Encounter Books, 2007); Yuri Felshtinsky and Vladimir Pribylovsky, *The Age of Assassins: The Rise and Rise of Vladimir Putin* (London: Gibson Square, 2008); Boris Volodarsky, *The KGB's Poison Factory: From Lenin to Litvinenko* (Minneapolis: Zenith Press, 2009); Arkadi Vaksburg, *Toxic Politics: The Secret History of the Kremlin's Poison Laboratory* (Santa Barbara, Calif.: ABC-CLIO, 2011).

41. Michael Schwirtz and Ellen Barry, "A Turncoat Spy Went Free. Putin Never Forgave Him," *New York Times*, September 10, 2018.

42. Alex Goldfarb with Marina Litvinenko, *Death of a Dissident: The Poisoning of Alexander Litvinenko and the Return of the KGB* (New York: Free Press, 2007); Sixsmith, Martin, *The Litvinenko File: The Life and Death of a Russian Spy* (New York: St. Martin's Press, 2007); Alan Cowell, *The Terminal Spy: The Life and Death of Alexander Litvinenko, A True Story of Espionage, Betrayal, and Murder* (London: Doubleday, 2008).

43. Goldfarb and Litvinenko, *Death of a Dissident*, 330.

44. Mark Urban, *The Skripal Files: The Life and Near Death of a Russian Spy* (New York: Henry Holt, 2018).

45. Ellen Berry, Michael Schwirtz, and Eric Schmitt, "U.K. Poisoning Investigation Turns to Russian Agency in Mueller Indictments," *New York Times*, July 16, 2018; Michael Schwirtz and Ellen Barry, "A Turncoat Spy Went Free. Putin Never Forgave Him," *New York Times*, September 10, 2018.

46. Lucie Beraud-Sudreau and Douglas Barrie, "Russia's Defense Spending: The Impact of Economic Contraction," *IISS*, March 6, 2017.

47. Mankoff, *Russian Foreign Policy*, 42, 44.
48. "Military Expenditure by Country, in Constant 2016 US\$," SIPRI 2018.
49. Ibid.
50. Douglas Schoen and Melic Kaylan, *The Russia-China Axis: The New Cold War and America's Crisis of Leadership* (New York: Encounter Books, 2014), 34.
51. "Status of World Nuclear Forces," *Federation of American Scientists*, Website.
52. "Military Spending and Armaments," SIPRI, website.
53. Ibid.
54. "Russia Military Strength," "United States Military Strength," *Global Firepower*, website.
55. Thierry Gongora and Harold von Riekhoff, *Toward a Revolution in Military Affairs?: Defense and Security at the Dawn of the Twenty-First Century* (New York: Praeger, 2000); Colin Gray, *Recognizing and Understanding Revolutionary Change in Warfare: The Sovereignty of Context* (Carlisle, Penn.: Strategic Studies Institute, 2006); Steve Metz and James Klevitt, *The Revolution in Military Affairs and Conflict Short of War* (Washington D.C.: Strategic Studies Institute, 2013); Emily Goldman, *Information and Revolutions in Military Affairs* (New York: Routledge, 2015).
56. Mark Galeotti, *The Modern Russian Army, 1992–2016* (London: Osprey Books, 2017); Bettina Renz, *Russia's Military Revival* (New York: Polity, 2018); Rene De La Pedraja, *The Russian Military Resurgence: Post-Soviet Decline and Rebuilding, 1992–2018* (Jefferson, N.C.: McFarland and Company, 2018).
57. Zoltan Barany, "Defense Reform, Russian-Style: Obstacles, Options, Opposition," *Contemporary Politics*, vol. 11, no. 2 (March 2005), 33–51; Tor Bukkvoli, "Iron Cannot Fight: The Role of Technology in Current Russian Military Theory," *Journal of Strategic Studies*, vol. 34, no. 5 (2011), 681–706; Christopher Chivvis, "Hybrid War: Russian Contemporary Political Warfare," Bulletin of the Atomic Scientists, vol. 73, no. 5 (2017), 316–21; Timothy Thomas, "The Evolving Nature of Russia's Way of War," *Military Review*, July-August 2017.
58. Kenneth Jensen, ed., *The Origins of the Cold War: Novikov, Kennan, and Roberts 'Long Telegrams' of 1946* (Washington D.C.: United States Institute of Peace Pres, 1995), 27–8.
59. Andrew Higgins, "Mixed Feelings in Russia about a Man They loved to Hate," *New York Times*, August 29, 2018.
60. Greg Miller, *The Apprentice: Trump, Russia, and the Subversion of American Democracy* (New York: Custom House, 2018), 177.

Chapter 5

1. Marshall Goldman, *The Privatization of Russia: Russian Reform Goes Awry* (New York: Routledge, 2004); Anders Aslund, *Russia's Capitalist Revolution* (Washington D.C.: Petersen Institute for International Economics 2007); Pekka Sutela, *The Political Economy of Putin's Russia* (New York: Routledge, 2012).
2. Gerald Easter, "Building Fiscal Capacity," in Timothy Colton and Stephen Holmes, eds., *The State After Communism: Governance in the New Russia* (New York: Rowman and Littlefield, 2006), 26; Hill and Gaddy, *Mr. Putin*, 86, 134.
3. Sakwa, *Russian Politics and Society*, 299, "Russia," *World Bank*, website.
4. Gerald Easter, "Building Fiscal Capacity," in Timothy Colton and Stephen Holmes, eds., *The State After Communism: Governance in the New Russia* (New York: Rowman and Littlefield, 2006), 32.

5. Ibid., 43–4.
6. Linda Cook, "State Capacity and Pension Provision," Timothy Colton and Stephen Holmes, eds., *The State after Communism: Governance in the New Russia* (New York: Rowman and Littlefield, 2006), 128–9.
7. "Russia Military Strength," "United States Military Strength," *Global Firepower*, website.
8. Brendan Conway, "Grant on Gazprom: 'Worst Managed Company on the Planet' Is a Buy," *Barron's*, May 5, 2014.
9. Mankoff, *Russian Foreign Policy*, 46.
10. Sakwa, *Russian Politics and Society*, 181.
11. Myers, *New Tsar*, 247.
12. Boris Berezovsky, Elena Bonner, Vladimir Bukovsky, Ruslan Khasbulatov, and Ivan Rybkin, "Seven Questions to President George Bush about his Friend Vladimir Putin," *New York Times*, September 23, 2003.
13. Myers, *New Tsar*, 251.
14. John Dunlop, *The 2002 Dubrovka and 2004 Breslan Hostage Crises: A Critique of Russian Counter-Terrorism* (Stuttgart: Ibidem-Verlag, 2006).
15. Zygar, *All the Kremlin's Men*, 318, 22.
16. Myers, *New Tsar*, 259–60.
17. Marie Mendras, *Russian Politics: The Paradox of a Weak State* (New York: Columbia University Press, 2012), 185.
18. Anders Aslund and Michael McFaul, eds., *Revolution in Orange: The Origins of Ukraine's Democratic Breakthrough* (Washington D.C.: Carnegie Institute of Peace, 2006); Anders Aslund, *How Ukraine Became a Market Economy and Democracy* (Washington D.C.: Peter G. Peterson Institute for International Economics, 2009); Marvin Kalb, *Imperial Gamble: Putin, Ukraine, and the New Cold War* (Washington D.C.: Brookings Institute, 2015).
19. Aslund, *How Ukraine Became a Market Economy*, 180.
20. Andrew Wilson, *Ukraine's Orange Revolution* (New Haven, Conn.: Yale University Press, 2005).
21. "Russian Legislative Election, 2007," *Wikipedia*, website.
22. Nikolai and Marina Svanidze, *Medvedev* (St. Petersburg: Amfora, 2008); Richard Sakwa, *The Crisis of Russian Democracy: The Dual State, Factionalism and the Medvedev Succession* (New York: Cambridge University Press, 2011); Joseph Black, *The Russian Presidency of Dmitri Medvedev, 2008–2012: The Next Step Forward or Merely Time Out?* (New York: Routledge, 2014).
23. Mankoff, *Russian Foreign Policy*, 15, 17.
24. Svante Cornell and Frederick Starr, eds., *The Guns of August 2008: Russia's War in Georgia,* (Armonk, N.Y.: M.E. Sharpe, 2009); Ronald Asmus, *A Little War that Shook the World, Georgia, Russia, and the Future of the West* (New York: Palgrave Macmillan, 2010); Elena Yost, *The Russia-Georgia War of 2008: Media Content and Public Opinion* (Frankfort: Akademikerverlag, 2014).
25. "Georgia," CIA World Fact Book, cia.gov.
26. Lincoln Mitchell, *Uncertain Future: U.S. Foreign Policy and Georgia's Rose Revolution* (Philadelphia: University of Pennsylvania Press, 2008).
27. Rice, *No Higher Honor*, 686.
28. Nalbandov, *Not By Bread Alone*, 255.
29. Myers, *New Tsar*, 352.

30. Hill and Gaddy, *Mr Putin*, 87; Myers, *New Tsar*, 355–56 Anders Aslund, Sergei Guriev, and Andrew Kuchins, eds., *Russian after the Global Economic Crisis* (Washington D.C.: Peter G. Peterson Institute for International Economics, 2010).
31. Myers, *New Tsar*, 382.
32. Ibid.
33. Zygar, *All the Kremlin's Men*, 204–5.
34. Ibid., 210.
35. "Russia's 2011 Duma Election," *Wikipedia*, website.
36. Nalbandov, *Not By Bread Alone*, 66.
37. Masha Gessen, *Words Will Break Cement: The Passion of Pussy Riot* (New York: Riverhead Books, 2014).
38. Greg Miller, *The Apprentice: Trump, Russia, and the Subversion of American Democracy* (New York: Customs House, 2018), 35–6.
39. Myers, *New Tsar*, 411–12.
40. Nalbandov, *Not By Bread Alone*, 102.
41. Robert Orttung, *Putin's Olympics: The Sochi Games and the Evolution of Russia* (New York: Routledge, 2017).
42. Andrew Wilson, *Ukraine Crisis: What It Means for the West* (New Haven, Conn.: Yale University Press, 2014); Marvin Kalb, *Imperial Gamble: Putin, Ukraine, and the New Cold War* (Washington D.C.: Brookings Institute, 2015).
43. Zygar, *All the Kremlin's Men*, 258.
44. Ibid., 260.
45. Conradi, *Who Lost Russia?*, 254.
46. Ibid., 262–3.
47. Myers, *New Tsar*, 462.
48. Hill and Gaddy, *Mr. Putin*, 283, 299.
49. Nalbandov, *Not By Bread Alone*, 453.
50. Michael Isikoff and David Corn, *Russian Roulette: The Inside Story of Putin's War on America and the Election of Donald Trump* (New York: Hachette Group, 2018), 49.
51. Kalb, *Imperial Gamble*, 29.
52. Conradi, *Who Lost Russia?*, 274–5.
53. Both quotes from Nalbandov, *Not By Bread Alone*, 73.
54. "Russia's 2016 Duma Election," *Wikipedia*, website.

Chapter 6

1. John Rhodehamel, ed., *George Washington: Writings* (New York: Library of America, 1997), 988.
2. Nalbandov, *Not By Bread Alone*, 106.
3. Angela Stent, *The Limits of Partnership: U.S.-Russia Relations in the Twenty-First Century* (Princeton, N.J.: Princeton University Press, 2014).
4. Myers, *New Tsar*, 182.
5. Conradi, *Who Lost Russia?* 121.
6. Strobe Talbott, *The Russian Hand: A Memoir of Presidential Diplomacy* (New York: Random House, 2002), 8.
7. Conradi, *Who Lost Russia?*, 133.
8. Ibid., 134.
9. James Dao, "Rumsfeld Calls on Europe to Rethink Arms Control," *New York Times*, June 11, 2001.

10. Conradi, *Who Lost Russia?*, 136–7.
11. George Bush, *Decision Points* (New York: Crown, 2011), 196.
12. Condoleezza Rice, *No Higher Honor: A Memoir of My Years in Washington* (New York: Random House, 2011), 63.
13. Patrick Tyler, "Putin, Sizing Up Bush, Says 'the Retinue makes the king,'" *New York Times*, September 3, 2001.
14. Ibid.
15. Angela Stent, *The Limits of Partnership: U.S.-Russian Relations in the Twenty-First Century* (Princeton, N.J.: Princeton University Press, 2014), 62–3; Conradi, *Who Lost Russia?*, 140–1.
16. Myers, *New Tsar*, 204.
17. "In 2 Presidents' Words: The 'New Relationship' Moves to Antiterrorism," *New York Times*, November 14, 2001.
18. Karen Hughes, *Ten Minutes from Normal* (New York: Viking, 2004), 284–5.
19. David Sanger, "Bush and Putin Agree to Reduce Stockpile of Nuclear Warheads," *New York Times*, November 14, 2001.
20. Elaine Sciolino, "New Allies: One Trusts, the Other's Not So Sure," *New York Times*, November 14, 2001.
21. Colum Lynch, "Russia Emerges as Top Customer for Iraqi Exports," *International Herald Tribune*, January 17, 2002; Sabrina Tavernise, "Oil Prize, Past and Present, Ties Russia to Iraq," *New York Times*, October 16, 2002.
22. Steven Myers and Michael Wines, "Russia's Overtures to 'Axis of Evil' Nations Strain Ties with U.S.," *New York Times*, September 1, 2002.
23. "From Bush, 'Formal Notice' of End of Pact," *New York Times*, December 14, 2001.
24. Michael Wines, "Facing Pact's End, Putin Decides to Grimace and Bear It," *New York Times*, December 14, 2001; Michael Wines, "Putin Sees Continued Alliance Despite the End of the ABM Pact," *New York Times*, December 18, 2001.
25. David Sanger, "U.S. Sees 'New Era'" *New York Times*, May 24, 2002; "A Treaty to 'Reduce and Limit" Warheads and a Declaration of a New Relationship," *New York Times*, May 25, 2002.
26. Patrick Tyler, "Bush and Putin to Sign Pact to Cut Nuclear Warheads; Weapons to be Stockpiled," *New York Times*, May 14, 2002; James Dao, "Senators Question Powell on Arms-Cut Treaty," *New York Times*, July 9, 2002.
27. Steven Myers, "Putin Says New Missile Systems Will Give Russia a Nuclear Edge," *New York Times*, November 18, 2004.
28. William Nester, *Haunted Victory: The American Crusade to Destroy Saddam and Impose Democracy on Iraq* (Washington D.C.: Potomac Books, 2012).
29. "Bush and Putin Stress Strong Ties," *International Herald Tribune*, May 23, 2003.
30. Hall Gardner, *NATO Expansion and the U.S. Strategy in Asia: Surmounting the Global Crisis* (New York: Palgrave Macmillan, 2013).
31. Hill and Gaddy, *Mr Putin*, 307.
32. Ibid., 308.
33. Conradi, *Who Lost Russia?*, 194.
34. Kalb, *Imperial Gamble*, 12.
35. Max Fisher, "The Putin Slouch," *Washington Post*, August 9, 2013.
36. Clinton, *Hard Choices*, 212.
37. Susan Nichols, *Vladimir Putin: Russia's Prime Minister and President* (New York: Enslow Publishing, 2019), 91.

38. Bill Browder, *Red Notice: A True Story of High Finance, Murder, and One Man's Fight for Justice* (New York: Simon and Schuster, 2015).
39. Kalb, *Imperial Gamble*, 11.
40. Steven Erlanger, Julie Hirschfield Davis, and Stephen Castle, "NATO Plans a Special Force to Reassure Eastern Europe and Deter Russia," *New York Times*, September 5, 2014.
41. Conradi, *Who Lost Russia?*, 302.
42. Scott Wilson, "Obama Dismisses Russia as 'Regional Power,' Acting out of Weakness," *Washington Post*, March 25, 2014.
43. David Leip, *2016 Election*, Atlas of U.S. Presidential Elections, website.
44. For the 2015 election, see: Larry Sabato, Kyle Kondik, and Geoffrey Shelley, eds., *Trumped: The 2016 Election that Broke All the Rules* (Lanham, Maryland: Rowman and Littlefield, 2017): Brian Schaffner and John Clark, eds., *Making Sense of the 2016 Election* (Washington D.C.: Congressional Quarterly Press, 2017). For biographies on Trump, see: Gwenda Blair, *The Trumps: Three Generations of Builders and a Presidential Candidate* (New York: Simon and Schuster, 2000); Tim O'Brien, *Trump Nation: The Art of Being the Donald* (New York: Hachette, 2016); Wayne Barrett, *The Greatest Show on Earth: The Deals, the Downfall, the Reinvention* (New York: Regan Arts, 2016); David Kay Johnson, *The Making of Donald Trump* (New York: Melville House, 2016); Michael Kranish and Marc Fisher, *Trump Revealed: The Definitive Biography of the 45th President* (New York: Scribner's, 2017).
45. Nicholas Confessore and Karen Yourish, "$2 Billion Worth of Free Media for Donald Trump," *New York Times*, March 15. 2016.
46. Isikoff and Corn, *Russian Roulette*, 2.
47. For Trump and Russia, see: Michael Isikoff and David Corn, *Russian Roulette: The Inside Story of Putin's War on America and the Election of Donald Trump* (New York: Hachette Group, 2018); Greg Miller, *The Apprentice: Trump, Russia, and the Subversion of American Democracy* (New York: Custom House, 2018); Seth Abramson, *Proof of Collusion: How Trump Betrayed America* (New York: Simon and Schuster, 2018); Malcom Nance and Rob Reisner, *The Plot to Destroy America: How Putin and His Spies Are Undermining America and Dismantling the West* (New York: Hachette, 2018); Stephen Cohen, *War with Russia?: From Putin and Ukraine to Trump and Russiangate* (New York: Hot Books, 2018); Seth Hettena, *Trump/Russia: A Definitive History* (New York: Melville House, 2018); Craig Unger, *House of Trump, House of Putin: The Untold Story of Donald Trump and the Russian Mafia* (New York: Dutton, 2018).
48. Conradi, *Who Lost Russia?*, 279.
49. Scott Shane and Mark Mazzetti, "The Plot to Subvert an Election," *New York Times*, September 20, 2018; Scott Shane and Sheera Frenkel, "Russian Election Effort focused on Influencing African-American Vote," *New York Times*, December 18, 2018.
50. David Sanger, Jim Rutenberg, and Eric Lipton, "Following the Tentacles of Guccifer 2.0 to Russia," *New York Times*, July 16, 2018.
51. Nichols Fandos and Michael Wines, "Russia Tried to Crack Voting Systems in at Least 18 States, Senators Say," *New York Times*, May 9, 2018.
52. Ostrovsky, *Invention of Russia*, x.
53. Isikoff and Corn, *Russian Roulette*, 55.

54. Company Intelligence Report, 2016, 80, 86, 94, 95, 97, 100, 102, 105, 111, 112, 113, 135, *Buzzfeed*, website; Scott Shane and Mark Mazzetti, "The Plot to Subvert an Election," *New York Times*, September 20, 2018.

55. Miller, *Apprentice*, 346.

56. For the most comprehensive account, see: Craig Unger, *House of Trump, House of Putin: The Untold Story of Donald Trump and the Russian Mafia* (New York: Dutton House, 2018).

57. Unger, *House of Trump*, 2–3.

58. Thomas Frank, "Secret Money: How Trump Made Millions Selling Condos to Unknown Buyers," *Buzzfeed*, January 12, 2018, website.

59. Miller, *Apprentice*, 101–2.

60. Unger, *House of Trump*, 38–9, 42–3, 53–4.

61. Ibid., 54.

62. Ibid., 51.

63. Isikoff and Corn, *Russian Roulette*, 221.

64. Ibid., *Russian Roulette*, 104–9.

65. Miller, *Apprentice*, 60.

66. Ibid., *Apprentice*, 82.

67. Isikoff and Corn, *Russian Roulette*, 226.

68. Unger, *House of Trump*, 180–90.

69. Miller, *Apprentice*, 84.

70. Woodward, *Fear*, 20–1.

71. Sharon LaFraniere, Matthew Rosenberg, and Adam Goldman, "Maria Butina Loved Guns, Trump, and Russia. It Was a Cover, Prosecutors Say," *New York Times*, July 17, 2018.

72. Matt Apuzzo, Katie Benner, and Sharon LaFraniere, "Russian Made Secret Push to Sway Policy, Charges Say," *New York Times*, July 17, 2018; Sharon LaFraniere, Matthew Rosenberg, Adam Goldman, "Prosecutors Say Russian Natives 3 Passions Were All a Ruse," *New York Times*, July 18, 2018; Matthew Rosenberg, Mike McIntire, Michael LaForgia, Andrew Kramer, and Elizabeth Dias, "Russian Sought Potent Friends beyond N.R.A.," *New York Times*, August 5, 2018.

73. Isikoff and Corn, *Russian Roulette*, 110–11.

74. Ibid., 111.

75. Ibid., 117–18.

76. Miller, *Apprentice*, 110–11.

77. Ibid., 75–6, 88.

78. Scott Shane and Mark Mazzetti, "The Plot to Subvert an Election," *New York Times*, September 20, 2018.

79. Nancy LeTournau, "The WikiLeaks-Russia Connection," *Washington Monthly*, January 25, 2019.

80. Michael Schmitt, "'Russia, if You're Listening…' Trump Said. Perhaps It was," *New York Times*, July 14, 2018; Marc Mazzetti and Katie Benner, "12 Russian Agents Charged in Drive to Upset '16 Vote," *New York Times*, July 14, 2018.

81. Conradi, *Who Lost Russia?*, 316.

82. Isikoff and Corn, *Russian Roulette*, 230–1.

83. Conradi, *Who Lost Russia?*, 326–7.

84. Isikoff and Corn, *Russian Roulette*, 213.

85. Ellen Nakashima, "Russia Government Hackers Penetrated DNC, Stole Opposition Research on Trump," *Washington Post*, June 14, 2016; Mike Morell,

"I Ran the CIA-Now I'm Endorsing Hillary Clinton," *New York Times*, August 5, 2016.

86. Isikoff and Corn, *Russian Roulette*, 224–5, 213–217.

87. Ibid., 251.

88. Terry Gross, "Russia's Connection to Brexit Is 'Opaque and Complicated,' Journalist Says," NPR, March 21, 2019.

89. Miller, *Apprentice*, 209–12.

90. Ibid., 215.

91. Ibid., 221–2, 254.

92. *Assessing Russian Activities and Intentions in the Recent US Election*, Intelligence Community Assessment, January 6, 2017, Directorate of National Intelligence, ICA 2017–01D.

93. James Comey, *A Higher Loyalty: Truth, Lies, and Leadership* (New York: Flatiron Books, 2018), 221.

94. David Sanger and Matthew Rosenberg, "From Start, Trump Has Muddied Clear Message: Putin Interfered," *New York Times*, July 19, 2018; Isikoff and Corn, *Russian Roulette*, 293.

95. Ronald Kessler, *Inside the Trump White House* (New York: Gallery Books, 2017); Michael Wolff, *Fire and Fury: Inside the Trump White House* (New York: Henry Holt, 2018); Bob Woodward, *Fear: Trump in the White House* (New York: Simon and Schuster, 2018).

96. David Barstow, Susan Craig, and Russ Buettner, "Trump Took Part in Suspect Schemes to Evade Tax Bills," *New York Times*, October 3, 2018.

97. Glenn Kessler, Salvador Rizzo, and Meg Kelly, "President Trump made 8,159 false or misleading claims in his first two years," Fact Checker, *Washington Post*, January 21, 2019.

98. Unger, *House of Trump*, 24.

99. Donald Trump and Tony Schwartz, *Trump: Art of the Deal* (New York: Ballantine Books, 2015).

100. Mark Landler, "In Russian Talks, Experts Fear U.S. Will Give Up Too Much," *New York Times*, June 29, 2018.

101. Ibid.

102. Woodward, *Fear*, 207.

103. Ibid., 301.

104. Nicholas Fandos and Maggie Haberman, "White House Whistle-Blower Tells Congress of Irregularities in Security Clearances," *New York Times*, April 1, 2019.

105. Woodward, *Fear*, 225, 263.

106. Ibid., xix.

107. Eric Schmitt, David Sanger, and Maggie Haberman, "Talks of Securing Election Included a Warning: Don't Tell Trump," *New York Times*, April 25, 2019.

108. Miller, *Apprentice*, 245–6, 262–5, 271, 277–9.

109. James Comey, *A Higher Loyalty: Truth, Lies, and Leadership* (New York: Flatiron Books, 2018).

110. James Comey, "How Trump Co-opts Leaders Like Barr," *New York Times*, May 2, 2019.

111. Miller, *Apprentice*, 285, 327–8.

112. Noah Weiland, Emily Cochrane, and Troy Griggs, "Mueller's Team: The Players and the Playbook," *New York Times*, December 2, 2018.

113. Marc Mazzetti and Katie Benner, "12 Russian Agents Charged in Drive to Upset '16 Vote," *New York Times*, July 14, 2018.

114. Sharon LaFraniere and Adam Goldman, "Maria Butina, Suspected Secret Agent, Used Sex in Covert Plan, Prosecutors Say," New York Times, July 18, 2018.

115. Adam Goldman, "U.S. Says Russians Led Online Drive to Tilt Midterms," *New York Times*, October 10, 2018.

116. Kenneth Vogel, Sharon Lafraniere, and Adam Goldman, "Lobbyist Guilty Over 4 Tickets for Inaugural," *New York Times*, September 1, 2018; Sharon Lafraniere, "Undeclared Lobbyist Is Given Probation," *New York Times*, April 13, 2019.

117. Sharon LaFraniere, "To Woo Trump, a Raft of Russian Suitors," *New York Times*, April 19, 2019.

118. Adam Goldman and Sharon LaFraniere, "New Filing Details Manafort's Lies in Several Contacts," *New York Times*, December 9, 2019; Sharon LaFraniere, "Manafort Given Less than 4 Years, Faced Long Term," *New York Times*, March 8, 2019.

119. Sharon Lafraniere, "Sentence Adds Time in Prison for Manafort," *New York Times*, March 14, 2019; William Rashbaum, "New York Accuses Manafort of 16 Crimes Not Eligible for Pardon," *New York Times*, March 14, 2019.

120. Unger, *House of Trump*, 165.

121. Mike McIntire, Megan Twohey, and Mark Mazzetti, "Cohen Plea Bares Russian Power Bid Deep in Trump's Run: Ex-Spymaster, Felon, Lawyer: Chasing a Project," *New York Times*, November 30, 2018; Mark Mazzetti, Benjamin Webster, Maggie Haberman, "Cohen Plea Bares Russian Power Bid Deep in Trump's Run: Presidential Hopeful Sought Closer Ties and a Deal, Too," *New York Times*, November 30, 2018; Sharon LaFraniere, Benjamin Weiser, and Maggie Haberman, "Hush Money Scheme—Prison Is Sought for Former Fixer," New York Times, December 8, 2018.

122. Benjamin Weiser and William Rashbaum, "Cohen Gets 3 Years in Prison for 'Smorgasbord of Fraudulent Conduct,'" *New York Times*, December 13, 2018.

123. "Full Transcript: Michael Cohen's Opening Statement to Congress," *New York Times*, February 27, 2019.

124. Sharon LaFraniere and Adam Goldman, "'You sold your country out': Judge Rebukes Flynn, Then Delays Sentencing," *New York Times*, December 18, 2018.

125. Sharon LaFraniere, "Witness in Mueller Inquiry Expects Charges of Lying," *New York Times*, November 13, 2018.

126. Mark Mazzetti, Eileen Sullivan, and Maggie Haberman, "Indicting Roger Stone, Mueller Show Link Between Trump Campaign and WikiLeaks, *New York Times*, January 25, 2019.

127. Charlie Savage, Adam Goldman, and Eileen Sullivan, "Britain Arrests Assange, Ending 7–Year Standoff," *New York Times*, April 12, 2019.

128. Nicholas Fandos, "Democrats Reveal Vast Scope of Trump Inquiry," *New York Times*, March 3, 2019; Nicholas Fandos, "House Investigations Have Begun Digging into President's World," *New York Times*, March 8, 2019.

129. Melissa Gomez, "Giuliani Says 'Truth Isn't Truth' in Defense of Trump's Legal Strategy," *New York Times*, August 19, 2018; Emily Cochrane and Catie Edmonson, "Giuliani Says 'There Is Nothing Wrong with Taking Money from Russians,'" *New York Times*, April 21, 2019.

130. Kit Gillet, "Giuliani Criticizes a Crackdown on Corruption in Romania," *New York Times*, August 30, 2018.

131. Woodward, *Fear*, 210–16.

132. Michael Shear and Katie Benner, "In a Reversal, Trump Pulls Back from Declassifying Russia Documents," *New York Times*, September 22, 2018.

133. Peter Baker, Michael Schmid, and Maggie Haberman, "Citing Recusal, Trump Says He Wouldn't Have Hired Sessions," *New York Times*, July 19, 2017.

134. Adam Goldman, Michael Shear, and Mitch Smith, "Trump Finds Attack Dog in Fight against Mueller," *New York Times*, November 10, 2018.

135. Eileen Sullivan, "Takeaways from The Times's Investigation into Trump's War on the Inquiries Around Him," *New York Times*, February 19, 2019.

136. "Mark Mazzetti, Maggie Haberman, Nicholas Fandos, and Michael Schmitt, "Intimidation, Pressure, and Humiliation: Inside Trump's Two-Year War on the Investigations Encircling Him," *New York Times*, February 19, 2019.

137. The best published version to date comes with an introduction by *Washington Post* reporters Rosalind Helderman and Matt Zapotosky: *The Mueller Report, presented with Materials by the Washington Post* (New York: Scribner, 2019).

138. Nicholas Fandos, Mark Schmidt, and Mark Mazzetti, "Barr Understated Mueller Findings, Some on Team Say," *New York Times*, April 5, 2019; Mark Mazzetti, "Mueller at Odds with Barr's View of Investigation," *New York Times*, May 1, 2019.

139. Robert Mueller, *Report on the Investigation into Russian Interference into the 2016 Presidential Election*, 2 vols. (Washington D.C.: Government Printing Office, March 2019), 1:5, 1:9, 1:173, 2:8.

140. John Cassidy, "Hundreds of Former Prosecutors Would Indict Donald Trump," *The New Yorker*, May 7, 2019.

141. Sharon LaFraniere, "Mueller, First Comments on Russian Inquiry Refuses to Clear Trump," *New York Times*, May 30, 2019.

142. Larry Buchannan and Karen Yourish, "The Mueller Report Is Highly Anticipated: Here's What We Already Know," *New York Times*, March 20, 2019; Mark Mazzetti and Katie Benner, "Mueller Finds No Trump-Russia Conspiracy," *New York Times*, March 25, 2019; Karen Yourish and Larry Buchannan, "Mueller Report Shows Depth of Connections between Campaign and the Russians," *New York Times*, April 19, 2019; "Charged in the Investigation, Connections to the President," *New York Times*, April 19, 2019.

143. Isikoff and Corn, *Russian Roulette*, 81.

144. Mark Landler, "In Russian Talks, Experts Fear U.S. Will Give Up Too Much," *New York Times*, June 29, 2018.

145. Mark Mazzetti, "Defense of Trump Shifts as Russia Evidence Mounts," *New York Times*, July 31, 2018.

146. Peter Baker, "Trump Says He'd Accept Foreign Dirt on a Rival," *New York Times*, June 13, 2019.

147. Benjamin Weiser and William Rashbaum, "Cohen Gets 3 Years in Prison for 'Smorgasbord of Fraudulent Conduct,'" *New York Times*, December 13, 2018; Mike McIntire, Charlie Savage, and Jim Rutenberg, "Tabloid Publisher's Deal in Hush-Money Inquire Adds to Trump's Danger," *New York Times*, December 13, 2018.

148. "Trump Has Publicly Attacked the Russia Investigation More than 1,100 Times," *New York Times*, February 19, 2019; Mark Mazzetti, Maggie Haberman, Nicholas Fandos, and Michael Schmitt, "Intimidation, Pressure, and Humiliation: Inside

Trump's Two-Year War on the Investigations Encircling Him," *New York Times*, February 19, 2019.

149. Woodward, *Fear*, 68.

150. Miller, *Apprentice*, 341–2.

151. Woodward, *Fear*, 65.

152. Julian Barnes, Katie Benner, Adam Goldman, and Michael Schmidt, "C.I.A. Scrutinized by Justice Dept. over Russia Case," *New York Times*, June 13, 2019.

153. Eileen Sullivan, "Trump Calls Intelligence Officials 'Naïve' After They Contradict Him," *New York Times*, January 30, 2019.

154. Emily Cochrane, "'That's My Kind of Guy,' Trump Says of Representative Lawmaker who Body-Slammed a Reporter," *New York Times*, October 19, 2018.

155. Woodward, *Fear*, 219.

156. Ibid., 276.

157. Ibid., *Fear*, 264.

158. Catherine Porter, "'That Relationship Is Gone,' After U.S.-Canada NAFTA Talks," *New York Times*, October 4, 2018.

159. Cathleen Camino-Isaacs and Jeffrey Scott, eds., *The Trans-Pacific Partnership: An Assessment* (Washington D.C.: Peterson Institute for International Economics, 2016); Timothy Barnes, *A Naked View of the Trans-Pacific Partnership* (Indianapolis: Dog Ear Press, 2016).

160. Jack Ewing, "Europe Cultivates New Partners as Old Ally Loosens Trade Ties," *New York Times*, July 18, 2018; Steven Erlanger and Jane Perlez, "'Trump vs. the World': Europe and Asia Rush to Bolster Global Order," *New York Times*, July 19, 2018.

161. Carl Roper, *Made in China: Trade Secrets, Theft, Industrial Espionage, and the China Threat* (New York: Taylor Francis, 2015); Steven Mosher, *Bully of Asia: Why China's Dream is the New Threat to World Order* (Washington D.C.: Regnery, 2017); Kai Fu Lee, *AI Superpowers: China, Silicon Valley, and the New World Order* (New York: Houghton Mifflin, 2018).

162. Woodward, *Fear*, 273.

163. Mark Landler, "Pence Sees China as Trying to Oust Trump," *New York Times*, October 4, 2018.

164. Woodward, *Fear*, xvii-xviii.

165. Ibid., xviii-xxii, 305–8.

166. Ibid., *Fear*, 280–1, 300.

167. Gardiner Harris and Choe Sang-Hun, "North Koreans Say U.S. Position is 'Gangster-like,'" *New York Times*, July 8, 2018.

168. Maggie Haberman, "When a President Believes He Is Entitled to His Own Facts," *New York Times*, October 19, 2018.

169. Reuters, "Trump Publicly Opposes Using CIA Informants against North Korea's Kim," *New York Times*, June 11, 2019.

170. Julie Hirshfeld Davis, "Spend or Else, President Warns NATO Countries," New York Times, July 3, 2018.

171. Marc Santora, "To the Baltic Nations with Russia Ties, NATO Is No Abstraction," *New York Times*, July 11, 2018; Steven Erlanger, Julie Hirschfield Davis, and Katie Rogers, "NATO Survives Trump's Disruption, but the Turmoil Leaves Scars," *New York Times*, July 13, 2018; Palko Karasz, "Experts Assess Barbs by Trump on Germany," *New York Times*, July 12, 2018; Steven Erlanger and Julie Hirschfield

Davis, "Merkel Replies to U.S. Attacks with Caution," *New York Times*, July 12, 2018.

172. Helene Cooper and Julian Barnes, "Rush to Protect NATO Accord against Trump," *New York Times*, August 10, 2018.

173. Eric Schmitt, "U.S. Military Is Training to Counter Russian Might," *New York Times*, June 30, 2018.

174. Steven Erlanger, Julie Hirschfield Davis, and Katie Rogers, "NATO Survives Trump's Disruption, but the Turmoil Leaves Scars," *New York Times*, July 13, 2018.

175. Andrew Higgins, "Russian War Games Plan Includes a Role for China," *New York Times*, August 29, 2018.

176. Julian Barnes and Helene Cooper, "Trump Discussed Pulling U.S. from NATO, Aides Say Amid New Concerns over Russia," *New York Times*, January 14, 2019.

177. Steven Erlanger, "In Trump's Chaos, Europe Sees a Strategy: Divide and Conquer," *New York Times*, July 14, 2016.

178. Julian Barnes, "NATO Works to Woo U.S. Conservatives," *New York Times*, September 15, 2018.

179. Stephen Castle and Julie Hirschfield Davis, "Trump Undercuts Leader of Britain after NATO Clash," *New York Times*, July 13, 2018; Julie Hirschfeld Davis, "Trump Tries to Mend Fences on Day 2 in Britain," *New York Times*, July 14, 2018; Stephen Castle, "May Says Trump Told Her to 'Sue the E.U.'" New York Times, July 16, 2018.

180. Avis Bohlen, William Burns, Steven Pifer, and John Woolworth, *The Treaty on Intermediate Range Nuclear Forces: History and Lessons Learned* (Washington D.C.: Brookings Institute, 2012).

181. David Sanger and William Broad, "Cold War Arms Treaty May Unravel, Creating a Much Bigger Problem," *New York Times*, December 10, 2018.

182. Andrew Kramer, "If U.S. Missiles Are Deployed, Putin Says, Europe at Risk of 'Counterstrike,'" *New York Times*, October 24, 2018.

183. Miller, *Apprentice*, 322.

184. Peter Baker and Sophia Kishkovsky, "Trump Signs Russian Sanctions into Law, with Caveats," *New York Times*, August 2, 2017.

185. Miller, *Apprentice*, 324.

186. Peter Baker, "Trump Praises Putin Instead of Critiquing Cuts to U.S. Embassy Staff," *New York Times*, August 10, 2017.

187. Isikoff and Corn, *Russian Roulette*, 304–5.

188. Julie Hirschfeld Davis and Katie Rogers, "On Eve of Talks, Trump Congratulates Putin and Calls E.U. a Trade 'Foe'," *New York Times*, July 16. 2018.

189. Julie Hirschfeld Davis, "Trump, with Putin, Attacks 2016 Intelligence," *New York Times*, July 17, 2018; Linda Qui, "Helsinki New Conference: Eight Suspect Claim," *New York Times*, July 17, 2018.

190. Ibid., Linda Qui, "Helsinki New Conference: Eight Suspect Claim," *New York Times*, July 17, 2018; Mark Landler, "From Trump, Disdain for U.S. Institutions and Praise for an Adversary," *New York Times*, July 17, 2018.

191. Michael Schwirtz and Kenneth Vogel, "Putin Singles Out Critic in an Offer to Mueller," *New York Times*, July 17, 2018.

192. Andrew Higgins and Steven Erlanger, "For Putin, the 'Summit He Dreamed of for 18 Years'," *New York Times*, July 17, 2018; Mark Landler, "From Trump, Disdain for U.S. Institutions and Praise for an Adversary," *New York Times*, July 17, 2018;

Julian Barnes, "Intelligence Chief Warns U.S. Digital Infrastructure 'Is Literally Under Attack,'" *New York Times*, July 14, 2018; Sherly Gay Stolberg, Nicholas Fando, and Thomas Kaplan, "Measured Condemnation But No G.O.P. Plan to Act," *New York Times*, July 17, 2018; Will Hurd, "Trump Is Being Manipulated by Putin. What Should We Do?" *New York Times*, July 19, 2018.

193. Katie Benner, "Justice Department to Crack Down on Foreign Agents of Discord," *New York Times*, July 20, 2018.

194. Nicholas Fandos and Sheryl Gay Stolberg, "Republicans Block Anti-Putin Resolutions, then Let One Fly," *New York Times*, July 20, 2018.

195. Miller, *Apprentice*, 343.

196. Gardiner Harris, "U.S. to Impose New Sanctions against Russia," *New York Times*, August 9, 2018.

197. Andrew Kramer, "U.S. Action on Russia Send Ruble into Tailspin," *New York Times*, August 10, 2018 Neil MacFarquhar, "Tighter Sanctions Rain on Putin's Parade," *New York Times*, August 13, 2018.;

198. Julian Barnes and Nicholas Fandos, "Lawmakers Fault White House Measure to Fight Election Interference," *New York Times*, September 13, 2018.

199. David Sanger, "President Loosens Secretive Restraints on Ordering Cyberattacks," *New York Times*, September 21, 2018.

200. David Sanger, "Russian Hackers Train Focus on U.S. Power Grid," *New York Times*, July 28, 2018; Nicholas Fandos and Kevin Roose, "Facebook Busts a Shadowy Plot to Jolt Elections," *New York Times*, August 1, 2018; David Sanger and Sheera Frenkel, "Russian Hacker Broaden Attacks to Conservatives," *New York Times*, August 21, 2018; Sheera Frenkel and Nicholas Fandos, "Facebook Says New Campaign Tried to Spread Global Discord," *New York Times*, August 22, 2018.

201. Andrew Kramer, "Bolton Says He Chided Russians for '16 Meddling," *New York Times*, October 23, 2018; Andrew Higgins, "Moscow Mocks Russian Aide Recruited by the C.I.A. as a Boozy Nobody," NYT, September 12, 2019.

202. David Sanger and Sheera Frenkel, "Cybersecurity Experts Expect Interference, but Not a Repeat of 2016," *New York Times*, November 5, 2016.

203. Carolyn Forrest, "Russia's Disinformation Campaign: The New Cold War," *Forum Committee of the American Bar Association*, vol. 33, no. 3 (Winter 2018), 2–5.

204. Michael Shear and Michael Wines, "Russian Threat to Midterms 'Is Real,' Trump's Top Security Officials Warn," *New York Times*, August 3, 2018; Nicholas Fandos and Catie Edmondson, "Promise from Senators to Punish Russia after New Reports of Hacking," *New York Times*, August 22, 2018; Julian Barnes and Matthew Rosenberg, "U.S. in the Dark on Russia's Plan for the Election," *New York Times*, August 25, 2018.

205. Unger, *House of Trump*, 215–19.

206. Gardiner Harris, "Poll Finds U.S. Popularity Nose-Dived Under Trump," *New York Times*, October 2, 2018.

207. "Trump Claims Inner Workings of Mueller Probe are a 'Total Mess'—but Gives No Evidence," *Washington Post*, November 15, 2018.

208. David Sanger and William Broad, "U.S. Departure from Arms Pact Is Said to Loom," *New York Times*, October 20, 2018; Mark Lander and David Sanger, "Trump Delivers a Mixed Message on his National Security Approach," *New York Times*, December 18, 2017; Ellen Nakashima, "Trump Chairs National Security

Meeting But Gives No New Orders to Repel Russian Interference," *Washington Post*, July 28, 2018.

209. Peter Baker and Adam Nossiter, "Trump Meets with France's President and This Time It's Not Buddy-Buddy," *New York Times*, November 11, 2018; Peter Baker and Alissa Rubin, "'America First' Draws Rebuke at Ceremony," *New York Times*, November 12, 2018; David Sanger, "U.S. Declines to Sign Macron Declaration against Cyberattacks," *New York Times*, November 13, 2018.

210. Katrin Bennhold and Steven Erlanger, "Merkel Joins Macron in Calling for Self-Reliance and a 'Real European Army,'" New York Times, November 14, 2018.

211. Kenneth Vogel, "Treasury Department Plans to Lift Sanctions on Russian Oligarch's Business," *New York Times*, December 20, 2018; David Sanger, Mark Landler, Helene Cooper, and Eric Schmitt, "U.S. Ends Mission in Syria as Trump Pulls 2,000 Troops," *New York Times*, December 20, 2018; Kenneth Vogel, "Deripaska and Allies Could Benefit from Sanction Deal, Document Shows," *New York Times*, January 21, 2019.

212. Steven Erlanger, and Katrin Bennhold, "Rift Between Trump and Europe Is Now Open and Angry," *New York Times*, February 17, 2019.

Chapter 7

1. Steven Erlanger, "Balkans Become a Testing Ground in a New Cold War," *New York Times*, April 11, 2018.

2. Per Hogselius, *Red Gas: Russia and the Origins of European Energy Dependence* (New York: Palgrave Macmillan, 2013); Sadek Boussena and Catherine Locatelli, "Gas Market Developments and their Effect on Relations between Russia and the EU, *OPEC Energy Review*, vol. 35 (2011), 27–46; Sadek Boussena and Catherine Locatelli, "Gazprom and the Complexity of EU Gas Market: A Strategy to Define," *Post-Communist Economies*, vol. 29, no. 4 (2017), 549–64.

3. Jeffrey Gedmin, "Beyond Crimea: What Vladimir Putin Really Wants," World Affairs, vol. 177, no. 2 (July/August 2014), 11.

4. Matt Apuzzo, "A Vital Mineral, a Toxic Metal and Fears of a Russian Power Play," *New York Times*, October 22, 2018.

5. S.V. Terebova, "Co-operation between Russia and the European Union from Importing to Exporting Technology," *Studies on Russian Economic Development*, vol. 28, no. 3 (2017), 327–37.

6. Alina Polyakova, "Strange Bedfellows: Putin and Europe's Far Right," *World Affairs*, vol. 177, no. 3 (September/October 2014), 38.

7. Nalbandov, *Not By Bread Alone*, 301.

8. Catherine Philip, "Moscow Meddling in US and Europe for the Past 20 Years," *The Times*, January 26, 2018.

9. Lucan Way and Adam Casey, "Russia Has Been Meddling in Foreign Elections for Decades. Has It Made a Difference?" *Washington Post*, January 8, 2018.

10. Stefan Kornelius, *Angela Merkel: The Chancellor and Her World* (London: Alma Books, 2013), 182.

11. Zygar, *All the Kremlin's Men*, 152.

12. Senate Intelligence Hearing on Russian Interference in European Elections, October 8, 2018, Senate website.

13. Tony Blair, *A Journey: My Political Life* (New York: Knopf, 2010), 484.

14. Conradi, *Who lost Russia?* 121.

15. Donette Murray and David Brown, *Power Relations in the Twenty-First Century* (New York: Routledge, 2018).

16. Zygar, *All the Kremlin's Men*, 43–4.

17. David Gowland, *Britain and the European Union* (New York: Routledge, 2016).

18. Karla Adam and William Booth, "British Alarm Rising over Possible Russian Meddling in Brexit," Washington Post, November 18, 2017; David Kirkpatrick and Matthew Rosenberg, "Kremlin's Links to Brexit Push Get a New Look," *New York Times*, June 29, 2018; David Kirkpatrick, "'Fake News' Investigations Rebuke Facebook," *New York Times*, July 29; 2018. Natasha Singer, "Democracy Under Siege on the Internet," *New York Times*, August 27, 2018.

19. Harold Clarke and Matthew Goodwin, *Brexit: Why Britain Voted to Leave the European Union* (London: Cambridge University Press, 2017); Graham Taylor, *Understanding Brexit: Why Britain Voted to Leave the European Union* (London: Emerald Publishing, 2017); Jason Farrell and Paul Goldsmith, *How to Lose a Referendum: The Definitive Story of Why the UK Voted for Brexit* (London: Backbite Publishing, 2017).

20. Stephen Castle, "Is Britain's Political System at the Breaking Point," *New York Times*, February 20, 2019.

21. Andrew Higgins, "In Interview with Two Russians, Credibility Is the Half of It," *New York Times*, September 19, 2018; Reuters, "E.U. Sanctions 4 Russians over Skripal Poisoning," *New York Times*, January 21, 2019.

22. Karla Adam and William Booth, "British Alarm Rising over Possible Russian Meddling in Brexit," Washington Post, November 18, 2017.

23. Adam Nossiter, David Sanger, and Nicole Periroth, "Hackers Came, but the French were Prepared," *New York Times*, May 9, 2017.

24. Ostrovsky, *Invention of Russia*, 7.

25. Jason Horowitz, "Five Star Was Against a Pipeline to Italy, Until the Election Was Over," *New York Times*, August 13, 2018.

26. Jack Ewing, "Why the World Should Care about Italy's Debt Woes," *New York Times*, October 24, 2018.

27. Jason Horowitz, "E.U. Rejects Italy's Budget as Populists Refuse to Bend," *New York Times*, October 24, 2018; Jason Horowitz, "Italy's Populists Relent and Reach Budget Deal with E.U., *New York Times*, December 20, 2018; Jason Horowitz, "Italy Weighs Debt Plan, Rattling Europe," *New York Times*, June 13, 2019.

28. Richard Perez-Pena, Adam Nossiter, and Jason Horowitz, "France Recalls Ambassador to Italy after Minister Meets 'Yellow Vest' Protesters," New York Times, February 7, 2019.

29. Myers, *New Tsar*, 321.

30. Andrew Kramer, "Estonia Says Putin's Plane Trespassed," *New York Times*, July 18, 2018.

31. Andrew Higgins, "In Elections, Latvia Ushers a Coalition of Populists," *New York Times*, October 8, 2018.

32. Patrick Kingsley and Benjamin Novak, "Hungarian Site Shows How a Free Press Can Die," New York Times, November 25, 2018; Patrick Kingsley, "Big News Outlets in Hungary Are Given to Entity Tied to Premier," *New York Times*, November 30, 2018.

33. Patrick Kingsley, "E.U.'s Leadership Seeks to Contain Hungary's Orban," *New York Times*, September 12, 2018; Patrick Kingsley, "Hungary's Democracy Is in Danger, E.U. Parliament Votes," *New York Times*, December 13, 2018; Marc

Santora and Steven Erlanger, "Party of Hungary's Autocratic Leader Is Suspended by Top E.U. Coalition," *New York Times*, March 21, 2019.

34. Allen Paul, *Katyn: Stalin's Massacre and the Triumph of Truth* (Urbana: Northern Illinois University Press, 2010).
35. Marc Santora, "Poland Purges Its Supreme Court and Protestors Take to the Streets," *New York Times*, July 4, 2018.
36. Marc Santora, "Crisis in Poland Deepens as Judges Scorn Their Own Tribunal's Leader," *New York Times*, July 6, 2018.
37. Marc Santora and Joanna Berendt, "Court Orders Poland to Reinstate Justices," *New York Times*, October 20, 2018; Joanna Barendt and Mar Santora, "To Appease E.U., Poland Reverses Purge of Top Court," *New York Times*, December 18, 2018.
38. Stanley Reed, "Burned by Russia, Poland Turns to U.S. for Natural Gas and Energy Security," *New York Times*, February 6, 2019.
39. Niki Kitsantonis, "Greece's Expulsion of 2 Diplomats Angers Russia," *New York Times*, July 20, 2018; Andrew Kramer and Liz Alderman, "Russian Hacker, Wanted in U.S., May Go to Russia," *New York Times*, September 5, 2018.
40. Marc Santora, "As Macedonia Votes on a New Name, Russia Sends in the Internet Trolls," *New York Times*, September 17, 2018; Marc Santora, "Little Solved in Macedonia after Vote to Change Name," New York Times, October 6, 2018 Helene Cooper and Eric Schmitt, "Work of U.S. Spies Uncovers Russian Link in Balkans Vote," *New York Times*, October 10, 2018.;
41. Emily Young, "Russian Money in Cyprus: Why Is There So Much?" *BBC*, March 18, 2013; Shaun Walker, "Cyprus Bailout—The Russian Angle, Vladimir Putin Hits out at 'Unjust and Dangerous' Bank Levy," *The Independent*, March 18, 2013.
42. Eileen Sullivan, "President Questions NATO's Mission of Mutual Defense," *New York Times*, July 19, 2018.
43. Barbara Surk, "Politicians in Bosnia Revive Old Divisions, To Russia's Satisfaction," *New York Times*, October 7, 2018; Barbara Surk, "Serb Nationalist Claims Victory in Bosnia," *New York Times*, October 8, 2018.
44. Milan Scheuer, "Russians Planned Attack on Lab, the Swiss Say," *New York Times*, September 15, 2018.
45. "Russia-EU," August 18–22, 2017, *Levada Survey* website.

Chapter 8

1. Mankoff, *Russian Foreign Policy*, 94.
2. Mankoff, *Russian Foreign Policy*, 84.
3. Richard Perez-Pena, "Russia Snarls Meeting on Chemical Weapons," *New York Times*, June 27, 2018.
4. Eric Miller, *To Balance or Not to Balance: Alignment Theory and the Commonwealth of Independent States* (Burlington, Vermont: Ashgate, 2004).
5. James Brusstar, "Russian Vital Interests and Western Security," *Orbis*, vol. 38, no. 4 (1994), 609–10.
6. Zygar, *All the Kremlin's Men*, 111.
7. Margarita Balmaceda, *Belarus: Oil, Gas, Transit Pipelines, and Russian Foreign Energy Policy* (London: GMB, 2006); Brian Bennett, *The Last Dictatorship in Europe: Belarus under Lukashenko* (New York: Oxford University Press, 2011); Andrew Wilson, *Belarus: The Last European Dictatorship* (New Haven, Conn.: Yale University Press, 2011).
8. Stent, *Limits of Partnership*, 168.

9. Eric Miller, *To Balance or Not to Balance: Alignment Theory and the Commonwealth of Independent States* (Burlington, Vermont: Ashgate, 2004), 107.

10. Andrew Kramer, "Leader of Ukrainians Separatists Is Killed in Bombing," *New York Times*, September 1, 2018.

11. Neil MacFarquhar, "Russia-Ukraine Tensions Set up the Biggest Christian Schism since 1054," *New York Times*, October 8, 2018; Neil MacFarquhar, "In Russia, Rift Grows Over Orthodox Church," *New York Times*, October 16, 2018; Neil MacFarquhar, "Ukraine Church Moves to Break with Moscow," *New York Times*, December 16, 2018.

12. Neil MacFarquhar, "Russia Puts Sanctions on Ukraine's Elite," *New York Times*, November 2, 2018.

13. Andrew Kramer, "Ukraine Says Russia Fired on Its Ships, Wounding Six," *New York Times*, November 26, 2018; Neil MacFarquhar, "Crimea Fight Moves Closer to Widen War," *New York Times*, November 27, 2018; Neil MacFarquhar, "How Did Ukraine Reach Point of Declaring Martial Law?" *New York Times*, November 29, 2018; Andrew Higgins, "Key Russian Weapon against Ukraine: Fear," *New York Times*, December 15, 2015.

14. Neil MacFarquhar, "Outrage Grows as Russia Grants Passports in Eastern Ukraine," *New York Times*, April 26, 2019.

15. Jelena Milic, "The Russification of Serbia," *Center for Euro-Atlantic Studies*, October 2014; Gordana Knezevic, "Putin's Orchestra in Belgrade," Radio Free Europe, Free Liberty, September 18, 2017.

16. Marc Santora and Neil MacFarquhar, "Putin Gets Red Carpet Treatment in Serbia, a Fulcrum Once More," *New York Times*, January 17, 2019.

17. Thomas de Waal, *The Great Catastrophe: Armenians and Turks in the Shadow of Genocide* (New York: Oxford University Press, 2015).

18. Bahruz Balayez, *The Right to Self-Determination: The South Caucasus Nagorno Karabakh in Context* (New York: Lexington, 2013).

19. Nalbandov, *Not By Bread Alone*, 270.

20. Suha Bolukbasi, *Azerbaijan: A Political History* (London: I.B. Tauris, 2011).

21. Nalbandov, *Not By Bread Alone*, 276.

22. Rob Johnson, *Oil, Islam, and Conflict: Central Asia since 1945* (London: Reaktion Books, 2007).

23. Nalbandov, *Not By Bread Alone*, 291.

24. Alexei Voskressenski, *Russia and China: A Theory of Interstate Relations* (London: Routledge, 2003); Bobo Lo, *Axis of Convenience: Moscow, Beijing, and the New Geopolitics* (Washington D.C.: Brookings Institute, 2008); Douglas Schoen and Melic Kaylan, *The Russia-China Axis: The New Cold War and America's Crisis of Leadership* (New York: Encounter Books, 2014).

25. Neil MacFaraquer, "Xi Jinping's Visit to Russia Accents Ties in Face of Tensions with U.S.," New York Times, June 5, 2019.

26. Mankoff, *Russian Foreign Policy*, 179.

27. Andrew Higgins, "Russian War Games Plan Includes a Role for China," *New York Times*, August 29, 2018.

28. "Attitudes Toward Other Countries," January 18–23, 2018; "Enemies," December 1–5, 2017, *Levada Survey* website.

29. Mankoff, *Russian Foreign Policy*, 180.

30. James Goodby, Vladimir Ivanov, Nobuo Shimotomai, *The Northern Territories and Beyond: Russia, Japanese, and American Perspectives* (Westport, Conn.: Praeger,

1995); Fiona Hill, "The Gang of Two: Russia and Japan Make a Play for the Pacific," *Foreign Affairs*, November 23, 2007).

31. Michael Schwirtz, "North Korea Is Abetted by Russia, Haley Says," *New York Times*, September 28, 2028; Andrew Kramer and Choe Sang-Un, "With U.S. Talks at a Standstill, North Korea Turns to Russia," New York Times, April 25, 2019; Andrew Kramer and Choe Sang-Un, "After Meeting Kim, Putin Backs Him (Not Trump) on Disarmament," *New York Times*, April 26, 2019.

32. Gardiner Harris, "U.S. Reimposes Iran Sanctions but Exempts Big Customers," *New York Times*, November 3, 2019.

33. Eric Schmitt and Thomas Gibbons-Neff, "U.S.-Russian Relations in Syria Are Less Rosy than Leaders Implied," *New York Times*, July 18, 2018; Kenneth Vogel, "Treasury Department Plans to Lift Sanctions on Russian Oligarch's Business," *New York Times*, December 20, 2018; David Sanger, Mark Landler, Helene Cooper, and Eric Schmitt, "U.S. Ends Mission in Syria as Trump Pulls 2,000 Troops," *New York Times*, December 20, 2018; Rod Nordland, "U.S. Exit Is Seen as an Abandonment of the Kurds and a Boon for ISIS," *New York Times*, December 20, 2018.

34. Ben Hubbard, "Foreign Powers See 'No Military Solution' in Syria," *New York Times*, September 8, 2018.

35. Hill and Gaddy, *Mr. Putin*, 293–4.

36. David Halbfinger and Ben Hubbard, "Israeli Leader Says Russia Agreed to Restrain Iran in Syria," *New York Times*, July 13, 2018; David Halbfinger and Andrew Higgins, "Putin Plays Down Israel's Role in Downing of Warplane by Syria," *New York Times*, September 19, 2018 Andrew Kramer and Isabel Kershner, "Eying Israel, Putin Pledges to Send Syria New Missiles," *New York Times*, September 25, 2018.

37. Eric Schmitt, "Moscow Gains Clout in Africa, Alarming West," *New York Times*, April 1, 2019.

38. Andrew Higgins and Ivan Nechepurenko, "In Africa, Murder of Journalists Put Spotlight on Kremlin's Reach," *New York Times*, August 8, 2018.

39. Hal Brands, *Latin America's Cold War* (Cambridge, Mass.: Harvard University Press, 2012); Marvin Astrada and Felix Martin, *Russia and Latin America: From Nation State to Society of States* (New York: Palgrave Macmillan, 2013).

40. Nalbandov, *Not By Bread Alone*, 413.

41. Zygar, *All the Kremlin's Men*, 179.

42. Nicholas Casey, "Crisis Grips Venezuela But It's Strengthening the President's Hand," *New York Times*, August 7, 2018.

43. Nicolas Casey, "Forecast for Inflation in Venezuela: 1,000,000%," *New York Times*, July 24, 2018.

44. Peter Baker and Edward Wong, "Intervening against Venezuela's Strongman, Trump Belies 'America First'" *New York Times*, January 24, 2019.

45. Ana Vanessa Herrero and Neil MacFarquhar, "Russia Warns U.S. Not to Intervene in Venezuela as Military Backs Maduro," *New York Times*, January 24, 2019; Kirk Semple, "With Spies and other Operatives, a Nation Looms over Venezuela's Crisis: Cuba," *New York Times*, January 26, 2019; Nicholas Casey, "Secret Venezuelan Files Target Maduro Confident," *New York Times*, May 3, 2019.

46. Nicholas Casey, "In Venezuela, A Brazen Act Deepens Crisis," *New York Times*, May 1, 2019; Mark Landler, "Pressure Rises after Failure in Venezuela," *New York Times*, May 2, 2019.

47. Mark Landler, "Trump Says He Discussed the 'Russia Hoax' in a Phone Call with Putin," New York Times, May 3, 2019.
48. Kirk Semple, "Nicaraguans Fleeing a Crisis Create One for Costa Rica," *New York Times*, September 23, 2018.
49. "Ortega Celebrates Putin's Nicaragua Visit as a 'Ray of Light,'" *Moscow Times*, July 13, 2014.

Chapter 9

1. Winston Churchill, *The Gathering Storm: The Second World War* (New York: Houghton Mifflin, 1948), 403.
2. Nalbandov, *Not By Bread Alone*, 86.
3. Ibid., 100.
4. Ibid., 37–8, 457; "The Perception of Stalin," *Levada Survey* website.
5. Gaidar, *Collapse of Empire*, xvi.
6. Figes, *Revolutionary Russia*, 295.
7. David Satter, *It Was a Long Time Ago, and It Never Happened Anyway: Russia and the Communist Past* (New Haven, Conn.: Yale University Press, 2012), 6.
8. Nalbandov, *Not By Bread Alone*, 19.
9. Myers, *New Tsar*, 208.
10. Nalbandov, *Not By Bread Alone*, 69, 76.
11. Edith Clowes, *Russia on the Edge: Imagined Geographies and Post-Soviet Identities* (Ithaca, N.Y.: Cornell University Press, 2011); Arkady Ostrovsky, *The Invention of Russia: The Rise of Russia and the Age of Fake News* (New York: Penguin, 2017); Alfred Evans, "Putin's Legacy and Russia's Identity," *Europe-Asia Studies*, vol. 60, no. 6 (August 2008), 899–912.
12. Sakwa, *Russian Politics and Society*, 216.
13. Andrey Kozyrev, "Russia: A Chance for Survival," *Foreign Affairs*, vol. 71, no. 2 (1992), 9.
14. Sakwa, *Russian Politics and Society*, 379.
15. Nalbandov, *Not by Bread Alone*, 36.
16. "Approval Ratings of Government Institutions," August 18–22, 2017, *Levada Survey* website.
17. "Donald Trump's Election," January 18–23, 2018, *Levada Survey* website.
18. Linda Cook, "State Capacity and Pension Provision," Timothy Colton and Stephen Holmes, eds., *The State after Communism: Governance in the New Russia* (New York: Rowman and Littlefield, 2006), 144.
19. Chen, *Return of Ideology*, 68.
20. Ibid.
21. Freedom House, website.
22. Dawisha, *Putin's Kleptocracy*, 314.
23. S.V. Terebova, "Cooperation between Russia and the European Union from Importing to Exporting Technology," *Studies on Russian Economic Development*, vol. 28, no. 3 (2017), 330.
24. CIA World Factbook, website.
25. David Holloway, "The Politics of Catastrophe," *New York Review of Books*, June 10, 1993.
26. "The World's Billionaires, 2019," *Forbes Magazine*, website.
27. Dawisha, *Putin's Kleptocracy*, 1.
28. Transparency International, website.

29. Chen, *Return of Ideology*, 69.

30. "Most Alarming Problems," August 18–22, 2017, *Levada Survey* website.

31. Myers, *New Tsar*, 403.

32. Henry Kissinger, "To Settle the Ukrainian Crisis, Start at the End," *Washington Post*, March 5, 2014.

33. Angela Stent, "Restoration and Revolution in Putin's Foreign Policy, *Europe-Asia Studies*, vol. 60, no. 6 (August 2008), 1090, 1089–1106.

34. Mankoff, *Russian Foreign Policy*, 16.

35. Andrei Grachev, "Putin's Foreign Policy Choices," in Alex Pravda, ed., *Leading Russia: Putin in Perspective, Essays in Honor of Archie Brown* (New York: Oxford University Press, 2005), 269.

36. Marcel Van Herpen, *Putin's Wars: The Rise of Russia's New Imperialism* (New York: Rowman and Littlefield, 2014).

37. Sakwa, *Russian Politics and Society*, 229; *CIA World Fact Book*, cia.gov.

38. John Lewis Gaddis, *Strategies of Containment: A Critical Appraisal of American National Security Policy during the Cold War* (New York: Oxford University Press, 2005), 231.

39. Sakwa, *Russian Politics and Society*, 384.

40. "Attitudes Toward Other Countries," January 18–23, 2018, *Levada Survey* website.

41. "Donald Trump's Election," January 18–23, 2018, *Levada Survey* website.

42. "Attitudes Toward Other Countries," January 18–23, 2018, *Levada Survey* website.

43. "Enemies," December 1–5, 2017, *Levada Survey* website.

44. Melissa Gomez, "Giuliani Says 'Truth Isn't Truth' in Defense of Trump's Legal Strategy," *New York Times*, August 19, 2018.

45. Hillary Clinton, Hard Choices (New York: Simon and Schuster, 2014), 245.

46. Peter Baker and Michael Crowley, "Trump and Putin Share a Chuckle about Meddling", *New York Times*, June 29, 2019; Andrew Kramer, "Putin Declares Liberalism 'Has Outlived Its Purpose'" *New York Times*, June 29, 2019.

Bibliography

Books

Abramson, Seth, *Proof of Collusion: How Trump Betrayed America*, New York: Simon and Schuster, 2018.

Aitken, Jonathan, *Margaret Thatcher: Power and Personality*, New York: Bloomsbury, 2013.

Albats, Yevgenia, *The State within the State: The KGB and Its Hold on Russia—Past, Present, and Future*, New York: Farrar, Straus, and Giroux, 1994.

Alekperov, Vagit, *Oil of Russia: Past, Present, and Future*, Minneapolis: East View Press, 2011.

Ambrosio, Thomas, *Authoritarian Backlash: Russian Resistance to Democratization in the Former Soviet Union*, Burlington, Vermont: Ashgate, 2009.

Andrews, Christopher and Vasili Mitrokhin, *The Sword and the Shield: The Mitrokhin Archives and the Secret History of the KGB*, New York: Basic Books, 1999.

Anisimov, Evgenii, *The Reforms of Peter the Great: Progress through Coercion in Russia*, New York: M.E. Sharpe, 1993.

Antonenko, Oksana, *The New Russian Analytical Centers and Their Role in Political Decisionmaking*, Cambridge, Mass.: Harvard University Press, 1996.

Applebaum, Anne, *Gulag: A History*, New York: Doubleday, 2003.

——, *Red Famine: Stalin's War on Ukraine*, New York: Doubleday, 2017.

Arbatov, Alexis, Karl Kaiser, and Robert Legvold, eds., *Russia and the West: The 21st Century Security Environment*, Armonk, N.Y.: M.E. Sharpe, 1999.

Aron, Leon, *Yeltsin: A Revolutionary Life*, New York: St. Martin's Press, 2000.

——, *Roads to the Temple: Truth, Memory, Ideas, and the Ideals in the Making of the Russian Revolution, 1987–1991*, New Haven, Conn. Yale University Press, 2012.

Arutunya, Anna, *The Putin Mystique: Inside Russia's Power Cult*, Northampton, Mass.: Olive Branch Press, 2014.

Aslund, Anders, *Russia's Capitalist Revolution*, Washington D.C.: Petersen Institute for International Economics 2007.

——, *How Ukraine Became a Market Economy and Democracy*, Washington D.C.: Peter G. Peterson Institute for International Economics, 2009.

——, and Michael McFaul, eds., *Revolution in Orange: The Origins of Ukraine's Democratic Breakthrough*, Washington D.C.: Carnegie Institute of Peace, 2006.

——, Sergei Guriev, and Andrew Kuchins, eds., *Russian after the Global Economic Crisis*, Washington D.C.: Peter G. Peterson Institute for International Economics, 2010.

Asmus, Ronald, *A Little War that Shook the World, Georgia, Russia, and the Future of the Wes*, New York: Palgrave Macmillan, 2010.

Astrada, Marvin, and Felix Martin, *Russia and Latin America: From Nation State to Society of States*, New York: Palgrave Macmillan, 2013.

Baker, Peter, and Susan Glasser, *Kremlin Rising: Vladimir Putin's Russia and the End of Revolution*, New York: Scribner, 2005.

Balmaceda, Margarita, *Belarus: Oil, Gas, Transit Pipelines, and Russian Foreign Energy Policy*, London: GMB, 2006.

——, *Energy Dependency, Politics, and Corruption in the Former Soviet Union: Russia's Power, Oligarch's Profits, and Ukraine's Missing Energy Policy, 1995–2006*, London: Routledge, 2008.

Balayez, Bahruz, *The Right to Self-Determination: The South Caucasus Nagorno Karabakh in Context*, New York: Lexington, 2013.

Barnes, Timothy, *A Naked View of the Trans-Pacific Partnership*, Indianapolis: Dog Ear Press, 2016.

Barrett, Wayne, *The Greatest Show on Earth: The Deals, the Downfall, the Reinvention*, New York: Regan Arts, 2016.

Bennett, Brian, *The Last Dictatorship in Europe: Belarus under Lukashenko*, New York: Oxford University Press, 2011.

Bennetts, Marc, *Kicking the Kremlin: Russia's New Dissidents and the Battle to Topple Putin*, London: Oneworld, 2014.

Behrman, Greg, *The Most Noble Adventure: The Marshall Plan and How America Helped Rebuild Europe*, New York: Free Press, 2008.

Billington, James, *The Icon and the Axe: An Interpretative History of Russian Culture*, New York: Knopf, 1966.

Black, Joseph, *The Russian Presidency of Dmitri Medvedev, 2008–2012: The Next Step Forward or Merely Time Out?* New York: Routledge, 2014.

Blackwell, William, *The Beginnings of Russian Industrialization*, Princeton, N.J.: Princeton University Press, 1968.

——, ed., *Russian Economic Development from Peter the Great to Stalin*, New York: New Viewpoints, 1974.

Blair, Gwenda Blair, *The Trumps: Three Generations of Builders and a Presidential Candidate*, New York: Simon and Schuster, 2000.

Blair, Tony, *A Journey: My Political Life*, New York: Knopf, 2010.

Blank, Stephen, ed., *Can Russia Reform?: Economic, Political, and Military Perspectives*, Washington D.C.: U.S. Army War College Strategic Studies Institute, 2012.

Bohlen, Avis, William Burns, Steven Pifer, and John Woolworth, *The Treaty on Intermediate Range Nuclear Forces: History and Lessons Learned*, Washington D.C.: Brookings Institute, 2012.

Bolukbasi, Suha, *Azerbaijan: A Political History*, London: I.B. Tauris, 2011.

Braithwaite, Roderic, *Afghantsy: The Russians in Afghanistan, 1979–89*, New York: Oxford University Press, 2011.

Brands, Hal, *Latin America's Cold War*, Cambridge, Mass.: Harvard University Press, 2012.

Bzezinski, Zbigniew, *Grand Failure: The Birth and Death of Communism in the Twentieth Century*, New York: Collier Books, 1990.

Browder, Bill, *Red Notice: A True Story of High Finance, Murder, and One Man's Fight for Justice*, New York: Simon and Schuster, 2015.

Brown, Archie, *The Gorbachev Factor*, New York: 0xford University Press, 1996.

Brown, Archie, and Lilia Shevtsova, eds., *Gorbachev, Yeltsin, and Putin: Political Leadership in Russia's Transition*, Washington D.C.: Carnegie Endowment for International Peace, 2001.

Bugajski, Janusz, *Cold Peace: Russia's New Imperialism*, Westport, Conn.: Praeger, 2004.

Bush, George, *Decision Points*, New York: Crown, 2011.

Bushkovitch, Paul, *A Concise History of Russia,* New York: Cambridge University Press, 2013.

Camino-Isaacs, Cathleen, and Jeffrey Scott, eds., *The Trans-Pacific Partnership: An Assessment,* Washington D.C.: Peterson Institute for International Economics, 2016.

Carlin, John, and Garrett Graff, *Dawn of the Code War: America's Battle against Russia, China, and the Rising Global Cyber Threat,* New York: Public Affairs, 2018.

Chen, Cheng, *The Return of Ideology: The Search for Regime Identities in Postcommunist Russia and China,* Ann Arbor: University of Michigan Press, 2016.

Chinn, Jeff, and Robert Kaiser, *Russians as the New Minority: Ethnicity and Nationalism in the Soviet Successor States,* Boulder, Colo.: Westview, 1996.

Chua, Amy, *World on Fire: How Exporting Free Market Democracy Spreads Ethnic Hatred and Global Instability,* New York: Doubleday, 2003.

Churchill, Winston, *The Gathering Storm: The Second World War,* New York: Houghton Mifflin, 1948.

Clark, Christopher, *The Sleepwalkers: How Europe Went to War in 1914,* New York: HarperCollins, 2014.

Clarke, Harold, and Matthew Goodwin, *Brexit: Why Britain Voted to Leave the European Union,* London: Cambridge University Press, 2017.

Clark, Wesley, *Waging Modern War: Bosnia, Kosovo, and the Future of Combat,* New York: Public Affairs, 2001.

Clinton, Bill, *My Life,* New York: Alfred Knopf, 2004.

Clinton, Hillary Rodham, *Hard Choices,* New York: Simon and Schuster, 2015.

Clowes, Edith, *Russia on the Edge: Imagined Geographies and Post-Soviet Identities,* Ithaca, N.Y.: Cornell University Press, 2011.

Cohen, Stephen, *Failed Crusade: America and the Tragedy of Post-Communist Russia,* New York: W.W. Norton, 2000.

——, *Soviet Fates and Lost Alternatives: From Stalinism to the New Cold War,* New York: Columbia University Press, 2009.

——, *War with Russia?: From Putin and Ukraine to Trump and Russiangate,* New York: Hot Books, 2018.

Coleman, Fred, *The Decline and Fall of the Soviet Empire,* New York: St. Martin's Press, 1996.

Colton, Timothy, *Yeltsin: A Life,* New York: Basic Books, 2008.

Colton, Timothy, and Michael McFaul, *Popular Choice and Managed Democracy: The Russian Elections of 1999 and 2000,* Washington D.C.: Brookings Institute Press, 2003.

Colton, Timothy, and Stephen Holmes, eds., *The State after Communism: Governance in the New Russia,* New York: Rowman and Littlefield, 2006.

Comey, James, *A Higher Loyalty: Truth, Lies, and Leadership,* New York: Flatiron Books, 2018.

Conquest, Robert, *Harvest of Sorrow: Soviet Collectivization and the Terror-Famine,* New York: Oxford University Press, 1986.

——, *The Great Terror: A Reassessment,* New York: Oxford University Press, 2007.

Conradi, Peter, *Who Lost Russia?: How the World Entered a New Cold War,* New York: Oneworld, 2017.

Cornell, Svante, and Frederick Starr, eds., *The Guns of August 2008: Russia's War in Georgia,* Armonk, N.Y.: M.E. Sharpe, 2009.

Cotton, Timothy, *Yeltsin: A Life,* New York: Basic Books, 2011.

Cowell, Alan, *The Terminal Spy: The Life and Death of Alexander Litvinenko, A True Story of Espionage, Betrayal, and Murder,* London: Doubleday, 2008.

Cracraft, James, *The Revolution of Peter the Great*, Cambridge, Mass.: Harvard University Press, 2003.

Crane, Keith et. al., *Russian Foreign Policy: Sources and Implications*, Santa Monica, Calif.: RAND, 2009.

Cummings, Bruce, *The Korean War: A History*, New York: Modern Library, 2010.

Dawisha, Karen, *Putin's Kleptocracy: Who Owns Russia?* New York: Simon and Schuster, 2014.

De La Pedraja, Rene, *The Russian Military Resurgence: Post-Soviet Decline and Rebuilding, 1992–2018*, Jefferson, N.C.: McFarland and Company, 2018.

Deane, John, *The Strange Alliance: The Story of Our Efforts at Wartime Cooperation with Russia*, New York: Viking, 1947.

Desai, Padma, *Conversations on Russia: Reform from Yeltsin to Putin*, New York: Oxford University Press, 2006.

Deutscher, Isaac, *Stalin: A Political Biography*, New York: Oxford University Press, 1967.

Diesen, Glen, *Russia's Geoeconomic Strategy for a Greater Eurasia*, New York: Routledge, 2018.

Doder, Dusko, and Louise Branson, *Gorbachev: The Heretic in the Kremlin*, New York: Penguin, 1990.

Dougherty, James, and Robert Phaltzgraff, *Shattering Europe's Defense Consensus: The Anti-Nuclear Movement and the Future of NATO*, Washington D.C.: Pergamon-Brassey's, 1985.

Dostoyevsky, Fyodor, *A Writer's Diary, Volume 1, 1873–1876*, Evanston, Il.: Northwestern University, 1994.

Dukes, Paul, ed., *Russia and Europe*, London: Collins and Brown, 1991.

Dunlop, John, *The Rise of Russia and the Fall of the Soviet Empire*, Princeton, N.J.: Princeton University Press, 1993.

——, *The 2002 Dubrovka and 2004 Breslan Hostage Crises: A Critique of Russian Counter-Terrorism*, Stuttgart: Ibidem-Verlag, 2006.

——, *The Moscow Bombings of September 1999: Examination of Russia Terrorist Attacks at the Onset of Vladimir Putin's Rule*, Stuttgart: Ibidem-Verlag, 2012.

Early, Pete, *Comrade J: The Untold Secrets of Russia's Master Spy in America after the End of the Cold War*, New York: G.P. Putnam's Sons, 2007.

Ellison, Herbert, *Boris Yeltsin and Russia's Democratic Transformation*, Seattle: University of Washington Press, 2006.

Evangelista, Matthew, *The Chechen Wars: Will Russia Go the Way of the Soviet Union?* Washington D.C.: Brookings Institute, 2002.

Farrell, Jason, and Paul Goldsmith, *How to Lose a Referendum: The Definitive Story of Why the UK Voted for Brexit*, London: Backbite Publishing, 2017.

Fedor, Julie, *Russia and the Cult of State Security*, New York: Routledge, 2011.

Felshtinskiy, Yuriy, and Vladimir Pribylovskiy, *The Age of Assassins: The Rise and Rise of Vladimir Putin*, London: Gibson Square, 2008.

Felshtinskiy, Yuriy, and Vladimir Pribylovskiy, *The Corporation: Russia and the KGB in the Age of President Putin*, New York: Encounter Books, 2008.

Ferguson, Niall, *The Pity of War: Explaining World War I*, New York: Basic Books, 1999.

Figes, Orlando, *A People's Tragedy: A History of the Russian Revolution*, New York: Viking, 1996.

——, *Natasha's Dance: A Cultural History of Russia*, New York: Picador, 2003.

——, *Revolutionary Russia, 1891–1991*, New York: Metropolitan Books, 2014.

Fish, Steven, *Democracy Derailed in Russia,* New York: Cambridge University Press, 2005.

Fitzgerald, Frances, *Way Out There in the Blue: Reagan, Star Wars, and the End of the Cold War,* New York: Simon and Schuster, 2000.

Foot, Peter, *The Protesters: Doubt, Dissent, and British Nuclear Weapons,* Aberdeen: Centre for Defense Studies, 1983.

Freeland, Chrystia, *Sale of the Century: Russia's Wild Ride from Communism to Capitalism,* New York: Crown, 2000.

Friedman, Robert, *Red Mafiya: How the Russian Mob Invaded America,* New York: Little Brown, 2009.

Frum, Donald, *Trumpocracy: The Corruption of the American Republic,* New York: Harper, 2018.

Fuller, William, *Strategy and Power in Russia, 1600–1914,* New York: Free Press, 1992.

Gaddis, John Lewis, *Strategies of Containment: A Critical Appraisal of American National Security Policy during the Cold War,* New York: Oxford University Press, 2005.

Gaddis, John Lewis, *The Cold War: A New History,* New York: Penguin, 2006.

Gaddy, Clifford, *The Price of the Past: Russia's Struggle with the Legacy of a Militarized Economy,* Washington D.C.: Brookings Institute, 1996.

Gaidar, Yegor, *The Collapse of an Empire: Lessons for Modern Russia,* Washington D.C.: Brookings Institute, 2007.

Galeotti, Mark, *Gorbachev and His Revolution,* London: Palgrave Macmillan, 1997.

——, *The Modern Russian Army, 1992–2016,* London: Osprey Books, 2017.

——, *The Vory: Russia's Super Mafia,* New Haven, Conn.: Yale University Press, 2018.

Gall, Carlotta, and Thomas de Waal, *Chechnya: Tragedy in the Caucasus,* New York: New York University Press, 1998.

Garcia, Oscar Martin, and Rosa Magnussorie, eds., *Rethinking the Cold War: Machineries of Persuasion,* Berlin: Oldenbourg-De Gruyter, 2019.

Gardner, Hall, *NATO Expansion and the U.S. Strategy in Asia: Surmounting the Global Crisis,* New York: Palgrave Macmillan, 2013.

Gatrell, Peter, *Russia's First World War: A Social and Economic History,* New York: Routledge, 2014.

Gessen, Masha, *The Man Without a Face: The Unlikely Rise of Vladimir Putin,* New York: Riverhead Books, 2012.

——, *Words Will Break Cement: The Passion of Pussy Riot,* New York: Riverhead Books, 2014.

Getty, Arch, Oleg Naumov, and Benjamin Sher, *The Road to Terror: Stalin and the Self-Destruction of the Bolsheviks, 1932–1939,* New Haven, Conn.: Yale University Press, 2010.

Gevorkyan, Natalyia, Natalya Timakova, and Andrei Kolesnikov, *First Person: An Astonishing Frank Self-Portrait by Russia's President Vladimir Putin,* New York: Public Affairs, 2000.

Goldfarb, Alex, and Marina Litvinenko, *Death of a Dissident: The Poisoning of Alexander Litvinenko and the Return of the KGB,* New York: Free Press, 2007.

Goldgeier, James, and Michael McFaul, *Power and Purpose: U.S. Policy toward Russia after the Cold War,* Washington D.C.: Brookings Institute, 2003.

Goldman, Emily, *Information and Revolutions in Military Affairs,* New York: Routledge, 2015.

Goldman, Marshall, *The Privatization of Russia: Russian Reform Goes Awry,* New York: Routledge, 2004.

——l, *Petrostate: Putin, Power, and the New Russia*, New York: Oxford University Press, 2010.

Gomart, Thomas, *Russian Civil-Military Relations: Putin's Legacy*, Washington D.C.: Carnegie Institute for International Peace, 2008.

Gongora Thierry, and Harold von Riekhoff, *Toward a Revolution in Military Affairs?: Defense and Security at the Dawn of the Twenty-First Century*, New York: Praeger, 2000.

Goodby, James, Vladimir Ivanov, Nobuo Shimotomai, *The Northern Territories and Beyond: Russia, Japanese, and American Perspectives*, Westport, Conn.: Praeger, 1995.

Gorbachev, Mikhail, *The August Coup: The Truth and the Lessons*, London: HarperCollins, 1991.

Goscilo, Helena, *Putin as Celebrity and Cultural Icon*, New York: Routledge, 2012.

Gower, Jackie, and Graham Timmins, ed., *Russia and Europe in the Twenty-First Century: An Uneasy Partnership*, London: Anthem Press, 2008.

Gowland, David, *Britain and the European Union*, New York: Routledge, 2016.

Gray, Colin, *Recognizing and Understanding Revolutionary Change in Warfare: The Sovereignty of Context*, Carlisle, Penn.: Strategic Studies Institute, 2006.

Greenburg, Andy, *Sandworm: A New Era of Cyberwar and the Hunt for the Kremlin's Most Dangerous Hackers*, New York: Doubleday, 2019.

Greene, Samuel, *Moscow in Movement: Power and Opposition in Putin's Russia*, Stanford, Calif.: Stanford University Press, 2014.

Gregory, Paul, *Terror by Quota: State Security from Lenin to Stalin*, New Haven, Conn.: Yale University Press, 2009.

Gustafson, Thane, *The Wheel of Fortune: The Battle for Oil and Power in Russia*, Cambridge, Mass.: Harvard University Press, 2012.

Hagenloh, Paul, *Stalin's Police: Public Order and Mass Repression in the USSR, 1926–1941*, Baltimore: Johns Hopkins University Press, 2009.

Hart, Peter, *The Great War: A Combat History of the First World War*, London: Profile Books, 2015.

Hastings, Max, *The Korean War*, New York: Simon and Schuster, 1988.

——, *Vietnam: An Epic Tragedy, 1945–1975*, New York: Harper, 2018.

Herring, George, *America's Longest War: The United States and Vietnam, 1950–1975* (New York: McGraw-Hill, 2013.

Hesli, Vicki, and William Reisinger, eds., *The 1999–2000 Elections in Russia: Their Impact and Legacy*, New York: Cambridge University Press, 2003.

Hennessey, Peter, *The Secret State: Whitehall and the Cold War*, London: Allen Lane, 2002.

Hettena, Seth, *Trump/Russia: A Definitive History*, New York: Melville House, 2018.

Hill, Fiona, and Clifford Gaddy, *Mr. Putin: Operative in the Kremlin*, Washington D.C.: Brookings Institute, 2013.

Hoffman, David, *The Oligarchs: Wealth and Power in the New Russia*, New York: Public Affairs, 2003.

——, *The Dead Hand: The Untold Story of the Cold War Nuclear Arms Race and Its Dangerous Legacy*, New York: Anchor, 2009.

Hogselius, Per, *Red Gas: Russia and the Origins of European Energy Dependence*, New York: Palgrave Macmillan, 2013.

Hollander, Paul, ed., *From the Gulag to the Killing Fields: Personal Accounts of Political Violence and Repression in Communist States*, Wilmington, Del.: Intercollegiate Studies Institute, 2007.

Hopf, Ted. ed., *Understandings of Russian Foreign Policy*, University Park: Pennsylvania State University Press, 1999.

Horvath, Robert, *Putin's Preventive Counter-Revolution: Post-Soviet Authoritarianism and the Spectre of Velvet Revolution*, New York: Routledge, 2013.

Hughes, Karen, *Ten Minutes from Normal*, New York: Viking, 2004.

Isikoff, Michael, and David Corn, *Russian Roulette: The Inside Story of Putin's War on America and the Election of Donald Trump*, New York: Hachette Group, 2018.

Jack, Andrew, *Inside Putin's Russia*, New York: Oxford University Press, 2002.

Jelevich, Barbara, *St. Petersburg and Moscow: Tsarist and Soviet Foreign Policy, 1814–1974*, Bloomington: Indiana University Press, 1974.

Jensen, Kenneth, ed., *The Origins of the Cold War: Novikov, Kennan, and Roberts 'Long Telegrams' of 1946*, Washington D.C.: United States Institute of Peace Pres, 1995.

Johnson, David Kay, *The Making of Donald Trump*, New York: Melville House, 2016.

Johnson, Rob, *Oil, Islam, and Conflict: Central Asia since 1945*, London: Reaktion Books, 2007.

Jones, Nate, *Able Archer 83: The Secret History of the NATO Exercise That Almost Triggered Nuclear War*, New York: New Press, 2016.

Judah, Ben, *Fragile Empire: How Russia Fell In and Out of Love with Vladimir Putin*, New Haven, Conn.: Yale University Press, 2013.

Kalb, Marvin, *Imperial Gamble: Putin, Ukraine, and the New Cold War*, Washington D.C.: Brookings Institute, 2015.

——, *Enemy of the People: Trump's War on the Press, the New McCarthyism, and the Threat to American Democracy*, Washington D.C.: Brookings, 2018.

Kasparov, Garry, *Winter Is Coming: Why Vladimir Putin and the Enemies of the Free World Must Be Stopped*, New York: Public Affairs, 2015.

Katz, David, and Fred Weir, *Russia's Path from Gorbachev to Putin: The Demise of the Soviet System and the New Russia*, New York: Routledge, 2007.

Keane, John, *The Life and Death of Democracy*, New York: W.W. Norton, 2009.

Kessler, Ronald, *Inside the Trump White House*, New York: Gallery Books, 2017.

Khlevniuk, Oleg, *The History of the Gulag: from Collectivization to the Great Terror* (New Haven, Conn.: Yale University Press, 2004.

Klebnikov, Paul, *The Godfather of the Kremlin: The Decline of Russia in the Age of Gangster Capitalism*, New York: Mariner, 2000.

Knight, Amy, *Spies without Cloaks: The KGB's Successors*, Princeton, N.J.: Princeton University Press, 1998.

Kochiw, J.V., *The Abuse of Power: Corruption in the Office of the President*, Reading, U.K.: Artemia Press, 2013.

Kolsto, Pal, and Helge Blakkisrud, *The New Russian Nationalism: Imperialism, Ethnicity, and Authoritarianism, 2000–2015*, Edinburgh: University of Edinburgh Press, 2016.

Kornelius, Stefan, *Angela Merkel: The Chancellor and Her World*, London: Alma Books, 2013.

Kotkin, Stephen, *Armageddon Averted: The Soviet Collapse, 1970–2000*, New York: Oxford University Press, 2001.

Kranish, Michael, and Marc Fisher, *Trump Revealed: The Definitive Biography of the 45th President*, New York: Scribner's, 2017.

Krivosheev, G.F. *Soviet Casualties and Combat Losses in the Twentieth Century*, London: Greenhill, 1997.

Langworth, Richard, *Winston Churchill, Myth and Reality: What He Actually Did and Said*, Jefferson, N.C.: MacFarland and Company, 2017.

Laqueur, Walter, *Russia and German,* New Brunswick, N.J.: Transaction Publishers, 1990.

Laruelle, Marlene, *Russian Eurasianism: An Ideology of Empire,* Baltimore: Johns Hopkins University Press, 2008.

——, ed. *Russian Nationalism and the Nationalist Assertion of Russia,* New York: Routledge, 2009.

Ledeneva, Alena, *Russia's Economy of Favors: Blat, Networking, and Informal Exchange,* New York: Cambridge University Press, 1998.

Ledeneva, Alena, *How Russia Really Works,* Ithaca, N.Y.: Cornell University Press, 2006.

——, *Can Russia Modernise? Sistema, Power Networks, and Informal Governance,* New York: Cambridge University Press, 2013.

LeDonne, John, *The Russian Empire and the World, 1700–1914,* New York: Oxford University Press, 1997.

Lee, Kai Fu, *AI Superpowers: China, Silicon Valley, and the New World Order,* New York: Houghton Mifflin, 2018.

Legvold, Robert, *Russian Foreign Policy in the Twenty-First Century and the Shadow of the Past,* New York: Columbia University Press, 2007.

Leichtova, Magda, *Misunderstanding Russia: Russian Foreign Policy and the West,* London: Ashgate, 2014.

LeVine, Steve, *Putin's Labyrinth: Spies, Murder, and the Dark Heart of the New Russia,* New York: Random House, 2008.

Lieven, Anatol, *Chechnya: The Tombstone of Russian Power,* New Haven, Conn.: Yale University Press, 1998.

Lieven, Dominic, *The End of Tsarist Russia: The March to World War I and Revolution,* New York: Penguin, 2015.

Litvinenko, Alexander, and Yuri Felshtinsky, *Blowing Up the Kremlin: The Secret Plan to Bring Back KGB Terror,* New York: Encounter Books, 2007.

Levitsky, Steven and Daniel Ziblatt, *How Democracies Die,* New York: Crown Publishers, 2018.

Lo, Bobo, *Axis of Convenience: Moscow, Beijing, and the New Geopolitics,* Washington D.C.: Brookings Institute, 2008.

Lucas, Edward, *The New Cold War,* New York: Palgrave Macmillan, 2008.

——, *Deception: The Untold Story of East-West Espionage Today,* London: Walker Books, 2012.

Lynch, Allen, *How Russia Is Not Ruled: Reflections on Russian Political Development,* New York: Cambridge University Press, 2005.

Lynch, Allen, *Vladimir Putin and Russian Statecraft,* Washington D.C.: Potomac Books, 2011.

MacKinnon, Mark, *The New Cold War: Revolutions, Rigged Elections, and Pipeline Politics in the Former Soviet Union,* New York: Carroll and Graf, 2007.

Makarychev, Andrey, and Andre Mommen, *Russia's Changing Economic and Political Regimes: The Putin Years and Afterwards,* New York: Routledge, 2013.

Malia, Martin, *The Soviet Tragedy: A History of Socialism in Russia, 1917–1991,* New York: Free Press, 1994.

Mankoff, Jeffrey, *Russian Foreign Policy: The Return of Great Power Politics,* New York: Roman and Littlefield, 2012.

Matlock, Jack, *Autopsy of an Empire: The Ambassador's Account of the Collapse of the Soviet Union,* New York: Random House, 1995.

Mayer, Arno, *The Furies: Violence and Terror in the French and Russian Revolutions*, Princeton, N.J.: Princeton University Press, 2000.

Maynard, Christopher, *Out of the Shadows: George H.W. Bush and the End of the Cold War*, College Station: Texas A & M University Press, 2008.

McAuley, Mary, *Soviet Politics, 1917–1991*, New York: Oxford University Press, 1992.

McFaul, Michael, *Russia's Unfinished Revolution: Political Change from Gorbachev to Putin*, Ithaca, N.Y.: Cornell University Press, 2001.

Meier, Andrew, *Chechnya: To the Heart of a Conflict*, New York: W.W. Norton, 2004.

Mendras, Marie, *Russian Politics: The Paradox of a Weak State*, New York: Columbia University Press, 2012.

Metz, Steve, and James Klevitt, *The Revolution in Military Affairs and Conflict Short of War*, Washington D.C.: Strategic Studies Institute, 2013.

Miller, Donald, *The Cold War: A Military History*, New York: Thomas Dunne, 2015.

Miller, Eric, *To Balance or Not to Balance: Alignment Theory and the Commonwealth of Independent States*, Burlington, Vermont: Ashgate, 2004.

Miller, Greg, *The Apprentice: Trump, Russia, and the Subversion of American Democracy*, New York: Custom House, 2018.

Mitchell, Lincoln, *Uncertain Future: U.S. Foreign Policy and Georgia's Rose Revolution*, Philadelphia: University of Pennsylvania Press, 2008.

Montefiore, Simon, *The Romanovs, 1613–1918*, New York: Vintage, 2017.

Mosher, Steven, *Bully of Asia: Why China's Dream is the New Threat to World Order*, Washington D.C.: Regnery, 2017.

Mueller, Robert et al, *Report on the Investigation into Russian Interference into the 2016 Presidential Election*, 2 vols., Washington D.C.: Government Printing Office, March 2019.

Mueller, Robert et al, *Report on the Investigation into Russian Interference into the 2016 Presidential Election*, presented with related materials by *The Washington Post*, Introduction and Analysis by Reporters Rosalind S. Helderman and Matt Zaptosky, New York: Scriber, 2019.

Murray, Donette, and David Brown, *Power Relations in the Twenty-First Century*, New York: Routledge, 2018.

Myagkov, Mikhail, Peter Ordeshook, and Dmitry Shaikin, *The Forensics of Election Fraud: Russia and Ukraine*, New York: Cambridge University Press, 2009.

Myers, Steven Lee, *The New Tsar: The Rise and Reign of Vladimir Putin*, New York: Vintage, 2015.

Nalbandov, Bruce, *Not by Bread Alone: Russian Foreign Policy Under Putin*, Lincoln: University of Nebraska Press, 2016.

Nance, Malcom, and Rob Reisner, *The Plot to Destroy America: How Putin and His Spies Are Undermining America and Dismantling the West*, New York: Hachette, 2018.

Nester, William, *Haunted Victory: The American Crusade to Destroy Saddam and Impose Democracy on Iraq*, Washington D.C.: Potomac Books, 2012.

Nichols, Susan, *Vladimir Putin: Russia's Prime Minister and President*, New York: Enslow Publishing, 2019.

O'Brien, Tim, *Trump Nation: The Art of Being the Donald*, New York: Hachette, 2016.

Orttung, Robert, *Putin's Olympics: The Sochi Games and the Evolution of Russia*, New York: Routledge, 2017.

Ostrovsky, Arkady, *The Invention of Russia: The Rise of Russia and the Age of Fake News*, New York: Penguin, 2017.

Ostrow, Joel, Georgiy, and Irina Khakamada, *The Consolidation of Dictatorship in Russia: An Inside View of the Demise of Democracy*, Westport, Conn.: Praeger, 2007.

Paul, Allen, *Katyn: Stalin's Massacre and the Triumph of Truth*, Urbana: Northern Illinois University Press, 2010.

Paulson, Arthur, *Donald Trump and the Prospects for American Democracy*, New York: Lexington Books, 2018.

Pipes, Richard, *Russia Under the Old Regime*, New York: Charles Scribners' Sons, 1974.

——, *The Russian Revolution*, New York: Knopf, 1990.

——, *The Formation of the Soviet Union: Communism and Nationalism, 1917–1923*, Cambridge, Mass.: Harvard University Press, 1997.

——, *Russian Conservatism and Its Critics: A Study in Political Culture*, New Haven, Conn.: Yale University Press, 2005.

Plokhy, Serhii, *The Last Empire: The Final Days of the Soviet Union*, New York: Basic Books, 2014.

——, *Chernobyl: The History of a Nuclear Catastrophe*, New York: Basic Books 2018.

Politkovskaya, Anna, *Putin's Russia: Life in a Failing Democracy*, New York: Metropolitan, 2005.

Pomerantsev, Peter, *Nothing Is True and Everyone Is Possible: The Surreal Heart of the New Russia*, New York: Public Affairs, 2014.

Pravda, Alex, ed., *Leading Russia: Putin in Perspective, Essays in Honor of Archie Brown*, New York: Oxford University Press, 2005.

Radanko, Laura, *The Russian Mafia in America*, Gainesville: University of Florida Press, 2011.

Ragsdale, Hugh, *The Russian Tragedy: The Burden of History*, Armonk, N.Y.: M.E. Sharpe, 1996.

Reddaway, Peter, and Dmitri Glinski, *The Tragedy of Russia's Reforms: Market Bolshevism against Democracy*, Washington D.C.: United States Institute of Peace, 2001.

Remnick, David, *Lenin's Tomb: The Last Days of the Soviet Empire*, New York: Random House, 1993.

——, *Resurrection: The Struggle for a New Russia*, New York: Random House, 1997.

Renz, Bettina, *Russia's Military Revival*, New York: Polity, 2018.

Rhodehamel, John, ed., *George Washington: Writings*, New York: Library of America, 1997.

Rhodes, Richard, *Arsenals of Folly: The Making of the Nuclear Arms Race*, New York: Vintage, 2006.

Riasanovsky, Nicholas, and Mark Steinburg, *A History of Russia*, New York: Oxford University Press, 2018.

Rice, Condoleezza, *No Higher Honor: A Memoir of My Years in Washington*, New York: Random House, 2011.

Romanov, Alexander Mikhailovich *Once a Grand Duke*, New York: Farrar and Rinehart, 1932.

Roper, Carl, *Made in China: Trade Secrets, Theft, Industrial Espionage, and the China Threat*, New York: Taylor Francis, 2015.

Rosenfeld, Ross, *The Slow Death of Democracy*, New York: Resistance Books, 2018.

Roxburgh, Angus, *The Strongman: Vladimir Putin and the Struggle for Russia*, London: I.B. Tauris, 2012.

Rychiak, Ronald, and Ion Mihai Pacepa, *Disinformation: Former Spy Chief Reveals Secret Strategies for Undermining Freedom, Attacking Religion, and Promoting Terrorism*, Washington D.C.: WND Books, 2013.

Sabato, Larry, Kyle Kondik, and Geoffrey Shelley, eds., *Trumped: The 2016 Election that Broke All the Rules*, Lanham, Maryland: Rowman and Littlefield, 2017.

Sakwa, Richard, *Putin: Russia's Choice*, New York: Routledge, 2007.

——, *Russian Politics and Society*, New York: Routledge, 2008.

——, *The Quality of Freedom: Khodorkovsky, Putin, and the Yukos Affair*, New York: Oxford University Press, 2009.

——, *The Crisis of Russian Democracy: The Dual State, Factionalism and the Medvedev Succession*, New York: Cambridge University Press, 2011.

——, *Putin and the Oligarch: The Khodorkovsky Affair*, London: I.B. Taurus, 2014.

——, *Putin Redux: Power and Contradiction in Contemporary Russia*, New York: Routledge, 2014.

Salisbury, Harrison, *Black Night, White Snow: Russia's Revolutions, 1905–1917*, New York: Doubleday, 1977.

Sanger, David, *The Perfect Weapon: War, Sabotage, and Fear in the Cyber Age*, New York: Random House, 2018.

Sargent, Greg, *An Uncivil War: Taking Back Our Democracy in an Age of Trumpian Disinformation*, New York: Custom House, 2018.

Satter, David, *Darkness at Dawn: The Rise of the Russian Criminal State*, New Haven, Conn.: Yale University Press, 2003.

——, *It Was a Long Time Ago, and It Never Happened Anyway: Russia and the Communist Past*, New Haven, Conn.: Yale University Press, 2012.

Schaffner, Brian, and John Clark, eds., *Making Sense of the 2016 Election*, Washington D.C.: Congressional Quarterly Press, 2017.

Schoen, Douglas, and Melic Kaylan, *The Russia-China Axis: The New Cold War and America's Crisis of Leadership*, New York: Encounter Books, 2014.

Sell, Louis, *Slobodan Milosevic and the Destruction of Yugoslavia*, Durham, N.C.: Duke University Press, 2002.

Serio, Joseph, *Investigating the Russian Mafia*, New York: Carolina Academic Press, 2008.

Shevtsova, Lilia, *Putin's Russia*, Washington D.C.: Carnegie Institute for International Peace, 2005.

——, *Russia—Lost in Transition: The Yeltsin and Putin Legacies*, Washington D.C.: Carnegie Institute for International Peace, 2007.

Simis, Konstantin, *USSR: The Corrupt Society, The Secret World of Soviet Capitalism*, New York: Simon and Schuster, 1982.

Sixsmith, Martin, *The Litvinenko File: The Life and Death of a Russian Spy*, New York: St. Martin's Press, 2007.

Soldatov, Andrei, and Irina Borogan, *The New Nobility: The Restoration of Russia's Security State and the Enduring Legacy of the KGB*, New York: Public Affairs, 2010.

Solnick, Stephen, *Stealing the State: Control and Collapse in Soviet Institutions*, Cambridge, Mass.: Harvard University Press, 1998.

Solzhenitsyn, Alexander, *The Gulag Archipelago, 1918–1956*, vols. 1–2, New York: Harper and Row, 1974.

Staar, Richard, *Foreign Policy of the Soviet Union*, Stanford, Calif.: Hoover Institute Press, 1991.

Stell, Benn, *The Marshall Plan: Dawn of the Cold War*, New York: Simon and Schuster, 2018.

Stent, Angela, *Russia and Germany Reborn: Unification, the Soviet Collapse, and Europe Reborn*, Princeton, N.J.: Princeton University Press, 1999.

——, *The Limits of Partnership: U.S.-Russia Relations in the Twenty-First Century*, Princeton, N.J.: Princeton University Press, 2014.

Stent, Angela, *Putin's World: Russia against the West and with the Rest*, New York: Twelve Books, 2019.

Stone, David, *The Russian Army in the Great War: The Eastern Front, 1914–1917*, Topeka: University Press of Kansas, 2015.

Strayer, Robert, *Why Did the Soviet Union Collapse?: Understanding Historical Change*, Armonk, N.Y.: M.E. Sharpe, 1998.

Sutela, Pekka, *The Political Economy of Putin's Russia*, New York: Routledge, 2012.

Svanidze, Nikolai and Marina, *Medvedev*, St. Petersburg: Amfora, 2008.

Talbott, Strobe, *The Russian Hand: A Memoir of Presidential Diplomacy*, New York: Random House, 2002.

Tamarov, Vladislav *Afghanistan: Soviet Vietnam*, New York: Mercury House, 1992.

Taubman, William, *Khrushchev: The Man and His Era*, New York: W.W. Norton, 2003.

——, *Gorbachev: His Life and Times*, New York: W.W. Norton, 2017.

Taylor, Graham, *Understanding Brexit: Why Britain Voted to Leave the European Union*, London: Emerald Publishing, 2017.

Thompson, William, *Khrushchev: A Political Life*, New York: St. Martin's Press, 1995.

Tishkov, Valery, *Chechyna: Life in a War-Torn Society*, Berkeley: University of California Press, 2004.

Treisman, David, *The Return: Russia's Journey from Gorbachev to Medvedev*, New York: Free Press, 2011.

Trotsky, Leon, *Terrorism and Communism: A Reply to Karl Kautsky*, New York: Verso, 2017.

Trump, Donald, and Tony Schwartz, *Trump: Art of the Deal*, New York: Ballantine Books, 2015.

Truscott, Peter, *Kursk: The Gripping Story of Russia's Worst Submarine Disaster*, London: Simon and Schuster, 2004.

——, *Putin's Progress: A Biography of Russia's Enigmatic President*, London: Simon and Schuster, 2004.

Tsygankov, Andrei, *Russia's Foreign Policy: Change and Continuity in National Identity*, New York: Rowman and Littlefield, 2013.

Urban, Mark, *The Skripal Files: The Life and Near Death of a Russian Spy*, New York: Henry Holt, 2018.

Unger, Craig, *House of Trump, House of Putin: The Untold Story of Donald Trump and the Russian Mafia*, New York: Dutton House, 2018.

Vaksburg, Arkadi, *Toxic Politics: The Secret History of the Kremlin's Poison Laboratory*, Santa Barbara, Calif.: ABC-CLIO, 2011.

Van Herpen, Marcel, *Putin's Wars: The Rise of Russia's New Imperialism*, New York: Rowman and Littlefield, 2014.

Verkhovsky, Alexander, ed., *Xenophobia and Radical Nationalism in Russia*, Moscow: Sova Center for Information and Analysis, 2013.

Volodarsky, Boris, *The KGB's Poison Factory: From Lenin to Litvinenko*, Minneapolis: Zenith Press, 2009.

Voskressenski, Alexei, *Russia and China: A Theory of Interstate Relations*, London: Routledge, 2003.

Waal, Thomas de, *The Great Catastrophe: Armenians and Turks in the Shadow of Genocide*, New York: Oxford University Press, 2015.

Walker, William, ed., *America in the Cold War: A Documentary History*, Santa Barbara, Calif.: ABC-CLIO Books, 2014.

Weeks, Albert, *Russia's Life Saver: Lend Lease Aid to the U.S.S.R. in World War II*, Lanham, Maryland: Lexington Books, 2009.

Wegner, Stephen, *Return to Putin's Russia: Past Imperfect, Future Uncertain*, New York: Rowman and Littlefield, 2013.

Wilson, Andrew, *Ukraine's Orange Revolution*, New Haven, Conn.: Yale University Press, 2005.

——, *Belarus: The Last European Dictatorship*, New Haven, Conn.: Yale University Press, 2011.

——, *Ukraine Crisis: What It Means for the West*, New Haven, Conn.: Yale University Press, 2014.

Woodward, Bob, *Fear: Trump in the White House*, New York: Simon and Schuster, 2018.

Wolff, Michael, *Fire and Fury: Inside the Trump White House*, New York: Henry Holt, 2018.

Wren, Christopher, *The End of the Line: The Failure of Communism in the Soviet Union and China*, New York: Simon and Schuster, 1990.

Yost, Elena, *The Russia-Georgia War of 2008: Media Content and Public Opinion*, Frankfort: Akademikerverlag, 2014.

Zygar, Mikhail, *All the Kremlin's Men: Inside the Court of Vladimir Putin*, New York: Public Affairs, 2016.

Articles

Aron, Leon, "Putinology," *The American Interest*, July 30, 2015.

Babayan, Nelli, "The Return of the Empire? Russia's Counteraction to Transatlantic Democracy Promotion in the Near Abroad," *Democratization*, vol. 22, no. 3 (2015), 438–58.

Barany, Zoltan, "Defense Reform, Russian-Style: Obstacles, Options, Opposition," *Contemporary Politics*, vol. 11, no. 2 (March 2005), 33–51.

Barrie, Douglas, and Tom Waldwyn, "Candid Debate Needed on Russian Air-Transport Plan," *International Institute of Strategic Studies*, August 23, 2018.

Beraud-Sudreau, Lucie, and Douglas Barrie, "Russia's Defense Spending: The Impact of Economic Contraction," *International Institute of Strategic Studies*, March 6, 2017.

Boussena, Sadek, and Catherine Locatelli, "Gas Market Developments and their Effect on Relations between Russia and the EU, *OPEC Energy Review*, vol. 35 (2011), 27–46.

——, "Gazprom and the Complexity of EU Gas Market: A Strategy to Define," *Post-Communist Economies*, vol. 29, no. 4 (2017), 549–64.

Brandenberger, David, "Debate: Stalin's Populism and the Accidental Creation of Russian National Identity," *Nationalist Papers*, vol. 38, no. 5 (2010), 723–30.

Bukkvoli, Tor, Iron Cannot Fight: The Role of Technology in Current Russian Military Theory," *Journal of Strategic Studies*, vol. 34, no. 5 (2011), 691–706.

Cassidy, Julie, and Emily Johnson, "Putin, Putiana, and the Question of a Post-Soviet Cult of Personality," The Slavonic and East European Review, vol. 88, no. 4 (October 2010), 681–707.

Charap, Samuel, "The Petersburg Experience: Putin's Political Career and Russian Foreign Policy," *Problems of Post-Communism*, vol. 51, no. 1 (January-February 2004), 55–62.

Chivvis, Christopher, "Hybrid War: Russian Contemporary Political Warfare," Bulletin of the Atomic Scientists, vol. 73, no. 5 (2017), 316–21;

Cottrell, Robert, "Putin's Trap," *New York Review of Books*, December 4, 2003.

Dawisha, Karen, "The Putin Principle: How It Came to Rule Russia," *World Affairs*, vol. 178, no. 1 (May–July 2015), 13–22.

Ellman, Michael, "Soviet Repression Statistics: Some Comments," *Europe-Asia Studies*, vol. 54, no. 7 (November 2002), 1151–72.

Evans, Alfred, "Putin's Legacy and Russia's Identity," *Europe-Asia Studies*, vol. 60, no. 6 (August 2008), 899–912.

Forrest, Carolyn, "Russia's Disinformation Campaign: The New Cold War," *Forum Committee of the American Bar Association*, vol. 33, no. 3 (Winter 2018), 2–5.

Gaddy, Clifford, "Putin's Third Way," *The National Interest*, (January-February 2009).

Gedmin, Jeffrey, "Beyond Crimea: What Vladimir Putin Really Wants," World Affairs, vol. 177, no. 2 (July/August 2014), 8–16.

Hill, Fiona, "The Gang of Two: Russia and Japan Make a Play for the Pacific," *Foreign Affairs*, November 23, 2007).

Ikenberry, John, and Charles Kupchan, "Socialization and Hegemonic Power," *International Organization*, vol. 44, no. 3 (1990), 283–315.

Kaylan, Melik, "Kremlin Values: Putin's Strategic Conservatism," *World Affairs*, vol. 177, no. 1 (May-July 2014), 9–17.

Kozyrev, Andrey, "Russia: A Chance for Survival," *Foreign Affairs*, vol. 71, no. 2 (1992), 1–16.

Lend Lease Shipments: World War II (Washington D.C.: War Department Chief of Finance, December 31, 1946).

Mileski, Toni, "Identifying the New Eurasian Orientation in Modern Russian Geopolitical Thought," *Eastern Journal of European Studies*, vol. 6, no 2 (December 2015), 177–87.

Monaghan, Andrew, "The Vertikal: Power and Authority in Russia," *International Relations*, vol. 88, no. 1 (2012), 1–16.

Polyakova, Alina, "Strange Bedfellows: Putin and Europe's Far Right," *World Affairs*, vol. 177, no. 3 (September/October 2014), 36–40.

Pomerantsky, Peter, "The Hidden Author of Putinism: How Vladislav Surkov Invented the New Russia," *The Atlantic Monthly*, November 7, 2014.

Stent, Angela, "Restoration and Revolution in Putin's Foreign Policy, *Europe-Asia Studies*, vol. 60, no. 6 (August 2008), 1089–1106.

Terebova, S.V., "Cooperation between Russia and the European Union from Importing to Exporting Technology," *Studies on Russian Economic Development*, vol. 28, no. 3 (2017), 327–37.

Thomas, Timothy, "The Evolving Nature of Russia's Way of War," *Military Review*, July-August 2017.

Index